Empire of Rags and Bones

Empire of Rags and Bones

Waste and War in Nazi Germany

ANNE BERG

OXFORD
UNIVERSITY PRESS

Oxford University Press is a department of the University of Oxford. It furthers
the University's objective of excellence in research, scholarship, and education
by publishing worldwide. Oxford is a registered trade mark of Oxford University
Press in the UK and certain other countries.

Published in the United States of America by Oxford University Press
198 Madison Avenue, New York, NY 10016, United States of America.

© Oxford University Press 2024

All rights reserved. No part of this publication may be reproduced, stored in
a retrieval system, or transmitted, in any form or by any means, without the
prior permission in writing of Oxford University Press, or as expressly permitted
by law, by license, or under terms agreed with the appropriate reproduction
rights organization. Inquiries concerning reproduction outside the scope of the
above should be sent to the Rights Department, Oxford University Press, at the
address above.

You must not circulate this work in any other form
and you must impose this same condition on any acquirer.

Library of Congress Control Number: 2023045502

ISBN 978–0–19–774400–0

DOI: 10.1093/oso/9780197744000.001.0001

Printed by Sheridan Books, Inc., United States of America

für Mama

Contents

Acknowledgments — ix
Abbreviations — xiii
Glossary — xv

Introduction: Rag and Bone Economics — 1

PART I ORDER

1. The Nazi Waste Regime — 19
2. Garbage Visionaries — 42
3. Garbage Community — 61

PART II EXTRACTION

4. Forged in Metal — 85
5. Rag Farming — 114
6. Waste Cycles — 137

PART III DESTRUCTION

7. Soap Bones — 161
8. Bombed Out and Trashed In — 184
9. Piles — 203

Conclusion: Hidden in Plain Sight — 225

Notes — 233
Bibliography — 297
Index — 331

Acknowledgments

When I first told friends and colleagues about the book I intended to write, I received some rather mixed responses, ranging from "sexy" to "you can't do that, that's sensationalizing atrocity" (I'm paraphrasing). Ultimately, they all made the same point: there's something illicit, taboo-breaking, about thinking of garbage and genocide together, particularly when the genocide in question is the Holocaust. But some thoughts cannot be unthought. It was the mundanity of garbage and the mindless, technocratic, everyday habits of dealing with it that monopolized my attention. Once I started looking, garbage was everywhere, even if not consistently keyworded in the ledgers of the archives. I combed through folders for several years and brooded over thousands of pages of archival copies for some more years. I gave talks and published articles that discussed waste management and waste avoidance in Nazi Germany and elsewhere but skirted around the main question: How and why were waste and recycling at the center of the Nazi genocide of the Jews and other targets of the regime? This book no longer skirts.

I would like to thank the many individuals and institutions that believed this project is licit and that the questions I ask and attempt to answer in this book are important. I also want to thank those individuals who remained skeptical or outright hostile; they forced me to think more deeply and argue more carefully; and they taught me to not only bring pen and notebook to each seminar room but also a *Kettenhemd*.

This book has received generous institutional support. I wish to thank the History Department at the University of Pennsylvania, the University of Pennsylvania Research Foundation, the University of Pennsylvania's School of Arts and Sciences, the Jewish Studies Program at the University of Pennsylvania, the History Department at the University Michigan, the Institute for Contemporary History in Potsdam, and the Shelby Cullom Davis Center at Princeton University for financial assistance. The expertise and guidance of the staff at archives and libraries has been crucial. I thank the *Mitarbeiter* at the Bundesarchiv Berlin, KZ-Gedenkstätte Mauthausen, Gedenkstätte und Museum Sachsenhausen, Gedenkstätte Bergen-Belsen, Archiv der Gedenkstätte Dachau, Stiftung Niedersächsicher Gedenkstätten,

Staatsarchiv Hamburg, Landesarchiv Berlin, Brandenburgisches Landeshauptarchiv Potsdam, Stadtarchiv Bielefeld, and the United States Holocaust Memorial Museum. In particular, I would like to thank Ralf Lechner, Volker Reißmann, and Klaus Tätzler.

I am immensely grateful to my editor, Susan Ferber, for her guidance and encouragement, and for her in-depth engagement with my writing. She embraced my vision for the book and improved it tenfold, eclipsing anything I expected or even had the sense to dream of. She also arranged for my travel to Wrocław for a most productive and intellectually stimulating manuscript workshop. I would like to thank Andrzej Kaminski, Tomasz Ochinowski, Martyna Grądzka-Rejak, Richard Butterwick, Anna Kalinowska, Eulalia Łazarska, Adam Kożuchowski, and Michał Przeperski for their feedback on the first draft of the manuscript, for their kind words of encouragement, and for their many helpful suggestions. I am, moreover, immensely grateful to the anonymous readers who reviewed the manuscript for Oxford University Press. Their comments, criticisms, and suggestions proved invaluable.

Special thanks are due to my colleagues in the History Department at the University of Pennsylvania; in particular, I wish to thank my department chairs, Antonio Feros and Sophie Rosenfeld, for critical support. I also wish to express my gratitude to our departmental staff for helping me navigate the institutional thicket. My students were often the first to be confronted with the most undercooked version of my ideas as I was designing courses to explore connections between concepts and categories rarely thought of together. In particular, I would like to thank the students in "Wastes of War" and "White Nationalism in the Age of Climate Change" for their doubts, their pressing questions, and their urgent presentism, for insisting on hope when all I had to offer was rage. They pressed me not only to articulate the connections between social and environmental history but also to explain why they matter in today's world.

Many colleagues and friends have provided guidance, assistance, encouragement, advice, mentorship, suggestions, criticisms, archival support, logistical support, and opportunities to share my work along the way. I thank Dolores Augustine, Etienne Benson, Dan Berger, Daniela Blei, Frank Bösch, Marc Bradley, Dorothee Brantz, Warren Breckmann, Marc Buggeln, Nathan Burtch, Kathleen Canning, Lee Cassanelli, Angela Craiger, Belinda Davis, Serawit Bekele Debele, Jacob Dlamini, Richard Ek, Heiner Fangerau, Jared Farmer, Ann Farnsworth-Alevar, Siyen Fei, Melissa Feinberg, Antonio Feros, Michael Gordin, Christoph Gunkel, Paul Hanebrink, Gabrielle Hecht, Peter

Holquist, Çiçek İlengiz, Harold James, Destin Jenkins, Nils Johansson, Jeff Kallberg, Annika Kirbis, Jonas Kreienbaum, Rita Krüger, Franziska Kuschel, Victoria Langland, Annette Lareau, Heikki Lempa, Alex Lichtenstein, Thomas Lindenberger, Christoph Lindner, Miriam Meissner, Johanna Mellis, Erica Milam, Yair Mintzker, Ben Nathans, Douglas Northrop, Tamar Novick, Amy Offner, Roberta Pergher, Maria Pirogovskaya, Anat Plocker, Brian Porter-Szucs, Uli Prehn, Simon Richter, Alana Rodriguez, Mark Rosemann, Sophie Rosenfeld, Mikkel Sack, Tiago Saraiva, Julia Sneeringer, Paul Steege, Nathan Stoltzfus, Marla Stone, Julia Adeney Thomas, Beans Velocci, Till von Raden, Adelheid Voskuhl, Nik Wachsmann, Keith Wailoo, Heike Weber, Bethany Wiggin, Michael Wildt, Thomas Zeller, Corinna Zeltsman, and Carl Zimring.

I spent my first ever sabbatical as a Davis Center fellow at Princeton University, where I had the opportunity to present draft chapters and learn from amazing scholars. I am particularly grateful to the Davis Center directors, David Bell and Isadora Mota, and the wonderful fellows Nicole Barnes, Rosie Bsheer, Sarah Cameron, Will Cavert, Ben Cohen, Reinaldo Funes Monzote, Camille Goldmon, Andrew Needham, Tiffany Nichols, and David Patterson. They read drafts, pushed me to clarify my arguments, write for different audiences, and engage with literature in different fields. In addition, Nicole Barnes, David Bell, David Crew, Geoff Eley, Simcha Gross, Christa Keister, Dirk Moses, Marcy Norton, Raz Segal, Sargeant Donovan Smith, and Melanie Tanielian read and commented on drafts, sometimes multiple versions. Their feedback and comments were invaluable. Over the past several years, I benefited from countless conversations, conference panels, seminar discussions, and email exchanges. As a result, my thinking took many turns, I changed arguments and their structures in response to such criticisms and suggestions, and other times I stubbornly dug in my heals. Naturally, any errors here are mine alone.

My friends, near and far, put up with my constant fixation on waste and waste management infrastructures, while making sure that I don't forget about life beyond garbage. I am particularly grateful to my Fishtown family, Raz, Anat, and Ella (and Willy the cat) for having me over on bad days and good days alike. Lastly, I thank Doug and Melanie for being there always and Emilio for leaving.

There's no way I could possibly describe the many ways in which the love and support of my family has been and continues to be central to absolutely everything. When it comes to this book, I am most grateful to them for pulling me away from work while supporting my obsession with it all the same. Mama, Papa, and Lisa are living evidence that miles don't produce distance. Lukas, Yannik, and Timo remind me that life happens in the present. They share distraction, laughter, and love as they pursue their own dreams now. Lukas makes sure the "ogre" drags herself to the gym instead of brooding over footnotes. He nutmegs me only gently and trades backrubs for "really good cultural-appropriation cooking." Yannik peppers my late nights with discussions of human evolution and politics, inserting occasional queries about pizza recipes. Plus, he heroically visited the Paris sewers with me (and yes, they reek). Timo keeps me on edge when flipping off cliffs and landing his stunts solidly, sometimes with a helmet, always with music. But he calls me afterward to tell me that "all is good" or "I may have broken my thumb." It is because of their lives and their futures that I refuse to think about end-times.

Abbreviations

AOK	*Armeeoberkommando* (Army High Command)
BEMAG	*Berliner Müllabfuhr Gesellschaft* (Berlin hauling company)
BDM	*Bund Deutscher Mädel* (League of German Girls)
BIWF	*Brauenschweigisches Institute für Wirtschaftsforschung* (Brunswick Institute for Economic Research)
DAF	*Deutsche Arbeitsfront* (German Labor Front)
DAW	*Deutsche Ausrüstungswerke* (German Equipment Works)
DESt	*Deutsche Erd und Steinwerke* (German Earth and Stone Works)
DFW	*Deutsches Frauenwerk* (German Women's Work)
DP	displaced person
DWB	*Deutsche Wirtschaftsbetriebe* (German Economic Company)
DWH	*Deutsches Wohnungshilfswerk* (German Tenement Relief Works)
EHW	*Ernährungshilfswerk* (Food Relief Works)
FBAmt	*Feldeisenbahnbetriebsamt* (Army Railway Operating Office)
FEKdo	*Feldeisenbahnkommando*
Gestapo	*Geheime Staatspolizei* (Secret State Police)
HJ	*Hitlerjugend* (Hitler Youth)
HTO	*Haupttreuhandstelle Ost* (Main Trustee Section East)
IKL	*Inspektion der Konzentrationslager* (Inspectorate of the Concentration Camps)
KdF	*Kraft durch Freude* (Strength through Joy)
KGL	*Kriegsgefangenlager* (prisoner-of-war camp)
KZ	*Konzentrationslager* (concentration camp)
KL	*Konzentrationslager* (concentration camp), official abbreviation
LWA	*Landeswirtschaftsamt* (regional economic office)
NS	National Socialist
NSDAP	*Nationalsozialistische Deutsche Arbeiter Partei* (National Socialist German Workers Party)
NSV	*Nationalsozialistische Volkswohlfahrt* (National Socialist People's Welfare)
OKW	*Oberkommando Wehrmacht* (Army High Command)
POW	prisoner of war
OSTI	*Ostindustrie GmbH*
RAD	*Reichsarbeitsdienst* (Reich Labor Service)

RIF	*Reichsstelle für industrielle* Fettversorgung as of 1942 *Reichsstelle für industrielle Fette und Waschmittel* (Reich Office for Industrial Fats)
RM	Reichsmark
ROGES	*Rohstoff und Handelsgesellschaft mbH* (Raw Material Trading Company)
RSHA	*Reichssicherheitshauptamt* (Reich Security Main Office)
RWM	*Reichswirtschaftsministerium* (Reich Ministry of Economic Affairs)
SA	*Sturmabteilung* (Strom Section)
SD	*Sicherheitsdienst* (Security Service)
SS	*Schutzstaffel* (Security Section)
SS-WVHA	*SS-Wirtschafts-Verwaltungshauptamt* (SS Main Economic and Administrative Office)
TexLed	*Gesellschaft für Textil und Leder Verwertung mbH* (Textile and Leather Utilization, Inc.)
T4	code name for Nazi murder of mentally and physically disabled and hereditarily ill, also referred to as the euthanasia program
Ufa	*Universum Film AG*
UNRRA	United Nations Relief and Rehabilitation Administration
VoMi	*Volksdeutsche Mittelstelle* (Coordination Center for Ethnic Germans)
VVG	*Verwaltung- und Verwertungsgesellschaft mbH* (Administration and Utilization Corporation)
Wifo	*Wirtschaftsforschungsgesellschaft m.b.H* (Economic Research Corporation)
WEK	*Wehrmachtserfassungskommando* (army requisition commando)

Glossary

Altmaterial	secondary material; old, out-moded material, recyclables
Altstoff	secondary material; old, out-moded material, recyclables
Altstoffhändler	secondary materials trader, rag-and-bone men
Anschluss	incorporation of Austria in the German Reich, 1938
Arbeitslager	labor camp
ausschlachten/ausgeschlachtet	exploit/exploited, the German term has a more violent connotation, as it is derived from butchering/slaughtering (*schlachten*)
Austauschjuden	exchange Jews, foreign national Jews retained from deportations for potential negotiations with Western Allies
Autarkie	economic self-sufficiency, resource independence
Baumwollkommando	cotton squad, forced labor detail for growing cotton
Baustoppverordnung	prohibition on nonstrategic construction projects
Beschlagnahme	confiscation, a "legal" tool
Betrieb	company
Beutegut	loot, requisition, or impounded material
Beutetrupp	booty crews, usually armed scouts securing loot
Beutepark	junkyard or storage lot for loot
Blockadesicherheit	security against blockade
Deutsche Ausrüstungswerke (DAW)	SS company, German Equipment Works included and expanded concentration camp workshops, mainly textile, cobbler, carpentry workshops
Deutsches Frauenwerk	German Women's Work
Deutschtum	an essentialized notion of German culture and language, racialized
Durchführung	execution (of an order or a task)
Durchgangslager	transit camp

Einsatzgruppen	mobile killing squads, subordinated to SS leadership, operating in Poland as of September 1939 and in Soviet territory starting in June 1941, primarily for the murder of Jews and other politically unreliable populations
Eisenbahnpioniere	railroad pioneers, scouts, part of the army railway authority
Endlösung	Final Solution, euphemism for the annihilation of the Jews
Endziel	final goal, end goal
Entlausung	delousing
Entwesung	decontamination/disinfection
Entwesungsbracke	decontamination/disinfection barrack
Entwesungskammer	decontamination/disinfection chamber
Erfassung	capture, also recordation
Erholungslager	convalescence camp, a euphemism for a camp to which prisoners were sent to die or miraculously recover without care, simply because of no labor exploitation
Ernährungshilfswerk (EHW)	Food Relief Works, part of the NSV
Erzeugungsschlacht	subsistence battle, envisioned by the Nazi regime as an all-out war for food independence
Feldeisenbahn	Army Railway Authority
Feldeisenbahnbetriebsamt	Army Railroad Operating Office
Feldeisenbahnkommando	army railroad commando/squad, essentially troops organizing rail traffic in active combat zones
Fusslappen	sock substitute, rag wraps for feet
Gau	contrived regional administrative unit that is larger than a municipality, but is not a state
Gauleiter	governor
Gefangenentuch	cheap, inferior cloth out of which prison uniforms *were fashioned*
Generalplan Ost	General Plan East, genocidal military and economic plan for the occupation of the Soviet Union
Gesellschaft für Textil und Lederverwertung (TexLed)	SS company for textile production
Grosswirtschaftsraum	greater economic space, generally referring to a European-wide economic sphere

Häftling	prisoner, usually concentration camp prisoner
Haupttreuhandstelle Ost (HTO)	Main Trustee Section East, organized to oversee and administer the gutting of Poland and later the Soviet Union
Hilfswillige	collaborators; literally, "those willing to help"; term obscures coercive context
Judenaktion	literally, "Jew action"; usually refers to massacres; prior to 1941 also used for acts of expropriation and plunder
Judensachbearbeiter	Jew clerk, clerk tasked with matters pertaining to the resettlement, deportation, and murder of Jews
Kahlfraßzone	territory designated for complete (economic) devastation
Knochenvernichtungsverbot	prohibition to destroy (animal) bones
Kriegsgefangene(r)	prisoner(s) of war (POWs)
Kriegsgefangenlager	prisoner-of-war camp
kriegswichtig/kriegsentscheidend	strategic, essential to, decisive for the war effort
Kriegszeug	war material, weaponry
Lager	camp; the Nazi regime had countless different kinds of camps, for youth as training camps, and a number of different prison and concentration camps
Lagerverwaltung	camp administration
Landeswirtschaftsamt (LWA)	regional economic office
Lebensraum	living space, a racialized concept of space, crucial to Nazi designs for imperial expansion
Leibbinden	body wraps, cloth to be wrapped around midsection as a form of undergarment for additional warmth
Löffelsammlung	collection of baking supplies by the spoonful by the NS women's organization to bake treats for the army
Luftwaffe	German air force
Lumpenwirtschaft	rag economy
Menschenmaterial	human (raw) material, usually referring to the humans to be exploited for labor (Jews, POWs); occasionally also used in reference to Germans to stress their superior quality; in either case use value was key
minderwertig	inferior, of lesser value
Müll	garbage, waste, trash, usually household waste

GLOSSARY

Müllbeseitigungsanstalt	Berlin's waste disposal company; literally, "garbage elimination facility"
Müllerde	garbage soil, compost derived from garbage
Müllspühlung	the flushing of garbage onto wetlands
Müllgemeinschaft	this author's term, a wordplay on people's community; a community organized around garbage and waste management
Müllwurst	garbage sausage
Nahrungsfreiheit	literally, "food freedom," meaning food independence
Nationalsozialistische Volkswohlfahrt (NSV)	National Socialist People's Welfare, main party-based welfare organization that organized collections, donations, social life, education, family planning and was involved in the abduction of "Germanizable" children from various European countries
Ostarbeiter/Ostarbeiterinnen	Nazi term for civilian laborers, male and female, forcibly deported from the eastern territories for labor in Germany
Ostbahn	term for railroad in Nazi-occupied Poland
Ost-Faser	state-controlled textile company operating in the occupied Soviet Union
Ostgesellschaften	state-controlled companies profiting from war
Ostindustrie (OSTI)	SS-owned company, formed by Odilo Globocnik, who oversaw the implementation of the Final Solution in Poland; its self-described purpose the utilization of Jewish labor
Ostland	Nazi administrative unit comprising the occupied Baltic states of Estonia, Latvia, and Lithuania
Ostmark	administrative unit referring to Austria, after its incorporation in 1938
Protektorat	Protectorate of Bohemia and Moravia, administrative unit for the former Czech territories
Räumungsgut	evacuated material, loot
Reichsbahn	Reich Railway Authority
Reichsbeauftrageter für Küchenabfälle	Reich Commissioner for Kitchen Garbage
Reichsbeauftragter für Altmaterialverwertung	Reich Commissioner for Secondary Material's Recovery
Reichskommissariat Ukraine	Nazi-occupied Ukraine

Reichsnährstand (RNS)	Reich Food Estate
Reichssicherheitshauptamt (RSHA)	Reich Security Main Office
Reichsstelle	office for the monitoring of industrial branch activities, setting of prices, allocation of raw materials, and regulation of trade
restlos	prevalent adjective meaning root-and-branch or total in Nazi speak; literally, "without remnant" or "remainderless"
Rohproduktenhandel	secondary materials trade
Rohproduktenhändler	peddler, secondary materials trader
Rohstoff	raw material
Rohstoffamt	Raw Materials Office
Rohstoffkreislauf	raw materials cycle
Rohstoff und Handelsgesellschaft mbH (ROGES)	logistics company; literally, "Raw Material and Trade Corporation"
Rollbahn	rail lines
Rückstand	remainder, residue
Russenlager	prison camps for people deported from the Soviet Union for labor inside Germany, a derogatory term; literally, "Russian camp"
Scheisskommando	shit squad, concentration camp labor detail for the removal of excrement from latrines
Schrott	junk, usually metal junk
Schrottaktion	junk recovery campaign/mission
Schwarzerdegebiet	black earth territory in Ukraine, designated for agricultural development
Sonderaktion	special action/mission/campaign
Sonderbehandlung	special treatment, euphemism for murder
Sonderkommando	camp labor detail tasked with the removal of bodies from gas chambers, "securing" hair, gold teeth, and other valuables before burying or burning the dead
Spinnstoff	textiles
Spinsstoffsammlung	textile collection
SS-*Bekleidungswerk*	clothing works, provisioning office for the Waffen-SS
SS-*Wirtschafts-Verwaltungshauptamt* (SS-WVHA)	SS Main Economic and Administrative Office, in charge of the SS economy of extraction and labor exploitation.

städtische Anstalten	municipal institutions such as prisons, correctional facilities, mental institutions, orphanages, etc.
Sterbelager	camp for the dying; see *Erholungslager* (convalescence camp)
Systemzeit	Nazi term for Weimar period
Tempowagen	funeral speed truck
Tierkörperverwertungsanlage	cadaver-processing plant, animal-rendering plant
Treuhänder	trustee; here, usually a German or ethnic German person or company entrusted with running a company or administering goods that have been looted on behalf of the Nazi state
Trockenabort	dry toilet; here, rudimentary dry outhouse
Trümmerverwertung	rubble processing, rubble recycling
Trümmerverwertungsanlage	rubble-recycling plant
Umwelt	environment; literally, "the world that surrounds"
Urbarmachung	agricultural development; literally, "to make habitable/usable"
Vierjahresplan	Four-Year Plan, with the purpose of gearing the entire economy toward war
Verwaltungs- und Verwertungsgesellschaft mbH (VVG)	state-controlled company for the administration and processing of loot and other materials in the Nazi-occupied east
verwerten	to utilize, use, use up, metabolize, recycle
verwertet	utilized, used up, metabolized, recycled
Verwertung	recycling, utilization, metabolization, processing
Verwertungsanstalten	recycling facilities
Volk	people, racialized understanding of the nation, epithet bestowing valorization and signaling a sense of belonging, exclusionary
Volksdeutsche/r	ethnic German
Volksgemeinschaft	people's community, national community, racial Community; a somewhat untranslatable term at the core of the Nazi vision for a social order based on duty and sacrifice, defining the exclusionist parameters of citizenship and national belonging
Volksgenosse	a member of the *Volksgemeinschaft*, invoking the socialist term of "comrade," translating it into the racialized, exclusionist category of people's comrade

Volksgut	people's property
Volksschädling	parasitic enemy of the people/race
Volkssturm	people's army, desperate mobilization of men 16–60, explicitly ordered to fight to the death
Volksvermögen	people's property, national property
Waldzone	forest zone, determined to be neglected after industry is scrapped and livestock, reserves, and consumer goods are extracted
Waffen-SS	part of the SS in charge of concentration camps; also the part of the SS in which ethnic Germans, who could not join the regular army, were allowed to serve
Warthegau	part of Poland incorporated into the Reich in 1939
wertlos	without value, worthless
Wehrmacht	German Army
Wehrmachterfassungskommandos (WEK)	army requisitioning commandos, hunting for loot
Wirtschaftsführungstab Ost	Economic Staff East, a link between the Four-Year Plan Authority and the military authorities in the occupied eastern territories
Zentrallageranstalten	central warehousing facilities

Empire of Rags and Bones

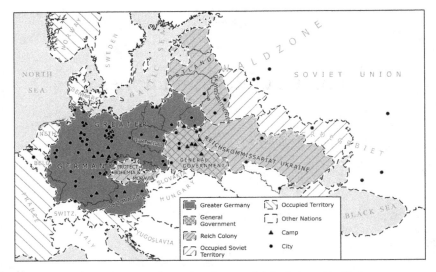

The Nazi Garbage Empire: Places, Borders, and Administrative Units

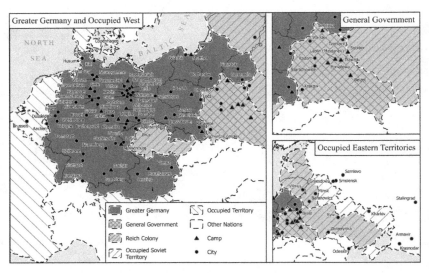

The Nazi Garbage Empire Up Close: Locations Referenced

Introduction

Rag and Bone Economics

As the Allies incinerated German cities and towns in the fall of 1944, Mr. M. A. Rothe faced a fire hazard of an altogether different kind. For over a year, dirty rags and polishing wool had piled up at his factory in Lössnitz.[1] Located in the Ore Mountains in Saxony, Rothe's Putzwolle Fabrik was one of two remaining manufacturers of cleaning products in Germany that also specialized in the recycling of used and dirty rags.[2] Given the pervasive reality of smoldering cities across Germany, Rothe worried that the piles of oil-drenched cleaning materials accumulating in his warehouse might self-ignite and set the whole factory on fire. Advertising himself as a master recycler in the name of the *Volksgemeinschaft* (people's community) and the war effort, the self-described "largest manufacturer of cleaning products in the entire Reich's territory" was trying to add urgency to his request for permission to expand his existing recycling plant. Cleaning supplies were not subject to rationing, but given the catastrophic conditions at the end of the war, they remained in high demand, and supply was running low.[3] Even armaments manufacturers could not obtain supplies to degrease their machinery.[4] After his initial request had been denied in March 1943, Rothe persisted, invoking regulations that required consumers to return used cleaning products in order to receive replacements.[5] He continued to send detailed letters to various offices, insisting on the strategic service that his company provided to the war economy at a time of excessive scarcity.

Putzwolle was generally manufactured out of reprocessed cleaning rags and other textile wastes, the allocation of which was centrally managed by the Reich Raw Materials Office (*Rohstoffamt*) and the respective *Reichsstellen* (industry-specific regulatory offices). Rothe had realized as early as 1936 that he would be able to exercise some control over his raw material supply and save money by investing in in-house recycling of dirty rags, while recovering oil and grease for reuse as well.[6] By September 1943, 1.3 million pounds of dirty rags had stretched his facility beyond its capacity as he waited for a favorable response from the various Reich offices. Meanwhile, truckloads of used and dirty materials kept rolling in, but raw material allotments did not. Whether out of conviction or habit, Rothe argued his case in Nazi speak. Accordingly, he foregrounded national priorities rather than self-interest and stressed the need to prevent "the degeneration of the still valuable fibrous materials and more importantly the degeneration of the oils still contained" therein. The expansion of his factory, so Rothe argued, would ensure the continued supply of much needed cleaning products for private consumers and industry alike. He finally received a positive response and allocations of forced laborers in October 1944 to start the expansion. But by January, the overall chaos that was engulfing Germany brought construction to a halt. Rothe was not discouraged. Instead, he continued to reiterate the importance of cleaning products to the war effort and promised his plant would be fully operational by the fall of 1945.[7]

The disconnect between Rothe's projections and wartime realities could not have been more extreme. Since the summer of 1944, Allied bombing of German cities had been relentless. In the east, the German occupiers hastily evacuated their positions as the Red Army pressed westward. Refugees piled into the Reich, and increasingly Germans themselves were on the move in desperate attempts to escape from bombs and enemy armies. In the west, the Allies steadily gained ground; the German authorities focused on the evacuation of loot and military equipment. Rescued loot—much of it waste—clogged transport routes; finished products and raw materials piled up in warehouses. The regime forcibly marched columns of half-dead concentration camp prisoners and forced laborers to new "strategic" destinations on notorious death marches.[8] To relieve the pressures on the war economy, additional labor was needed to unload shipments, declog railways, and distribute and process materials. And yet, the regime systematically murdered its slave-labor force. Internally, the SS and Gestapo ramped up their terror, indiscriminately targeting all "subversive elements," executing forced laborers, shirkers, deserters, soldiers who had gotten cut off from their regiments, and civilians who had abandoned their posts or whose inefficiency, panic, or disorientation posed obstacles to the war effort. Transportation bottlenecks, infrastructural collapse, breakdown of communication, and provisioning chaos characterized the final months of Hitler's "Thousand-Year Reich." In the context of rapid implosion, the very notion that recycling cleaning rags would be of utmost strategic importance appears rather strange, if not utterly delusional.[9]

Even in early 1945, the language of resource extension and waste reclamation had lost none of its power. To the contrary, in the face of endemic shortages and mass destruction, making something from nothing or turning waste into a resource resonated precisely because nothing but waste was available in abundance. Since 1936, waste avoidance and waste reclamation had been central pillars of the Nazi economy, encouraging ordinary citizens to conserve and extend the Reich's resource base at every turn. In the absence of resource-rich colonies, the self-described people without space (*Volk ohne Raum*) bought into the fantasy of a circular economy that could cycle raw materials through the production process indefinitely long before wartime shortages necessitated such thinking.[10] Therefore, Rothe was hardly alone, as he focused on the hidden value of accumulated garbage. Miracle weapons aside, waste reclamation had become the only language that Germans could employ to redress and reverse the fortunes of war.[11]

Until the very end, Nazi authorities freighted tons of metal scrap, airplane junk, broken down military equipment, rags, old shoes, and textile waste back to the Reich, in a futile effort to close the raw material cycle and stopgap the imploding economy through the brutal extraction of labor from the depleted bodies of Jews, concentration camp inmates, and forced laborers. For years, waste materials had been celebrated as the solution to all of Germany's resource problems and raw material shortages; by 1945, they filled warehouses and stressed fuel reserves. Still, Nazi children continued to chase after metal junk and secondary materials; they had gotten used to "rescuing" iron bolts from railroad tracks and carrying their family's rags and kitchen bones to designated collection points for recycling. Old habits die slowly. The quasi-religious hunt for junk glutted a destructive cycle until it, too, ground to a halt, buckling under its own weight. Rothe's persistent attempts to secure both labor and materials for his recycling endeavors amidst the regime's implosion illustrate the extent to which Germans desperately held on to Nazi ideas of order.

The Nazi Empire was a waste regime.[12] Imagining Germans as a spaceless people, strapped for raw materials, surrounded by powerful adversaries, and threatened by internal enemies, the regime developed an economic rationale that linked waste utilization (recycling) and internal purging. Framing questions about national security as a matter of racial purity and territorial expansion, the regime refracted racist ideas in economic terms, focused around *Blockadesicherheit* (security against blockade), *Nahrungsfreiheit* (food freedom), and *Autarkie* (resource independence), deliberately reimagining conquest and oppression as defensive strategies.[13] Waste and squander were crimes against the nation, frugality and thrift the unquestioned responsibility of every member of the people's community. Inner enemies depleted scarce resources and threatened national health. While internal enemies were the responsibility of the SS, the war against waste and squander engaged ordinary Germans from the start.[14] By scrapping and skimping, recycling and salvaging, they supported a system that ultimately didn't work for them, but nonetheless buttressed social structures that underwrote the brutal exploitation and murder of millions.[15] As the example of Rothe illustrates, by the end of the war, the unquestioned assumptions about cleanliness and resource-savviness that drove imperial expansion, shaped the concentration camp complex, and became central to the Nazi genocide of the Jews and other minorities informed the economic considerations of private individuals as well.

Nazi economic common sense became a function of total resource exploitation, dubbed zero-waste today. Initially, zero waste was only a matter of rhetoric. But with the 1936 Four-Year Plan, the Nazi regime wrote the maximization of resource use and extraction into law.[16] Nothing of value, no matter how small, was to be wasted. During the war, everything became subject to extraction—from sewage to potato juice, from coal dust to kitchen garbage, from rags and old shoes to airplane junk and rusted tanks. With hidden value lurking everywhere, citizens, entrepreneurs, and policymakers conjured up countless schemes to squeeze value from waste or invent new uses for defunct, outmoded, or spent material, no matter the cost. The materials from which no more value could be squeezed were removed and destroyed.

The fanatical obsession with waste and resource extensions at least partially explains the glaring economic dysfunction that characterized the Nazi regime in its final years, when genocidal practice decisively interfered with strategic imperatives by depriving the war economy of its labor force.[17] Waste was simultaneously a contaminating threat, a sign of administrative inefficiency or personal failure, and a precious resource. Given that most of the labor performed in ghettos and camps was waste labor, even when in the service of strategic goals, the experts who managed the slave labor complex and allocated raw materials constantly adjusted the economy of value, moving people and things into and out of the category of waste in a desperate effort to meet competing demands.

When the initial military successes of the summer of 1941 provided a near infinite supply of slave labor in the form of Soviet POWs and enemy civilians, the Nazi leadership shifted its thinking about Europe's Jews, whom they saw as both a security threat and "unnecessary eaters," and moved from a policy of expulsion and resettlement toward annihilation.[18] However, even then, Hitler made it very clear that at no point was the solution to the "Jewish question" to interfere with the Reich's economic (war-making) priorities, implying that if strategically necessary, Jews would be put to work rather than murdered.[19] Plenipotentiary of Labor Fritz Sauckel explained that providing rations to people merely to keep them alive without extracting "equivalent performance, must be regarded from the point of view of the national war economy as a pure loss."[20] The Nazi economy was running on war, not profit. War prioritized winning. Once winning appeared clearly utopian, the hierarchy of priorities crumbled. Extracting labor from Jews and murdering them collapsed into a single strategy.[21] Eventually, this genocidal system of hoarding and forced labor, of plunder and murder spiraled toward collapse. Even as wastes glutted and ultimately paralyzed both transportation networks and production, Germans clung to the fantasy that emaciated prisoners would turn rags into uniforms and junk into weapons of war. To illustrate and explain the origins and internal logic of the Nazi waste regime's genocidal and ultimately self-devouring excess is the purpose of this book.

Rags Don't Eat

Nazi Germany, World War II, and the Holocaust are among the most thoroughly studied subjects in human history. Yet, the question that continues to be asked is: "How could it happen?"[22] This passive framing and the non-naming of either object or subject create the impression that these events lie outside history, even as scholars have provided names, descriptions, and explanations.[23] At times, intense debates have characterized this burgeoning field, arguing over Hitler's personal role and intentions versus the self-radicalizing dynamics of the Nazi state and its bureaucratic apparatus,[24] over Nazism's "modernity,"[25] over the Holocaust's singularity and the nature of antisemitism,[26] and most recently over the ethics and necessity of comparative approaches.[27] In conversation with these debates, *Empire of Rags and Bones* argues that the mundane practices of cleanup, salvage, and waste reclamation cast Nazi imperial destruction and its genocidal rationality in a new light. In Nazi Germany, economic common sense was uncoupled from profit. The underlying rationale was not the growth of the economy but the growth of the regime's annihilative capacity. Accordingly, "the market" as an objective determinant of value ceased to exist, and economic rationales shifted.[28] Instead, the regime subordinated the economy to its political agenda and attempted to lead, fully and unapologetically, a world order in which racial hierarchies forged through war determined the distribution of resources.[29]

Nazism broke the fourth wall of racial capitalism. Racial capitalism surreptitiously reproduces White supremacy, while insisting that racial inequalities are inadvertent side-effects of market-based dynamics.[30] Nazism had no need for such deception. Instead, it enlisted market-based principles to build a self-consciously racist world order. Nazi ideologues outright rejected universal ideas of freedom and equality that crystalized at the very moment that Europeans built the structures that engendered systematic inequality, violent oppression, and, indeed, genocide (and ecocide) as an equally universal reality.[31] Instead, Nazism saw systematic inequality and race war as foundational to the geopolitical order and key to its own ascent. Accordingly, racial and economic goals were not hierarchical but identical.[32] War was the only strategy that could address both goals simultaneously. Waste reclamation served as an intermediate but crucial bridge between presumed resource scarcity and imagined imperial riches that would propel the engines to "final victory." The resulting hunt for inferior materials—rags, bones, metal junk— knew no bounds. Since, in the eyes of the regime, Jews had no intrinsic value besides their labor output, the resulting economic logic boiled down to a simple fact—rags don't eat. Heinrich Himmler and SS leaders in Nazi-occupied Poland, together with economic managers and civil administrators, reasoned that even minimally fed people process more rags than they carry on their bodies. Accordingly, the SS kept alive the minimum number of Jews needed to process the material remnants of the "surplus" populations. In the end, the Nazis rescued rags and murdered people.

The framework of the waste regime offers a window onto how Nazi racism operated and how ideas about waste and recycling informed calculations about labor exploitation and murder. Historians agree that racial ideology provided a key organizing principle for state power in Nazi Germany, even if they increasingly question the extent to which racism and antisemitism provide the best explanation for the widespread consent to, complicity with, and participation in the regime's genocidal war and the destruction of the Jews.[33] The concept of "the racial state" serves as a crucial descriptor of the

Nazi regime's organizing principles, but it does not sufficiently explain the thoughts and actions of ordinary Germans.[34] It is precisely the crude functionality with which racial maxims were invoked when policies and actions flew in the face of conventional (economic) wisdom that cuts to the core of their power. Rather than a primary driver of individual action, racial ideology gave Germans a way to explain the necessity of their behaviors to themselves and each other after the fact.[35] This is not to say that Germans did not hold racist beliefs, but rather that these beliefs alone cannot explain their continued participation in a genocidal war that in their eyes was "both unpopular and legitimate."[36] Rather, Nazi racism circumscribed "dangers" and offered "defensive" frameworks for justifying actions that were clearly amoral and outright criminal.[37]

Waste management was the glue that bound ordinary Germans to the Nazi regime and cemented its genocidal logic in everyday practice, precisely because salvaging, scrapping, and extending resources were seen as inherently good and orderly behaviors. After the proclamation of the Four-Year Plan in September 1936, the idea of a closed-loop economy undergirded Nazi preparations for war and provided the rationale for the extraction of value from waste and secondary materials for its duration. Anticipating an economy of scarcity, the Nazi regime enlisted ordinary Germans in the performance of frugality and thrift and increasingly relied on their cooperation to return every bit of valuable material to the cycle in support of the growing demands of the war economy. Waste avoidance and waste reclamation provided the organizing framework, guiding political activism and social policing.[38]

Even when it was not essential to citizens' self-understanding, Nazi racism ordered social relations in unmistakable terms. The garbage economy of the Third Reich offered local functionaries, industrialists, and ordinary citizens ample space for political action and self-actualization; the Nazi racial order provided a framework for imagining the war as both essential and defensive, rather than merely expansionist. This total, genocidal war ultimately produced incontrovertible evidence for otherwise baseless claims of German lack of space and resource poverty. Ordinary Germans found entry into this system through skimping and salvaging rather than racist sloganeering in ways that did not require political consciousness or conviction, but rather fostered it.

Scarcity had affected large segments of German society intermittently since World War I.[39] Once in power, the Nazi regime deliberately rearmed at the expense of consumer society, artificially extending experiences of scarcity beyond economic recovery and the return to full employment in 1936 and throughout its brutal war, all the while promising prosperity for a postwar future.[40] During the war, scarcity became a harsh reality anticipated and experienced by most Germans. Conserving resources, collecting recyclables, and, ultimately, cleaning up the mess of war, Germans actively forged the Nazi racial order and, knowingly or not, accepted the necessity of a war of extraction and imperial conquest. However, skimping on meat and collecting bottle caps and kitchen scraps are hardly the kinds of practices that inspire wholesale enthusiasm in their own right, satisfy desires for consumer goods and comforts, or assuage very real experiences of loss and want.[41] Such daily demonstrations of good citizenship were designed and advertised to extend the war-making capacity of the regime. Germans understood their momentary sacrifices and daily recycling labor in light of the promised reward of a postwar future of plenty, premised on genocidal destruction, slave labor, plunder, and systematic exploitation of colonial resources. In the context of wartime destruction, Germans recast the violent extraction of labor and material as a matter of national survival.

Garbage Empire

Empires bleed value from people and the land. Diamonds and gold, stimulants and spices, timber, cotton, and fossil fuels are the stuff of empire.[42] The imperial visions of the Third Reich, too, were focused on natural resources, such as iron, oil, and fertile soil, and the Nazis robbed whatever luxury goods they could get their hands on.[43] But in the end, whether for textiles or gold, the Nazi Empire mined people rather than land, not as a matter of principle but as a matter of wartime contingency and expedience. To be clear, there were elaborate plans and truncated attempts to build up more traditional structures of imperial extraction, but those were ground down by war.

A growing number of historians have emphasized the imperial nature of the Nazi state and its colonizing ambitions.[44] Others have begun to examine direct linkages between the Nazi imperial project and imperial Germany's colonizing efforts overseas.[45] This book shows how Nazi Germany developed both novel imperial structures and actively adapted lessons from Germany's own colonial history and the larger European colonial repertoire in the attempt to conquer, depopulate, and colonize the east.[46] Nazi imperial planning anticipated the starvation of millions of people as an inevitable side-effect of German expansion.[47] The regime considered the allocation of resources (food, clothing, and shelter) to internal enemies (Jews) and subjected (colonial) populations wasteful and out of line with its economic imperatives. Accordingly, allocation of food and other bare necessities followed calculations familiar from other imperial contexts.[48] An environmental—that is, an extractivist—framework makes visible the connections between Nazism and its colonial precursors.

The process of resource extraction is profoundly violent, destroying human and non-human actors and environments in the pursuit of profit.[49] In the context of the Nazi waste regime, the concept of extraction did not involve the profitability usually associated with imperial extraction of gold, timber, oil, or cotton. Rather than a linear process of taking from nature to produce goods that will eventually become waste, the Nazi regime's focus on secondary and waste materials meant that extraction operated at multiple points in a supposedly infinite cycle of resource production and regeneration by eliminating waste rather than by making profit. The goal of this "zero-waste" economy was not growth per se but the extension of its murderous capacity. In Nazi practice, extraction fed the cycles of destruction.

Because of the short-lived nature of its existence, an existence entirely overshadowed and shaped by war, Nazi Germany focused almost exclusively on exploiting secondary and waste materials that war and genocide generated in abundance. The piles of shoes, garments, glasses, and other items that visually encoded the destruction of humanity and a break in civilization also render visible these practices of resource extraction and the excruciating labor that went into producing them.[50] But even when it comes to silver or iron ore, resources are never merely there, waiting to be claimed. To understand extraction as resource production makes labor visible.[51]

Through the perspective of the waste regime, the linkages between the racist, expansionist, and extractivist objectives of the Nazi Empire become recognizable. Waste reclamation and ruthless labor regimes together affixed the stigma of filth to "racial inferiors" and "social misfits" through carceral systems of labor exploitation that reduced people's existences to "bare life."[52] It was on the very bodies of Jews, Soviet POWs, *Ostarbeiter* (eastern workers),[53] so-called asocials, racial "inferiors," and "criminals," that the twin logic of imperial extraction and genocidal destruction operated. By 1944, columns of slave laborers—inmates from correctional facilities, concentration camp prisoners, POWs, and civilians deported from enemy nations—constituted almost the entirety of the regime's labor force.[54] Not only were forced laborers deployed in strategic industry, they also cleaned up the rubble, unloaded trains stuffed with junk, recycled garments, and scrapped machinery. Germans found their racial and cultural "superiority" affirmed and turned away in disgust as these bedraggled masses did society's "shit work."[55] Waste labor invariably mapped human value onto Nazi racial hierarchies. In the face of certain defeat, Germans only aligned themselves more firmly with the structures of policing that promised safety from contamination and pollution. By the end of the war, millions of Germans unthinkingly acted within the parameters set by the Nazi waste regime, exacerbating its genocidal practice and inadvertently accelerating its collapse.

A focus on resource extraction (recycling) and waste eradication shows that value systems are forged, painfully, brutally, and usually on the backs of the most vulnerable people.[56] It is evident from the General Plan East, the central genocidal plan for the colonization of Eastern Europe, and other planning documents that the regime intended to build up infrastructures for mining, industrial production, and agriculture.[57] War just jinxed the timing. Together with wholesale and unlimited plunder, the comprehensive collection, freight, and recycling of waste and secondary materials were not goals in their own right. Instead, they were strategies to bridge the resource gap and carry the war economy toward final victory, which would, in the Nazi imagination, provide the pioneer space to build up infrastructures of extraction familiar from other settler colonial and imperial contexts.[58] The hunt for waste, secondary, and base materials and their subsequent recycling within a proliferating complex of forced labor took the place of oil fields, cotton plantations, and silver mines. In the Nazi Empire, recycling *was* extraction.

In this book, extraction is employed in two distinct ways. On the one hand, extraction is what the Nazis did as they violently squeezed value from people and things. On the other hand, extraction conceptually links the Nazi regime to imperial projects in different times. Like other colonial powers, the Nazi regime exploited local labor and indiscriminately plundered materials from its empire.[59] At the same time, Nazi imperialists zeroed in on inferior materials, wastes, and secondary materials to maximize their destructive capacity. Based on the premise that Germany lacked essential resources, the regime targeted wastefulness as a matter of principle and devised routines to squeeze the maximum yield out of raw materials and its slave-labor force. At the most basic level, then, the Nazi waste regime did not distinguish between junk and jewels; everything from which some value might be squeezed was subject to deportation and extraction, including humans. The regime selectively extracted labor from its own and subjected populations based on the sociobiological hierarchy codified by the Nazi racial state. At the end of this violent dynamic, the materials that had been *ausgeschlachtet* (exploited) and people who had been bled dry were cast aside, buried, burned, or left to rot. The only limitations were logistical.

Environments of Destruction

The environment and how the Nazi regime understood the environment are crucial to this story of expansion, extraction, and destruction. Nazi Germany was neither preservationist nor conservationist, and it most certainly was not green.[60] While Nazi ideologues idealized the German forest and experimented with biodynamic food production, there simply is no evidence that the Nazi fetishization of primordial nature translated into environmental stewardship or care. But that does not mean National Socialists didn't have ideas about the environment (*Umwelt*), even if they had little use for the term itself.[61]

Nazi ideology theorized nature as vast, if not limitlessness. Accordingly, expansion and resource exploitation were of particular importance to the Nazi environmental imagination. The key concept was not "the environment" but *Lebensraum* (living space, literally, the "space that sustains life"), indicating both the essential and the subservient role nature played in the Nazi imagination. Moreover, the concept of *Lebensraum* was premised on the imagined compatibility between race and space. Supposedly, the biogeological qualities of any given space would reach for racially compatible inhabitants and naturally "eject" populations whose nature (i.e., race) did not correspond to the unchangeable qualities of the soil, Nazi ideologues mused.[62] Grounded in human exceptionalism, National Socialists understood the relationship between humans and their environments not only in hierarchical and utilitarian terms, but also imagined an exploitative symbiosis as natural.[63] In other words, National Socialist understanding of the environment was extractivist.[64]

Unlike the United States, the Nazi regime had not yet reached the outer edges of its "frontier" and hence did not need to concern itself with preservation or conservation.[65] To the contrary, the entire Nazi project was premised on expanding frontiers.[66] Accordingly, the regime operated with the notion of a passive environment that lay in waiting—to be seized, *erschlossen* (cultivated), and mined. Conservation, not of nature but of resources, was a temporary necessity rather than a goal in its own right. In the Nazi imaginary, resources were not finite, they were just elsewhere. The conquest, cleansing, and settling of *Lebensraum* would provide the natural environment in which the German "race" could flourish and prosper.[67]

Privileging the regime's extractivist practice rather than Hitler's ideas about nature, this book examines how Nazi imperialism fundamentally restructured the environments of Europe. It is informed by studies that show how National Socialists acted on the environment while focusing on economic utility, agricultural yield, popular consent, and population control.[68] Ultimately, the environment National Socialists inhabited was an environment made by war. Environments of war involve human technology, geography, weather, pests, and disease, among other factors.[69] This book is populated by rats, flies, livestock, and pathogens, even if they rarely function as the main actors. It does not attribute explanatory power to the cold, the weather, or climate directly. Rather, it shows how Nazi war making produced particular kinds of environments that heightened the sensibilities of authorities and ordinary Germans toward dangers posed by natural forces and racial enemies, reordering the perception of an existential threat in line with the ideological imperatives of the Nazi regime. Environments of war thus shaped the social and material worlds of occupiers and occupied, of soldiers and citizens, of slave laborers and their oppressor in fundamentally unequal terms, radicalizing Nazi visions for racial mastery. Nazi Germany reordered the racial and physical environments of the continent, but rather than fostering industrial production in an economically unified Europe (*Grosswirtschaftsraum*), war making mined inferior raw materials and forged environments of destruction.[70]

Ideas about "purity" were crucial to this worldview and ultimately shaped the racial, social, and economic thinking of ordinary people around the putatively apolitical and timeless principle of cleanup, underwriting the brutal labor regimes that connected fantasies of racial purification to the eradication of unproductive or "unworthy" people.[71] Hitler's antisemitism certainly occupied a central position in this matrix and shaped the particular virulence with which the Nazi regime pursued the destruction of European Jews. The destructive dynamism of the Nazi waste regime readily accommodated antisemitism without making it a necessary precondition for participating in its resource fetishizing, genocidal operations.

Waste and Excess

The concept of waste and the histories of recycling, then, are crucial for understanding the ways in which racial and economic rationales intersected.[72] Rather than a single physical category, this book contends that material substances of waste and wastelike matter (dirt, dregs, discards, recyclables, debris, rubble, etc.) moved between categories and changed over time—metabolically and in the eyes of beholders. Even as a "basic sign" left behind by living animals in the form of excrement, waste's nature constantly shifts and remains both transient and reversible.[73] Here, waste differs from residue, which is usually understood as an irreversible and permanent, often toxic, remainder.[74] While waste is neither dirt nor merely "matter out of place," the conceptual confluence of dirt, filth, waste, discards, and so forth underscores the power of social taboos and cultural norms to evoke emotional reactions. It is never really clear whether waste is an actual object that threatens to contaminate and pollute or merely an idea that produces the same kind of reflexive response as a result of social processes of ascription. As a result, waste is a unique social force that inspires the constant desire to fixate, to regulate, to order.[75] Authorities readily respond to the sense of disorder that the presence of waste matter invariably produces.[76]

In Nazi Germany, waste was an economic category, a racial category, and an environmental one. Waste was central to the Nazi conceptualization of "order" and merged notions of purity and efficiency, which ultimately depended on the complete, remainder-less exploitation of value and the equally total eradication of valuelessness from inanimate matter and human labor.[77] It was simultaneously reimagined as a valuable resource and experienced as a "revolting object" or idea.[78] This contradictory simultaneity of waste underscores the dynamic nature of the Nazi waste regime as it oscillated between extraction and destruction.

By the end of the war, wastes of varying sorts piled sky-high, structuring German experiences of defeat and shaping the world's understanding of the German crimes. The regime's murderous reordering of life and death etched its presence into the environment: mountainous accumulations of secondary material, junk, and rubble were the defining topographical features of Germany in the spring of 1945. Bone fields still stretch across vast territories in Eastern Europe, and in some places, when the snow melts and the earth settles, femurs and skulls well up from the ground.[79] In Germany, corpses were stacked and scattered next to the pits and piles of ash and bone fragments in Nazi concentration camps when coal delivery failures interfered with the burning of the dead. By 1944, it did not require measurements by the air quality control institute to register the dramatic increase of particles (dust and ash) in the vicinity of sites of industrial mass murder such as Auschwitz.[80] A simple human nose was refined instrument enough. The piles of corpses, rubble, personal items, hair, and household goods not only capture the enormity of the Nazi crimes against Jews, Roma, and the peoples of Eastern Europe, but also the back-breaking labor that went into sorting, cleaning, and recycling these materials. They are moreover a record of the violence that actively shattered social worlds, ripped families apart, dragged people from their homes, and willfully destroyed the lives of millions. Resembling trash heaps, these piles of stuff have long since served as visual shorthand for the inexplicable madness and irrational excess of the Nazi regime. The excess is beyond dispute, yet the neatly sorted piles betray allegations of irrationality.[81]

This is not a comfortable book to read, nor is it meant to be. While most readers will expect to encounter narratives of cruelty, murder, and destruction in a book on the Nazi genocide, the everyday structures of the Nazi waste regime show the embeddedness of mindless violence, of decay, of rot, of the decomposition of human and nonhuman life in the face of technopolitical performances of efficiency and plain apathy. This book draws attention to the visceral nature of killing and dying, to the stench of decomposing corpses, to bodies plagued by sickness and lice, to obliterated cities teaming with vermin, to environments suffused with death, and to people going about their business in the midst of it. For all its technological precision and industrial scale, murder was a personal, an intimate affair.

The juxtaposition of garbage and genocide will make many readers uneasy. To look at the Nazi crimes through the prism of waste and recycling is not meant to sensationalize. Instead, it is intended to illustrate how mundane, seemingly innocuous, unquestioned assumptions about cleanliness and order were central to the apparatus of policing and the practice of mass murder. This book emphasizes that death was an all-pervasive presence and visceral reality that structured the lives of killers, collaborators, facilitators, bystanders, onlookers, and away-lookers in ways that call the separateness of these very categories into question. Garbage and waste management touched the lives (and hands) of all Germans, no matter the role they played in the destructive matrix of killing and dying that governed Nazi-occupied Europe.

Empire of Rags and Bones is organized in three parts that follow the Nazi waste regime from its origins to its violent implosion. While the narrative proceeds along chronological lines, each part has a distinct thematic focus. Part I, "Order," illustrates how waste management became central to the new social order Nazism envisioned and ultimately enforced. Chapter 1 delineates the contours of the Nazi waste regime in comprehensive terms to set the framework for the chapters that follow. It further explains the ideological linkages between race thinking and waste management, focusing on the language around purity, health, and order. However, as Chapter 2 illustrates, the Nazi waste regime did not simply spring from the minds of Nazi ideologues. Instead, it was the result of a vision that relied on bottom-up initiatives to coordinate waste infrastructures in line with state imperatives. Since those imperatives were only developing, local initiatives by scrap merchants, municipal officials, and individual businessmen, like the cleaning rag expert Mr. Rothe, shaped the developing structures as well as hardened ideological principles by grounding them in practice. Detailing how peacetime propaganda campaigns set the stage for the total mobilization of the population, Chapter 3 zeroes in on the role played by ordinary citizens and describes the Nazi party's efforts to enlist them in comprehensive recycling schemes. In scrapping, salvaging, and other waste-focused initiatives, citizens recognized readily accessible, seemingly apolitical, ways to participate in a regime premised on imperial conquest and genocidal extraction. By the height of the war, scrapping had become a routine, unquestioned part of everyday life for the vast majority of Germans.

Part II, "Extraction," shifts the focus toward the complex administrative apparatus dedicated to material and labor extraction. Since the Nazi regime was particularly concerned with armaments production and the reduction of imports, imperial plunder focused on metals and textiles.[82] Chapter 4 traces the development of the complex for metal requisitioning from 1939 to the collapse of the regime. Detailing the ever-proliferating structures of mafia-esque booty-hunters in Nazi-occupied Europe, this chapter illustrates the increasing competition between strategic and economic priorities. Rags, and textiles more generally, constitute the focus of Chapter 5, which examines the development of an apparatus of pilfering in the Nazi-occupied east. At the center of this chapter lies the destructive entrepreneurship of the so-called *Ostgesellschaften*, companies that merged administrative and market-based structures for the purpose of gutting enemy territory, ostensibly "developing" the colonial lands. The disregard for civilians and laborers reached its apex in the landscape of camps. Chapter 6 demonstrates how Nazi racism and zero-waste rationality worked in tandem. Science, technology, administration, bureaucracy, and industry converged, accepting forced labor as an indispensable necessity in the face of resource scarcity and labor shortages, ultimately cementing the link between forced labor and recycling in carceral settings—from ordinary prisons to the concentration camp complex. Camps, this chapter shows, became a crucial component of the regime's waste management infrastructure.

The final part of this book, "Destruction," shows how purification fantasies and imperial extraction congealed into a matrix of violent destruction. Focused on soap production, Chapter 7 highlights the connections between Nazi slave labor and wartime recycling to show how ideas about cleanliness and hygiene readily coalesced with Nazi racism inside the Nazi camps—environments designed as rubbished spaces. This chapter shows how SS ideas about racial pollution and mantras of total extraction came together in a destructive cycle of plunder, sanitization, and murder. Chapter 8 examines the final fits of the Nazi waste regime before it suffocated in the glut of materials freighted back to Germany. Juxtaposing the fantasy built around garbage technology with the realities of military implosion and infrastructural collapse, the chapter shows that despite the reeking matter that accumulated inside Germany—garbage, rubble, sewage, corpses—Germans clung to the idea that hundreds of thousands of dying prisoners would turn waste into essential goods for final victory. Chapter 9 details the collapse of the Nazi waste regime and surveys the landscape of piles it left in its wake. Focusing on the last months of the war and the hellscape of Bergen-Belsen concentration camp, this chapter illustrates how through the rot of death and the violence of implosion, Germans held on to ideas about cleanliness and order that had powered the Nazi waste regime, reaffixing the stigma of filth to survivors and displaced persons. Cleaning up the mess of war, first forced and then with self-satisfied conviction, Germans all but erased the evidence that the Nazi regime's extractivist rationality had recorded in a landscape of piles.

PART I
ORDER

1
The Nazi Waste Regime

Imprisoned at Landsberg and reminiscing on his "schooling," Hitler had lots to say about refuse (*Unrat*) and filth (*Schmutz*). Throughout the ramblings that made up his political testament *Mein Kampf*, Hitler returned time and again to metaphors of waste, decay, and dirt as well as the associated sights and smells to describe the existential threat "the Jew" supposedly posed to the "German race" and *Kultur*. His views were likely shaped by his own earlier descent into abject poverty and less than immaculate cleanliness—his most eminent biographer describes the young Hitler as "thin and bedraggled, in filthy, lice-infested clothes"—when in 1913 he moved into one of Vienna's recently established shelters for the homeless.[1] His subsequent projections of impurity and filth onto his most loathed enemy became a regular feature of his political rants. Hitler insisted that the lack of "moral and other purity of this people [Jews]" was a sticking point for him and crucial to the development of his "insight" into the historical accuracy and political necessity of antisemitism:

> That we are not concerned with water-lovers, was obvious from their mere appearance, unfortunately, often in evidence even with one's eyes closed. Later, I found myself nauseated by the smell of these kaftan-wearers. Plus, the unclean clothing and the less than heroic veneer. All of this was quite unappealing; yet one was revulsed when discovering in addition to the bodily squalidness the moral stains of this chosen people.[2]

National Socialists were hardly breaking new ground when maligning racial others as filthy and dirty, when aligning them with waste and shit, all the while actively designing living and working conditions that would provide "evidence" for the unalterable essence of those they designated as subhuman.[3] Hitler could look back on a long tradition of Western philosophers, thinkers, and statesmen when clinging to metaphors of purity (*Reinheit*) and cleanliness (*Sauberkeit*) to express a racist worldview.[4]

The emphasis on "purity" and the importance of "cleanup" resonated in the context of interwar disruption, cultural revolution, economic uncertainty, and political polarization. For National Socialist ideologues, racial, environmental, and economic thinking readily congealed, and cleanup was central to all.[5] The problems Nazi Germany defined for itself—resource scarcity, racial pollution, encirclement by powerful enemies, proliferating degeneracy within the national body among them—could be solved. The national body could be cleansed, waste could be transformed into a resource, something could be made of nothing, and with strength, determination, and will enemies could be repelled and the geopolitical realities remade.

Resource thinking and obsessions with cleanliness thus moved to the core of the regime's conception of order. Over the course of the 1930s, waste and waste management came to play a crucial function in bridging the gap between rhetoric (labeling as filthy and unproductive) and practice (exorcising those labeled as filthy and unproductive), taking the policing of biosocial and racial others to new extremes. Since waste functioned as both stigma and potential resource, the potency of waste cut two ways. On the one hand, the concentration of "undesirable" people in camps and ghetto affixed the stigma of waste and wastefulness to those individuals whom the regime understood and treated as "lesser." On the other hand, the regime fetishized waste products that could be reclaimed, reused, or recycled as a most precious resource of national political importance. To return this valuable matter to the raw material cycle, the regime increasingly extracted labor from racial and biosocial others. The stench, filth, rot, and decay associated with waste and garbage became instead equated with those whose labor transformed waste into resource. Waste practices ranging from frugality and thrift to salvage and recycling, to burning and dumping provided cohesion to the Nazi system and opened multiple, seemingly apolitical points of entry into the Nazi racial state.[6]

Waste management provided opportunities for participation and innovation long before the war necessitated resource conservation. Initially based on individual initiative, as of 1936, the Four-Year Plan stipulated waste avoidance and regulations for total recycling, ordering social relations in comprehensive terms. Administrative responses to problems posed in the language of garbage seemed neither foreign nor radical to most people after Hitler assumed the chancellorship of the Weimar Republic.[7] The geopolitical relevance of collecting and recycling secondary materials readily escaped most people. In the context of protracted scarcity, it just made good sense.

The Biosocial "Environment"

It is tempting to read Hitler's utterances about filth as precipitating the subsequent development of eradicative practices when, in fact, common German discourse conveyed racial difference, social deviance, degeneracy, and criminality as the inverse of cleanliness and orderliness. For Hitler, historian Gisela Lebzelter argues, "the term 'Neger' [Negro] was code for everything despicable, 'black' a synonym for evil, inferior, un-German."[8] Hitler's worldview formed in the context of European empire-building, and his entry into politics was shaped in part by the realization that the lost war also meant an end to German colonial expansion and rule.[9] Hitler's ideas were certainly extreme, but his reactions toward the German geopolitical demotion and its forced exit from the imperial stage were representative of a large cross section of German society.[10] While much of bourgeois society in Weimar Germany was alienated by Hitler's violent antisemitic rhetoric, a much narrower contingent had compunctions about German imperial ambitions or anti-Black racism.[11] Even the political factions of the left that opposed imperialism in theory responded with outrage to the presence of French colonial troops on the Rhine.[12] The widespread consensus about racial hierarchies, insisting on the cultural, intellectual, and moral superiority of White Europeans over "the colored hordes," was further cemented by anthropological research conducted during the war.[13] With access to "specimens" in prisoner of war (POW) camps, German anthropologists broke "new ground" by deploying the theoretical apparatus of racial science to the comparative study of European and non-European prisoners. As historian Andrew Evans shows, "[T]he camps placed Europeans into subject positions that were almost identical to those of many non-Europeans in similar camps created during earlier colonial wars" and, not surprisingly, in the prison environment "the distinction between European and non-Europeans quickly collapsed," producing the "evidence" for the racial inferiority of Jews, Sinti, Roma, and Slavs as "asiatic peoples."[14]

The trauma and devastation of war exacerbated fears of racial decline and population quality that had shaped the outlook of social reformers, cultural pessimists, social Darwinists, and eugenicists since the late nineteenth century.[15] During the same period, the expansion of urban sanitation infrastructures similarly reinforced ideas of a social order premised on biracial and social-hygienic considerations.[16] Unsurprisingly, municipal policing developed in parallel to enforce the proliferating ordinances and regulations intended to guarantee public health and social order.[17] In fact, the German term "Polizei" denoted an entire science (*Polizeiwissenschaft*) devoted to governance and administration with the goal of producing order.[18] Only over the course of the nineteenth century did police become a force patrolling the streets in Europe. Initially, police were saddled with responsibilities to enforce regulations such as vagrancy laws, anti-dumping ordinances, street cleaning ordinances, and poor laws that marked an underclass of "idlers" who periodically threatened to erupt into riots. The crime-fighting fiction of policing developed only in the context of urban growth and industrialization. Throughout the so-called West, understanding of social hygiene and urban order was intimately connected to and only hardened further in the face of the social disruptions brought by war and revolution.[19]

The moral, sexual, and cultural panic that characterized different parts of German society from the far right to bourgeois reform movements echoed widely across Europe.[20] These trends attained a new urgency in the aftermath of war and the context of a global flu pandemic, shaping views about social contamination and racial contagion.[21] Accordingly, popular fears of disease, the scientific discovery of pathogens, and the role of insects (lice) in spreading disease, typhus in particular, merged with sociological observations of the negative effects of poverty, overcrowding, lack of ventilation, unsanitary conditions, and infestation of vermin in urban settings on the spread and fatality of disease. Race scientists and social reformers thus drew on biomedical metaphors in their attempt to "treat" the social body of the city or the nation.[22]

Ideas about biosocial dangers were shared widely across the political spectrum.[23] By the early 1930s, the practice of casting social problems in the language of waste and decay, entomology and disease, and of course race was not peculiar to Nazi Germany.[24] Over the first half of the twentieth century, the biopolitical paradigm shaped social and national security considerations across Europe and grounded the emerging Nazi emphasis on purity in a broader scientific consensus.[25] Concerned about poverty, noise pollution, crime, air and water quality, pathogens and disease, urban planners, medical professionals, and social reformers tried to manage social and natural environments, particular in large cities.[26]

National Socialists, too, sought to design and manage a "healthy" environment (*Umwelt*).[27] Unlike conservationists, Nazi ideologues were less preoccupied with pristine nature or its protection than with access to nature, whether as a reservoir of natural resources or leisure spaces that would allow workers to recharge their bodies.[28] But nature was hardly the only or primary focus of National Socialists. Without using the term *Umwelt*, National Socialist ideologues and planners were concerned with environments more broadly conceived: On the one hand, they focused on land as an exploitable resource. On the other hand, they worried about the spatial, racial, microbial surroundings and their potentially adverse effects on the health and vitality of the nation.

Accordingly, the Nazi regime managed environments to increase yield and eradicate sources of potential danger or contamination.[29] How best to achieve these goals was not always clear and often contested. Ideas about land use, for example, were rife with contradiction. Some ideologues supported conservationist efforts to protect the German forests and nature preserves, yet at the same time they recast the practice of rubbishing the countryside as "soil melioration."[30] Under the premise of *Urbarmachung* (development), Nazi administrators pushed for the use of unprocessed garbage and untreated sewage as fertilizer to increase agricultural yields.[31] Scientists "confirmed" that concerns about typhus contamination were "exaggerated."[32] With respect to built environments, too, ideas about what constituted healthy environments and how to achieve them were not preordained. After the city of Hamburg had razed one of the congested alley quarters to the ground in 1934, the regime-friendly sociologist Andreas Walther argued against slum clearance, noting that Hamburg ended up displacing and dispersing the "*gemeinschaftsschädigende* [malignant]" inhabitants after obliterating this "site of infection."[33] Overturning conventional wisdom, he subsequently advocated for containment and concentration of "asocial elements" to facilitate their control, a practice that became the defining feature of Nazi social policy.[34] Walther, too, invoked nature to underwrite his analysis, insisting that the terms "*gemeinschaftsschädigend*" and "*volksschädigend*" do not pass moral judgment, but rather, "foreground the effect" that "degenerate" individuals would have on healthy environments.[35] This way of thinking was not particularly Nazi, nor was Walther alone in thinking about environments, particular urban environments, in biosocial terms. His work was informed by the longitudinal studies conducted by eugenicist E. J. Lidbetter, who theorized that debased individuals naturally flock together and generally marry within their own ranks, and hence "only several thousand clans in each generation account for the mass of those who burden and pollute the general community."[36] The ideas of social Darwinists clearly shaped the understanding of the environment's social effects; fittingly, the

British philosopher Herbert Spencer introduced the term "environment" into English-language scientific discourse.[37]

Ideas about the environment were premised on the concept of the "organism," which was readily extended from individual members of a species and applied to societies as a whole.[38] In the context of World War I, the concept of the environment came to include natural resources, their unequal distribution across the globe, and the energy flows necessary for their extraction because they were perceived as central to the social organism's function under conditions of total war and potential blockade across the belligerent nations of Europe.[39] In Germany, the ideas of biologist Jakob von Uexküll best encapsulate this way of thinking. Uexküll coined the term "*Umwelt*," which he defined as the essential surroundings and perceptual reality (*Merkwelt*) of an organism.[40] After the war, Uexküll explicitly extended the interdependence between organism and environment to entire nation-states.[41] While the organism depended on the environment to sustain its unique *Stoffwechsel* (metabolism), Uexküll conceived of the state as an organism that depended on *Menschenmaterial* (human material), which it cycled through carefully calibrated *Menschenwechsel* (literally "human exchange"), conceived as complex overlaying networks of human-chain production.[42]

In order to naturalize his justification for hierarchy and inequality, Uexküll compared the state to an orchestra in which every instrument had a specific role to play, and all instruments played to the tune of the conductor.[43] Uexküll pitted his biology of planning and regularity against the scientific theories that stressed the randomness of natural selection and the cosmic chaos of quantum physics.[44] Even though his relationship with the Nazi regime remained ambivalent at best, Uexküll's anti-Marxism, his antisemitism, and his scientific support for the morality of eugenic measures aided the positive reception of his reissued book *Staatsbiologie* (*Biology of the State*) in 1933 and ensured the regime's continued support of the Institute of Environmental Research (*Institut für Umweltforschung*) in Hamburg.[45] Uexküll, who identified working-class solidarity as the main enemy of the state and attributed the state's pathologies to the effect of "inner parasites," not only shared fundamental ideological principles with National Socialists, but his *Staatsbiologie* also provided a scientific framework to model political systems on organizations found in the natural world.[46]

Nazi Germany thus inherited and tapped into a number of different popular and scientific models for understanding humans and their surroundings. Their strategies for molding both social and natural environments built on the work of race scientists, social reformers, economists, eugenicists, and biologists, grounded in a popular rather than scientific consensus.[47] Hitler's own musings are illustrative here. He readily cast social problems in terms of tigers and wolves, of foxes and horses, and speculated about the connections between race and climate in a crazed attempt to invoke nature as an underwriter of his racial utopia.[48] In Hitler's understanding, the environment was not a separate category, whether as *Lebensraum* or *Grosswirtschaftsraum*, but was fundamentally bound up with ideas about race and *Volk*. Following his lead, Nazi ideologues ultimately tried to sell a biopolitical regime of extraction as the inevitable expression of a biological, geographical, and climatological destiny.

Zero Waste

Initially, extraction started at home and focused on waste and secondary materials. The language around cleanup and resource poverty resonated with large segments of German society, since unemployment, economic uncertainty, and political turmoil had characterized everyday life since the Great Depression. Against this backdrop, most Germans experienced the period between 1935 and the end of military victories in late 1942 as "good" times.[49] In contrast to the mass unemployment and economic uncertainty of the Depression era and the endemic scarcity amidst wartime destruction, the period of economic and military expansion was relatively quiet and unremarkable for the majority of Germans who were neither targeted by antisemitic measures nor scrutinized for suspicious political activities. However, in terms of living standards, the Third Reich hardly ushered in an age of comfort. Economic recovery was geared toward armaments production, which accounted for the reduction in unemployment but did not bring a comparable increase in private consumption. As historian Adam Tooze shows, the majority of German workers earned modest wages and prices remained high. An unskilled worker spent half a day's wages on a kilogram of bacon and half an hour's worth on a loaf of bread.[50]

The Third Reich was plagued by policies that routinely prioritized the regime's annihilative capacity over people's comfort. With foreign exchange in exceedingly short supply, the required imports of grains and animal feed to supply the protein-rich diets Germans expected moved agriculture to the center of economic policy. The abundant harvest of 1933 proved to be an exception. Grain yields declined the following year, forcing the regime to dig deep into reserves. The potato harvest of 1935 was dismal, and the Reich Food Estate (hereafter referred to as the *Reichsnährstand* [RNS]) decided to cull a large number of pigs, diverting potatoes for human consumption and driving up the price of pork. Bread rations, discussed earlier that summer, were still a political impossibility, but the regime silently rationed meat and butter by the fall of 1935, requiring retailers to keep customer lists for equitable distribution.[51] Germans did not face actual food shortages, but the continuing crisis in foreign currency pitted necessary imports against each other. In 1936, Germany imported more than a million tons of grains.[52] Food and clothing (textiles accounted for over 20 percent of German imports) thus were in direct competition with rearmament.[53] The regime therefore waged the so-called *Erzeugungsschlacht* or subsistence battle on a number of different fronts—increasing production, economizing consumption, utilizing waste products—with the ultimately utopian goal of making Germany food-independent. It was clear to Germany's economic managers that only a massive landgrab in the east could ensure the country's food security.[54]

In Hitler's mind, the territorial expanse of the United States and Soviet Union explained their respective potential to develop into world powers.[55] So, too, did he see that imperial expansion had propelled an island nation to world dominance a century earlier. But rather than emulating the British model of a discontinuous empire cemented in structures of economic exploitation through indirect rule, Hitler looked toward territorially continuous empires that harnessed natural resources through exploitative labor regimes and technological modernization for inspiration.[56] But until the resource-rich landmass could be secured, Nazi Germany decided to innovate its way into a position of military preeminence.[57] Just as Nazi technopolitics offered opportunities for scientists, engineers, administrators, and entrepreneurs in areas ranging from chemical engineering to weapons design and medical research, waste reclamation provided yet another field in which innovation and political zeal congealed.[58] Ultimately, commitments to recycling (regeneration) prevailed even as political zeal waned.

The transformation of waste into resource became a fundamental conceptual pillar of the Nazi economy long before war produced widespread scarcity. Whether reverse-engineering kitchen scraps into bacon, meliorating the soil with urban garbage and sewage, spinning fish protein into synthetic fibers, mining human bodies for precious metals, or mandating the comprehensive collection of secondary materials, the Third Reich's garbage economy fostered innovation for individual entrepreneurs, scientists, and local functionaries. While initial experiments with waste utilizations had a bottom-up character, from the moment the Four-Year Plan was announced in 1936 to the final collapse of the regime, waste anchored Nazi ideas of self-sufficiency and resource independence in collective (often mandatory) practice. Economic policy hardly proceeded according to a masterplan but was often reactive, even chaotic, and shaped by the initiatives of individuals and agencies with overlapping and at times competing competencies.[59] The crystallization of the Nazi waste regime followed a similar trajectory. It started with an ideological *Leitmotif* that inspired a flood of decrees and directives, followed by propaganda and ideological schooling that inspired initiatives at various levels in the administration, the party apparatus, industry, and the proliferating complex of policing, which radicalized both zeal and repression.[60] Rhetoric around frugality and thrift inspired a bottom-up approach toward revaluing waste as a resource that energized entrepreneurs and administrators alike.

The drive for autarky—the political goal to achieve German resource independence—ushered in a new phase of top-down planning.[61] An important ideological pillar for Nazi economists and certainly for Adolf Hitler and Hermann Göring, the concept of economic self-sufficiency deliberately obscured the imperial subtext on which it was premised and allowed Nazi ideologues to cast their expansionist drive as a defensive measure.[62] It was a key strategy for purchasing the allegiance of large parts of a population that had little appetite for war. Starting in 1936, the regime placed the economy on a war footing with the expressed goal of being ready for armed conflict (conquest) by 1940 at the latest. It is in this context that wastes of all sorts were reconsidered as a resource and their systematic extraction envisioned on a general scale, inspiring new, more radical initiatives, fine-tuning at every level, and harsh sanctions for those who did not comply with the proliferating regulations. In light of the regime's self-described resource poverty, squander was akin to treason, a crime against the nation and the race, a crime against nature.

Economic wisdom in the Depression-stricken United States continued to emphasize the importance of replacing old, outmoded, or broken goods as a means of revitalizing production and protecting jobs even as people skimped and salvaged. Nonetheless, consumption rather than conservation remained key, and scrapping although pervasive became a political characteristic of the war economy only.[63] Nazi Germany, in contrast, deliberately constricted consumption, ensuring that private savings bolstered the cash reserves of the regime by guaranteeing the solvency of banks and finding their way into the regime's coffers through constant collections for donations—monetary and material—for the Winter Relief Works and the National Socialist People's Welfare (*Nationalsozialistische Volkswohlfahrt*, NSV).[64] Nazi propaganda effectively cast Germany's relative austerity as a fundamental critique of Anglo-American consumerism, in which Germans' savvy resourcefulness served as its ideological counterpart.[65]

The reimagination of waste products as resources was an important first step in the development of much more comprehensive waste management goals. Claus Ungewitter's *Verwertung des Wertlosen* [Utilization of the Worthless] captures the comprehensiveness of National Socialist ideas about waste and recycling, while powerfully illustrating the transnational nature of the discussion.[66] Originally published in German in 1938, the book was translated into English in 1944 and reissued in London under the title *Science of Salvage*. Written with a particular interest in the chemical industry and salvaging of residues, wastes and by-products of chemical manufacturing, the book drew on diverging experiences in Europe and the United States. The British edition hoped to utilize "the survey in this book . . . by competent experts" to economize resources and fight poverty in the postwar years.[67] During wartime, salvage drives, recycling initiatives, and waste avoidance characterized the economies of all belligerent nations to combat shortages and, more importantly, to offer opportunities for the citizenry to contribute to the war effort.[68]

In contrast, in Germany comprehensive recycling was understood as resource production, as the only viable means to bridge the resource gap that imperial conquest would close for good. Accordingly, the main goal of the original German edition of Ungewitter's book was to identify additional venues for resource recovery from manufacturing processes, sewage, air, minerals, ash, forest products, secondary materials, and municipal waste. World War I, Ungewitter argued, witnessed the first systematic collection of scrap and worn materials.[69] But, in his view, Germany's scrap collection was not particularly efficient and lagged behind similar U.S. efforts.[70] Drawing on examples of resource reuse by private enterprises across Europe and the United States, Ungewitter advocated the systematic reclamation of value from wastes, old materials, and low-grade materials as a political task to enlarge the national economy.[71]

Since it proved difficult to increase agricultural output, the idea of avoiding squander and rot became imperative. Richard Walther Darré, in his dual function as the Reich peasant leader and minister of food and agriculture, mobilized German farmers in the struggle for subsistence, which he announced in the fall of 1934. Darré's immediate subordinate and righthand man, the state secretary Herbert Backe, directed the business group "nutrition," which translated large-scale national imperatives into expectations for ordinary citizens.[72] Together, the two men reimagined the inheritance law for ancestral estates and reorganized the *Reichsnährstand* as the entity that managed agricultural production and distribution with strict price controls for farmers and associated industries.[73] During the war, Backe became indispensably involved in genocidal practice in the occupied east, maintaining close relationships with both Himmler and Göring, whereas Darré's esoteric agrarian idealism was ill suited for wartime realities.[74] The tensions between the two men only grew over the next several years, until Backe, as a minister without portfolio, essentially took over the Ministry of Food and Agriculture in 1942.[75] War left little room for the romantics among the Nazi elite but instead played into the hands of ruthless technocrats. No less ideological, those wartime managers were determined to impose the Nazi order at all costs.

In the years after the promulgation of the Four-Year Plan, Göring, Backe, the newly minted *Reichsbeauftragte für Altmaterialverwertung* (Reich Commissioner for Secondary Materials Recovery) Wilhelm Ziegler, and an increasingly complex network of visionaries and enforcers saw to it that waste avoidance and material recovery extended beyond the collection of scrap from individual households but became a priority for every administrative office, political organization, and industrial branch. The emerging waste regime replaced the existing network of scrap collectors, ragpickers, and peddlers, and it soon pervaded and intensified the interplay of party organs, state bureaucracy, industry, the military, and Himmler's matrix of policing.[76] In this context, the seemingly innocent term of Ungewitter's title "*Verwertung*," usually translated as "recycling" or "utilization," connoted more violent meanings since it can also be translated as "to metabolize" or "to use up." The violence became apparent once the regime insisted on the complete use or "*Verwertung*" of labor. The waste regime provided the economic rationale for exploiting people in a total fashion, using up their labor power until it was spent.

Accordingly, at the moment that Germany reached full employment, Himmler reimagined the concentration camp complex with an eye toward labor exploitation. The early camps were holding pens for political opponents, but from 1936 onward the regime continuously expanded its use of forced labor, building a slave labor complex that expanded to massive proportions during the war. It included concentration camps, prison labor, POW camps, and camps for forced foreign laborers abducted from the occupied territories, particularly from Nazi-occupied Poland and the Soviet territories under German control.[77]

As of 1939, war was the main driving force behind the concerted effort to transform waste into resource and forced labor became central to this process. The regime embarked on a campaign to eradicate waste and excess by cycling materials through the production process indefinitely.[78] The initial successes of *Blitzkrieg* highlighted the precarious state of raw material provisioning at the same time that they spawned the grandiose planning projects for a Thousand-Year Reich.[79] By 1940, the management of waste had become routine, even if the much championed "efficiency" never materialized. The regime readily compensated for lack of efficiency and yield with cruelty toward forced laborers when production and transportation bottlenecks confronted its zero-waste fantasies with real, hard limitations.

Reich Commissioner for Secondary Materials Hans Heck, who replaced Ziegler in 1940, explained that "the squandering of all kinds of raw materials is economically devastating." While the regime was particularly concerned with junk and scrap metal, since the "ore reserves in German soil are limited even with the newly won territories in the East," ultimately it was the hunt for "lesser" materials, such as rags and bones, that shaped the structures of material and labor extraction.[80] Turning metal junk into war material was difficult, costly, and required both skilled labor and high-tech facilities. Shredding rags into fibers, spinning and weaving them into cloth, and sewing cloth into uniforms, however, were labor-intensive, grueling, and often unsanitary work, as was stewing animal bones to extract fats and glycerides for soap production, but such tasks could be carried out by an unskilled, slave-labor force without expensive machinery.

Throughout the war years, the Nazi regime hunted for, collected, counted, and stored war debris, such as bombed out tanks and destroyed military equipment, and wastes of various sorts all over Europe with the goal of exploiting its value onsite or transporting it back to processing facilities inside Germany. The regime fanatically targeted waste and wastefulness, dirt, decay, impurity, and contamination not just when expedient or economically necessary but as a matter of principle. Master scavenger Hans Heck explained:

> Since resources do not multiply by growth, they will eventually, when all have been extracted, cease to exist. To delay this process as long as possible and to enjoy a raw material advantage over other peoples who did not economize as frugally, is the prime goal of the extreme exploitation of all secondary materials . . . and [this process] further renders Germany as independent as possible from foreign countries.[81]

Summarizing the importance of the secondary materials to the German war economy, Heck used familiar talking points about German autarky efforts that sought to minimize or replace imports in an effort to save foreign currency and increase German independence from foreign trading partners. Heck conveniently glossed over the fact that such efforts depended on both rapid territorial expansion by way of conquest and the brutal regimes of forced labor. Instead, he argued his case for secondary materials in abstract terms. The health of the race and the nation,[82] the preservation of the German forest and German living space,[83] the flourishing of German art,[84] the well-being of members of the *Volksgemeinschaft*, and national prosperity were all premised on imperial expansion and extraction, conveniently rebranded as self-sufficiency with waste reclamation as the magic bullet. Over the course of the war, zero-waste economics became a key yardstick by which the regime measured administrative efficiency.[85]

The actual extraction of value from secondary and waste materials took place in a haphazard and uneven fashion. There was no overarching strategy that coordinated policy across different spheres of influence and priorities. Even the counting was inaccurate, in most cases. Yet, priorities around resource extension and waste eradication—framed in political terms around "autarky" and in moral terms around frugality and obligation—provided a shared language and shared goals across different sectors of the state bureaucracy, the party apparatus, the business community, and the kitchens of ordinary citizens.

Garbage Speak

The connections between racial policy and zero-waste economics in Nazi Germany can be understood through the discursive conventions that anchored fanaticism in practice. As Claus Ungewitter's *Verwertung des Wertlosen* illustrates, the regime took seriously the possibility of metabolic circularity that had fascinated thinkers of radically different political persuasions.[86] Following the discovery of the fertilizing properties of *guano*, the "odiferous excreta of Peruvian seabirds," the exiled French Socialist Pierre Leroux lamented the wastefulness of London in the 1850s and fantasized about perfecting the conditions under which man can live off of the generative power of his "own excrement."[87] Similar fantasies energized scientists like Ungewitter, politicians like Göring, and a host of entrepreneurs in Germany in the early 1930s as Nazi propaganda was beating the drums of frugality, thrift, and resourcefulness.[88]

Entrepreneurs and local politicians seeking to increase their political currency developed new mechanisms for extracting value from useless matter and by cleaning up their cities and towns. Local and individual initiatives often preceded official policy. Waste avoidance, too, was key, as was the revaluing (*Aufwertung*) of matter by redesignating garbage as a resource; waste as *Altstoff* effectively turned trash into treasure. Household waste (*Müll*) was considered in terms of its *Brennwert* (metabolic value) and sewage (*Abwasser*) was scrutinized for its fertilizing properties, for example.

At the same time, the idea of a closed-loop economy was intimately connected to fantasies of racial purification and the total eradication of racial others and social "misfits." Hitler and Nazi ideologues made clear from the beginning that national unity and health, racial purity, resource independence, economic prosperity, and territorial expansion were premised on the total destruction of Weimar democracy, the eradication of "community aliens," the destruction of internal and external enemies, and, eventually, the annihilation of European Jews. Long before Hitler became chancellor, he ranted against *Entartung* (degeneracy) *Verseuchung* (contamination), *Abschaum* (scum), *Zersetzung* (debasement), and *Verfall* (decay). Like other cultural pessimists at the time, he lamented the adverse biological effects of modernity, the deteriorating "national health," and the declining birthrate of "the racially valuable."[89] Once in power, his government eradicated ideas, practices, and cultural products that were deemed to be dangerous, alien, or impure. This sort of labeling, in turn, stimulated the rhetoric surrounding *restlose Ausschöpfung* (complete, literally leftover-less, extraction) of resources and the *restlose Durchführung* (complete execution) of administrative tasks, indicating zero tolerance for remainders of any kind, bolstering fantasies of economic extraction and national purification.[90] Nazi rhetoric implied that only absolute ruthlessness would guarantee total extraction.[91] Words and deeds operated in multifaceted feedback loops, experiencing successive radicalization. What is more, the practice of resource exploitation was initially geared toward inanimate objects, most of which had been historically undervalued and whose revaluation opened up spaces for zealots and opportunists alike to ensure their standing within the National Socialist people's economy.

Rather than predetermining genocidal action, Nazi linguistic extremism gives some indication of the importance that total processes and purification fantasies occupied in the Nazi imagination. The utilization of fish products is an interesting case. Claus Ungewitter details the manifold usages to which fish waste can be put and the "immense value" that could be derived for the people's economy. Fish glue, supposedly odorless and of "immense adhesive force," could be derived by boiling heads and skins to separate the fats and oils. The residue didn't have to go to waste either; it could be processed into fishmeal (a supplementary feed for hogs in feedlots). Simultaneously, scientists conducted experiments to make plastics out of fish scales and worked to improve the isolation of fish protein—which could both be used as animal feed or for the production of fish-based rayon. The spinning of fish protein supposedly rendered a tear-resistant and durable fiber, which allegedly had the additional advantage of being cheaper than wool.[92]

However, as one imagines the odors associated with these production processes, it is obvious that mass production of such scientific discoveries was somewhat complicated. Even the *Vierjahresplan* magazine admitted that "this was less than pleasant work," and due to imperfect hygienic processes and odor pollution, animal rendering was not yet fully developed, leading to the destruction of much valuable material.[93] By 1938, the trade journal *Die Umschau in Wissenschaft und Technik* reported on the first floating fishmeal factory, which processed the waste products of deep-sea fishing far out at sea. This motorized vessel could process the bycatch that was normally thrown overboard. Together with the fish scraps, the bycatch was then minced, cooked, and predried. Fats and oils were removed; the residue, once dried and ground into fishmeal, could be stored in sacks. "In this way, the complete utilization of the entire catch is realized, whereby the economic efficiency of the shipping company is improved, and valuable feed and oil for food and industrial purposes obtained."[94] In this example, the regime's focus rested on squandered material, rather than on the workers. Once the regime relied exclusively on slave labor, considerations for workers disappeared entirely.

The language around total recycling (*restlose Wiederverwertung*) obscured the fact that waste labor was hard, dangerous, and dirty. Not just the language

Figure 1.1 An official of the railway authority demonstrates the process of lightbulb recycling by prison inmates. Courtesy of Bundesarchiv.

around waste utilization but even the photographs of waste work—whether they depicted lightbulb recycling or the collection of kitchen scraps for the hog farms of the NSV—presented a sanitized fiction of clean efficiency. The dirtiness of recycling hardly fit the purification fantasies of the Reich. Therefore, the regime increasingly turned to prisoners and concentration camp inmates for this kind of work. It associated dirtiness and filth with criminals, Jews, social "misfits," POWs, and enemy civilians, rather than with the processes of imperial extraction itself. Exhortations about handwashing graced the walls of concentration camps, while work uniforms were not provided.[95] Public notices informed the residents in the ghettos in occupied Poland of their responsibility—under penalty of punishment—to ensure the order and cleanliness of streets and public places, as well as building interiors.[96] At the same time, the regime administered ghettos and camps in a way that made hygiene and sanitation impossible by design.

Hitler left no doubt about his views on the importance of cleanliness and the need to outsource certain kinds of work, such as earth moving, trench digging, and all forms of "shit work" to a biosocial underclass.[97] He recognized that even the German people didn't come by their current standard of cleanliness and purity by virtue of nature alone, stressing instead that "cleanliness

Figure 1.2 Workers empty barrels of kitchen garbage into a truck that transports the waste to NSV hog farms. Courtesy of Landesarchiv Berlin.

is the result of continuous education to *discipline*."[98] The party newspaper *Völkische Beobachter* illustrates the linguistic acrobatics that linked personal cleanliness to national dominance:

> Without cleanliness, inside and out, there is no order. And without order, on a small or an exceedingly large scale, chaos is guaranteed. If you don't clean up your kitchen, don't wash your dishes, if dirt suffocates your office, if you can write your name in dust everywhere, then you are worthless. Since time immemorial, in Germany we are used to order; exemplary is our

homeland in the gigantic struggle against the slovenliness [*Verlotterung*] of the whole world.[99]

However, labeling people "trash" or "vermin" did not seamlessly translate to or necessarily anticipate their murder. Such rhetoric did not automatically precede systemic oppression nor was there a direct causal relationship between linguistic slippage and the boundaries of the category of the human. While propagandists in both Germany and the United States certainly moved "people *out* of the category of human" and moreover "*into specific categories* of the non-human," the implied ease for subsequent murder remains unsubstantiated and impossible to prove.[100] As perpetrator testimony makes clear, German *Einsatzgruppen* and police battalions had no illusions about the fact that the victims they murdered were, in fact, people. The regime moreover realized that linguistic extremism was hardly sufficient to convince German killers of the task at hand and hence shipped truckloads of alcohol to the killing fields in the east.[101] The planners and architects of the Nazi genocide also left no doubt about their intent to murder people.[102] Planning documents such as the General Plan East made their case for starving millions of people to death in plain bureaucratic German. The SS directives routinely deployed obfuscating, euphemistic language that coded mass murder as "resettlement" and "special treatment" for those who had to actually carry it out.[103] The linguistic acrobatics of dehumanization cement categories of (imagined) existential threats and allow perpetrators to rationalize their actions as defensive and necessary, often after the fact. The alignment of racial and economic fanaticism took time, practice, and war. But linguistic extremism was cheap and readily available to Germans looking to burnish their National Socialist credentials.

Apparatus of Extraction

Nazi ideas around waste were fairly clear in theory, but they did not readily translate into practice and thus offer limited insight into everyday activity. Ideology provided a framework within which individual executors of the garbage economy intuited economic priorities, experimented with new methods of salvage, constructed environments of extraction, and competed with each other for political currency and power. Since their individual power and influence grew regardless of whether schemes actually extended the war economy or merely articulated the promise to do so, the success of specific initiatives was less important than the zeal and ruthlessness with which they were pursued. Failure of any given innovation could readily be attributed to a number of factors—shortages, misallocations, misdirected shipments, military developments, bureaucratic lethargy, or sabotage by forced laborers. Only zeal and determination mattered. Accordingly, waste reclamation enjoyed the same kind of radicalization that characterized Nazi political action writ large.[104]

The remainder of this book lays out the ways in which waste and recycling practices affected and structured social life for Germans and the people the Nazi regime subjugated; here the apparatus that developed as of 1936 can be described in broad brushstrokes.[105] The Nazi waste regime and its subsequent development had numerous authors and executors. Before the regime stepped in to regulate garbage matters in 1936, an underclass of peddlers and rag-and-bone men handled the collection of secondary materials.[106] The Four-Year Plan charged Gau commissioners with enforcing the closing of the *Rohstoffkreislauf* (raw materials cycle) by ensuring the swift, orderly, and remainder-less return of any and all secondary materials. However, Göring's insistence on hunting down the tiniest shred of "wood, rags, paper, and bones" hardly guaranteed seamless raw material provisioning.[107] In November 1936, Göring entrusted Walther Köhler with overseeing the secondary materials trade and issued the first torrent of instructions and regulations.[108] Less than a year later, he considered it necessary to coordinate the activities in a separate office; he created the office of the Reich Commissioner for Secondary Materials Recovery (*Reichsbeauftragte für Altmaterialverwertung*) and appointed Wilhelm Ziegler to oversee the comprehensive utilization of garbage (*Müll*), with the exception of kitchen scraps.[109] Ziegler was technically in charge of the efforts of the individual Gauleiter whose already proliferating competencies now included the prickly title of regional executor of the waste economy.[110] When Göring first attempted to organize the secondary materials economy, he stipulated that "under no circumstances may this campaign lead to the creation of a special new administrative apparatus." Instead, an advisory task force, including representatives from the National Socialist Women's League (NS-*Frauenschaft*), the existing peddling trades (*Rohproduktenhandel*), and the director of the local propaganda office, was charged with coordinating the increased collection activities.[111] Over the next several years, a number of institutions and organizations in party, state, army, and industry were enlisted in the ever-proliferating attempts to extend the Reich's raw material base. Like elsewhere in the Nazi administration, competences overlapped, pitting individual functionaries against each other and fostering zeal and radicalism, often at the expense of efficiency.

As of 1937, towns with more than 35,000 inhabitants were required to separate secondary materials from regular household waste.[112] That year, Jews were pushed out of the peddling trades and the regime increasingly relied on the massive volunteer staff from the NSV, the Hitler Youth, and other party organizations.[113] Initially, this restructuring mainly benefited large- and medium-size distributors, whereas small firms and individuals, often stigmatized as "asocial," were pushed out. Jews, who constituted a sizable contingent in the secondary materials trades, additionally found themselves targeted by antisemitic measures.[114] As of 1938, monthly and yearly reports on the materials collected by the growing volunteer army under the direction of the various Gau commissioners attested to their "success," and a year later volunteers all but replaced the existing structures of *Rohproduktenhändler*.[115] Directives stressed coordination with the existing structures of middlemen and distributors for the secondary materials trades to ensure quality control. Both Ziegler, and as of 1940 his successor Hans Heck, anticipated that the reliance on volunteers would be temporary. However, volunteers remained crucial to the recycling apparatus when it came to collecting and recording both donations and discards from within the *Volksgemeinschaft*. For the processing of wartime loot of textiles, metal scrap, and various other "recyclables," the regime increasingly relied on forced laborers and concentration camp prisoners.

In 1939, the Ministry of Economic Affairs bragged to Göring about the immense increases in secondary materials retrieved from the rubbish of 160 municipalities participating in the initial experiment. In addition, the collection of secondary materials from households increased. Between 1936 and 1939, a total of 1 million metric tons of recyclable paper, 55,000 tons junk metal, 8,000 tons of rags, 2,000 tons of bones, and a further 1,200 tons of scrap metal had been secured for the people's economy.[116] Berlin alone was allegedly able to isolate the equivalent of 10,000 metric tons of scrap metal from household waste in 1936.[117] As these numbers signal, numerical recording was "*infinitely* difficult." Ultimately, the numbers did not matter because even in the late 1930s, collecting was one thing, but recycling quite another.[118]

In the prewar years, household waste constituted a special focus because it allowed the regime to do what it did best—inundate the population with "enlightening" information by way of massive propaganda campaigns, which was subsequently followed by an equally massive flood of directives, which then required the recruitment of volunteers for the ever-proliferating collections.[119] Special initiatives or collection drives started in peacetime and became endemic during the war, extending from textiles, woolens, and metal wares to bottles, books, sheet music and musical instruments, gramophones and records, and even spoonfuls of sugar and flour to the point that the population complained "what the state grants for Christmas the party promptly collects."[120] From the beginning of state-coordinated collection of secondary materials, propaganda campaigns encouraged small- and medium-size businesses to return industry-specific wastes and leftover materials in close consultation with the peddling trades.[121] Ongoing attempts to collect wastes from industries and business placed increasing responsibility on the individual managing directors.[122]

War not only heightened the urgency and inspired the fanatical zeal of party functionaries at every level but also set in motion the large-scale recordkeeping, reclamation, collection, and reuse of industrial wastes.[123] Scientists continued their efforts to utilize remainders and waste products from chemical processes, mining, iron-smelting, and manufacturing industries in an ever more comprehensive fashion. In 1938, Ungewitter had already proposed catching *Flugstaub* (metal dust) and mining it for precious metals, collecting coal dust for briquette making, increasing agricultural yields by irrigating fields with raw sewage, using garbage slag for cement making or road construction, and extracting oil for soap making from tomato seeds. During the war, such ideas energized scientists and guided experiments in factories, mines, waste management facilities, SS-owned industries, and concentration camps.

By the 1940s, scrapping and salvaging were readily extended to the occupied territories, carried out by violent force rather than volunteerism. Inside the Reich, Germans collectively reimposed order on the chaos of war by collecting and reclaiming materials from waste. Naturally, whatever value they were able to extract and return to the cycle by default powered the very motor of destruction. The regime amassed mountains of what hitherto would have been considered garbage. The "*totale Erfassung*" or "total collection" was a principal political goal.

The actual reuse of the yield was more difficult and required the coordination of transport, technical know-how, fuel, factories, furnace capacity, and labor. By the end of the war, none of those were available. War produced more and more junk, broken down tanks, airplane scrap, and rubble. The regime's attempt to freight the unfathomable amounts of material collected (and robbed) in the occupied territories back to the Reich brought the infrastructures to the brink of collapse and exacerbated fuel shortages. Inefficiencies and logistical backlogs were endemic but that did not stop Germans from collecting and storing "valuables" in junkyards all across Europe. By 1943, Göring ordered the requisitioning and transport of all waste, secondary, and booty materials in occupied Europe. The hunt for junk and material of all kinds often relied on the army and army-adjacent units. At the same time, the genocidal collaborations of Heinrich Himmler, Herbert Backe, Hans Frank, Fritz Sauckel, and Hermann Göring seemingly "solved" the labor problem by condemning scores of concentration camp prisoners and POWs to recycle *Beutegüter* (loot) extracted from the conquered nations of Europe.

The war unfettered the morbid creativity of the SS. The SS rationalized camp kitchens to avoid the squandering of resources—which explains why the commander of the KL Buchenwald mandated the use of water in which potatoes had been soaked overnight so as not to waste the starch that seeped into the soaking liquid. In 1942, the regime began to conceive of wastewater in concentration camps and Waffen-SS barracks as a resource and required the installation of fat skimmers to reclaim the meager amounts of grease in concentration camp kitchens for the production of soap, laundry detergent, and machine grease. Apparently, the commandants of concentration camps and Waffen-SS barracks did not think that regulations about skimmers applied to them. The SS Main Economic and Administrative Office (*SS-Wirtschafts-Verwaltungshauptamt*, SS-WVHA) drew attention to "difficulties with the collection of grease from dishwater" and reiterated that concentration camps, too, were required to install skimmers, adequately clean them every four weeks, and deliver the salvaged sludge to approved soap manufacturers.[124]

Retrofitting meat-processing facilities and industrial-scale kitchens with skimmers became a priority as early as 1940 and justified exemptions from building prohibitions (*Baustopverordnungen*). Two years later, the Plenipotentiary for Construction informed the *Reichsstelle* for industrial fats and detergents (*Reichsstelle für Industrielle Fette und Waschmittel*, RIF) that "a general permit for the installation of skimmers cannot be issued under the current extremely tight conditions in the construction industry."[125] Increasingly, secondary material recovery competed with production and construction, whose progress it was supposed to enable. As a matter of compromise, skimmers and regenerating factories already operational were exempt from the broad-spectrum electricity cuts that affected industry more generally.[126] By 1944, transport and fuel capacities were so strained and railway transport containers were so scarce that operators of slaughterhouses and industrial kitchens had to use buckets, cans, lidded tubs, or jars to transport wastewater sludge to the designated collection points.[127]

As in so many recycling endeavors, the energy expended to recover fats from wastes was hardly justified in traditional economic terms, yielding only a minuscule fraction of the raw materials needed for soap and detergent production. The reclamation was a political imperative. Squander of untapped resources, even if yield was minuscule, was anathema. In many cases, recycling became deadly by design. In ghettos and camps in Nazi-occupied Poland, Jews and other prisoners deemed fit to work turned the garments of the victims murdered by the Nazi killing machine into Wehrmacht uniforms and prisoner cloth. As the Nazi killing peaked, slave labor was literally *verwertet*, used up.

By the end, the wastes of war restructured the environments of much of Europe. The Reich itself resembled a wasteland—destruction arrived from the skies by way of Allied aerial bombardments and from the east as a dual function of the destruction wielded by the Red Army's advance and the scorched earth practices of the Wehrmacht's retreat. As if the reclamation of waste had the power to halt and reverse its impending collapse, the regime set out to battle the effects of its own destruction, which manifested Nazi fears about filth, disease, degeneration, social dissolution, and moral decay in material reality. Waste—rubble, debris, household garbage, ashes, corpses, and broken-down material—was everywhere.

Anticipation of resource scarcity and production bottlenecks drove the regime's politics of recycling and continued to power them through the end. Individual and industrial efficiency, reclamation, and extraction were supposed to combat the chronic shortages and conserve precious resources. While lower-level officials and certainly individual citizens could convince themselves of the apolitical nature of their collective hoarding delusions, the upper echelons of the Nazi administration were all too conscious of the political implication of the various campaigns designed to stretch the Reich's resource base and their ultimate convergence with the politics of social hygiene, imperial conquest, racial persecution, and genocide.

2
Garbage Visionaries

In December 1935, the director of a potato-processing factory, Mr. A. Pütter, wrote to the Regional Office for Water, Soil and Air Hygiene (*Landesanstalt für Wasser-, Boden—und Lufthygiene*). He wished to offer the priceless gift of his personal genius as a state secret to the German nation and its Führer, Adolf Hitler. Without going into technical detail, Pütter revealed that he was the only person in the world who was able to fully isolate—without using chemical additives—protein from the liquid residue that accrues when processing potatoes. He promised that this protein, once solidified, keeps eternally and never expires. It could therefore be pressed, he ventured, into pills that could serve as a meat substitute and substantially enhance the battle-readiness of German troops in an eventual war.[1] After the regime began rationing meat and butter in the fall of 1935, Pütter was hardly alone in trying to develop a technique to utilize the nutrient-residue of *Kartoffelsaft* (potato juice).[2] In fact, he joined a long list of pioneers and innovators who saw an opportunity to express both their National Socialist devotion, while hoping for recognition, perhaps even fame, but at least some tangible monetary gain.

The *Landesanstalt* was not interested in pressing potato protein into pills for German warriors. Rather, Pütter's and other such schemes sparked interest because they promised to effectively remove organic residue from the wastewater of food-processing plants, which could pollute rivers and streams and disrupt the nitrogen balance.[3] Pütter's suggestion inspired further experiments and comparisons with alternative methods of removing protein from effluents. His potato protein turned meat substitute received no further attention. As it turns out, Pütter was a few years ahead of his time.

Pütter's discussion of his "discovery" reveals the pervasive shifts in how citizens thought about and understood the importance of resources in the first few years after the Nazis took power. Nazi rhetoric about autarky and resource independence connected with the experiences of prolonged scarcity and economic uncertainty that had shaped the outlook of Germany's business community over the past decade.[4] The *Landesanstalt* retained its regulatory focus and considered Pütter's proposal not for its contribution to the national economy but for its potential to remove organic pollutants from effluents; the high modernist projects—such as wastewater management—aligned with Nazi rhetoric about cleanliness and sanitation, at least initially. By the early 1940s, however, the managers of the war economy deprioritized concerns about industrial pollution. In the context of war, pollution came to be understood primarily in racial terms; the sort of resource thinking that characterized Pütter's fascination with "potato juice" carried the day and inspired businesses and administrators alike to innovate value out of waste.

Questions about garbage had predated the Nazi assumption of power in 1933. In fact, the regime's growing obsession with waste and material remainders, though clearly shaped by ideological considerations, was also inspired by bottom-up initiatives that recognized opportunities for political power or material gain. In the context of the Nazi "revolution" and in light of the social and economic uncertainty that continued beyond the end of the Weimar Republic, there was significant room for low-level functionaries, entrepreneurs, scientists, volunteers of various sorts, and self-anointed spokespersons for the *Volksgemeinschaft* to shape the parameters of the new regime.[5] Whether "working toward the Führer," establishing their National Socialist credentials, or vying for lucrative business opportunities, individual *Volksgenossen* were quick to discover in garbage a nearly inexhaustible realm for action.[6] Those with knowledge of or experience in the "regeneration" of various kinds of secondary materials saw opportunities to rehabilitate stigmatized forms of labor, previously associated with rag-and-bone men, as selfless contributions to the national economy.[7]

Many of the initiatives the regime introduced with the Four-Year Plan and expanded over the course of the war had roots if not actual historical precursors in pre-1933 practices. Nazism's political emphasis on resource independence brought local administrators and private enterprise together, until official policy caught up with and outstripped local initiatives after 1936. Over the course of the 1930s, waste issues blurred the boundaries between social, economic, and racial concerns. In the context of war, they narrowly reframed the questions of material utility in national-political terms, linking resource extraction with practices geared toward guaranteeing social cohesion, public health, and order in the abstract.

Starting in 1936, the Nazi regime legislated and attempted to centrally manage the root-and-branch return of all kinds of wastes. Rooted in communal practice, individual entrepreneurship, and local initiatives, their heavy-handed approaches continued to rely on the active participation and resourcefulness of the *Volksgemeinschaft*. Much like the rest of the Nazi warmaking apparatus, the Nazi waste regime did not spring solely from the pens of Nazi bigwigs like Hermann Göring and Herbert Backe, but involved lower-level functionaries and local entrepreneurs.[8] Interestingly, innovators looked to the past for inspiration.

Rubbished *Lebensraum*

Toward the end of the nineteenth century, garbage captured the imagination of urban planners, sanitary engineers, and administrators. The rapid growth of European cities rendered previous methods of dealing with refuse insufficient. In most cities, human and animal waste were hauled beyond the city gates by private entrepreneurs—separated at the source according to trade.[9] Rag-and-bone men bought secondary materials from households, which they then sold to middlemen. Combustibles were burned in kitchen stoves and backyards. Together with ashes, sweepings, and kitchen garbage, wastes were often dumped into pits and ditches, rivers and inner-city waterways or carted off for a fee by haulers. Haulers sold organics to farmers, unspoiled scraps were used as hog feed, and rotting matter fertilized fields. Nightsoil men emptied cesspools and latrines, selling the feces as fertilizers to surrounding farmers.[10] An even poorer underclass dredged the inner-city waterways to peddle reusable materials and cart organic matter to farmers in the countryside. Private firms cleaned the streets of rubbish, ashes, leaves, and animal feces, based on a concession system. Dead animals, frequent in predominantly horse-drawn societies, were "the job of the city knacker."[11]

Until the industrial production of chemical fertilizers in the second half of the nineteenth century, raw sewage and animal wastes had been coveted by farmers for their fertilizing properties. Bacteriological science and recurring cholera epidemics at the end of the century rendered urban garbage and sewage particularly suspect as agents of disease.[12] Increasingly, not only public health officials and administrators but also the general public recognized the incessant accumulation of waste and refuse as a danger to public health.[13] The installation of sewer systems, the organization of standing police forces, and inner-city decontamination projects preceded the establishment of municipal garbage collection.[14] In Berlin, sewer construction commenced in the late 1870s, and by the 1890s most houses in the city were connected. Smaller towns and rural areas relied on privy middens, pits, cesspools, and ash closets.[15] Disease and epidemics, mortality rates, crowding, urban poverty, and filth inspired administrative responses in sanitation and policing.

The accumulation of refuse in urban centers slowly captured the attention of the state, increasingly pressured by scientific and medical experts, who underscored the linkages between public health and urban order.[16] Toward the end of the nineteenth century and into the first decades of the twentieth century, cities moved from merely regulating waste disposal by way of police ordinances toward regular garbage collection as part of municipal services that obligated every property owner to pay monthly service fees. Nonetheless opportunities arose for private entrepreneurs to offer "solutions" to cities' growing refuse problems.[17]

By the time the Nazis came to power, Berlin, like many cities of its size, had a real garbage problem.[18] Its population had reached more than a million inhabitants in the 1880s at a density without comparison in all of Europe. Berlin did not have an official dump site for garbage (*Müllabladeplatz*) until 1887 but even then, garbage collection remained in private hands. There were hardly any rules about garbage until 1893 when two police ordinances attempted to get a handle on the wild (unregulated) dumping of wastes and mandated the registration of dump sites.[19] By the turn of the century, four main garbage companies organized collection in Berlin. With waste disposal within city limits declared illegal, haulers looked to the surrounding countryside for suitable disposal sites.[20]

The police ordinance of January 30, 1895, decreeing that all garbage must be transported in dust-proof and perfectly sealed containers, put many haulers out of business. A cooperative of Berlin property owners, initially formed for the purpose of neighborhood policing, effectively monopolizing garbage collection until inflation and economic crisis put an end to its operation in 1922. Shortly thereafter, two leading Berlin haulers formed the *Berliner Müllabfuhr-Aktiengesellschaft* (BEMAG), in which the city held 25 percent of the shares. In the wake of scandals and corruption, the city came to control the leadership and operated as a majority shareholder.[21] Leadership changed again in 1933, now chosen for their political reliability. In 1935, the BEMAG dissolved and the operations transferred to the *Müllbeseitigungsanstalt*, literally "garbage elimination facility," formally part of Berlin's municipal administration.[22]

The increasing economic importance of garbage during and after World War I inspired approaches that imagined disposal in terms of usefulness.

Sanitary engineers had experimented with incineration and "reduction"—the stewing of garbage in large vats for the extraction of fats and glycerine—to identify more efficient ways of getting rid of urban garbage.[23] Hamburg invested in incineration, but Berlin's garbage was considered too wet. Therefore, the best alternative—or so it appeared to opponents of urban dumpsites (*Halden*)—was the use of garbage for soil melioration projects.[24] Over the course of the 1920s and 1930s, dumping garbage into low-lying wet- and badlands became reimagined as a way of turning useless land into productive agricultural soil.[25] For Berlin, this was a relatively cheap way of getting rid of noxious stuff, and for the surrounding rural communities selling dumping licenses was an important source of communal revenue.

The dumping of Berlin garbage in Ketzin, a small town southwest of Berlin, started in 1928 after years of negotiations between the municipal authorities and Berlin haulers. Residents soon complained.[26] But Mayor Karl Reumschüssel estimated that the municipality derived an annual income of 200,000 RM from the dump sites and brushed their concerns aside.[27] Despite complaints about odor and vermin, the district medical officer asserted that citizens' health implications could not be substantiated.[28] As financial benefits took priority, the practice of rubbishing the countryside pitted property owners against municipalities during the last years of the Weimar Republic.

Under the Nazis, turning badlands into potential wheat fields became a political imperative. The Berlin-based company Aretz Faserstoffplatten GmbH attempted to perfect its mechanism of pressing garbage into building boards, while the Mast corporation experimented with a new method of flushing garbage onto wetlands.[29] Both initiatives appealed to Mayor Heinrich Sahm and BEMAG Director Richard Rautenberg, but only flushing of garbage moved beyond the experimental stage. In response to Berlin's consistently growing refuse volume, National Socialist authorities quickly revoked the 1927 law that had turned the Brandenburger wetlands into a protected nature preserve, and the flushing of garbage onto the wetlands west of Potsdam commenced in earnest.[30]

The first experiment in the marshes at Golm started in March 1933. The process was crude and simple. A manmade breach in the levee ensured the constant moderate flushing of the area designated to be rubbished while a large dredger hurled the garbage delivered by the BEMAG several meters into the swamp, which would then be evenly dispersed by the water flushing through, eventually settle, and slowly fill the lowland. The water was supposed

Figure 2.1 *Spühlbagger* or dredger that flushes garbage into the Golmer Luch. Courtesy of Bundesarchiv.

to clear itself as it made its way through the peat and loam sediments before returning by way of the smaller creeks to the Havel, the main river in this watershed.[31] The press readily proclaimed the imminent transformation of wetlands into wheat fields through nothing but garbage.[32]

Such pronouncements were gross exaggerations. Even though the volume of garbage was initially relatively small, it did not take long for residents to complain about the stench emanating from the putrid water. Both residents and the office for hydraulic construction (*Wasserbauamt*) began to worry about potential contamination of the watershed through the runoff, though authorities in 1935 still maintained that the unappealing yellow tint of the runoff was not a cause for concern.[33] Expert testimony insisted that the flushing of garbage "is of outmost importance" for the national economy.[34] Only in rare cases was resistance powerful enough to prevent the rubbishing of particular sites. In Mellensee, for example, Dr. Leonardo Conti, a key author of the Nazi euthanasia program (T4), threatened to take matters to the Reich's secretary in order to put an end to the dumping in the vicinity of his villa.[35] In Golm, garbage flushing continued despite complaints. From 1933 to 1936, the volume was still relatively small, but in subsequent years, with flushing at capacity, the containment of the foul-smelling garbage waters, ranging in tint from yellowish brown to putrid black, became a serious problem. The contaminated waters flowed into adjacent fields and meadows, seeping into wells and affecting the irrigation systems on which local farmers relied.[36] After farmers sprayed vegetable beds with the contaminated water, the plants shriveled up and died.[37]

A 1937 investigation found that garbage-contaminated water decimated the fish reserves in the Wublitz river.[38] That August, the hydraulic construction authority of Potsdam discovered breeches in the levee and confirmed the suspicion that perilous water flowed back into the watershed, unfiltered, black, putrid, and reeking of sulfides.[39] It ordered rectification and contemplated fully prohibiting garbage flushing, arguing the volume was too great to ensure proper purification by the time the water reached the pumping station at Geltow. Over objections of company management, authorities started the process of planning necessary upgrades to the levees and pumping stations, recognizing the extent of the contamination.[40] In the meantime, flushing continued. Even when the improvements were completed in 1939, contaminated waters continued to pollute the watershed. In the eyes of Göring and Backe, Germany's food independence was paramount. Accordingly, they ignored the noxious realities of the garbage experiment at Golm and held on to the fantasy that the process would eventually yield arable land.[41]

Before the flushed marshes could support the growth of robust grasses for animal feed, the "meliorated soil" required heavy labor to thoroughly plow the garbage under, facilitate the sinking of debris, and rotate fertile soil upward. The Mast corporation relied on conscript prison labor for this hazardous and unsanitary work. Convicts trudged through the sodden, liquified garbage to retrieve mattresses, furniture pieces, and secondary materials, yet previously sunken decaying objects constantly resurfaced.[42] It became increasingly apparent that flushing 500 tons of garbage into the Golmer Luch daily was not turning marshes into wheat fields but only creating a growing environmental hazard.[43] Nonetheless, the project, heightened in importance by war, continued.

By 1941, Potsdam attempted to expand efforts in light of the pressing *Erzeugungschlacht* (subsistence battle) and suggested utilizing untreated urban sewage for irrigation purposes as well.[44] "The most valuable urban waste products are undoubtedly fecal matter," argued a senior regional economic councilor in Berlin in an attempt to assuage "fearful minds" who "unnecessarily" worried about adverse health effects of raw sewage for plants and humans alike.[45] Since the Potsdamer wastewater treatment plant was

Figure 2.2 Worker dredging through the garbage waters in Golm. Courtesy of Bundesarchiv.

overwhelmed and on the verge of collapse in 1941, local authorities invoked soil melioration as a safe, healthy, and productive solution to Potsdam's sewage crisis.[46] The official rhetoric of the regime stressed "productivity" and invited scientists to "prove" that waterborne pathogens did not pose a danger when irrigated onto fields.[47] Betraying their own assertions about the safe nutritional benefits of sewage, experts contemplated whether disinfecting powders (chlorides) could be added to wastewater to reduce the risk of bacterial infections. Prior to the war, only the use of certain types of agro-industrial wastewater was deemed safe for irrigation, but under wartime conditions, "experts" found concerns about pathogen contamination "unsubstantiated" and "exaggerated."[48] Even as pathogens—typhoid bacilli in particular—had been found in large quantities in urban wastewater, authorities continued to argue that "in light of the current food situation," shutting down irrigation of untreated sewage "could not be justified."[49]

Garbage Domestic Product

In contrast to later desperate measures, in the first few years after the Nazis took power, ideas and proposals for various kinds of waste-utilization projects still glistened with innovative zeal. By the mid-1930s, Nazi rhetoric about subsistence battles and an all-out war against rot and decay, together with fantasies about closed raw material cycles, inspired numerous individuals to write to their local officials to share their outlandish ideas for economic revitalization. Some of these propositions bordered on garbage alchemy.

In October 1935, Berliner Harry John made the case for the essential role of potato peels in the national economy. In a letter to superintendent Dr. Julius Lippert in Berlin, John obsequiously described himself "as a tiniest cog in the wheels of the people's community" who nonetheless wanted "to contribute to the Führer's great idea" of making "the German fatherland independent from foreign interests." In numerous conversations with housewives John had learned of the abominable squander of precious *Volksvermögen* (national property).[50] While the poor traded potato peels for firewood, in the better neighborhoods of Berlin garbage cans were overflowing with potato peels, he explained.[51]

John wanted to end this wastefulness and insisted that by way of propaganda in radio and press "every housewife must learn that the squandering of potato peels constitutes an act of pilferage against the nation's wealth." He proposed that homes be outfitted with specially marked bins for potato peels and that the *Nationalsozialistische Volkswohlfahrt* (National Socialist People's Welfare, NSV) should ensure the proper collection of valuable hog feed. Potato peels thus secured could even be used in city-owned feedlots.[52]

Although, Lippert never responded to John's letter, in 1936 an eerily similar proposal became the pet project of Hermann Göring, while Lippert was promoted to mayor the following year.[53] Perhaps it was a coincidence, but Lippert may have gotten Göring's ear.[54] What is more, Lippert's garbage credentials were impeccable—he had overseen the negotiations with Aretz Faserstoff GmbH to press garbage into fiberboard and remained chiefly involved in the garbage flushing experiments in Golm. Thus, it is quite possible that he relayed the contents of John's letter to Göring, perhaps even passing them off as his own idea.[55] A similar undertaking was in the works in late 1936, and Berlin led the way in the separate collection of kitchen garbage as hog feed. In its ultimate implementation, the scheme ended up costing the Reich upward of 40 million RM.[56]

The Four-Year Plan buzzed with militarized language about agricultural production, detailing progress in Germany's subsistence battle and combating Germany's perilous raw material basis. After the dismal potato harvest of 1935, the regime resorted to culling the pig population, driving up the price of pork.[57] The scheme of raising pigs on garbage promised concrete and immediate relief. The Four-Year Plan, or so the Führer reasoned, would at least ensure that Germans would not be short of bread, butter, and bacon. Accordingly, the regime spared neither cost nor effort to guarantee the food supply for the German population; by resorting to plunder and investing in "magic."

Whether inspired by the citizen's letter or not, in the fall of 1936, Hermann Göring, together with Herbert Backe, aggressively pushed for the systematic collection of food waste—from food-producing industries as well as households. In November, Backe charged the NSV with organizing the collection of kitchen garbage as hog feed. The 1.5 million volunteer staff of the NSV, Backe reasoned, was ideally positioned to guarantee "the root-and-branch collection of all reusable scraps at minimal cost."[58]

Feeding garbage to swine was hardly a new idea, through it had not been widely practiced in Germany.[59] By 1936, Berlin's population of 4.2 million produced around 3,000 metric tons of garbage daily. Claus Ungewitter, author of the Nazi garbage bible *Verwertung des Wertlosen* (Utilization of the Worthless), estimated that the average *Volksgenosse* accounted for approximately half a kilo to a kilo worth of garbage per day, 16 percent of which were kitchen scraps. In Berlin alone, the daily accumulation of potential hog feed thus amounted to approximately 480 metric tons.[60]

In the fall of 1936, the office of the Four-Year Plan created the Food Relief Works (*Ernährungshilfswerk*, EHW) and anticipated the wholesale collection of kitchen scraps from private households. Technically, the EHW was a subsidiary within the NSV but even Backe conceded that its legal status was somewhat in limbo. Over the course of the next several years, the collection of kitchen garbage became the fiscal responsibility of the Reich because it had to bail out the NSV, a party organization, which, in turn, funded the massively unprofitable feedlots operated by the EHW. From its inception and throughout, Göring's effort to reverse-engineer kitchen scraps back into bacon ultimately served propagandistic rather than financial or nutritional objectives.[61]

In January 1937, haulers of the Berlin *Müllbeseitigungsanstalt* began to collect kitchen garbage separately and delivered it to EHW feedlots with support from the NSV volunteers. NSV leader Erich Hilgenfeldt, promptly advanced to the newly created post of Reich Commissioner for Kitchen Garbage (*Reichsbeauftrager für die Erfassung und Verwertung von*

Küchen- und Nahrungsmittelabfällen) and was charged with oversight of NSV-run piggeries. In smaller communities, the NSV worked with local farmers rather than invest in separate hog farms. Given the quantities, the separate collection and swift transportation of kitchen garbage and its conversion into consumable calories faced some inherent challenges. The whole undertaking proceeded at a snail's pace since vehicles and fuel for transport were both in short supply and feedlots had to be sited and constructed. A year later, the Reich Commissioner for Kitchen Garbage requested a 15 million RM loan from the Reich Ministry of Finance to support the projected costs for the fiscal year of 1938–1939: 10 million RM for the acquisition of pigs, 5.6 million RM for additional concentrated feed, 5.6 million RM operating costs for the collection of kitchen garbage, 400,000 RM for insurance purposes, 260,000 RM for veterinarian care, and another 4.7 million RM to cover the operating costs of the feedlots—including wages, coal, light, and material for the stables. Hilgenfeld insisted that it was impossible to cover the entire 25 million RM using the budget of the NSV, and the Reich stepped in.[62]

In early 1938, the NSV was responsible for 60,000 pigs. The propagated tenfold increase never materialized since there was not enough concentrated feed available to justify an increase in the number of NSV pigs. These realities did not lead to an adjustment of the plan to raise 1 million pigs feasting on German garbage. Göring insisted that the propaganda value of the endeavor outweighed financial considerations.[63] At its peak in August 1940, 300,000 hogs were being sustained but not exactly fattened in NSV feedlots. Even modest increases proved difficult. For municipalities with populations under 100,000, the construction materials and labor could not be allotted, and the leadership of the National Socialist German Workers Party (*Nationalsozialistische Deutsche Arbeiter Partei*, NSDAP) encouraged them to finance the collection of kitchen scraps out of their own budgets.[64] To ease the burden, the Reich minister of labor permitted the use of POWs for essential building projects and in agriculture.[65]

Although the regime could prioritize NSV feedlots, it was unable to control the "quality" of the garbage, which continued to decline along with diminishing food rations and waste. By 1940, the pigs were skinnier and less healthy, and they were often slaughtered prematurely as the composition of their feed changed. As a result, a fattening period, usually six months, did not achieve the desired weight; many animals were slaughtered before reaching their target weight, while others were sickly and died.[66] Accordingly, the cost of meat production increased consistently, raising the price of NSV pork from 1.05 RM per kilo in 1938 to 1.38 RM per kilo in 1940. Despite its goal of the "complete utilization of all scraps," the monthly losses incurred by the NSV rose to around 700,000 RM.[67]

By the end of 1941, still half, if not more, of the collected kitchen garbage spoiled due to fuel shortages and transportation difficulties; the requisitioning of vehicles for strategic purposes made the delivery of garbage from households to feedlots impossible in some areas. To remedy the situation, the authorities contemplated collecting potato peels separately to minimize spoilage. In addition, hydroxypropionic fermentation (first steaming and then pickling the collected garbage) promised to prevent spoilage and preserve raw garbage for years but required additional personnel and fuel resources, and therefore could not be implemented on a significant scale. Supplementary feed was expensive and by February 1942, the number of NSV pigs had dwindled from 300,000 to 171,200 animals. The EHW operated 1,325 feedlots, but many of the stables remained empty. The hunt for kitchen garbage continued nonetheless, as if more garbage was going to provide the solution.[68] The NSV contemplated ways to procure food waste from the Wehrmacht, free of charge. Backe ordered the Reich minister of finance to provide an interest-free loan to the NSV in order to cover the losses of 30 million RM incurred by the Food Relief Works.[69]

In May 1942, Göring and Backe decreed that all previously unexplored sources of food waste should be exploited and used for agricultural purposes. However, potato shortages and ration cuts further decreased the caloric value of the collected waste. What is more, the Reich started to feed raw scraps to hogs, exacerbating potential risks of infection, but the EHW facilities for steaming garbage (to kill bacteria) were at maximum capacity. Circulars compelled municipal garbage collection to make vehicles and labor available for the separate collection of food waste, and private haulers, horse-drawn if need be, were called on to ensure the complete use of all food waste. When possible, hog farmers were encouraged to collect the feed with their own vehicles either from individual households or municipal collection points. Housewives were singled out for education and supervision to improve their collection habits and efficiency.[70] In blatant disregard for the realities of war, propaganda continued to reinforce the strategic importance of the separate collection of kitchen garbage. From May 1941 to the end of 1942, financial losses grew from 14 million to almost 42 million RM.[71] By the end of 1943, the Reich refused to subsidize the project.[72]

Institutionalized Surplus

The implicit logic that informed the regime's attempts to transform badlands into wheat fields and household waste into bacon was perhaps most clearly captured by the title of Claus Ungewitter's treatise *Verwertung des Wertlosen* (Utilization of the Worthless).[73] While Ungewitter explicitly focused on the extraction of value from various waste products, his emphasis on utility characterized the Nazi economy of value more generally, which extended "norms of efficiency" from industrial processes to the population itself.[74] In addition to racial others (Jews in particular) and people with hereditary illnesses, designated by the regime as a biological threat to the health of the nation, the SS soon targeted individuals who deviated from ideas of purity and productivity—criminals, the mentally ill, and the socially deviant—as burdensome to society and resolved to extract useful labor from those populations.[75]

Economic and racial hygienic reasoning in relation to waste management initially crystalized around prisons, sanatoria, hospitals, and mental institutions.[76] Beyond the biological paradigm that undergirded applied science during the Weimar period, economic imperatives and, particularly, fantasies of waste avoidance played an equally important role in transforming the state from a more or less militant custodian of ill or deviant populations into a hyper-vigilant executioner of an imperial logic based on extraction and eradication.[77] Changing medical approaches to labor characterized German practice during the Weimar years and prefigured the extraction of labor from institutionalized populations under the Nazi regime.[78]

During the Nazi period, the reformists' conceptions of labor were retained for rhetorical flourish but more often deployed as a means of abuse and mockery, as the universal inscription of "Arbeit macht frei" on concentration camp gates illustrates. A near immediate shift occurred in 1933 as the Nazis consolidated their hold on institutions. Given the economic pressures experienced by municipalities as a result of the Depression, the Nazified state apparatus approached populations in prisons, workhouses, and mental institutions as useless and burdensome eaters—"*unnütze Fresser.*" School books illustrated the pervasiveness of this economic logic by introducing math examples that asked students to compare the cost of "a cripple, a reform school inmate, a mentally ill person, a deaf-mute or criminal" to the income of workers, white-collar employees, or civil servants in order to calculate the losses to the people's community by the uncontrolled reproduction of social "parasites."[79] By 1938, Ungewitter found it unremarkable that it had become customary "for quite some time to use prisoners in the processing of secondary materials."[80]

Public institutions, such as prisons and mental hospitals (*Städtische Anstalten*), were an obvious starting point for zealous Nazis in municipal administrations to think about minimizing costs and extracting potential value from people deemed "worthless." In 1933, Heinrich Sahm, mayor of Berlin, turned toward *Städtische Anstalten* as an additional source of potential revenue and economic innovation. The two main strategies were to recover valuable materials from waste and to treat the inmates' bodies themselves as a source of revenue.

These strategies converged in the first intervention as Sahm contemplated how to legally requisition gold teeth and precious metals from the dentures of deceased inmates and patients. On February 27, 1933, Sahm changed the regulations for Berlin hospitals and mental institutions, ordering that teeth and dentures worth less than 10 RM were not to be returned to a released patient or a deceased patient's relatives. Instead, the precious metals in dentures were to be removed by workers or patients under a dentist's supervision, the yield returned to the institution, and the useless dental matter destroyed.[81] Apparently, not all hospitals welcomed these changes. Collecting precious metals from dentures required significant labor, and not everyone was convinced that it would be worth the effort. One institution even questioned whether the institutional dentist could reasonably be burdened with such tasks. The city refused to provide special compensation to the workers who had to break apart patients' gold teeth.

Some hospitals displayed enthusiasm for compliance, questioning whether the extracted materials would best be appraised by a pawnshop expert (*Altgoldhändler*) or whether it would be more efficient to centrally collect the dentures and supply the extracted gold to a gold refinery. By November, Sahm's clerical assistant reported that even though enforcement of the changes decreed in February did not cause difficulties, the matter "was dealt with in an irregular fashion" by different institutions.[82] Some districts reported that material had been returned, others expressed discomfort with the new guidelines, and many institutions remained suspicious of, if not explicitly opposed to, extracting wealth from the bodies of their deceased patients.[83] Others were quite eager to comply with the new measure. The Rudolf-Virchow-Krankenhaus, a Berlin hospital, for example started to inventory the value of dentures when admitting a new patient, a practice

Berlin's mayor promptly recommended be adopted broadly.[84] Sahm rejected outright some hospitals' request to simply forgo the reclamation of precious metals from dentures. After all, the *Heil-und Pflegeanstalt Buch*, a mental hospital, reclaimed 68 grams of platinum and 15 grams of gold (carat unspecified), extracting a total value of 250–300 RM from the dentures of a mere 200 patients.[85] Even in this most celebrated example, the yield amounted to less than 1.50 RM per patient.

The *Heil-und Pflegeanstalt Buch* was particularly zealous in resource recovery. After the Nazi assumption of power, the hospital underwent rapid and thorough political cleansing. The oversight board "voluntarily" stepped down, and Direktor Johannes Birnbaum, an internationally distinguished psychiatrist, was removed from his post under the aryan paragraph of the Law for the Restoration of the Professional Civil Service of 1933.[86] Within a few months, Buch had been thoroughly Nazified. By the end of the year, Buch's institutional administration was soliciting quotes from Berlin scrap dealers and rag-and-bone men (*Altstoffhändler*) for a wide range of secondary materials, inviting the tradesmen to scrutinize the materials for sale on weekday mornings.[87] Offers rolled in quickly—differentiating between up to ten different type of rags and offering to pay 0.25 RM for 1,000 kilograms of wastepaper.[88]

Less than a year later, on October 2, 1934, Mayor Sahm insisted that all hospitals and mental institutions investigate the extent to which they might increase the reuse of waste materials in order to ease the Reich's dependence on imported raw materials. In particular, he wanted to know which kinds of waste products had been deemed completely useless to date (such as bones, tin cans, and slag); how institutions had hitherto disposed of those wastes; and whether or not there were new ways to utilize those wastes.[89] By mid-November, he received confirmation that all hospitals and mental institutions simply tossed tin cans and kitchen bones into the rubbish and carted them off with the rest of the garbage or buried them onsite. Berlin promptly negotiated with prospective buyers of bones and cans. Sahm asked that in the interest of the national economy and national tin production, all empty cans be dutifully collected. On November 26, 1934, he tapped Wilhelm Schumann Gmbh, which the *Städtische Anstalten* offered to pay 17.50 RM for 1,000 kilograms of empty tin cans.[90]

The utilization of wastepaper had already been addressed by a 1931 decree, but Sahm also insisted on the comprehensive, centrally regulated collection of rubber and metal scrap from public offices.[91] Sahm's initiative preceded the Four-Year Plan by over a year. In July 1935, the public health department in Berlin followed up and ordered the systematic utilization of secondary materials in hospitals and mental institutions with a particular focus on bones, tin cans, and slag.[92] The city surveyed all public offices and institutions about the yearly amount of slag that accrued, who had thus far hauled away slag, under what conditions, and how much of it was used for production in municipal enterprises.[93]

By 1936, it had become standard practice for the secondary materials trade to inquire about valuable refuse at hospitals and mental institutions, and individual scrap merchants fiercely competed among themselves over old linens, mattresses, blankets, rags, and other textile wastes. Some *Altstoffhändler* specialized in specific materials, while others took virtually everything that was not perishable, including junk and metal scrap, textiles and discarded linens, and wastepaper, such as old files and correspondence.[94] Scrap merchants had been inquiring about secondary materials for years, but until Sahm's comprehensive garbage regime, hospitals and other public institutions had simply dumped or burned secondary materials.[95]

The Four-Year Plan provided the legal framework for the comprehensive exploitation of the Reich's garbage reserves. Even the food scraps in medical and mental institutions were subjected to scrutiny.[96] Noting the shortage of sheet metal and tin and citing the constant administrative reprimands for frugality, Max Gottesmann wrote to the *Heil-und Pflegeanstalt Buch* on September 2, 1936, to implore them to collect floor polish cans. Gottesmann offered to compensate them with requisite deliveries of floor polish in exchange.[97] In October 1936, Sahm's successor, Dr. Oskar Maretsky, solicited information from the district mayors about the extent to which tin cans had been collected and sold to scrap dealers in the past. Before long, buyers of tin cans had established regular contracts with *Städtische Anstalten* and were able to haggle with the city over price.[98] In January 1938, Mitteldeutsche Seifenfabrik Gmbh, a soap manufacturer, offered to purchase the fats collecting in the mud of the sinkholes and drains, an initiative that was taken up in a comprehensive fashion by the Four-Year Plan Authority in 1940, when the regime mandated the installation of fat skimmers for the public sector.[99]

The Four-Year Plan set in motion comprehensive waste reclamation at the national level. On September 18, 1936, the Ministry of Economic Affairs decreed that "in the interest of conserving raw materials, secondary materials accruing internally must be systematically collected and where possible returned and reused, root-and-branch."[100] Accordingly, the Berlin *Müllbeseitigungsanstalt* was required to expand its existing garbage-sorting facility in Schöneberg to ensure the retrieval of all valuables from household waste. Immediately, the *Mülllbeseitigungsanstalt* noted that the laborers employed—usually former employees who, because of age or disability, were no longer able to work as haulers—hardly earned their keep. "Their efforts left much to be desired," the *Müllbeseitigungsanstalt* noted with reference to the *Ausklauber* (garbage pickers). It argued that Four-Year Plan or not, the retrieval of reusable materials did not fall into its realm of responsibilities since technically its job was to make the waste disappear, rather than sort it. Instead, it suggested outsourcing the reclamation of reusable materials to a third party.[101]

The inmates in prisons and mental institutions were quickly tapped by the regime for the processing of the very materials collected.[102] Prisoners (*Strafgefangene*) were "employed" by the joint venture of flushing garbage into the Golmer Luch to retrieve bulk and secondary materials from the "meliorated" soil.[103] Patients and inmates were deemed a logical resource for sorting and processing.[104] Secondary materials that could be recycled within the *Anstalt* were exempted from the large-scale requisitioning drives, as long as institutions did not "hoard massive amounts of secondary materials" for later use.[105]

Mayor Maretsky insisted that low-quality waste products that secondary materials traders refused to purchase should be delivered to mental hospitals, "even if they can only be described as rags" for they could be used for "occupational therapy" by patients. There was nothing therapeutic about the grueling labor of manually shredding raggedy textiles into fibers so that they could be spun into yarn. The mental hospital in Berlin-Buch was not the only institution in which inmates were used for the realization of the Four-Year Plan's recycling goals.

Dr. Conti, still serving as the Prussian state counselor, reminded all medical facilities in Berlin to take the necessary measures to utilize all waste and secondary materials in the context of the national campaign *Kampf dem Verderb* ("War against Rot") that commenced in January 1937.[106]

Prison labor was also deployed to these ends.[107] The workhouse in Berlin Rummelsburg established a workshop for the sorting and recycling of secondary materials. The main benefit, aside from contributing to municipal income, was that the inmates were exposed to useful labor, claimed Mayor Lippert. Prisoners repaired outmoded household gadgets and appliances, but if that seemed uneconomical, they disassembled them and collected reusable materials separately. They sorted various metals, separated iron from machine parts, disassembled lightbulbs, and collected nails, wire scrap, tubes, cans, unused tools, and sheet metal. Metals such as lead, aluminum, copper, tin, and nickel were sold to scrap merchants. Paper and cardboard from files, newspapers, magazines, books, and various kinds of packaging materials were also sorted at Rummelsburg. Inmates separated textiles of all sorts into fibers, a laborious and demeaning task done by hand. They shoved the oily and used cleaning rags—potentially flammable—into metal containers, all in the name of resource recovery.[108] As the garbage regime matured, material and labor, no matter how "inferior" their value by official standards, had to be exploited.

By the end of 1937, the public health department brokered an arrangement between the prison in Berlin-Tegel and *Heil-und Pflegeanstalt Buch* for patients at Buch to sort waste materials from the prison under the guise of "occupational therapy." The prison administration was responsible for the transport of 1,000 kilograms of wastepaper (prisoner files). The mentally ill received detailed instructions about the proper procedure: paper was sorted and baled by color, folder covers and envelopes were baled separately, and twine and string and other filaments were collected and stuffed into sacks.[109] By 1939, the inmates in the mental institutions Buch, Herzberge, and Wittenau shredded thousands of kilograms of string and twine by hand for return to the Kabelfabrik Landsberg, which produced mechanical wires, cable, and rope.[110] The prisoners in Brandenburg-Görden penitentiary had been tasked with similar work until 1937, but with growing labor shortages, healthy male prisoners were increasingly forced to work in agriculture, construction, railroads, and garbage collection.[111]

Behind institutional walls, society's most vulnerable populations increasingly had to "prove" their value to the *Volksgemeinschaft*. The initial parity between prisoners and patients of mental institutions tilted rather dramatically as prison, prison camp, and concentration camp populations increased steadily.[112] Even at its peak, inmate labor at Buch was far from universal. In 1938, 65 percent of men and 38 percent of women worked in various workshops (slipper manufacturing, mattress recycling, knitting, and sock mending), in farming 50 acres of land, or in kitchen and maintenance work. Of the nearly 3,000 inmates at Buch in 1938, less than half were well enough to work.[113] With the expansion of the concentration camp complex after 1936—camps that served as *Arbeitslager* or labor camps—prison labor became an essential component of the Nazi economy and much of it was dedicated to waste labor. By contrast, the labor of the mentally ill no longer made sense in the regime's cost–benefit calculations. Dr. Conti's involvement in the far-reaching attempts to extract value from *Heil- and Pflegeanstalten* and his subsequent role as one of the chief architects for T4 euthanasia program, code for the systematic murder of individuals with hereditary illnesses, the mentally ill, and the physically disabled, likely signals the "lessons" learned from the Berlin garbage economy.[114]

Nazi careerists like Conti were not alone in linking the extraction of resources to the elimination of unproductive and unworthy people. Other garbage initiatives followed similar calculations. Racial others, those deemed social ballast, enemy populations, and POWs could not prove their inherent value, no matter their effort. Instead, the garbage economy opened up spaces in which one temporarily demonstrated one's usefulness—if the perceived gain their labor power accrued to the regime exceeded the calories they consumed, they might live. By the end of the war, not only Nazi ideologues but also prison and camp populations had come to understand the "common sense" of the Nazi waste regime.

3
Garbage Community

Addressing the nation from the Berlin *Sportpalast* on September 28, 1936, Hermann Göring, the newly minted plenipotentiary for the Four-Year Plan summarized his charge as "a clear task" and promised "to protect the German honor and to secure German life."[1] In his speech, Göring belabored and lamented the fact that Germany "had been robbed" of its colonies and as a result lacked essential raw materials for production. He fulminated "first they pillaged Germany, bled her white, and then declared 'why do you want colonies, just pay with your gold.'" Preparing his audience for future privations of butter, eggs, and meat, Göring bragged about having lost 20 pounds himself simply by having eaten less butter, using this to signal the iron will that would, under his guidance, drive Germany toward resource independence and food security. He called on inventors, scientists, and technicians to forge the resources Germany needed out of whatever the soil yielded. He presented a vision of massive factories that would produce rubber, cellulose, and textiles. He promised petrol and well-smelling soap, all made from coal and German ingenuity.[2] Göring, who seemingly channeled the platitudes of Leni Riefenstahl's two-hour docudrama *Triumph of the Will*, prophesied that "nothing in the world fails as long as the will does not fail." He charged Germans with embracing the momentary austerity and urged them to get to work. He neglected to mention that the life and honor of the German nation were to become dependent on garbage.

Germans were decidedly unenthusiastic about the introduction of rationing in 1935, but they participated quite eagerly in the many salvaging drives and large-scale collections of recyclable materials.[3] The belligerent rhetoric that characterized Göring's September address was unrelenting, yet donating old textiles or collecting tins tubes and bottle caps must have, at least initially, felt like an act of care rather than of war. As the regime reversed the "injustices" of the Versailles Treaty and Hitler's popularity soared, ordinary citizens were eager for opportunities to put their National Socialist zeal on display and to contribute to building Greater Germany. They collected scrap while Germany rearmed rapidly, reinstituted the draft, incorporated the Saar, remilitarized the Rhineland, and actively pursued an irredentist agenda of reclaiming German speaking lands. In 1938, Hitler engineered the *Anschluss* of Austria and a crisis in the Sudetenland that precipitated the disintegration of Czechoslovakia and the incorporation of the remaining Czech territories into a *Grossdeutsches Reich*. The garbage community channeled popular enthusiasm and energy into action.

Garbage provided citizens with an arena to put their conviction and indeed fanaticism on display. Party organizations such as the National Socialist People's Welfare (NSV), the Reich's women's organizations, the Hitler Youth (*Hitlerjugend*, HJ), and the League of German Girls (*Bund Deutscher Mädel*, BDM), and the Reich Air Raid Protection League, as well as local cell and block leaders, were crucial for whipping up popular enthusiasm for the collection of secondary materials and soon occupied a central logistical function in their neighborhoods. Nonetheless, to Claus Ungewitter, the author of a scientific treatise on recycling, the collection activities were hardly satisfactory. He lamented the "insufficient willingness of the general public to actively commit themselves to simplifying the return of secondary materials to the energy cycle."[4]

Consensus-motivated activism continuously waned in the context of war, but compliance remained constant; the collection of secondary materials became not simply routine but mundane and burdensome. Soon the reality of wartime scarcity cast frugality and thrift as necessities in their own right, and thus the political nature of waste-consciousness and salvage was easily obfuscated and ignored. The greater the demands and disorder of the war, the more these war-extending garbage practices attained the quality of a set of chores that good citizens grudgingly but diligently completed. Separating kitchen scraps from combustible waste, mending worn clothing or donating it to be recycled, saving paper while waiting for letters to arrive, collecting bottles and metal scrap for the military, sending woolens to the front, and clearing the streets of rubble became essential to maintaining a sense of order amidst the chaos of war.

The performative display of virtue and zeal receded with the progression of war, but citizens "did their bit," even though the collection frenzy made little demonstrable difference in the lives of individual consumers.[5] Citizens unthinkingly backed the logic of the war economy, lived in conditions of austerity, and responded to constant demands for higher levels of personal sacrifice while holding onto the hope of final victory and future prosperity. Even in the face of impending collapse, citizens continued to wage the battle against waste and disorder in increasingly desperate attempts to cope with shortages that plagued pantries and dinner tables and paralyzed the war economy.

Although the Nazi ideal of the *Volksgemeinschaft* never materialized as the harmonious, classless community propagated by Goebbels' ministry, it nonetheless structured German society and shaped German experiences in very real terms. The *Volksgemeinschaft* is best understood as a vehicle by which citizens asserted their own sense of belonging to an exclusionist state, made claims upon that state, policed themselves and each other, and found venues for political participation.[6] Participation in Nazi Germany took many different forms, ranging from all-out careerism within the Nazi bureaucracy, to volunteer work in the various party organization, to performances of nationalist zeal and political loyalty in offices, on the shop floor, or within the neighborhood. Politics also extended into the lives of ordinary citizens whose everyday diligence and resourcefulness assured their place within the people's community, whether they were true believers or mere opportunists.[7] Referring to Germans as a garbage community or *Müllgemeinschaft* is intended to underscore the significance of collective salvage and how seemingly mundane activities were translated into publicly legible acts of Nazi citizenship.

This chapter focuses on everyday trashers and gleaners and the roles they played in their neighborhoods and in the imagination of the Nazi propagandists and party officials. Neither the comprehensive campaign *Kampf dem Verderb* or "War against Rot," a large-scale propaganda action to raise awareness among housewives about spoilage and pests, nor the various collections of secondary materials had significant effects on the overall availability of foodstuffs or raw materials. Nonetheless, they effectively initiated Germans of all stripes and backgrounds into a community militantly organized around cleanliness, frugality, and thrift.

The War against Rot

The earliest efforts to mobilize the people's community around issues of garbage were not particularly comprehensive or original. Instead of interventions of strategic relevance, the regime organized low-tech propaganda actions that focused on the individual household and the labor of housewives with the goal of transforming shopping and consumption habits and getting all Germans accustomed to economizing. In the minds of its authors, there was no doubt about the purpose of the Four-Year Plan: it was a plan for a war of production (*Erzeugungsschlacht*) that would enable the subsequent war of conquest.[8] Given the catastrophic shortages during World War I, it was framed around public initiatives to secure the food supply.[9]

Launched in late September 1936, the propaganda campaign War against Rot aligned with the general trend of flooding the population with radio, film, and print messages about National Socialist achievements and ongoing efforts. The regime was determined to teach people how to be good Nazis.[10] As the Reich reimagined productive work for men by idealizing manual and agricultural labor, the War against Rot was geared primarily toward women, housewives, and mothers, and centered on the home. The message was clear: women's dedication, love, and care should no longer solely focus on husbands and children, but serve the nation at large.[11]

The exhibit "Battle over 1.5 Billion," which the *Reichsnährstand* (RNS) organized in Cologne in October, was modeled after "Green Week," an international Berlin-based exhibit on nutrition, agriculture, and horticulture.[12] Like Green Week, its opening act targeted urban visitors in order to educate them about the pervasiveness and cost of rot, decay, and squander in agriculture and the household, as well as wastage and material losses in industry and public administration.[13] But the heart of the campaign was geared toward addressing housewives and reining in their wasteful habits.

The *Reichsnährstand* spared no cost or effort. Spending a total of 167,000 Reichsmark (RM) on the many posters, pamphlets, illustrated books and booklets, and film shorts, it proselytized "ten commandments" for German housewives.[14] These included pearls of wisdom such as "what the seasons yield is cheap and healthy"; "a purposeful use of leftovers proves the skill of the good housewife"; and "exterminate pests wherever you find them."[15] Over the summer of 1936, in anticipation of the exhibit, the *Reichsnährstand* and the German Women's Work (*Deutsches Frauenwerk*, DFW) joined efforts with a number of different film companies to produce 16mm shorts as well as projection stills for use in movie theaters. Ufa, Germany's largest film production company, agreed to develop four separate subjects to be included in the weekly newsreels. In addition, the Reich Women's Work took charge of the four-part cinematic treatment to popularize the War against Rot. The first explained the reasons for this urgent battle against decay. The second introduced the main enemies of German foodstuffs. The third detailed the responsibility of the German housewife and the last touched on the role of food retailers. Not only did the experts within the *Reichsnährstand* calculate that Germans wasted 1.5 billion RM of foodstuffs, but they also explained how moisture, warmth, light, dirt, dust, and general uncleanliness produced environments conducive to putrescence.

In the age before refrigerators became a standard household fixture, stockpiling and hoarding perishable foods were not possibilities.[16] Consumption levels in Germany declined after the Nazi assumption of power, and thus the campaign effectively conjured up a lifestyle of abundance that was far from the reality of most Germans. It also blamed individuals for profligacy, carelessness, and squander. Ignorance and carelessness may have been easiest to combat, but they were hardly the greatest obstacle to German "food freedom." By targeting the German housewife, the campaign effectively distracted from the government's failure to increase living standards as promised. Instead, Nazi propaganda cast women as both the cause of and cure for endemic squander—the knowledge, skill, and cunning of the housewife were the most effective weapons in the war against rot caused by female carelessness and ignorance.

However, the film made clear that National Socialism had to first retool the housewife into the nation's armor against rot. The script for the film treatment featured a short history of female development from girl to housewife, comparing traditional women of imperial Germany (i.e., the good old times), the new women of the Weimar "system," and finally, the consciously economical Nazi homemaker. It painted a simplistic picture: prior to World War I, girls learned from their mothers so that upon finishing school, each girl was already "an almost independent little housewife." In contrast, women during the Weimar period entered into marriage without proper domestic education, so too much food spoiled and the household fell into debt. Starting in 1933, National Socialism restored lost wisdom and ensured the proper training of women in the art of homemaking and the virtues of the household economy to ensure marital harmony.[17] By blaming negligent German women, the film and other propaganda regurgitated simple tales that urged people to pass judgment on their neighbors and position themselves as guardians of the new Nazi order through simple acts, such as cooking one-pot meals on Sundays or separating out their kitchen scraps as hog feed.[18]

Propaganda effectively merged different campaigns in its attempt to reinforce the message to housewives that they stood at the center of economizing German food consumption. The short animated color film *Eine nette Schweinerei* [A Nice Mess] (1938) commissioned by the RNS, cast housewives as the natural link between the War against Rot and the NSV hog farms. Picturing rot as a sluglike black monster that penetrates walls and pantries and that cuts deeply into the Reich's food reserves, the film presents women's careless squander as the real reason for shortages of meat and fats in the form of a nursery rhyme. Singing piglets counter the wasteful habits of German housewives and jollily assert that "what disappeared here without use, would taste to pigs so very good." The enlightened housewives quickly adjust their habits and feed food scraps to the dancing pigs, which will soon turn into ham and bacon. By diligently separating kitchen scraps, they help raise 1 million pigs. The film concludes on a congratulatory note, ignoring the ill-fated and massively expensive NSV waste-to-pork program and leaves the viewer with a simplistic message about female duty:

> German housewife, it's up to you
> The Four-Year Plan needs you, too
> Thrift, you've proven frequently
> Now, too, save foreign currency.
> Whatever kitchen scraps you shed
> Collect to fatten hogs instead.

While the Nazi regime insisted on the separation of public and private spheres in principle, propaganda campaigns such as this one reminded Germans that family and home had strategic roles under the Four-Year Plan and were ultimately subservient to national-political considerations.

Most of the propaganda for the War against Rot targeted urbanites, who were supposedly estranged from the soil and manual labor and spoiled by the conveniences of modern life. But the film short *War Against Pests* was tailored toward a rural audience, who found themselves confronted with pests that adversely affected harvests and destroyed stored foodstuffs and seeds.[19] While the Nazi censor lauded the film as "a tremendous success," the production was plagued by problems with its animal actors and illustrates the disconnect between the imagined and actual concerns that shaped the lives of Germans.[20] The campaign War against Rot pitted the *Volksgemeinschaft* against imaginary enemies of pests and squander, but its belligerent language around full-fledged mobilization anticipated the regime's planning for scarcity of an entirely different order of magnitude. The exhibit Battle over 1.5 Billion drew over 80,000 visitors and set an important precedent for

Figure 3.1 Eine nette Schweinerei, 1938. Production still.

the role of propaganda for the mobilization of the garbage community in wartime.

From Waste Trade to Garbage Community

Alongside the *Reichsnährstand*'s propaganda campaigns, the regime articulated policies for comprehensive waste recovery.[21] Conceptually, questions about waste focused not on disposal but on erasure. To reduce waste, substantial amounts of it were redesignated as secondary material and thus could, in principle at least, be returned to the system as a resource. The redefinition of waste as a resource was an important first step in the development of a comprehensive program to eliminate waste altogether. As of November 27, 1936, Göring decreed the mandatory collection of waste and secondary materials in households and commercial businesses in coordination with the existing non-Jewish *Rohproduktenhandel* (secondary materials' trade).[22] The regime necessarily relied on the roughly 25,000 to 30,000 rag-and-bone men, who traditionally collected secondary materials from the individual households, passing through neighborhoods and loudly announcing their intention to purchase rags, bones, paper, glass, and other materials. They peddled their wares to registered scrap and secondary material traders. In 1933, the secondary materials trade comprised 6,571 businesses, only 5 percent of which were larger firms, slightly less than two-thirds were one-man businesses, and the remainder businesses with five or fewer employees. Such trades with low barriers for entry drew large numbers of unskilled predominantly poor, disadvantaged, and uneducated individuals. During the Depression, peddling was often the only source of income for unemployed as well as for physically disabled veterans.[23] Prior to the regime's interventions in this economy, a significant number of traders were Jewish, which explains Göring's insistence on organizing household collections in coordination with "aryan" peddlers only.[24]

Rhetoric around frugality and thrift characterized the Nazi regime from the beginning, but the progressive centralization of raw material allocation, beginning in the textile sector in 1934, accounted for an important uptick in propaganda geared toward heightening people's awareness of the necessity to collect and return, rather than throw out, valuable secondary materials.[25] This sudden intensification in programs around waste was largely an ideological phenomenon, rather than a true reflection of a transformed economy or the increased resale value of scrap. It emboldened housewives to demand higher prices for their suddenly precious seeming wastes, though all the talk about the hidden utility of garbage did not actually increase its resale value. The peddlers thus found themselves squeezed between housewives on the one hand and the regime's desire to extract as much value as possible on the other. In 1937, the regime subjected the secondary material industry to price controls as part of the Four-Year Plan's comprehensive program of resource management and allocation.

The NSV, supported by volunteers from the Nazi youth organizations, crystallized as the natural link between national imperatives, propaganda, and the individual household.[26] Party-based volunteers not only replaced the labor and profit of the rag-and-bone men (essentially eliminating costly middlemen), they also helped reframe the discourse around secondary materials in terms of sacrifice rather than profit. If neighborhood volunteers gave their time to return precious materials to the national economy, it was only reasonable to expect individual households to donate their old textiles and scrap metal to the people's community rather than selling them to raggedy, shifty entrepreneurs. The Nazi press did their part to continue to stigmatize secondary materials traders, facilitating their replacement by the NSV, the Reich Women's Work, the Hitler Youth, and the League of German Girls.[27]

The transition from trade to sacrifice happened gradually and almost organically. Intermediaries in the scrap trade had to work with party officials and NSV staff to resell collected materials, an arrangement that was concluded largely at the expense of the peddlers, anticipating the subsequent restructuring and aryanization of the secondary materials economy.[28] As a result, the for-profit trade found itself in intense competition with a zealous army of NSV volunteers. Historians have described such overlap in competences within the Nazi administration and between offices as an "organized chaos" that established hierarchies based on "Darwinian" logics of institutional survival and advancement.[29] In this instance, the party-based collections ultimately won out, first controlling and then largely replacing the bottom rung of the trade.

During this transition, Reich Commissioner for Secondary Materials Recovery Wilhelm Ziegler, together with Reichsführer SS and Chief of German Police Heinrich Himmler, subordinated the "non-Jewish" secondary materials trade to the oversight of the party organs and the surveillance of municipal police forces, recognizing the need to monitor the trade and expel the many "dishonest and asocial elements."[30] As in other parts of the economy, aryan competitors did not wait for anti-Jewish legislation before mobilizing Nazi racial imperatives for their personal gain.[31] Already in 1934, secondary materials traders offered their services and expertise as "purely aryan firms," expecting and achieving a clear advantage over their Jewish competitors.[32] The first regulations that followed from the Four-Year Plan stressed that waste reclamation "must under all circumstances be organized in mutual agreement with the non-Jewish secondary materials traders."[33] Thus, aryanization progressed before the law of December 12, 1938, that comprehensively excluded Jews from the German economy.[34]

None of this followed a preordained plan. Rather, eager Hitler Youth boys and other party volunteers, inspired by the War against Rot and the general discourse around frugality, started to collect materials such as bottle caps and metal tubes that were practically worthless to rag-and-bone men. Soon party organizations expanded their efforts and happily accepted everything a household was willing to offer, thus duplicating and eventually thwarting the interests of peddlers.[35] The NSV slowly prepared Germans to surrender secondary materials as a selfless act of national importance.[36] Waste peddlers, in turn, found themselves stigmatized and targeted as "asocials" by the regime and their former clients.[37] The German garbage community took their place, offering tenacity, diligence, and a sense of duty as collective sacrifice to the Führer and soon to his war.

Figure 3.2 Hitler Youth boys dress up as metal tubes to encourage scrap collection, 1938. Courtesy of Bundesarchiv.

A Crush on Metal

A close look at the broad-spectrum state-mandated activism that the Four-Year Plan inspired further elucidates the comprehensive reorganization of the secondary materials trade. Given the focus on heavy industry, Göring and the newly minted office of the Reich Commissioner for Secondary Materials aimed at increasing the collection of metal scrap in order to reduce scrap imports, save foreign currency, and channel raw material "reserves" in the form of "orphaned junk" into armaments manufacturing.[38] The collection of recyclables in households and small businesses, which became mandatory in September 1936, was neither immediately enforceable nor capable of producing the magical statistical increases that could prove the Four-Year Plan's success. Göring admitted that he was reorganizing the German economy "not as a big econ-head and even bigger entrepreneur, but with untrammeled will."[39] His "untrammeled will" neither readily translated into increases in metal reserves nor foreign currency, but the Nazi party organizations and adjacent federations could be mobilized to provide the labor force necessary to implement various blitz missions for the collection of scrap. Walther Köhler, who oversaw the group for raw material redistribution within the administrative machinery of the Four-Year Plan, coordinated the implementation of the first such propaganda campaign in the spring of 1937.[40] Köhler commissioned the SA, the SS, and the National Socialist Motor Corps for the "Decluttering of the Countryside and the Village" and charged volunteers with the root-and-branch requisitioning of every outmoded or useless agricultural implement; of iron scrap dumped into gravel pits, road-side ditches, and ravines; and of scrap amassed on farmsteads or dump sites. If farmers were not willing to donate their precious junk, the Reich paid them. However, the propaganda that saturated airwaves and print media left no doubt about the regime's expectations to receive the iron scrap that blighted the countryside as donations to the *Volksgemeinschaft*.[41]

The regime was nothing if not comprehensive in its approach to metal junk. A similarly focused special mission (*Sonderaktion*)—the first *Schrottaktion* or junk campaign—targeted manufacturing and industry, but without much of the propagandistic fanfare. The German Labor Front (*Deutsche Arbeitsfront*, DAF) conducted internal propaganda campaigns to requisition tools, machines, pipes, and assembly materials that accumulated in storage halls, attics, and basements of factories and businesses.[42] In the summer of 1938, the regime expanded its hunt, ordering the comprehensive recovery of sheet metal. Based on the decluttering campaign of the countryside, where the SA, Hitler's personal army, had been tasked with the retrieval of secondary materials from people's attics, ostensibly to remove potential fire hazards, the SA requisitioned sheet metal from public offices.[43] The SA was entitled to half of the revenue; the remainder flowed into accounts of the Four-Year Plan administration.[44]

Contemporaneously, Göring mandated the dismantling of iron fences— first from public institutions and then from private front yards. Since the process would have been very costly for property owners, the SA, the Soldiers and Veterans Association (*Kyffhäuserbund*), and the Technical Emergency Relief Association volunteered to remove the requisitioned fences.[45] The *Gauleiter* (governors) organized task forces that consisted of a representative of the respective volunteer organizations, a representative from the building police, and a representative of the municipal administration, who then negotiated with property owners and businesses. In addition, the task forces identified park fences, side railings, posts, and traffic signs on country roads and highways for removal.[46] Berlin set aside 35,000 RM to remove iron fences from houses and insisted that the owners be convinced it was for aesthetic improvements of the neighborhood.

A flood of subsequent regulations was enacted to curb overeager gleaners who removed precious historic latticework as well as essential infrastructural fortifications. Accordingly, the regime clarified: iron railings at embankments, in front of cellar shafts, at road crossings, and at schoolyards or hospitals were exempt from these collections, as were historical monuments, and fences deemed necessary for the protection of public buildings. In August 1938, the collection mania was extended to cemeteries where fences and iron grave crosses were dismantled by plainclothes SA men. The circular was not propagated; allegedly, in the interests of piety. Nonetheless, such raiding of graves prompted popular outrage. Göring, who relied on his "own observations" as well as on "reports from involved officials" and tip-offs, declared that all resistance to these collections, active or passive, was a crime against the nation.[47] The police lent a hand, "educating" the population about the importance of metal collections, monitoring compliance, and guarding the makeshift storage facilities against theft.

The collective zeal and volunteerism that arose between 1936 and 1939 quickly produced transport bottlenecks. On August 31st, the day before Germany invaded Poland, the *Reichsbahn* (railway authority) explained backlogs were due to "the intense foreign policy situation" and insisted that collection of scrap continue, and the yields be stored for immediate use upon availability of railcars.[48] Otherwise, the transportation of junk would have directly interfered with the mobilization efforts of the regime. War only exacerbated this particular phenomenon.

While smelting and transportation capacities were finite, collective sacrifice was an infinitely expandable category—at least in the minds of the managers of the war economy. Accordingly, Hermann Göring decided in February 1940 that it was time to round up every metal ashtray, ornament, kettle, plate, goblet, and emblem and offer them, together with dispensable signs, hooks, door hinges, banisters, and metal-made household wares, as a tribute of the *Volksgemeinschaft* to Hitler's fifty-first birthday on April 20th.[49] Somehow the framing was magic. For the better part of three years, the people's community had been subjected to the collection frenzy of the party and, had their enthusiasm been as total as the Reich's propaganda machine envisioned, no metal would have been left for the Führer's birthday present. But that was not the case. While many Germans had viewed the salvaging campaigns pushed by party organs with suspicion, their enthusiasm knew no limits when asked to make a personal sacrifice to Hitler himself. Industry, party offices, and the public sector over-exerted themselves; they removed bells from churches, city halls, and ships; households parted with decorative objects, tin plates, and beer jugs. Office workers dismantled metal plaques, signs, and hinges from administrative buildings and hospitals. Individuals who had no metal wares to spare went to collection points and instead offered cash as a present to the Führer.[50] By April 19th, the Germans had donated 50,000 metric tons of metal.[51] How much of this material was actually recycled went unrecorded, but the quantities collected were so staggering that transport to ironworks and smelting facilities could not keep pace. Vast

Figure 3.3 Metal collection, 1940. Courtesy of Bundesarchiv.

Figure 3.4 Metal collected in Berlin is loaded onto barges for transport. Courtesy of Bundesarchiv.

Figure 3.5 Bells weather the elements in Hamburg's harbor, 1947. Courtesy of Bundesarchiv.

quantities still weathered the elements in storage lots years after the war had been lost.[52]

Bottlenecks

The birthday collection set the tone for future Reich collections by explicitly connecting personal sacrifice and Hitler's gratitude.[53] Subsequent collections, ranging from textiles to gramophones, were modeled after this success story. On October 23, 1941, the High Command of the Wehrmacht tasked Hans Heck with immediately mobilizing 60,000,000 empty bottles through a nationwide campaign. These bottles were to be filled with much needed "warming beverages"—wine and spirits—and distributed to the troops fighting on the eastern front.[54] Planned as a blitz, the collection was set for November 8th.[55] To ensure that the refilled bottles would reach their destination before extreme cold could burst them, they had to embark on their journey before the end of the month.

When Walter Tiessler, the leader of the Reich Ring for National Socialist Propaganda, made his way home on the evening of November 10, 1941, he noted that his fellow Berliners had conscientiously followed instructions and lined up their empties in front of doors and along sidewalks. The *Müllgemeinschaft* had once again proven its willingness to sacrifice. Across the Reich, empty bottles were waiting to be picked up, filled, and sent eastward. Once again, the Reich was overwhelmed with the task of collection.[56]

The *Reichsflaschentag* was quickly earning its name, irrespective of the fact that the Reich's propaganda office insisted it be called "Bottle Collection for Our Army."[57] The glaring potential for mockery inherent in any composite of the word *Flasche* (bottle), which also translates as "dud" or "wimp," was a justified concern. When bottles remained on the doorsteps beyond the scheduled pick-up date, the collection was likely mocked as the "Reich duds' day" or "Reich wimp action." The Reich Propaganda Office decreed a new "language rule" to avert such ridicule in the face of logistical difficulties.[58]

Hans Heck erroneously dismissed the need for large-scale propaganda, claiming "the purpose of the collection is readily self-evident."[59] He was correct in estimating German compliance. By 1941, the people were well accustomed to collection drives and anything headed for the front had a different status of urgency. But precisely why German soldiers required special rations of liquor in the fall of 1941 likely still escaped most civilians. The implications of the bottle collection are sinister. Starting immediately with the invasion of the Soviet Union in June 1941, mobile killing squads (*Einsatzgruppen*), Waffen-SS, Wehrmacht soldiers, and police battalions began to systematically murder Polish and Soviet Jews, rounding up and liquidating the populations of entire towns and villages in occupied Poland and the Soviet Union. As historian Christopher Browning details, the Reich carted truckloads of alcohol to the killing fields to ease the grim task of shooting women and children, the frail, the infirm, and the elderly at point-blank range and wash away the memories of splattered brains and splintered bones in the aftermath.[60]

The campaign Bottles for Our Army coincided with the deportation of German Jews to the east, which began in October 1941.[61] Germans watched with outward curiosity and glee as their neighbors were taken away or simply turned away, pretending not to notice.[62] In contrast, the bottle collection drew over 500,000 devoted citizen-volunteers and a compliant population.[63] In big cities and rural areas, people dropped off their bottles at predetermined collection points at schoolyards and mayors' offices to avoid the expenditure of door-to-door collection.[64] In small- and medium-sized towns, citizens placed bottles outside their doors just before the scheduled pick-up time to avoid theft and breakage. The Wehrmacht provided fuel, vehicles, and additional manpower to transport the bottles to preselected bottling companies. The Reich had identified more than 300 suitable companies to refill the collected bottles with spirits.[65] Leaflets and posters were printed despite the growing paper shortage, and the press, radio, and film industry were enlisted to ensure that every single German would donate at least two empty bottles on November 8th.[66] Propaganda combined with door-to-door activism proved effective.[67]

In several cities and regions, the army simply lacked the necessary fuel reserves to collect and transport the empty bottles to designated bottling plants. The Office for Secondary Materials and local party offices reassured the affected district leaders that the collection would be completed by the end of the week. No effort was too great, even horse-drawn carts were brought into play. But in many cities and towns, the bottles remained where they had been placed. The military mobilized regular troops to sort bottles and transport them to the requisite filling centers. The allocation of vehicles and fuel received top priority by order of the High Command. By November 21st, the concerted efforts of Wehrmacht personnel, the Reich Security Service, the National Socialist soldier's league, the SS, and regular police units ensured the successful removal of collected bottles.[68] However, most were never filled and fewer were delivered to soldiers on the eastern front.[69]

Woolens for Christmas

On the surface, the bottle collection appears to be a rather curious example of the Reich's resource recovery efforts. In fact, it anticipated the genocidal implications of wartime recycling, at home and in the occupied east. Directly connected to Nazi extermination policies, it offered invaluable propaganda lessons that subsequent collections, which faced the same transportation difficulties, were largely able to avoid. When General Ernst Jodl requested a renewed collection of woolens in December 1941, the party was already so overwhelmed with collections that voices from within the ranks opined that everything expendable had already been donated. Goebbels brushed these reservations aside, if he "were to call upon the population because the front needs woolens, then the population would donate sufficient woolens." Cautionary voices insisted that the population would not understand why this collection only commenced in December and warned that they would further object to such sacrifice if it became obvious that the materials simply ended up in storage facilities. Indeed, this campaign ran up against some very real, undeniable logistical difficulties.[70]

Transportation bottlenecks were so severe that the party headquarters contemplated encouraging everyone to send warm clothing directly to their loved ones at the front and requiring that letters and other mail be included with the donations so as not to overburden the *Reichsbahn*. The idea was quickly tossed aside. Instead, the Propaganda Ministry issued an urgent official call across all German radio stations for a woolens collection to commence on December 23rd. Its motto called for "Woolens collection for the front: The Christmas present for our soldiers."[71] Scheduled to run through January 2nd, the collection obliged every member of the people's community to "completely exert" all possibilities. However, Goebbels forbade the use of the term "sacrifice," because it, he insisted, was exclusively reserved for the service provided by the men fighting on the front. Posters, leaflets, image reports, and shop-window displays announced the collection, and the Hitler Youth was mobilized to collect whatever warming textiles the *Volksgemeinschaft* had left and cart them to collection points.[72]

On December 19, 1941, the army leadership encouraged the collection but advocated against delivering the materials directly to the soldiers on the front lines. Instead, this last reserve ought to be stored in the textile repositories of the Wehrmacht at the railroad end points in the east, since the troops were well provisioned with winter clothing.[73] In light of this, the Führer himself demanded clarity. Either the collection should be completed as planned and the materials delivered to the front, or the campaign should be announced as a collection of future reserves. Military leaders disagreed among themselves. Chief of the Army Administration Herbert Osterkamp insisted that the troops were outfitted sufficiently, but the Quartermaster General Eduard Wagner ordered the woolens to be delivered to the front at once. While the propaganda office was still working out the precise wording of the Führer's orders, transportation holdups threatened the delivery. Major Froneberg, in charge of the allocation of vehicles, announced that the Wehrmacht could not provide vehicles for transport. Coordination between the Ministry of Transportation and the army could not be concluded prior to the beginning of the collection.

Nonetheless, on December 20th at 8:00 p.m., Goebbels announced the woolens collection in a nationwide broadcast by every radio station. Hitler Youth paraded through the streets, singing songs and chanting in honor of the collection. Donations were stored in schools. Since schools and gyms were not heated, volunteers staffed collection points in shifts to manage exposure to the cold.[74] The textiles then needed to be sorted. Volunteers separated out articles that were not suitable for use by the troops to avoid outfitting German soldiers with women's fur coats; apparently, women donated their furs in such enormous quantities that the Reich deemed it necessary to refuse such items.[75] At collection points, female volunteers offered advice and altered or mended donations on the spot.[76] Party offices at the Gau, district and municipal levels, organized transport to the train stations, relying on the Hitler Youth with pushcarts and other volunteers to transport the precious *Volksgut* to railway stations.[77] At the last minute, Tiessler expressly included skis and ski boots among desirable items.[78]

Less than a week into the collection, Fritz Sauckel reported that the Gau Thüringen had collected 8,000 pairs of woolen socks; 5,000 woolen sweaters, shirts, and underpants each; 10,000 head-warmers and mittens; and 1800 fur coats and vests.[79] Across the Reich, the collection delivered more than 9.5 million items before year's end.[80] Since Reich collections were specifically reserved for citizens, collectibles of interest were simply requisitioned from

Jewish households.[81] Goebbels lauded the woolens collection not only for having demonstrated the indestructible spirit and will of the people's community and the organizational acumen of the party, but also for giving the population something meaningful to do during the Christmas period, distracting from gloomy speculations about the future.[82] The campaign was so successful that Hitler agreed to extend it by another week.[83] On January 4th, a report was composed for Hitler, announcing that in just eight days 32,144,201 items had been collected at 40,417 different collection points, which had been staffed by 1,976,352 volunteers. The zeal of the population exceeded expectations and, quite predictably, the capacities of the *Reichsbahn*. In just two weeks, the people's community had stockpiled almost 70 million items.[84] To hide the transportation backlogs, the army started to allocate woolens and winter clothes to troops that were being relocated eastward from the western territories under the mantle of utmost secrecy.

The Christmas collection of woolens produced extraordinary results. It was exemplary in that the regime measured success not primarily in weight or bulk or the number of items, but in its ability to make visible popular support and volunteerism as well as the smooth and frictionless operation of the party organization. It was unusual because compliance with and yield of the collection exceeded subsequent efforts. The year 1941 was the first winter when German soldiers found themselves on Soviet territory, as well as one of the coldest winters on record. In comparison to the infamous Russian winter and the "barbaric" enemy that Nazi propaganda conjured up, privations shouldered by citizens inside the Reich were still rather manageable. The generosity of the population likely stemmed from the rapid military successes of the previous summer and unrealistic hopes for a speedy victory.

To capitalize on the huge propaganda success of the woolens campaign, the propaganda ministry announced wide-ranging additional collections. There would never be a better time to requisition church bells.[85] Perhaps it was the Christmas spirit Goebbels unleashed that explains the initiatives of the nurses of the Albrecht-Krankenhaus who volunteered to repair, alter, or mend any of the collected woolens. Perhaps it also explains why within a week, the Finnish women's organization, Lotta Svärd, sewed snowsuits out of requisitioned hotel linens for the entire Finnish army, who were fighting alongside the Germans.[86] But such initiatives did not mark a new norm. Citing the embarrassment of the bottle collection, the ongoing collection of books, a collection of tools, an NSV collection of furniture for soldiers' barracks, the musical instrument and sheet music collection, the gramophone and record collection, the regular school collections, "Sacrifice Sundays" designated for donations to the Winter Relief Works, and the street collection of the Winter Relief Works—all of which took place in November 1941—the propaganda office in Bavaria cautioned against collections becoming excessive. "It appears," the report noted, "that the collections are not coordinated from a central office" but rather implemented in a haphazard way.[87] Over subsequent months, Germans grumbled about the reductions in bread rations starting in February, and their willingness to donate anything was quickly reaching its limit.[88]

Little Garbage Heroes

Collections naturally overlapped and competed for train space, fuel, and storage facilities. By the last week of 1941, collections of secondary materials had to expand into gyms and other facilities since schools were overwhelmed by woolens and had served as collection facilities for more than a year.[89] In November 1936, Wilhelm Ziegler had still prohibited schools from accepting secondary materials that students might bring from home.[90] Before long the regime realized that schools could serve as natural hubs for secondary materials, especially after countless schools closed due to teachers being drafted en masse.[91] Eager pupils made for an army of dutiful collectors. In January 1937, Göring, in response to successful trials, permitted the utilization of schools and students for the collection of soup and kitchen bones.[92] War only accelerated and intensified the reliance on schools.[93] When Hans Heck took over the office of the Reich Commissioner, he focused on the systematic reorganization of scrap collections in light of wartime contingencies. Starting in January 1940, Berlin schools called out particularly zealous students and rewarded those who brought in large amounts of bones or secondary materials with books, and reprimanded those less eager.[94] Schools turned collecting into a competition. By May 1941, Berlin schools could pride themselves on an exponential increase in materials gathered. While they had netted 84.9 tons of secondary materials (bones, rags, paper, non-ferrous metals, and others) between January and March 1941, in May they doubled the efforts of the previous months.[95] In September, the mayor of Berlin personally congratulated the winning school, and four exemplary students received paid trips to Vienna.

Middle school students—driven by the reward structure; the constant exhortation about duty in light of the war effort; and a sense of independence, accomplishment, and adventure—went overboard. They incurred the wrath of secondary materials traders since they stood in line for hours to obtain secondary materials at shops and stores. Often, they decided for themselves what could and could not be deemed secondary materials. Especially after the Reich's textile collection decreased the amount of rags in circulation, students sought out such riches as hydrogen and acid cylinders, railroad bolts, lugs and shims, clamps and setup hooks, and the metal covers of city drainage systems.[96] A year later, a points system was in place to keep better track of student efforts. By November 1942, the scrap and junk amassed in schools required the disposition of special vehicles for transport. The following summer, eager collectors were rewarded with candy and the fifteen best students received a radio set.[97] Parents complained that their children were subjected to punishments if they did not meet desired delivery quotas.[98] But as the war dragged on, even pupils saw diminished returns in hunting after junk when it had long since become a defining characteristic of urban life amidst the ruins.

The collections nonetheless continued. But the turn of military events over the course of the winter of 1942–1943 affected the willingness of ordinary people to exhaust themselves by participating. They felt they had nothing left to give, no more patience, no more strength, and certainly no more stuff. Bombs rained on German cities, destroying infrastructure and impeding provisioning and relief efforts. In this context, the public performance of NSV volunteers was a sign of privilege, in sharp contrast to the pervasive hardships and a general downturn experienced by most Germans. When the National Socialist women's organization came around to collect flour, sugar, and butter by the spoonful in a so-called *Löffelsammlung* to bake sugary treats for the Wehrmacht, the population openly complained about the voracious greed of the party. Complaints were so severe that the NSV shelved a number of planned collections.[99]

Propagandists like Goebbels continued to imagine resources where there were none. By the summer of 1943, Goebbels was convinced that, in light of the unrelenting air war, it would be necessary to organize a collection for safety goggles through the Reich Motor Corps.[100] Apparently, a lot of the rescue workers incurred severe eye infections during and after the massive attacks on the industrial areas in the Rhineland.[101] That same summer, the Reich Consortium for Damage Prevention attempted to enlist party officials to collect boxes to transport other materials, but Heck stepped in, believing that collections were going overboard.[102] Apparently, the Reich Ministry for Economic Affairs in conjunction with the *Reichsstelle* for paper and packing materials plotted to send local volunteers from door to door to find empty boxes.[103] The correspondence between the Reich Chancellery and the Propaganda Ministry illustrate the complete disconnect of bureaucrats from the realities on the ground.[104] Volunteers were stretched thin. People worked long hours, stood in line to obtain necessary provisions, and ran for shelter during constant air raid alarms. The *Müllgemeinschaft* was running out of steam.

PART II
EXTRACTION

4
Forged in Metal

Georg Hörrmann did not know anything about construction. Yet, by 1943, he found himself on the side of the road, day in and day out, guarding a contingent of forced laborers whose work, he claimed, he didn't understand. After seventeen months of active duty on the eastern front, Sergeant Hörrmann, a non-commissioned officer, was back in the Reich when he learned about the defeat of the Sixth Army at Stalingrad. Perhaps he was bored and alienated by his work. Perhaps he felt disempowered and simultaneously deprived of a more meaningful opportunity to contribute to the war effort because on March 8, 1943, he wrote to the personal staff of the Reichsführer SS and Chief of German Police Heinrich Himmler with a grandiose proposal: a massive junk reclamation mission in German-occupied Soviet territory.

Informed by his own experiences in the east, Hörrmann described a landscape littered with recklessly abandoned, unused riches. Millions of Reichsmark were at stake, he claimed. Bombed out tanks and military vehicles, heavy artillery, pieces of machinery, shells, cartridges, and tires were falling victim to the wind, weather, and civilian exploitation. These "resources" were permanently lost to the Reich's armaments industry, Hörrmann lamented. If no action was taken, the Russians would seize this booty, transform it into new tanks, and deploy them against the Germans with lethal force, Hörrmann worried. To avert this fate, he proposed the organization of small, nimble special units that would salvage the junk and return it to the German armaments industry.

The proposal was hardly altruistic, even if the sergeant's primary goal was to contribute to securing final victory. Hörrmann offered to lead one of the very units he proposed be dispatched, perhaps hoping to put an end to his mundane guard duty and return to active duty.[1] It is unclear what became of Hörrmann. At the time he wrote to Himmler, Hörrmann was likely in his forties. Since 1917, he had worked as an automotive engineer and mechanic and had put his vehicular expertise at the service of the Reich after 1941. From his somewhat cryptic descriptions, it appears that his main task as a soldier was to drive, moving within and between the rearward army territory and the active front, either to ensure the delivery of supplies and provisions or, more likely, to repair military vehicles and other equipment. Deployed along the northern and the southern parts of the eastern front, Hörrmann recounted numerous trips along the road connecting Białystok and Vilnius as well as in the Kuban territory between Krasnodar and Armavir. The same bombed out tanks and army vehicles that Hörrmann encountered during the army's advance greeted him upon his return, though covered in thick layers of rust and the rubber stripped off their wheels. Hörrmann intuited that Soviet civilians used the cut tires to sole their shoes; he started to worry about what an advancing Red Army might accomplish with rusted tanks.[2]

The descriptions in Hörrmann's letter echoed Hermann Göring's admonitions from November 1941. Addressing the *Wirtschaftsführungsstab Ost* (Economic Staff East) in a secret meeting, Göring noted that the "Russian campaign" had brought "some surprises, which could have easily had devastating consequences" and reminded his audience that "peace only lies beyond victory."[3] Stressing the need for machine tools and raw materials, such as fuel, rubber, and iron, he imagined junk "littered the Russian landscape in obscene quantities."[4] When Hörrmann's letter reached Himmler's staff, the Wehrmacht had turned Göring's imagination into reality, wreaking indescribable havoc on cities and towns. The Nazis alternatively scattered and stored massive amounts of junk and other war debris in the eastern

Figure 4.1 Hörrmann's junk paradise. Courtesy of Bundesarchiv.

territories. Although framed as an original intervention, Hörrmann's letter indicated his awareness of elaborate structures in place to rescue metal junk in the areas under German occupation. Rather than proposing a fundamentally novel approach, Hörrmann's obsequious letter was an indictment of the pervasive inefficiencies that characterized the German war economy, especially metal reclamation.

To systematically dismantle all movable assets, metal above all, the regime created the Organization Schu, which ensured the removal of all metal reserves, junk, scrap, and other secondary materials in the occupied lands. Increasingly, however, waste recovery and recycling exacerbated the very problems they were supposed to address. Metal scrap in particular promised to backstop German industry until the acquired "living space" provided the resource base to sustain the Nazi Empire.[5] Accordingly, a focus on metal reveals the glaring disconnect between the rhetoric around resource extension and recovery. and the actual efficacy of the regime's efforts to turn scrap into weapons of war.[6] Nazi Germany administered the conquered lands in the east as colonial overlords. But instead of mines and metal works, it sited junkyards. Booty crews followed the advancing Wehrmacht to locate assets that the Organization Schu then dismantled and shipped off.

The ensuing chaos helps explain the muted frustrations Sergeant Hörrmann expressed in his letter to Himmler in the summer of 1943. Despite a massive apparatus developed for requisitioning all kinds of material, the Reich's efforts to secure the "millions worth" of abandoned riches Hörrmann painstakingly listed could hardly keep pace with the Wehrmacht's production of junk as it shelled cities, blasted infrastructure, and sacked military installations and depots. In the end, whether scattered across the terrain or stockpiled in designated storage facilities, junk remained everywhere the Germans went in Europe despite the massive efforts of railway workers to freight dismantled assets and loot back to the rapidly shrinking territory under German control. Having internalized the imperatives of the Nazi waste regime, Hörrmann had to grapple with the fact that the Wehrmacht produced more junk than the regime could transport home, let alone recycle.

Setting Up Shop

If the proclamation of the Four-Year Plan in 1936 had shifted the focus toward resource extension, the invasion of Poland and its subsequent occupation shifted the focus yet again from mandatory salvage in preparation for war to wholesale plunder. Germany invaded Poland on September 1, 1939, and on September 17th, the Soviet Union launched its assault from the east, executing the secret provision in the German–Soviet non-aggression agreement that anticipated the division and occupation of Poland. By the end of September, the Germans had concluded their blitz campaign and started to set up shop. With such rapid victories shaping expectations for future campaigns, Hitler's popularity soared, and Germans seemed willing to ignore the heavy losses the Polish army inflicted in the fierce defense of their country.[7] Initially, the Germans did not have clearly articulated plans for how to manage the conquered Polish territories.[8] The precise structures crystalized over the course of the fall 1939. Ultimately, the western parts of Poland were incorporated into the German Reich as the *Reichsgaue Wartheland* (also referred to as *Warthegau*), Danzig, and West Prussia. The eastern part, the General Government, functioned as a *Nebenland* or side country, which the Germans administered like a slave colony under Governor Hans Frank.[9] Hitler entrusted Heinrich Himmler, in his new capacity as the *Reichskommissar für die Festigung deutschen Volkstums* (Reich Commissioner for the Consolidation of German Nationhood), with "Germanizing" the new *Reichsgaue* by clearing the annexed parts of Jews and those Poles, who could not be Germanized.

The precise competencies, responsibilities, and hierarchies continued to take shape over the next few months. Heinrich Himmler, his deputy Reinhard Heydrich, and the *Judensachbearbeiter* (Jew clerk) Adolf Eichmann forged their own designs for spatial engineering in Poland.[10] The ultimate goal was to remove all Jews and a regionally specific number of Poles from the incorporated territories.[11] Multiple plans circulated, differing in range and urgency; they anticipated the forcible resettlement of roughly 600,000 to 1,000,000 Polish Jews, an unspecified number of Poles, and 30,000 Sinti and Roma from the Reich in the General Government or "the 'Reich ghetto' as Heydrich called it."[12] Between September 1939 and March 1940, approximately 128,000 people were forced from their homes, often with just a few hours' notice to pack their belongings, and crammed into the General Government.[13] The goal was to make room for the anticipated resettlement of Germans from the Reich and so-called *Volksdeutsche* (ethnic Germans). The General Government was supposed to generate the resources and labor necessary to support the German military occupation and subsequent military expansion. However, this systematic campaign of ethnic cleansing soon conflicted with the Frank's administrative priorities for the General Government.[14] When Frank complained about the dramatic influx of people, Goebbels noted in his diary that "everyone wants to dump their rubbish in the General Government. Jews, sick people, idlers. Frank is resisting. Not entirely unjustified." But Goebbels sharply criticized Frank's desire to turn "Poland [into] a model colony," invoking the "Führer" who insisted that Poland be mined for labor. "From where can we otherwise take the missing labor for menial tasks. Afterall, we have to take them from somewhere," Goebbels mused.[15]

Hitler, who rarely concerned himself with the practicalities of actual governance, insisted that none of the population measures and administrative battles were to interfere with his economic interests.[16] According to Frank, Hitler did not decide until January 1940 whether to "keep" the General Government or transform it into a "Polish rump state or something similar."[17] Nonetheless, in his decree from October 17, 1939, Hitler maintained:

> It is not the task of the administration to turn Poland into a model province or a model state of the German order or to rehabilitate the country economically or financially. It must be prevented that a Polish intelligentsia sets itself up as a leading class. A low standard of living is to remain in the country; we merely want to extract labor there. Poles should also be utilized to administer the country. However, the formation of national cells must be prevented. . . . Methods will be incompatible with our other principles. . . . The Polish economy shall flourish. The leadership must enable us to cleanse the Reich territory of Jews and Polacks as well. Cooperation with other *Reichsgaue* should only take place for the purpose of resettlement. Prudence and ruthlessness in this ethnic struggle must spare us from having to go to the battlefield once again because of these lands.[18]

Other than such general directives, Hitler left it to Himmler, Frank, and Göring to work out the details, which led to some serious turf wars between Himmler's SS and Frank's "civilian" administration. Himmler was in charge of the "resettlement program" and oversaw the *Einsatzgruppen* and supporting police forces that systematically murdered the Polish clergy, intelligentsia, and top military officials. Over the next two years, Himmler, Heydrich, and Frank enforced the systematic ghettoization of Polish Jews in the General Government in anticipation of more comprehensive and even "final solutions."[19] Major General Robert Bührmann stressed that the

General Government constituted something entirely new, "an experiment, comparable to those made in colonial countries [sic], like Africa."[20] The structures the German administrators put in place enabled an unfettered economy of extraction and, ultimately, served as a laboratory for genocide.

On October 19, 1939, Herman Göring created the *Haupt Treuhandstelle Ost* (HTO) or Main Trustee Section East to capture, secure, and transport the property of the former Polish state; to requisition designated private property from Poles and Jews; to regulate the credit and monetary system; and to oversee the reorganization of the economy in the General Government and territories incorporated into the Reich.[21] The HTO became the main body to coordinate and assert control over the rapid ransacking of Poland. Until year's end, responsibilities remained somewhat opaque, as Göring, representatives from the HTO, the Reich Ministry of Economic Affairs (*Reichswirtschaftsministerium*, RWM), and the emerging civilian administration under Hans Frank were working out the precise structures that would govern the pilfering of Poland.[22] While the plunderers were debating whether to create an administration and processing company that would oversee and finance shipments of assets back to the Reich, Göring designated Major General Robert Bührmann as the Commissioner for Raw Materials Requisitioning. To rein in the spontaneous, unauthorized fleecing of Polish assets, Göring threatened imprisonment for anyone who attempted to acquire any goods or raw materials either from official or private sources without coordinating with Bührmann's staff.[23]

By the end of the year, the preliminary structures were in place. Hans Frank had become the plenipotentiary for the General Government and served as part of the Four-Year Plan's administrative complex, with Robert Bührmann as his immediate deputy. The HTO, with its nine different departments (*Fachabteilungen*) and offices in Łódź, Gdańsk, Poznań, Ciechanów, Katowice, and Krakow, was in charge of requisitioning all raw materials and assets. It, too, was part of the Four-Year Plan Authority, with Director Dr. Max Winkler directly subordinate to Hermann Göring.[24] The staff of Major General Bührmann was thus an important link between the HTO, Frank's civilian administration of the General Government, and the military. Bührmann reported to Winkler. In many ways, these structures anticipated the amalgamation of military, industry, and civilian administrative competences that characterized the German war economy until its collapse in 1945. They further contributed to the fierce competition between Hans Frank and Heinrich Himmler, which ultimately ended in a lopsided truce that recognized Himmler's de facto authority. In addition, the appointment of Fritz Sauckel as the plenipotentiary of labor in March 1942 further eroded Frank's independence.[25]

While Himmler and the SS ultimately determined the day-to-day experiences of the population, Göring's influence remained crucial in the economic realm. Genocide and extraction developed interconnected structures. By late fall, Göring resolved to form the Administration and Utilization Corporation (*Verwaltungs- und Verwertungsgesellschaft Ost m.b.H.*, VVG) as the corporate arm of the HTO to ensure the smooth dispositioning of assets through the state-controlled Economic Research Corporation (*Wirtschaftsforschungsgesellschaft*, Wifo) and trusted intermediaries in business and industry. Unlike the Wifo, the VVG was a nominally independent entity and functioned as the liaison between the Four-Year Plan Authority and private industry.[26] Its name suggests that it was likely anticipated to deal primarily with inferior and secondary materials.

The organization of the VVG reflected the Reich's economic priorities. The corporation had three separate departments designated for metal requisitioning, one for iron and steel, one for nonferrous metals and precious metals, and one for scrap and junk. Additional departments were designated for oils and fats for the chemical industries; for rubber, carbon black, and asbestos; for machines of all sorts; for leather, skins, and furs; for textiles; and for secondary materials. Theoretically, all material subject to requisitioning and transport were of two kinds: *Beutegut* (loot) that included all property of the former Polish state, the property of Jews, and the property of most Poles, and *Kaufgut* (purchased goods) that were acquired from private companies and persons that retained permission to do business in Poland. These complex structures administered the local economy and governed the aryanization of Jewish property.

Initially, operations ran less than smoothly. Even before the VVG was officially incorporated, its managing directors, Ernst Ranis, Erich Bauwerker, and Erich Marschner, complained about overlapping competencies, lack of cooperation between various offices, and widespread disorganization. In particular, these three economic experts lamented that the "necessary connection or constant contact between the Military Economic Inspectorate Ober-Ost and the Commissioner for Raw Materials Requisitioning, Major General Bührmann, is almost completely missing."[27] Instead of railcars filled with metal for the German armaments industry, by the end of November, the Wifo branch office in Łódź had received only six wagons with rags and an additional three with wool.[28] Ultimately, what appeared to be mismanagement or organizational difficulties mirrored some of the misalignment of the Reich's plans for extraction. The obvious importance of metal to the war effort shaped the initial plans for extraction, but the shipment of textiles proved no fluke.

While textile mining was intimately connected with people (and their systematic murder), the plans Nazi administrators and businessmen spelled out with respect to metal reclamation were entirely devoid of people. Instead, their discussions revolved around demolition and shipping, inventing Poland as an unpeopled place. The plans for dismantling metal objects and machines provided a blueprint for the German approach to asset stripping. This meant removing almost all raw materials, secondary materials, and junk, in addition to machines and assets, from the General Government that could be of use to the German war economy.

Acknowledging the military necessity of booty, Hans Frank nonetheless objected to the continuing wild confiscation by armed personnel as well as the comprehensive and organized pilfering by way of trusteeship. Frank maintained that "it's essentially the same, whether one founds a corporation, whose supervisory boards are located in Germany but whose financial underpinnings are exclusively in the General Government or whether one seizes, heavily armed, a pig in the country road." Originally, the idea was that Poland would be fleeced without restraint: "[W]hat isn't bolted down is dragged off and even what is bolted down is tried to be taken out."[29] In Frank's mind, this "inner-territorial booty-extravaganza" directly interfered with his "absolute autarky" ambitions for the General Government."[30] Accordingly, he spent the first six months of the occupation trying to rein in the salaciousness for booty and plunder.[31] While Frank objected to such interference with his authority, the arbitrary and self-interested confiscation of foodstuffs, goods, and factories was an essential part of the terror inflicted on the population.

At the same time, the population politics of the SS actively depopulated the *Warthegau* and turned the General Government into a dumping ground for Poland's Jews. No provisions were made for them. Hans Frank made it clear that "the Jews don't interest me one bit. Whether they get any fodder to eat or not, is the very last question for me."[32] For Poles in the General Government, Frank was willing to entertain "possibilities of nutrition" but categorically ruled out regular rations.[33] At the same time, large numbers of Polish citizens were deported for forced labor inside Germany.[34] Göring insisted that all businesses "that are not absolutely necessary for the emergency maintenance of the bare life of the inhabitants must be transferred to Germany."[35] Göring ordered the gutting of Poland with no consideration for international law; his only worry was enemy propaganda capitalizing on German misconduct.[36] His single-minded focus on extraction ultimately played into Himmler's hands.

Frank, by contrast, had plans for the industrial development of the General Government and meticulously recorded the availability of all raw materials including secondary materials.[37] Metal and metal junk were of particular importance to the authorities in Berlin, who had rather outlandish ideas with regard to the quantities of junk they would be able to obtain. The Four-Year Plan Authority apparently expected to receive 2 million metric tons of iron and metal junk, 1 million from Warsaw alone. Major General Bührmann tried to adjust their expectations and explained that, even if everything were to be indiscriminately scrapped, a maximum of 700,000 to 800,000 metric tons could be mobilized. But since "the policy has changed and a sizable armaments industry has been built up, so that many factories won't be scrapped" as initially anticipated, expectations ought to be adjusted.[38]

By early 1940, the Reich looked eerily westward, preparing for imminent conflict with France and Great Britain, whose declaration of war on September 3, 1939, had accelerated German mobilization efforts and armaments production.[39] As Hitler gave and withdrew numerous orders to advance westward, Göring not only ramped up the disassembly of assets in Poland, but also extended his efforts inside Germany and proceeded to capture every non-essential piece of metal, from barriers and fences, to hinges and doorplates, to beer jugs and ashtrays, for the German war economy.[40] Göring recalled the massively belated, incomplete, and ultimately ill-fated attempts to supplement German metal supplies with voluntary donations of household items and requisitioned metal objects from government buildings during World War I and was determined not to make the same mistakes. Without acknowledging the already chaotic situation that characterized Germany's procurement and allocation of raw materials in the fall of 1939 and the spring of 1940, he claimed to act "preemptively" and ordered the requisitioning of all metal objects in party headquarters, administrative offices, libraries, universities, hospitals, mental institutions, and other public buildings.[41] This represented the launching of an intra-governmental treasure hunt to ensure that the Reich would lead by example before kicking off the Reich's widespread metal collection, conceptualized as a mass action in honor of Hitler's 51st birthday.

Inside the Reich, such collections could count on the eager participation of the population and the volunteer staff to support municipalities that coordinated the recording and transport of the amassed donations. In the aftermath of the metal collection in honor of Hitler's birthday, the action was extended to German businesses, which were encouraged to donate metal wastes and outmoded equipment or sell them to scrap dealers. After having cleaned out their own closets, unscrewed their hinges, and donated family tin plates and the like, workers became outraged at managers, arguing that companies were sabotaging Göring's explicit orders by selling wastes that should instead have been donated.[42]

Organizing a metal collection in the occupied territories, the regime didn't have to worry about such misplaced zeal. When Major Hartog reported on the yield, Governor Hans Frank made it clear that sentimentality would be misplaced and "one mustn't stop at Pilsudski monuments."[43] There, the regime could not avail itself of a massive voluntary effort and resorted to coercion and plunder.[44]

Schu's Empire

The gutting of Poland enabled the rapid growth of the sphere of influence of Rittmeister Hans Schu, the demolition expert at the VVG. Ultimately, Schu recorded his success in the mountainous accumulation of materials.[45] The exorbitant steel and metal requirements of Hitler's ammunitions plan, in part, explain this frenzy.[46] The *Reichsbahn* was overwhelmed, the *Ostbahn* (as the Germans referred to the remaining rail system in occupied Poland) was barely staffed, and backlogs were the order of the day. This exacerbated shortages and particularly endangered coal deliveries to German industry, without which production would lay fallow.[47]

Once the military campaign against France concluded in the summer of 1940, Göring charged Schu with systematically collecting junk and metal scrap in Western Europe. He had already demonstrated his success in building a junk empire in Nazi-occupied Poland. By his own accounting, Schu and his staff captured, processed, and shipped over 200,000 metric tons of scrap, usable metals, semi-finished goods, raw iron, and an additional 55,000 metric tons of secondary metals from Poland between October 15,

1939, and June 30, 1944.[48] By the summer of 1940, Schu was in charge of all junk recovery in the west from headquarters in Brussels.[49]

From his own reports and reports based on investigations of his organization, Schu appears to have been a shrewd individual, well-connected to high functionaries both within the Four-Year Plan Authority and the Army's High Command. His extensive ties to private scrap metal dealers enabled the flow of the recovered junk to manufacturers for processing. Schu operated without constraints or oversight, particularly once his ruthless successes led to the expansion of his responsibilities.[50]

In June 1941, Schu's charge was extended to the Balkans, and in July, less than three weeks after the invasion of the Soviet Union, he was entrusted with metal reclamation for the entire occupied territories.[51] Schu and his staff formed a sort of second front, trailing behind the advancing Wehrmacht, securing enemy military equipment, and hunting for additional mobile metal assets. Scouts, essentially bands of armed men, focused on defunct war machinery (tanks, canons, sunken ships, and munitions) and destroyed military barracks facilities, bridges, and ports, as well as the contents of enemy scrap storage facilities. They also "rescued" all sorts of secondary materials and returned them to the Reich or placed them in designated storage facilities. Squadrons of forced laborers disassembled, sorted, stored, and loaded materials onto train cars for transport back to the Reich.[52] As the organization's reach expanded, so, too, did its responsibilities. In November 1940, the Army High Command relied on Schu to process weapons and decommission munitions. In May 1942, when the Wehrmacht started a metal collection in the households, businesses, and public offices in the eastern territories, Schu's organization processed the "donations," ranging from copper household goods to shattered church bells.

The boundaries between various kinds of transportable materials—loot, merchandise, and "donations"—became increasingly blurred since nearly all of it was invoiced as loot. Naturally, shipments got mixed up, documentation was lost or delayed, and material was mislabeled, mispackaged, and misdirected as the volume strained the Reich's transportation capacities.[53] For example, in August 1942, an aluminum and smelting plant in Nuremberg received a boxcar filled with aircraft scrap, which upon inspection turned out to contain mainly wood and canvas, apparently the debris of gliders, instead of the anticipated scrap metal.[54] Similarly, Hansa Leichtmetall A.G. in Berlin received a train car filled with mixed iron scrap instead of aluminum, which was sent to the Eisen und Metall A.G. in Düsseldorf by mistake.[55]

In 1941, Schu's organization had 50 commanding and special officers, roughly 250 sergeants and 15 additional employees, but the brunt of the actual work was done by forced laborers. Similarly, the growing web of subcontracted demolition companies requested allocations of forced laborers for the grueling work of scrapping as well as for the loading and unloading of shipments.[56] On the receiving end, German scrap dealers and manufacturers were coordinated into consortia that by 1942 also relied almost exclusively on forced labor when processing reclaimed materials.[57] Allocations of both loot (*Beute*) and army goods (*Wehrmachtsgut*) required the approval of the various *Reichsstellen* that, in turn, coordinated with the Raw Materials Office. Words like "allocation" and "coordination" betray the brutality and utter chaos that characterized junk reclamation by booty crews (*Beutetrupps*) and army requisition commandos (*Wehrmachtserfassungskommandos*, WEK). Chaos and brutality, too characterized the demolition, disassembly, decommission, and freight organized by Schu in conjunction with the consortia of scrapping companies before the material was the sighted, weighed, accounted, and ultimate paid for by defense contractors, who then deployed the same callous force against the forced laborers they exploited. Working long hours, insufficiently clothed, and housed in appalling conditions, forced laborers were required to first make their own tools on site and out of the material to be scrapped.[58]

When the copper mining corporation Mansfelder Kupferschieferbergau Aktiengesellschaft found live ammunition in one of their shipments, they immediately announced that they would hold the Wehrmacht accountable for any resulting accidents and injuries. They further noted that because they had to rely exclusively on "Russian POWs" and other forced laborers, they were unable to guarantee the complete removal of explosives. However, the Wehrmacht, or to be precise, Schu's organization, was equally dependent on POWs and accordingly insisted that it, too, could not be held liable.[59] Since there was limited German military personal available to "supervise" the workers, Hermann Göring, in his capacity as Reich minister of aviation and the commander of the Luftwaffe, explained that neither "damage" nor the "malicious adding of explosive devices" was entirely preventable.[60]

In August 1943, the Army High Command argued that, of the 300,000 metric tons of scrap metal shipped monthly, only a relatively small contingent contained decommissioned munitions (*Munitionsschrott*), and careful inspections of shipments would guarantee reasonable safety.[61] Recipients complained about negligence. The Wehrmacht argued that accidents occurred because of insufficient supervision. Schu insisted that accidents involving explosives had been minimal, pointing out that he had personally overseen the shipping of 5 million metric tons of booty material to the Reich. He, too, noted repeatedly that throughout his operations he was "forced to mainly employ foreign laborers and prisoners, who naturally lack the requisite knowledge about live munitions." Rather than conceding the possibility that forced laborers and POWs knew precisely why they packed explosives into shipments headed for smelting facilities, Schu insisted that dangerous explosives were thrown into open railcars along the long transit route.[62] Explosives continued to find their way into plundered junk.

A key component in this apparatus of plunder and slave labor was the Raw Materials and Trade Corporation (*Rohstoff und Handelsgesellschaft mbH*, ROGES), which was responsible for logistics and invoicing of materials shipped back to manufacturers inside the Reich and thus linked the militarized extraction run by the Wehrmacht with the private sector of the German economy. The ROGES was founded in December 1940 to formalize the sale of extracted materials from the western territories to manufacturers as part of "normal" economic transactions.[63] It would keep separate the two economic sectors—the east, which was ruthlessly exploited, and the west, which was to form the basis for the new economic order of Europe. With a registered capital of 1,000,000 RM, the ROGES functioned as the logistics company for the proliferating array of shipments from the occupied westen territories, but it nonetheless constantly invoiced shipments of loot and other materials from the eastern territories. The regime held the majority share in this "independent" corporation that bore the cost for the financing and transport of the massive junk recovery mission and soon for the evacuation of the amassed loot.[64]

After the war, the Allies did not regard the ROGES as one of the *Ostgesellschaften* or *Kriegsgesellschaften* (war corporations) since it operated on an "exclusively commercial basis." Accordingly, the ROGES continued to work under the supervision of the British authorities after the war's end.[65] Similarly, the courts in the Federal Republic of Germany, which oversaw the cases over remaining accounts receivables well into the 1950s, claimed that the requisitioning of war-relevant materials was in keeping with international law.[66]

Playing by the "Green Book"

The occupation of Poland had been chaotic, but it provided the space for experimentation with war and resource extraction, especially by members of the SS.[67] The lessons learned in the sacking of Poland subsequently shaped the colonization of the *Ostland* and the *Reichskommissariat* Ukraine. The attempts at comprehensive resettlement of Germans in the parts of Poland incorporated into the Reich, and the forcible removal of Jews and Poles to the General Government, ultimately threatened to fragment the economic structures in both parts of Poland.[68] Accordingly, no comprehensive resettlement scheme was thought up for the Soviet Union. Similarly, while marauding bands of soldiers and Waffen-SS indiscriminately disassembled all movable assets in the General Government, such an endeavor would have been logistically impossible in the occupied Soviet territories.[69]

The occupation relied heavily on the security forces to "pacify" the territory, secure main roads and throughways, and buttress the thinly stretched administrative structures. At the peak of German expansion in the fall of 1942, the German occupying forces had to administer 1 million square kilometers of Soviet territory. Each installed military governor oversaw between 80,000 and 100,000 square kilometers and was thus responsible for local populations of 6 to 9 million people.[70] Within the rearward army territory, the Economic Staff East—which merged civilian and military principles and was formally part of Göring's Four-Year Plan Authority—operated first twenty-three and then later fifty economic command centers (*Wirtschaftskommandos*) with outposts in most larger cities and sizable towns. At the bottom end of the structure were the *Landeswirtschaftsführer* (La-Führer) or regional economic leaders, who were responsible for the registration of the population and exploitation of agriculture. Ultimately, 12,000 La-Führer were installed across the occupied territory. In small towns and villages, the La-Führer and their small staff were often the only Germans remaining behind, effectively acting as commanders on the ground.[71]

In anticipation of the invasion, Göring and the Economic Staff East worked out a comprehensive plan for the colonial administration of the Soviet territories west of the Ural Mountains, which they laid out in the infamous *Grüne Mappe* (Green Book) and a number of supplemental documents that formed the core economic blueprint of the *Generalplan Ost* (General Plan East).[72] The Green Book established the guidelines for economically gutting the eastern territories and defined the underlying principles for what would later be referred to as the Hunger Plan, the deliberate starvation of tens of millions of Soviet citizens. It further explained the division of Soviet territory into surplus and subsidy zones, depending on their environmental potential. The "subsidy zones" (the *Waldzone* or forest zone) were rich environments—in terms of forest, livestock, and industry. The forests could be mined at the Germans' leisure, whereas livestock was transported west, and whatever industry remained was simply scrapped. The Germans evaluated the environments designated as "surplus zones" (*Schwarzerdegebiet* or black earth territory) based on energy extraction (oil) and, more importantly, their potential to produce foodstuffs and natural fibers.[73] Consumer goods from subsidy zones in the northern forested parts of the Soviet territory would subsidize the population of the surplus zones in Ukraine, whose surplus of grains, agricultural products, and natural resources would flow to Germany. The Green Book planned for genocide in the passive voice.

Unlike in Poland, planners insisted that "the conquered [Soviet] territory mustn't be seen as an object of exploitation on the whole."[74] Instead of the strategic murder and universal pillage that characterized Polish operations, the Germans proceeded to strategically pillage and leave to die or migrate the citizens who could not provide for their own subsistence. Jews were the exception; in both cases, Jews would be indiscriminately pillaged *and* murdered.[75] The economic planners proposed a differential treatment for agriculturally developed areas, realizing that "without the willing cooperation of the farmers, a significant collection of grain will be impossible in the long run."[76] The environmental categorization of the Soviet Union had both ethnic (racial) and economic components. The Baltic states were integrated as the *Ostland* and administered like the Protectorate of Bohemia and Moravia, relying on ethnic Germans and "Germanizable" others. The Economic Staff East foresaw some difficulties with respect to Belarus, declaring that it would be difficult to build up a suitable leadership class since "the Belarussians are intellectually far behind the Russians, Jews, and Poles there."[77] The managers of the war economy urged restraint with respect to the treatment of the Belarussian population to exploit the "natural antagonism" between them and the Russians.[78]

The regime's main interests lay in the fertile regions of the *Schwarzerdegebiet* or black earth territory of Ukraine, which was administered as the *Reichskommissariat* Ukraine. The rationale was very straightforward and unequivocally genocidal.[79] In order to satisfy the needs of the Reich and supply large parts of Nazi-occupied Western Europe from the grain reserves of Ukraine, the Reich anticipated the starvation of millions of people in the *Waldzone* or forest zone to the north, which included "the important industrial centers of Moscow and Petersburg." Alternatively, the Green Book suggested that faced with starvation, the population of the *Waldzone* could be induced to "migrate" to Siberia.[80] Colonizing efforts were reserved for the fertile black earth of Ukraine and the oil-rich territory in the Caucasus—a measure that was considered necessary to guarantee the food and energy security of Europe.[81] The regime used household goods and clothing to purchase the "loyalty" of populations on whose cooperation the occupiers in the so-called surplus zones of Ukraine depended. Inevitably, "this would lead to the dying off of industry and large parts of the population in the subsidy zones."[82]

While Economic Staff East alternatively considered the transport of livestock to Germany or the preservation of enclosed hog farms in the *Waldzone*, they speculated that consumer goods and textiles from the *Waldzone* would be of inferior quality and thus unacceptable for export to the Reich.[83] The Nazi regime made it clear that, for Soviet citizens, food and clothing would be available only in exchange for labor.[84]

As historian Adam Tooze points out, the "planning" of Backe and Göring for mass starvation of the civilian population "had a more abstract quality."[85] The Soviet population did not simply allow themselves to be passively starved, and the German military presence was too limited to administer Russia's vast territories, as in Poland. Therefore, the German occupiers competed with "Russian partisans" over the resources of the territory "secured" by the Wehrmacht. Accordingly, by the end of 1941, the army had permission to plunder territory under their control indiscriminately. In such *Kahlfraßzonen*, literally zones of complete devastation, the occupiers recklessly carted off foodstuffs, agricultural products, and goods; depleted grain and seed storage depots; and thus made it impossible for even minimal subsistence to be provided to the working population, let alone foodstuffs to cities and towns. By December 1941, hunger was endemic. Populations suffered unequally, but even rural populations faced severe and persistent hunger, resulting in mass death the following spring.[86]

The Wehrmacht also saw itself in competition with cities, which relied on food deliveries from the countryside. Even though the recruitment of collaborators and establishment of localized structures for the extraction of goods and labor took time, violence was ever-present. The Germans ultimately depended on existing communal administrations to execute their policies, to distribute meager provisions, to "recruit" *Hilfswillige* (collaborators) for the army and police force, to mobilize the forced laborers the authorities required, and to coordinate labor allocation.[87] Local administrations were entirely overwhelmed by resource scarcity. In the event of mutinous or riotous hungry village populations, Wilhelm Keitel proposed mass executions.[88]

Göring reminded the Economic Staff East that "unlike with other prisoners, we are not bound by international obligations when it comes to provisions for Soviet POWs."[89] The German Chief of the Counter-Espionage Office (*Amt Ausland Abwehr*) Wilhelm Canaris noted his objections to the rationale behind the treatment of Soviet POWs, to no effect. The Nazis essentially argued that service in the Soviet military constituted a crime and refused to recognize that citizens were obligated to serve in the army.[90] The Germans took 3.35 million Soviet POWs in the first few months after the invasion. By the end of 1941, only 1.1 million were still alive. The German Wehrmacht shot 600,000 prisoners under the Commissar Order; the remaining prisoners died of deliberate starvation, neglect, and disease.[91]

Even if the mass starvation of the Soviet population was not as effortless as the Economic Staff East anticipated, these terrifyingly destructive policies effectively criminalized anyone who refused to work for the German authorities. In turn, the Germans punished any act of noncompliance with the utmost ruthlessness, institutionalizing indiscriminate terror wherever it was deemed expedient.[92] The Green Book made it very clear that when it came to Soviet territory, the regime's concern was not with managing or moving populations. Instead, it was focused on the extraction of key resources, raw materials, finished products of all kinds, and ordinary household and consumer goods. The Economic Staff East had no illusions about the magnitude of these tasks, particularly since it lacked lower-tier administrative structures. There simply were not enough German soldiers to fight a war and simultaneously administer such a massive territory. Accordingly, Göring stressed the importance of personal initiative, enthusiasm, and operational readiness of the officers in charge on the ground, arguing that "men who do not possess such initiative are useless for the task and should be replaced as soon as possible." He had no tolerance for indecision. Officers and soldiers alike "had to realize that they were on their own and could not wait for written or telephone orders from above," given the distance that separated them from their superiors.[93]

By 1943, Sergeant Hörrmann had seemingly internalized these admonitions and demonstrated the kind of initiative and esprit de corps that Göring had written into the *Generalplan Ost*. When Hörrmann wrote to Himmler in the spring of 1943, he clearly recognized the limitations of transport and labor capacity of the army's booty hunters (*Beutetrupps*) who, barely able to cope with the transport of weapons, munitions, reusable tools and equipment, invariably left a lot of junk behind. Whether inspired solely by Hörrmann's letter or a more general response to the chaos of war, on May 31, 1943, Chief of the Army General Staff Kurt Zeitzler authorized the *Groß-Schrottaktion*—a massive junk recovery mission. Its goal was to completely clear the eastern territories under Wehrmacht control "of all scrap iron, useless vehicles, tanks, and munitions, in short of all metal pieces including tin cans."[94]

The High Command planned to reach beyond even Hörrmann's wildest dreams and return to the Reich not only junk, scrap metal, service parts of machines, salvageable equipment, vehicles, tanks, and rubber, but also all sorts of recyclables such as empty bottles and cans, and secondary textiles.[95] In July, Himmler personally endorsed the *Groß-Schrottaktion* and requested that higher SS functionaries in the east order the removal of all junk from destroyed Russian villages and towns.[96] The director of the Reich Raw Materials Office, SS Standartenführer Albert Kloth, was on convalescence leave as the planning commenced, so his qualifying remarks were considerably delayed. Citing difficulties encountered in Greece during the recovery of junk from disarmed shells, Kloth sought to refute the commonly held misconception that "the availability of junk metal already guarantees the recovery of iron."[97] Instead, he stressed the very limited capacity of blast furnaces in the Reich and pointed out that the collected junk could not possibly be processed. Even so, Himmler demanded that the collection proceed, but all shipments would require his explicit authorization.[98] Accordingly, the Nazis not only religiously collected but also stored rubbish all over Europe.[99]

Infrastructures of Extraction

To understand the coexistence of detailed plans, grandiose initiatives, massive backlogs, constant shipments, and complete chaos, it helps to examine the infrastructures of extraction the regime created during the fall and winter of 1941–1942. Even though the "planners" spent considerable time imagining ways to increase agricultural output in Ukraine, war conditions did not lend themselves to such a build-up.[100] Regardless of discussions about the different treatment of subsidy and surplus zones, the first order of business was to establish the rails on which loot and eventually grains could travel westward. The gutting of "Russia" proceeded along existing rail lines, as roads were often in terrible condition and seasonally impassable. The rails were of a broader gauge and, in order to be used by German trains, needed to be retracked. Army railway commandos or *Feldeisenbahnkommandos* were key, building colonial outposts in the rearward army territory from where booty crews could conduct their raids and scouting expeditions. The *Feldeisenbahn* built railway transfer stations and, almost everywhere, they retracked railroad lines to fit German standards and guarantee the transport of troops, provisions, and loot.[101]

Again, the experiences in occupied Poland served as a guide. Within the first few weeks and months after the invasion of Poland, the Germans had issued an uncanny number of rules and decrees—to no avail. As the governor of the Lublin district, Dr. Ernst Zörner, remarked in June 1940, the problem was the transportation system. The roads were terrible, the trains slow and insufficient. Moreover, the desperately hungry Polish workers needed to be fed since without them the *Ostbahn* wouldn't roll and the loot wouldn't move. The Wehrmacht grudgingly agreed to step in and guarantee provisions to keep the trains moving.[102]

The *Feldeisenbahn* was new. In anticipation of the invasion of the Soviet Union, the Wehrmacht hastily assembled *Feldeisenbahnkommandos* in the spring of 1941.[103] Given the vast distances, snow-packed roads in the winter, sodden, muddy roads in the fall, thaw-induced flooding in the spring, and lack of reliable fuel depots, it had become clear that only the military authorities had the logistical capacity to ensure the upgrade and operation of the transportation infrastructure. Army railway commandos consisted of a military and a technical staff, which oversaw the *Feldeisenbahnbetriebsämter* (FBAmt) or army railway operations offices that managed traffic after the railway pioneers had secured lines and assessed damage.[104] Equipped with a truck and car, these pioneers would set off along the tracks and explore surrounding areas. They sent daily reports that included their location, anticipated destination for the following day, and detailed observations of destruction of railroad lines or stations. They further relayed what materials they discovered, what means for transport existed onsite, and estimated the numbers of personnel necessary to occupy and secure the stations. Moreover, the scouts decided which rails would be converted and when forced labor columns could start working.[105]

Nonetheless, the logistical development and transportation security of the occupied territories was rather chaotic as a railway worker's report in the area around Brest-Litowsk between June 22 and August 9, 1941, illustrates. Scouts set out on foot from Terespol (Nazi-occupied Poland) to determine whether the main station of Brest had already been taken. They occupied and secured select railroad lines, retracked some lines to standard gauge, and started organizing regular rail traffic for supply operations and the removal of booty. The first trains left only two days after the invasion commenced, before the area was "pacified." Scouts continued to follow the advancing army to identify destroyed bridges and tracks, do repair work, organize traffic, and load 2,483 train cars with war booty.[106]

However, military agencies seem to have been somewhat unaware of the organization and responsibilities of the army railway commandos, and some may not have known of the *Feldeisenbahn*'s existence at all. The AOK 2 (Army High Command 2) was a case in point. Between Czeremcha and Baranowicz, the army's chief transportation officer had set up makeshift railway operations using captured Polish locomotives and train cars. When the *Feldeisenbahn* took over the rail lines, the second army refused to cease operations. Individual commanding officers refused to accept "orders" from the dispatcher and plowed a makeshift train transporting tanks into a trolley that had not yet been removed from the tracks. In another instance, the military had confiscated the local station in Lesna, set up its staff, and subsequently refused to vacate the facilities.[107]

Since the army initially advanced exceedingly fast, the railway pioneers were completely overwhelmed by the tasks before them. After the initial chaos, the railway commandos relied on Polish workers and forced Jews to clean the station facilities. Reflecting on his memories after leaving Minsk, a city devasted by German troops, Hans Peter Hagedorn, a member of Army Railroad Commando 2 (FEKdo 2), not only noted the destroyed houses and the toppled tram cars, but also described the insides of the buildings "covered knee-high with filth and rubble" and wondered whether the local population "really saw the Germans as liberators." He decided not to fret since his unit was responsible for ensuring the continuous flow of supplies to the front, which had reached Smolensk where 9 million men rallied to the fight.[108]

By the end of October, the FEKdo 3 was stuck in the mud in Ukraine, delaying deliveries of supplies, building materials, and laborers needed for repairs of the important intersection at Zhmerynka to direct traffic to Odessa and Kyiv. In anticipation of the winter, "the Chief of Transportation ordered the 'Eastern Program' for the restoration of the railroad lines" and two months later the Führer headquarters followed up with the "immediate program."[109] Hitler could issue orders, but he did not command the weather.

The winter of 1941–1942 was one of the coldest on record. On some days in January and February, the cold left 80 percent of standard-gauge and 60 percent of broad-gauge locomotives inoperable. In addition, heavy snowstorms, resembling hurricanes, caused snow drifts of several yards and brought operations in Ukraine to a near standstill. Since the troops had used most of the snow fences for firewood, the *Feldeisenbahner* barely managed to keep the trains running.[110]

Figure 4.2 A snowed in locomotive near Smolensk, 1941. Courtesy of Bundesarchiv.

Figure 4.3 Railway worker digging out a locomotive. Courtesy of Bundesarchiv.

The situation was similar for FEKdo 2, which followed the troops in the *Waldzone* eastward from Brest-Litowsk. With temperatures of negative 58°F, the locomotives froze onto the tracks, and railway workers lacking sufficient clothing clung to liquor for warmth.[111] Hagedorn, stuck with his staff in a train without heat, put his own suffering into perspective:

> [B]ut what was all that, compared with the men on the locomotives and in the uncovered sheds, compared with the soldiers in earth bunkers! Finally, what did the members of our staff personally have to do with the meter-high masses of snow that clogged the lines other than worry about conquering them. But even that was managed with the help of the population.[112]

Hagedorn's compassion did not extend to the forced laborers who using only their hands had to shovel out the locomotives from underneath the mounds of snow. The German war against "Russian" nature expended people as *Menschenmaterial* (human raw material) without flinching.[113] In the spring of 1942, the Plenipotentiary of Labor Fritz Sauckel wrote of the hardships of German soldiers from the comforts of his desk in Berlin. He was particularly taken with the bad weather, which he thought compounded in immeasurable ways "the bestial brutality" of the enemy. He therefore praised German troops for their

> endurance of hardships unprecedented in history, of a severe winter, unsurpassed in cold, ice, snow, and storm for 140 years. Overcoming the unprecedented difficulties associated with such a climate and such exceptionally bad weather conditions, measured against the previous human and soldierly achievements of all time, our soldiers on the eastern front—it may be said without exaggeration—rise to the level of supermen.[114]

Smolensk, deep in the forest zone, became a major transportation hub for those German "supermen" and their extractivist operations. It was one of the few areas where the German occupiers outnumbered the local population by a wide margin.[115] When the *Feldeisenbahnbetriebsamt* 6 (Operating Division 6) arrived, they built water towers and ramps and took control of fuel storage facilities. The barracks—little wooden houses in the forest outside of Gniesdowa (Gnezdevo)—had already been occupied by Organization Todt, and the staff of the FEKdo 2, which included six operating divisions, three machine divisions, and three workshop divisions, moved into three special trains for the duration of their first year before making their home in an abandoned "mosquito village."[116] They secured the rail lines to enable the provisioning of the fighting troops. Their two main functions—sending building materials, weapons, and provisions eastward and transferring booty and loot westward—required labor-intensive repairs and the extension of infrastructures to stations further east.[117] Over the course of 1942, the *Feldeisenbahn* converted large contingents of the railroad network, including rolling stock, to standard-gauge.[118] They built various storage facilities within the area in and around Smolensk, including army equipment storage, a butchering division, a construction yard, and numerous warehouses for building materials, clothing, provisions, munitions, and fuel.[119]

Schrottschu, as Rittmeister Hans Schu's junk recovery organization had come to be known, set up operations in Smolensk early in 1942 and soon maintained a number of warehouses, workshops, and storage facilities. Schu's main role was to secure junk and scrap metal. In addition, his crews were charged with the recovery of enemy tanks and the return of broad-gauge locomotives to the Reich for scrapping. Usually, locomotives were taken apart for transport. In one instance, workers managed to heave the entire

Figure 4.4 Forced laborers retracking railroad. Courtesy of Bundesarchiv.

machine onto the train car, but the load exceeded the permissible height and ripped off heating pipes as it left Smolensk station.[120]

In the junkyards and workshops maintained by Schu, battalions of forced laborers and Soviet POWs collected, sorted, cut, and processed massive amounts of junk and scrap, forging tools and replacements from the available material. Ideally, the material required for infrastructure-related repairs and extensions would be recovered from scrap and loot since replacement parts for rails and railroad facilities were not provided by the Reich. By the summer of 1942, almost all of the pillaged materials had been used up. There was a shortage of railroad sleepers and no hope for replenishments to arrive from Germany. The *Feldeisenbahner* started to ration materials and recycle the used and slightly damaged sleepers of less trafficked lines. In anticipation of the coming winter, railroad workers were admonished to collect scattered scrap metal, particularly pieces of iron scrap that were strewn everywhere. Insisting that shortages could have been avoided the previous winter, had instructions been properly followed, the command staff mandated that "all materials found suitable for reuse shall be properly stored and accounted for as inventory. Small iron must be stored in sealed containers. Theft or use for other purposes must be prevented at all possible cost."[121]

Figure 4.5 Sunbathing railway workers, summer 1941. Courtesy of Bundesarchiv.

Accordingly, *Schrottschu*'s booty crews were essential in providing much needed supplies. Most of the work was done by POWs and forced laborers. The local population, including large numbers of women, were conscripted for labor and meagerly compensated in foodstuffs and tobacco products. Starting in the fall of 1941, POWs had been deployed in work battalions. The labor was excruciating, and provisions were appalling. Countless prisoners died of hunger, cold, and exhaustion. The Germans pushed the remaining POWs beyond the human limit. Their explanation that many of the tasks "could not have been completed with civilian laborers" hinted at the brutality

Figure 4.6 Recovered locomotive designated for scrapping. Courtesy of Bundesarchiv.

of the coercion.[122] In the end, it turned out that the tasks the Nazis set for themselves could not be completed at all.

Backtracking

Along the southern front, pressures mounted with the encirclement of the Sixth Army at Stalingrad in November 1942. By February 1943, railroad workers, too, were frantically organizing their retreat. Supply chains broke down as parked railcars clogged stations and crossings. Freezing temperatures and snowstorms exacerbated an already chaotic situation. As the front was crumbling, the railroad workers evacuated westward, sometimes on foot, leaving almost all tools, machines, material, even the Wehrmacht property, railroad equipment, and rolling-stock behind. The surviving men of the FEKdo3 arrived in Kharkiv after daylong marches, but the report lamented that "many thousands of boxcars had to remain behind."[123]

The *Feldeisenbahner* detailed their experiences in carefully illustrated reports. These series of photographic narratives on the building projects, with sparce explanatory captions, present an eerie summary of the "infrastructural achievements" of the Wehrmacht in the area in the summer of 1943. The report of FEKdo 2 from May 1943 in Smolensk began with photographs of recently completed buildings such as a sentry box and a sawmill. But the railway workers also detailed numerous instances of reclamation, including the massive junkyard where the secured metal junk was sorted, cut, and loaded for transport.[124] The report from July 1943 contained an addendum with photographs taken that March in Semlewo (Semlevo), which depicted the deliberate destruction of infrastructure such as water towers, bridges, and fuel tanks.

The photos anticipated the fate of Smolensk in September 1943, when the Wehrmacht not only abandoned positions and rescued as much *Räumungsgut* (loot) as possible but also deliberately demolished water towers, bridges, and fuel tanks as well as the rebuilt sentry box and sawmill. Six trains were supposed to transport the forced laborers and essential materials needed for the next mission. The remaining materials, junk and all, were moved to the Białystok region, designated as the next main junk storage location about 700 kilometers westward. Even the orderly report did not manage to hide the chaos that unfolded as the Wehrmacht scrambled to

Figure 4.7 Junkyard in Smolensk. Courtesy of Bundesarchiv.

evacuate their own staff of roughly 100 men, along with 1,500 forced labors, and civilians also forced to leave the area in treks. In addition, trains were loaded with tons of equipment, including almost 300 metric tons of metal junk in a few days' time. Accidents abounded. When the Germans burned down "Russian houses," they accidentally set the station on fire. The wholesale destruction, usually by fire, of entire towns and villages and the forced evacuation of civilians were part of the German military strategy to ensure that neither equipment nor labor fell into the hands of the advancing Red Army.[125] On some days, more than sixty trains left Smolensk, but massive backlogs spanned the length of forty whole trains. In total, the Wehrmacht logged 11,903 railcars filled with barracks, junk, and military vehicles, all of which headed for designated storage areas further west. On September 24th, as the last train left the station, the Smolensk main station was blown up.[126] Naturally, some junk remained.

Organization Schu was chiefly responsible for evacuating territories and disassembling the outposts the Wehrmacht had built for loot. With the advance of the Red Army westward and the progressive loss of territory in 1944, Schu's organization shrank; numerous branch offices had to be closed in both the east and west, and Schu increasingly tried to replace the lost sources of scrap by establishing task forces in German cities that focused on reclaiming scrap from the damage inflicted by enemy aircraft. War was good business. Schu prided himself on having salvaged 80,000 metric tons of junk a month from the rubble.[127]

The omnipresence of junk and debris only increased as the Germans retreated and razed cities and towns, including the buildings and infrastructure they had cobbled together during their short stint as colonial overlords. When Hörrmann wrote to Himmler in 1943, he attempted to explain the turned fortunes of the war and to formulate a strategy for redress and reversal. Like many other Germans, he had internalized the imperatives of the Nazi waste regime. Wastes continued to energize the fantasies of economic circularity and to be seen as the solution to the shortages that hemorrhaged the German war economy. Only toward the end of the war did the chaotic character of scrap metal requisitioning, which constituted only one facet of the massive secondary materials recovery, become clearly visible. The crumbling of the Third Reich illuminated the extent to which personal careerism and business interests found new forms of expression in the structures that legitimized ruthless extraction. When the imperial framework disappeared, the former state-sponsored enterprises claimed to have been private businesses and, when that proved unsuccessful, their leadership invoked the corporations' legal status as business entities to evade personal responsibility.[128] Schu, on the other hand, simply disappeared from the archive, and with him all traces of the wealth he had extracted and likely pocketed during the war. The records on forced labor remained.

5
Rag Farming

"The more torn, the better," advertised Emil Otto in 1942. His sock-resoling company reasoned that the more raggedy the sock, the more worthwhile the repair. The only requirements his company made of customers were that the leg length of the sock or stocking was still intact and the remnants properly washed. The elastic "Otto seam" would then attach a new, tear-resistant bottom to the worn-out sock in a matching color, extending the lifespan of the original garment. The company specialized in the repair of woolens, including sweaters, jackets, underwear, and children's rompers, and promised inexpensive, fast, expert service. They also repaired silk stockings, leaving them "as good as new." Three years into the war, the business was especially timely, as scarcity, particularly in the textile sector—something widely anticipated—had become endemic.[1]

Headquartered in Goslar, Otto's company prided itself on being the second largest special repair company for knitwear in Germany. With more than 7,000 individual drop-off locations, it offered repair services in nearly every city in the Reich.[2] It understood itself as providing a crucial service to the war economy. To prevent socks that had outlived their use-value from being utilized as cleaning rags or tossed in the rubbish, Otto saw his main function as closing an important loop in the nation's raw material cycle.[3] Insisting that "textiles are precious people's property," he patented a mechanism of stitching new soles onto old, ragged, hole-ridden socks—the Otto-*Ansohlverfahren*. Emil Otto proudly put his company at the service of the Reich's efforts to manage the production, distribution, and consumption of textiles. Taking textile rations as the basis for his calculations, he estimated that his company saved the Reich 249,000 kilograms of raw material or twenty-five railcars full of virgin wool in 1941 alone. Through his technique of harvesting material from the worn soles for respinning, the business model depended on minimal virgin raw materials. For example, every 65,000 kilograms of expended raw material was offset by 57,000 kilograms of textile waste the firm recovered in-house. Otto framed his contribution as a sacrifice to the war economy, when in fact this scheme enabled him to supply 87 percent of his raw material requirements from his own production process.[4]

Devoted to the National Socialist cause, Otto nonetheless knew that he had to keep his business running or face being drafted to the front. In the business plan he sent to the *Reichsstelle* for textiles in 1942, he scaled up the company's experiences from 1941 to make a case for increased raw material allocations. The question he posed to the *Reichsstelle* was simple, if rhetorical: What could an expanded Otto-*Ansohlverfahren* contribute to the German war economy? Proposing a modest yearly consumption of five pairs of socks or stockings per person—a total of 400 million pairs—he underscored his company's potential contribution. If only 20 percent of those 400 million pairs would be resoled rather than replaced each year, the raw material savings and the net accumulation of recyclable wastes would be enormous. He estimated that 1,400,000 kilograms of textile waste otherwise lost could be recovered, in addition to 200,000 kilograms in secondary materials as a result of the many other repairs his company provided. In total, Otto boasted, his company could save the Reich 10,920,000 kilograms of raw materials without negatively impacting consumers.[5] Of course, he conceded, he would need additional labor to accomplish this feat, but asserted that finding 2,500 women who could do the work from home would be easy. The only remaining, urgent difficulty would be the swift allocation of approximately 1,000 *Ostarbeiterinnen* (female workers from the east).[6]

Emil Otto and his sock-mending scheme offers a near perfect example of the race-conscious, gendered, technocratic exercises in salvage and waste reclamation that characterized the regime at large. What's more, they are indicative of the extent to which the business model that undergirded the so-called *Ostgesellschaften* informed the calculations made by ordinary German businesses. While metal was of utmost importance to the Reich's armaments industry, it played a less noticeable role in the lives of individuals than textiles. In addition to civilians, soldiers, SS men, concentration camp guards, mobile killing squads, and members of the occupying administration needed to be clothed. This strategically important industry made legible the racial dynamics of wartime extraction on the surface of bodies and the land: from rags barely covering the skin of slave laborers who fashioned uniforms for German soldiers to the marks left in the snow by felt boots or bare feet.

Anticipating Scarcity

For most branches of German industry, the Four-Year Plan introduced new levels of state control and centralized management. By contrast, the textile sector had already experienced state intervention during the 1934 foreign exchange crisis.[7] When the unfavorable exchange rate of the Reichsmark exacerbated the dynamics of declining exports, imports for raw materials and foodstuffs remained high. The whole system of prices and wages in Germany was out of step. Given Germany's high levels of international debt and Hitler's unwillingness to consider devaluing the currency, Germany had to selectively reduce imports.[8] The problem was military spending. Hjalmar Schacht, the president of the Reichsbank, would have jeopardized his position in the Nazi hierarchy if he supported cuts to the military budget. Instead, the textile industry was squeezed, which directly affected armaments production.[9] In 1933, textiles had accounted for 20.4 percent of all German imports and thus offered a natural target for state intervention and management.[10] The Reichsbank started to reduce the monthly foreign exchange quotas for German importers, and the Reich Ministry for Economic Affairs created monitoring agencies that oversaw and rationed industrial raw materials and foreign exchange permits. Five of the eighteen monitoring agencies, which prefigured the later *Reichsstellen*, were devoted to the management of textiles.[11]

Textiles thus lay at the heart of a new system of "comprehensive bureaucratic control" of the German economy.[12] On March 22, 1934, the regime announced the state management of cotton, wool, and bast fibers, decreeing an intermittent import moratorium and subsequently adding regulations for fibrous materials that culminated in the Reich Textile Law of December 12, 1934.[13] At first, the monitoring agency reduced work time for textile manufactures to 36 hours per week, in the hope of throttling their use of raw materials. But the firms just moved through the same amounts of raw materials in less time. Hence, the Reich Textile Law was changed to centrally allocate raw materials, rather than legislating work time.[14]

As the Reich attempted to decrease its dependence on imported textiles, a flood of regulations shifted technical innovation toward increasing synthetic fibers (I.G. Farben was the main pioneer in rayon production). They also aimed to increase sheep stock, expand the production of flax and hemp, and fully exploit waste and secondary materials. In 1936, economists estimated that only a quarter of the 240,000 metric tons of textile waste (trimmings, thread, yarn waste) and rags (worn fabric as well as cleaning material) were reused. By 1937, the self-sufficiency of the German textile industry had increased to 37.4 percent, as compared to 16 percent in 1932. Comprehensive regulation as well as the large-scale exploitation of waste material explains this shift more so than the moderate increase in the use of synthetic fibers.[15]

The Four-Year Plan mandated the systematic management of rags and textile wastes. The monitoring agency for wool and other animal hair now allocated these raw materials. The Reich Commissioner for Wool (*der Reichsbeauftragte für Wolle*), Dr. Toepfer, thus was in charge of the *Lumpenwirtschaft* (the rag economy) and accordingly set prices for different kinds of textile wastes and different categories of rags.[16] He moreover authorized the operation of sorting plants, reserving the right to withdraw operating licenses at any time.[17] Two interrelated goals are important here. On the one hand, the regime desperately tried to increase the recovery of rags and textile wastes for reuse, and on the other, it wanted to purge the existing secondary materials trade of Jewish peddlers, middlemen, and reprocessors by building up parallel collection structures.[18]

Over the next few years, the rag economy expanded significantly as the regime mobilized its volunteer army of scrap collectors and increased the recovery of rags from garbage dumps and rubbish pits.[19] War shifted the focuses of the *Reichsstellen* from managing raw material distribution toward rationing consumption in anticipation of raw material shortages and increased Wehrmacht demand. As Germany marched into Poland, six different *Reichsstellen*, each overseeing product-specific divisions, managed the Reich's textile industries.[20] During the first two months of war, the Reich introduced additional regulatory mechanisms. On September 3, 1939, Dr. Friedrich Bauer was appointed the Special Commissioner for Textiles (*Sonderbeauftragter für die Spinnstoffwirtschaft*) entrusted with the monitoring and regulation of the entire textile trade.[21] Bauer was supposed to coordinate the work of the separate *Reichsstellen* to ensure consistently integrated production and distribution of goods and raw materials. His main wartime tool became confiscation, which permitted him to seize raw materials and finished products and determine their appropriate distribution to manufacturers and consumers alike.[22] The introduction of a point system for the allocation of textiles to consumers on September 7, 1939, subjected clothing and other textiles (including yarn, thread, fabric, and finished goods) to rigid regulation and rationing. Soon the special commissioner was overwhelmed by the tasks before him, and in April 1942, he was replaced by an entire office: *Reichsstelle für Textilwirtschaft* (for textiles), which oversaw five of the six subordinate *Reichsstellen*.[23] The ad hoc nature of this proliferating bureaucracy illustrates one of the main strategies with which the regime addressed shortages—they created commissioners and offices to manage the shortages more efficiently.[24]

The responsibilities and importance of the Reich Commissioner for Secondary Materials Requisitioning expanded in a similar fashion during the war in ways that created some murkiness when it came to rags and textile wastes. Technically, the matter was very clear, at least on paper. The procurement (collection, washing, and sorting) of rags and related materials fell under the purview of this office, but the processing of such waste was the responsibility of the *Reichsstelle* for wool and animal hair. Difficulties arose as the regime increasingly targeted industrial textile wastes such as fabric cuttings, yarn, and filament wastes, and other trimmings that accumulated during the production process.

As industrial waste became a prime target, the regime extended the hunt for rags. The practice of retrieving rags from municipal garbage dumps continued during the war, relying on a combination of paid pickers and convict labor. In addition, the regime introduced school collections in 1941, which mainly gathered worn clothes, dishrags, and other old household fabrics. That same year, the party announced regular textile collections—*Spinnstoffsammlungen*—that appealed to ordinary citizens to sort through their closets and donate all worn and outmoded clothing and other items such as curtains and bedding. Despite these efforts, the volume of textiles collected inside the Reich declined over the course of the war, likely the result of the war-induced frugality of the population.[25] As the regime pushed out peddlers and small-scale entrepreneurs inside the Reich, it built up a slave-labor complex for textile production in occupied Poland. By the late summer of 1944, textiles flowing into the Reich, whether raw materials or finished goods, were the result of requisition or, more accurately, plunder.[26]

Captive Lint

Łódź, Poland's center of textile production and trade since the late nineteenth century, was the city in which the Nazi occupiers set up their administrative headquarters, facilitating the pilfering of textiles.[27] In the first weeks after the German conquest, the status of the city had been undetermined. Later in the fall of 1939, renamed Litzmannstadt and divided into a Polish and a German sector, Łódź was incorporated into the Reich.[28] As Łódź was transformed into a German city, its 160,000 Jewish residents fled or were forced to take up residence in the Łódź ghetto, which was completely sealed off from the rest of the city by April 30, 1940.[29] Since the textile industry was predominantly Jewish, the Germans considered the "exploitation of available, experienced Jewish craftsmen" strategic and relied on textile workshops behind the ghetto walls for the production of goods to German specifications.[30]

The HTO (Main Trustee Section East) functioned as the eastern arm of the Four-Year Plan Authority. It oversaw material requisitioning and wielded the powers of confiscation in the eastern territories, through nine different departments. Department 1 was in charge of iron, steel, and junk. Department 6 was responsible for all textiles and fibers, including wool and "other animal hair."[31] Department 9 was entrusted with the capture and disposition of secondary materials. Additional departments for chemicals, for leather, for oils and fats, for nonferrous metals, for machines, and for demolition also answered to the office of the Commissioner for Raw Materials Requisitioning, then led by General Bührmann and headquartered in Łódź.[32] Starting in the fall of 1939, Department 6 sent out standardized questionnaires—in quadruplicate—to Polish firms known or assumed to be part of the textile- or leather-processing industries and trades.[33] Companies were required to describe their operations and products, available machinery, production and sales statistics for 1938, number of employees, all raw materials, semi-finished and finished products. In addition, companies had to list all auxiliary materials such as fuel, fats, dies, and so forth and provide a separate inventory for waste products, such as hair or rags.[34]

In the General Government, the Nazis confiscated all assets of military or economic importance, including textiles, and placed them at the disposal of the German war economy.[35] In November 1939 alone, the *Verwaltungs- und Verwertungsgesellschaft* (VVG) oversaw the transport of 38 railcars stuffed with textiles, among those 7 cars filled with cotton, 8 containing linens, 2 carrying yarn, 7 packed with rags, and 14 with wool. Most of this booty benefited the Wehrmacht and police, satisfying the growing demand for uniforms and other essentials.[36]

Since the center of Polish textile production was formally incorporated into the Reich, the regime did not indiscriminately freight their loot back to companies in Germany, but rather exploited the existing infrastructure to build a hub for reprocessing rags, recycling old textiles and wastes, and manufacturing goods for the Wehrmacht and the police formations from impounded raw materials. Department 6 constantly communicated with the various *Reichsstellen* to record and distribute available assets, determining which Polish manufacturers would receive raw material allocations to produce various goods for the war economy and which materials would be shipped for processing. The occupiers could rely at least in part on the important textile sector in Łódź, ethnic German collaborators, and Germans who had established trade relations with "aryan" Polish textile firms when confiscating machinery and materials from Jewish businesses.[37] Department 6 confiscated assets and installed ethnic Germans to administer "unreliable" Polish and all Jewish firms. Trustees further oversaw storage facilities and helped manage the dispersal of raw materials, textile wastes, and finished products to designated manufacturers in Germany and throughout occupied Poland.

Department 6 regularly sent inquiries to keep track of inventory and to instruct Polish firms about the importance of textile wastes of various sorts. After learning that Otto Kampf in Alexandrow had purchased some yarn waste in January 1940, Department 6 sent him a questionnaire that he "was to promptly fill out and return," since all purchases made after December 21, 1939, had to be reported.[38] It also inquired about the total 3,063 kilograms of thread waste and sweepings in Kampf's last inventory, to root out as of yet unregistered suppliers.[39] For all the newly created administrative offices and empowered officials, these examples illustrate the dependence of German occupiers on Poles and ethnic Germans to report to and comply with the directives of their new masters. Initially at least, existing trade networks and social ties limited the absolute economic control of German authorities despite the excessive terror the Nazis unleashed against the population.[40]

For German companies, the occupation of Poland raised hopes of acquiring production materials that were already in short supply. Like vultures, they circled around the Commissioner for Raw Materials Requisitioning. The main ticket producer for the German *Reichsbahn*, for example, tried to procure old worn-out train tickets from the district of Poznań, in a successful attempt to cut middlemen out of the secondary materials trade.[41] Every shipment, every purchase order, every production run required permission of the *Reichsstellen* and their eastern representative in the HTO. The authorities were certainly aware of the chaos the proliferating decrees and regulations caused on the ground. In his comments to the economic managers of the General Government in the summer of 1940, Hans Frank reminded his subordinates that the work is not done "just because one has a regulation or because one sends paperwork from one room to the next." Instead, he insisted that the urgent task is "the most immediate management of reality."[42] However, reality seemed unmanageable a lot of the time.

Regulations, orders, and decrees continued to proliferate as the occupiers attempted to catalogue Polish companies according to industrial branch, specialization, and racial reliability and to track their assets. The HTO sent inspectors to the Polish cotton weavers in Łódź for firsthand observation. The inspectors not only counted the number of looms, but also remarked on the condition of the buildings, the equipment, and the workspaces. They took note of the cleanliness and ventilation of the facilities and reported whether or not the company appeared to be managed in an orderly fashion. In addition, they recorded owners as "aryan" or "Jewish." For example, the inspector described the Textil-und Maschinenbau-Werke Widzewer Manufaktur Aktiengesellschaft as having 3,129 looms, apparently located in a shed, and as being "old, dark, very bad. Machines old, terrible, unclean." He noted up front: "Jewish business."[43]

Jewish-owned businesses had to register their assets and inventory with the police.[44] From the beginning, the Nazi occupiers attempted to draw a hard line between the "civil" administration of the former Polish territories and the SS, which was in charge of the racial reordering.[45] The army registered no formal objections to the division of military authority and was regularly informed of the "progress" of the ethnic cleansing campaigns undertaken against "inner enemies"--Jews and politically unreliable Poles.[46]

As with so many of the Nazi plans, reality turned out to be more complicated. The occupiers depended on the local rag-and-bone men who stood at the heart of the rag trade in Poland, but most of whom were Jewish. H. F. Wegener, head of Department 6, put it bluntly:

> I have nothing to do with the collection of old rags by the Jews. I am only interested in those rags when they are sorted, baled, and brought to market. Because it is then that they are subject to my confiscation to be properly dispositioned for military purposes.[47]

How the rags got into his possession, Wegener did not care to know. He left that to the SS.

During a meeting with Major General Bührmann and representatives of the HTO on November 30, 1939, Wegener drew attention to the "unfortunate difficulties resulting from the fact that often orders placed by the army are given to Jewish firms because they are equipped with better machinery."[48] Illustrating the willingness of German economic staff to work around the lines drawn by antisemitism, the language obscures the antisemitic violence that was instrumental in the process of raw material extraction and textile production. As of October 18, 1939, the *Lodscher Warenhandelsgesellschaft* functioned as the de facto trustee administering all Jewish property.[49] Invoking the Ordinance against Jewish Hoarders of Textiles and Leather, Department 6 appealed to the chief of police in Łódź, speculating that large quantities of cotton and yarn wastes and the like were probably among the inventory registered with the police, but could better be utilized as raw material by cleaning-rag producers.[50] Upon request by Department 6, the *Warenhandelsgesellschaft* took over unused inventory held for immediate disposal by the Reichsführer SS.[51]

While Polish producers of bandages and dressings had to wait months for raw material allocations, leaving hospitals and apothecaries unable to dress wounds, the SS was empowered to enforce the release of raw materials for their own purposes and needs.[52] They might have preferred to procure clothing and linens produced by "aryan" manufacturers, but ultimately the SS did not have the luxury to make such distinctions and placed orders with firms irrespective of their racial credentials or inspection reports. The SS "Death's Head" Units (*SS Totenkopfverbände*) ordered their cardigans, sweaters, and woolen stocking from the spinning mill of Hugo Flaker, an "aryan" company that inspectors had described as "completely torn apart. Machines partly housed in basement. Workrooms poor. Continuation of this spinning mill cannot be considered under any circumstance."[53]

The SS troops became one of the most significant end-users of requisitioned materials "since the procurement of accommodation laundry for SS troops deployed in Poland can no longer be carried out in the Altreich."[54] On February 3, 1940, the SS Main Office of Budgets and Buildings requested the release of raw materials for the production of 30,000 pairs of socks, gloves, and wristlets to the company of N. Eitington, a "Jewish business" in Łódź, according to the inspection report. Additional raw material was released for the production of 30,000 sweaters, head guards, and body-wraps, as well as underwear, and fabric for towels, and much more.[55] The deployment of police ended up being much more exhaustive than anticipated; accordingly, the original 35,000 sets of bed linens ordered had to be amended by an additional 25,000 sets.[56] Essentially, Polish textile firms were forced to outfit the professional killers of the *Einsatzgruppen* and Order Police who terrorized the population and executed the Polish leadership class, clergy, intellectuals, and writers, as well as politically "suspect" individuals.[57]

Given the voracious demands of the occupying Germans, careerists competed to advance their positions within the Nazi hierarchies. In addition, the occupiers' comprehensive attempts to get their hands on anything of value blurred the boundaries between raw materials and secondary materials. Accordingly, the raw material "rags" pitted two departments of the Office for Raw Materials Requisitioning against each other. In early February 1940, Wegener demanded clarification from SA-Oberführer Ackermann. The subsequent back-and-forth between the heads of Department 6 (textiles) and Department 9 (secondary materials) reveals the confusion and bulldog-like territorialism that underwrote Nazi careerism. Ackerman insisted that rags, as secondary materials, fell under his jurisdiction.[58] For about a month, he ignored the instructions from superiors at the HTO until ultimately Wegener involved Major General Bührmann and prevailed. Ackerman's department was responsible for the collection of rags from private households through the existing rag trade, but industrial wastes, whether rags, yarn waste, or sweepings already in the possession of manufacturers, were off limits to peddlers and could not be dispositioned by Department 9.[59] Accordingly, the sweepings and trimmings from shop floors were considered industrial wastes and therefore raw material, closing another avenue to rag-and-bone men and women confined behind ghetto walls.

The requisition chaos reflected in the official records of the Nazi administrators obviously affected the population of Łódź in acute and often violent ways. Dawid Sierakowiak, a Polish Jew, commented on the wanton ransacking of private households by the German occupiers. "There's something sick about the Germans," the 15-year-old Sierakowiak recorded in his diary in November 1939. "Yesterday they started horrible, chaotic looting. They were taking everything: furniture, clothes, underclothes, food. Poles and Jews are ordered to turn in all their shovels and pickaxes."[60] Sierakowiak's personal diary routinely lambasts both the German occupiers and Mordecai Chaim Rumkowski, the Chairman of the *Judenrat* or Jewish Council.[61]

Charged with administering the ghetto, Rumkowski built a sizable network of administrative units, offices, and commissions that employed 10,000 people at its peak.[62] Even before the ghetto was formally sealed off from the city and disconnected from municipal services in May 1940, Rumkowski established a great number of workshops in the ghetto, provided detailed lists to the mayor of Łódź of what the ghetto was able to produce, and submitted requests for orders from the German occupiers.[63] At its peak in 1943, the 117 workshops employed a total of about 83,400 workers, roughly 85 percent of the population.[64] While textile workshops were the most numerous, other workshops included a feather- and down-sorting workshop, rug-making workshops, an old clothing depot, a chemical waste utilization workshop, slipper departments, shoemaker workshops, clothing- and undergarment-sorting departments, an empties department, a wire and nail factory, a wood shavings department, and various kinds of wood and metal workshops.[65]

Most workshops produced for the Wehrmacht and the Reich Labor Service or *Reichsarbeitsdienst* (RAD). The ghetto administration confiscated secondary material, such as old clothes and rags, as well as junk and refuse, as raw material, which workshops then transformed into goods for German military and police formations.[66] Over the summer of 1941, the existing workshops were expanded and new ones were established, leading Sierakowiak to mock the "glorious development" of the ghetto's "Jewish Industrial District."[67] Unskilled workers, many of them old people and children, shredded rags, spun the fibers into yarn, and wove yarn into cloth that made garments for the Germans.[68]

Such low skilled labor was also performed in the so-called Gypsy camp.[69] Throughout the ghettos and camps of Nazi-occupied Eastern Europe,

Figure 5.1 Jewish men working in a textile workshop in the Łódź ghetto. Courtesy of the United States Holocaust Memorial Museum.

the Germans harvested textile fibers by forcing "expendable" populations to manually shred rags and fabric. Economic experts in the General Government not only acknowledged such work but also spelled out the precise percentages with which such waste-derived fibers had to be mixed with wool in order to yield suitable fabric for clothing for not just camp and ghetto populations but farmers and industrial workers in the occupied territories as well.[70]

Ghetto labor was grueling, the workshops unsanitary and crowded, and the "prisonlike atmosphere" punctuated by screaming and yelling supervisors.[71] After the deportations started in the spring of 1942, child labor became endemic as parents believed that useful toil was the only defense against deportation.[72] The network of workshops and factories continued to grow, "reaching out their tentacles now for the last reserves of children (even those younger than ten) and adults who are barely able to work."[73]

These laborers were suffering from acute hunger, since the ghetto-made food was in short supply and consisting mainly of waste products:

> A typical example of this "food industry" in the ghetto was the manufacture of the so-called "*salatke*" and cottage cheese. "Vegetable salad" was manufactured from vegetable scraps (leaves, the good bits from rotten potatoes, and the like) and old bread that had begun to mold. The production of these so-called "ghetto preserves" rose from 380 kilos in January 1941 to 29,000 kilos in May 1942.[74]

By 1942, large contingents of the population were starving. Provisions were entirely insufficient, and doctors allocated yeast supplements and potato peels as extra rations for people with all kinds of ailments until the lines grew so enormous that kitchens refused to dole out peelings to "strangers," Sierakowiak confided in his diary.[75] On August 18, 1943, at age 19, Dawid Sierakowiak died of tuberculosis, starvation, exhaustion, and what they called "ghetto disease."[76] The Nazis cleared the Łódź ghetto in a final wave of deportations in 1944, eliminating the workshops as well as the workers.

Scaling Up

All along, Nazi imperialists had set their sights on the Soviet Union. Poland had no place in Hitler's imperial fantasies, but it provided the SS with a laboratory that lastingly shaped the connections between material extraction and genocide that the war against the Soviet Union unfettered on an even larger scale. Hitler imagined the invasion of the USSR as a massive land grab that would guarantee the future viability of the Third Reich. There was a growing consensus among military, political, and economic leaders that victory would provide the basis for a European *Großraumwirtschaft* based on imperial rule and colonial extraction.[77] More than a million Soviet citizens were compelled to work for the Wehrmacht and the police, and additional hundreds of thousands were drafted into local administrations and the economic apparatus, a level of recruitment unparalleled in Hitler's Europe.[78] But the long-term visions of the Reich and short-term needs of the Wehrmacht made for a poor match. On the one hand, the conquered territory was supposed to be strategically developed, particularly as an agricultural base for the German Empire. On the other hand, short-term priorities to sustain the Wehrmacht's war-making capacity and to supply the German occupying forces from local resources were not carried out with patience or moderation. Essentially, these parallel yet competing priorities pitted plunder against development.

State-controlled corporations that gutted the occupied territories scaled up the economic logic that characterized Emil Otto's sock-mending scheme. Otto's savviness relied not on technological innovation, but on the maximum exploitation of materials through labor. With the "natural laws" of the market suspended, the magical relationship between supply and demand essentially fixed in utter disarray, the malleable (i.e., expandable) factors in the economic equations were waste products and labor. Since those categories, however, had very clear, natural limits, Otto realized that profit had to be measured differently—as value registering in his bank account and as a form of political currency wedded to the regime's racist ideas of the "common good." Otto intuitively understood that in order to function in an economy that was subservient to politics, the market responded to racial and strategic considerations, rather than to such abstractions as "supply" and "demand."[79]

The same calculations shaped the economic structures in the east. Just a few weeks after the Wehrmacht crossed into Soviet territory, Walther Funk and Hermann Göring resolved to form a private company for the purpose of organizing the textile industries in the occupied eastern territories. Egged on by Hans Kehrl, one of the central managers of the textile industry within the Four-Year Plan Authority, they incorporated the Ost-Faser-Gesellschaft mbH in August 1941 with subsidiaries in the Baltics and Ukraine and installed

Kehrl as chairman.[80] At its peak, it managed more than 400 companies operating as trustees. The expressed purpose of this textile conglomerate was nothing short of the takeover of the entire textile and paper industries in the east.[81] Kehrl explained his rationale for approaching Göring with the idea of founding a textile concern in the occupied-east as follows:

> I knew for sure that the Wehrmacht's demand for textiles, due to the enormous wear and tear in such a large war, would decisively worsen my overall textile balance, even if the demand of the civilian population of the occupied territories, which also had to be covered somehow at some point, could initially be budgeted as modest.[82]

Kehrl realized that under the current conditions a successful enterprise was an enterprise shaped by and subordinated to political priorities—the priorities of war and conquest. Individual entrepreneurial ingenuity would need to develop and thrive within politically set parameters, meaning that politics should instrumentalize and unfetter the self-interest of the profit-oriented businessman, directing ambition rather than strangling it.[83] Kehrl used his business model to catapult himself into positions of power: in 1942, he advanced to leadership of the Main Office for Industry in the Department of Economic Affairs, and by 1943, he simultaneously served as chief of the Planning Office within the Four-Year Plan Authority and chief of the Raw Materials Office in the Ministry of Armaments and War Production, headed by Speer.[84] What Emil Otto attempted to accomplish with a scheme to mend socks in light of the unchanging demand for warm feet, Hans Kehrl and the Ost-Faser G.mbH implemented in the east, when the cultivation of cotton, flax, raffia, and hemp in Ukraine did not reach its desired targets.[85]

Regardless of their personal motivations, neither Hans Kehrl nor Emil Otto had any compunctions about the use of forced labor for their admittedly quite different enterprises. Both adapted their business strategy to fit the tenor of the times. Both turned to waste products as a main source of raw material supply. The war economy imposed certain constraints on businesses with respect to quotas, prices, production specifications, and raw material allotments, but within these constraints, they operated with a freedom unencumbered by ethical considerations. Roughly 800 Germans oversaw the operations of the Ost-Faser and managed a staff of close to 50,000 local employees.[86] Forced laborers who worked in the fields or on the shop floors of spinning, ginning, weaving, and paper mills and other factories and workshops are likely included in these statistics. The report mentions the Ost-Faser's unusual ambition of recruiting locals into leadership positions.

The surviving records carefully obscure the Ost-Faser's dual purpose of plunder and waste utilization. The Ost-Faser streamlined and centrally coordinated extraction of any and all textile fibers, raw materials, secondary materials, wastes, and finished products. Initially, it set out to expand crops of flax, hemp, and cotton to inculcate the war economy against the danger of blockades and guarantee raw material independence for the German Empire. But the Ost-Faser proved more successful in farming rags than crops of textile fibers. Of the nearly 1,779,158 acres of flax crops that it took over in 1941, only 716,600 acres remained in 1943. Similar declines characterized the production of hemp. In both cases, shortages of labor and seed played a crucial role in the rapid decline of cultivated fields.[87] The most important factor, however, was the war itself.

In light of the German onslaught, the Red Army had evacuated, initially in a chaotic fashion, most of the official functionaries of the state, party, and police apparatus, in addition to skilled workers and children under 15. By July 1941, the Red Army managed to evacuate entire population segments, removing most individuals fit for work and military service, leaving a society consisting mainly of women, children, the old, and the infirm, entirely stripped of elites. The Wehrmacht imprisoned men and women, deporting them to the Reich as slave labor after Hitler authorized the transport of "Russians" for use within the Reich in October 1941. In addition, the fighting and movement of armies wrought havoc on villages and fields. The Wehrmacht deliberately left a desolate wasteland in its wake.[88]

Accordingly, the Ost-Faser's efforts to increase agricultural production were short-lived. They nonetheless attempted to plant cotton in the south and southwest of Ukraine and in Crimea, despite the less-than-ideal climate and provisions of fuel, seed, and labor. They subcontracted this particular endeavor to the *Baumwoll-Aktiengesellschaft* that deployed squadrons of forced laborers to till 200,000 acres and work the land by hand in the absence of suitable machinery. The anticipated expansion of crops to 435,000 acres did not happen. Nonetheless, the Ost-Faser was able to squeeze 4,300 metric tons of raw cotton from the local producers in the 1942 harvest. By the time machinery finally arrived from Germany, the fortunes of war had turned, and the railway pioneers backhauled the equipment and blew up the newly built ginning mill. Wool production also proved difficult, as war decimated the sheep population to less than half its prewar numbers.[89]

Despite all its plans and talk about development, the Ost-Faser ended up transporting and reallocating the raw materials extracted from existing businesses and the local population rather than building up production. In the fiscal year 1941–1942, the one year of relatively unencumbered operations, it freighted raw materials worth 52,404,000 RM back to Germany. Ultimately, its main task was to transition the textile industry in the occupied territories from high-quality raw materials to inferior inputs that could be locally produced or requisitioned from the population, such as rags, reprocessed wool, woolen wastes, fluffed raffia, and animal and human hair. Forced labor turned rubbish into *Wehrmachtsgut* (goods for the army). As the annual report of the Ost-Faser indicates, some waste materials were transported back to the Reich. For example, the report notes that 10,000 tons of cotton were "found" in the Baltic and Russian territories and dutifully freighted westward at the end of 1942. Of those, an estimated 2,000 metric tons were lint and various kinds of textile wastes. Similarly, 1,770 metric tons of rags made their way back to Germany as loot. But the majority of rags and wastes collected for local production—3,725 metric tons of rags that were "donated" in the context of the secondary materials' collection conducted within the eastern territories in July 1942 alone—were coerced from the already massively underresourced populations.[90]

The precise operations of the Ost-Faser cannot be reconstructed from existing records, but such a large-scale enterprise of agricultural production, raw material production from natural fibers and secondary materials, and the dispositioning of various plundered finished products and virgin raw materials presumably involved both a collaborating office staff, supervisors, and guards, as well as countless slave laborers. Workers grew natural fibers such as raffia and hemp; others turned those materials into thread and cloth. In addition, and particularly as a result of the difficulties in increasing the cultivation of natural fibers, many workers were recycling secondary textiles and rags by shredding and respinning them. For finished products, the Ost-Faser relied instead on the specialized workshops in the ghettos of Nazi-occupied Poland—predominantly in Łódź and the Białystok region—that filled Wehrmacht orders for troops stationed in Ukraine.[91] The company reports mask the violence that undergirded its operation in sanitized business-German. In requisitioned factories and workshops under German or ethnic German supervision, workers were unpaid and carried out grueling manual labor to obtain minimal provisions of food and other necessities.

While most of the managerial personnel deployed in the east were German men (a total of 484) who relied on a secretarial staff of German women (138), the reports do not note the gender of the thousands of local workers. But the vast majority of those carrying out unskilled manual labor were women. Ignoring the gendered nature of labor, the company statistics do catalogue fluctuating employment numbers by ethnicity. Therefore, the business report notes—without commentary—that of the 1,076 Jews employed by the Ost-Faser in the Baltic states in 1939, none remained in 1943.[92] The Ost-Faser, like many German corporations, continued to present their own operations as merely commercial or industrial. The political umbrella of the Nazi Empire removed both a sense of responsibility or shame; otherwise, the Ost-Faser surely would have attempted to obfuscate the statistics or omitted the purging of its Jewish workers. Rather, it operated consciously and unapologetically within a genocidal framework.

The Ost-Faser's annual report does not mention the fact that none of the laborers were compensated.[93] The fact of this widespread practice only becomes evident when the German managers entertain the possibility of introducing minimal monetary rewards or increases in food deliveries to boost performance.[94] In his letter to Dr. Toepfer, the head of the *Reichsstelle* for wool, in December 1944, Friedrich Dorn, the managing director of the Ost-Faser, was slightly more explicit:

> The well-known development in the supply of consumer goods had a strong inhibiting effect on performance. There is no doubt that the general economic situation, especially the military developments and the resulting transport situation, made it impossible to adequately cover the demand for consumer goods. However, the fact that in some areas, especially in Ukraine and Belarus, the population was dependent on barter transactions on the black market even for the minimum subsistence level, had a debilitating effect on performance.[95]

Of course, Dorn blames the war for shortages, rather than acknowledging that scarcity was the result of official German policy and part of the Ost-Faser's business model. In fact, by 1943, the management at Ost-Faser realized that productivity in the *Ostland* was only a fraction of what could have been achieved had they instead transported the same forced laborers and materials to Germany. The relative unproductiveness of the Ost-Faser became even more apparent after the "losses [sic] of the majority of Russians and all of the Jews."⁹⁶ That both the Russians and the Jews were "lost" to the Ost-Faser because of the Nazis' genocidal violence Dorn carefully omitted. Holding fast to their long-term plans of building up considerable production in the eastern territories, the Ost-Faser insisted on the political importance of continuing production even under less-than-optimal conditions, suggesting that they had a key role to play in the Germanization of the territory.

Over the course of 1942, the main focus of the Ost-Faser shifted toward the rationalization of production of local firms. Fifty-four percent of all textiles produced in the combined eastern territories were Wehrmacht deliveries. The remaining production was geared toward civilian consumption in keeping with the usual racial differentiations, meaning they were mainly serving the occupiers as well as ethnic Germans and other *Hilfswillige*. Rigid quotas determined who was to receive what kind of allotments in the eastern territories. While Germans and ethnic Germans received close to what they would have gotten in the Reich, the local population was essentially left to fend for itself, living with what they wore on their skin. The Germans called them *Selbstversorger* or "autark individuals."⁹⁷

The occupiers had stripped the urban populations of the entirety of their possessions and ruthlessly extracted foodstuffs, seed, and livestock from the rural population. Any form of provisions, whether food, clothing, or medicine, was contingent on performing work for the Germans. The "payment" structure served as an instrument of terror, a scheme to extract more labor from a population that literally slaved merely to survive. For example, clothes could be obtained in exchange for deliveries of agricultural products, ensuring that the rural population provided foodstuffs, secondary materials, or raw textiles to Germans in exchange for goods.⁹⁸ The occupying authorities regularly threatened to confiscate the entire food supply of a given region if delivery quotas were not met.⁹⁹

The inadequate provisions made for local laborers not only failed to incentivize productivity but also made increases in output impossible.¹⁰⁰ In 1941, the occupiers set weekly maximums for the "nonworking" population and generally only provided food in exchange for labor. Those working for German companies, the occupying administration, the army, or various collective farms (*kolkhozes*) usually received meager provisions at their workplaces. Only at the end of 1942, after catastrophic hunger had plagued large segments of roughly 55–65 million Soviet citizens under German occupation did authorities consider general provisioning, including those who "due to no fault of their own" found themselves without work.¹⁰¹

Large-scale famine at the rear of the fighting front posed a serious security threat. Hunger increased the likelihood of epidemics and jeopardized the Germans' economic operations by further decimating the slave-labor force.[102] With endemic hunger and mass starvation in the spring of 1942, the Germans talked about improving conditions for the population or alternatively congregating starving people in a "hunger ghetto," but ultimately little changed.[103] To control the population at large, the occupiers introduced the general *Arbeitspflicht* in 1943, which compelled everyone aged 14 to 65 to work and forced large segments of the population into camps, from where they were deployed in labor squadrons.[104] Such concentration facilitated control but did not improve provisioning.

The Ost-Faser, too, economized, closing unprofitable factories or consolidating them in order to save labor and fuel. Instead of relocating labor and machinery westward, the Ost-Faser created a massive storage facility in Riga to concentrate valuable goods to avoid having to guard individual factories against theft and attacks from "marauding bands of partisans." The SS ramped up the fight against "partisans," hunting after hungry civilians who hid in the forest during the day and raided German outposts at night.[105] Since people fled from labor camps and Soviet collective farms (*kolkhozes*), which the Nazis often retained for purposes of control, German police and Wehrmacht formations retaliated with particular virulence against so-called partisans in the countryside. They incinerated entire "partisan villages" and massacred their populations, including women and children. Historian Dieter Pohl estimates that the Germans likely murdered more than 200,000 Soviet citizens in their fight against partisans.[106]

Despite the constriction of the labor force, the Ost-Faser continued production, geared exclusively toward the demands of war. The "new" raw materials such as reprocessed wool, reprocessed rags, and animal hair were key in the production of the so-called Ostland cloth, entirely fashioned out of secondary and inferior raw materials. Some factories generated their own raw materials from wastes. In one factory in the *Wirtschaftsinspektion Mitte* (economic inspection center), 2,500 laborers produced 700,000 meters of cloth, of which 450,000 meters consisted of so-called *Gefangenentuch* or prisoner cloth made of cottonized or fluffed raffia fibers produced onsite.[107] Inside the Reich, similar efforts were under way with the goal of manufacturing work clothes for eastern workers from cloth made exclusively from reprocessed rags.[108] The Nazi imperial economy readily registered its "success" in the utilization of wastes and inferior materials by slave laborers.[109]

Valenki

One of the most horrendous applications of the Nazis' zero-waste economics was the production of shoes from the by-products of genocide. Felt boots, a type of footwear that the Germans copied from those worn by the Red Army after the freezing winter of 1941, were one of the few products whose production the Ost-Faser's operations actually expanded. Felt boots, called *Valenki* in Russian, were fortified with leather and provided the best possible protection against wintry conditions. These boots were exclusively produced for the Wehrmacht and "the organizations used by the Wehrmacht," by which the Ost-Faser likely meant all those extermination squads active in the immediate war zone, such as Waffen-SS, police battalions, and *Einsatzgruppen*. In the first half of 1942, only 52,000 *Valenki* boots were produced in small workshops. Over the subsequent six months, production nearly tripled. In November 1943, the Reich Commissioner for the *Ostland*, Hinrich Lohse, reported that 200,000 pairs of felt boots had been delivered the previous fiscal year.[110]

Felt boots could be made almost entirely with inferior raw materials. Their production utilized large quantities of human hair—most of which

Figure 5.2 Jewish workers making felt boots. Courtesy of the United States Holocaust Memorial Museum.

was shorn from the heads of Jewish women murdered in the extermination camps across Nazi-occupied Poland. The hair was collected, sanitized, stored in sacks, and shipped to felt manufacturers across the Nazi-occupied territories and to Germany.[111] Since most of the Ost-Faser's records did not survive, it is impossible to reconstruct the quantities or precise number of shipments received, but the use of human hair in the production of felts is well documented, as is the fact that hair was collected from those murdered in Nazi death camps.[112] In a secret memo, the SS Main Economic and Administrative Office (*SS Wirtschafts-Verwaltungshauptamt*, SS-WVHA) from August 1942 aimed to "secure" the raw material, ordering that "the hair of female prisoners be stored after disinfection" and noting further that hair from male prisoners had to be 20 millimeters in length in order to be utilized.[113]

The supplemental use of human hair in the felt industry allowed for the reduction of wool, an expensive and scarce raw material. Initially, in 1937 and 1938, the numbers were inconsequential, less than two tons of hair were used for the production of technical felts.[114] By 1939, they had increased to 129 tons, still likely the result of contracts between felt-makers and hairdresser and barbershops.[115] By early 1943, the felt-making industry was using large

Figure 5.3 Bales of hair from female prisoners discovered at Auschwitz postliberation. Courtesy of the United States Holocaust Memorial Museum.

amounts of human hair, mixed with other animal hair (such as horsehair), as well as reprocessed textiles for the production of technical felts. Technical felts were rolled and pressed, rather than woven and thus able to utilize fibrous material unsuitable for spinning.[116] Stringent restrictions delineated the permissible mixture of raw materials and the uses to which such felts could be put, prioritizing strategic military and industrial needs over household and office applications. Permitted usages included powder boots, railroad worker boots, and other footwear, particularly footwear designated for the needs of the Wehrmacht and other public sector organizations.[117] These innovations were introduced in early 1943, at the very moment when the amount of human hair registered in the ledgers of the *Reichsstelle für Wolle und andere Tierhaare* (Reich Office for Wool and Other Animal Hair) exploded. By February 1943, the *Reichsstelle* allocated 530 metric tons of "other animal hair" per month for the production of felt products. It also provided the exact mixing ratio for felts specifically designed for the "shoe program," which required "14 tons of hair, 15 tons of animal hair, and 1 ton of wool."[118]

As a general rule, once the massive amounts of human hair were used in production, the statistics obfuscated its use.[119] But the correspondence within the SS-WVHA or the *Reichsstelle* for wool did not take such precautions. As of the second quarter of 1943, numerous German manufacturers used sizable amounts—a total of 530,000 kilograms—of hair in their regular production process.[120] Among them, the felt factory Alex Zink GmbH in Nuremberg received regular shipments of hair arriving from concentration camps inside Germany. Camp administrators lamented that "the construction of a workshop for utilizing the cut hair of male prisoners in one of the concentration camps is currently still impossible for technical reasons."[121] These technical abilities were in place in the factories of the Ost-Faser; they were likely also in place at Filzfabrik Gebr. Frejmark & Co and the Filzindustrie A.G., both in Łódź.[122]

When the Germans evacuated their positions in the fall of 1944, the Ost-Faser packed up the robbed and extracted materials, the raw fibers, the processed wool, the bales of rags, the carefully catalogued wastes, the bolts of prisoner cloth, and warehouses stuffed with finished or semi-finished products for transport back to the Reich.[123] During its evacuation, the Ost-Faser, according to Friedrich Dorn, "did everything in its power to enable our local workers to leave and cared for them as best as we could upon their arrival in the Reich."[124] Surely, care was only extended to the German staff, rather than the workers of the Ost-Faser's felt boot factory in Ukraine, who likely trekked westward on foot like the workers and civilians who cleared Smolensk in September 1943.[125] As historian Dieter Pohl illustrates, the faster the Red Army gained ground, the more ruthless the methods the Germans employed. The Wehrmacht forcibly evacuated civilians in the east. In many cases, entire villages were burned down and their populations marched westward.[126] The more certain defeat, the more the Ost-Faser clung to the illusion that it was merely a private corporation, even though it had been fully embedded in the imperial project and an active participant in the business of genocide.

With few records surviving, little has been written about the Ost-Faser, and its role as a corporation specializing in the utilization of waste and secondary materials has been entirely missed, in large part because the surviving records do their best to conceal the company's actual operations and inflate their productivity. However, a careful reading of the surviving documents in light of the context of occupation, forced labor, extraction, and wholesale murder in the east reveals the violent destruction of slave labor in the utilization of inferior, waste, or secondary materials.

6
Waste Cycles

In 1943, Ernst Günther Schenck, a medical doctor and nutritional scientist, conducted experiments at Mauthausen concentration camp with prisoner *"Kost"* (diet) to test the effects of various kinds of crudely designed foods. These experiments centered around the "east diet" and "yeast diet" to establish not just caloric minimums, but to strategically add or omit certain nutrients.[1] The so-called *Ostkost* or east diet was premised on the assumption that Slavs have more robust digestive tracts and therefore can survive longer on an all-vegetarian (starch-based) diet. The yeast diet or *Hefekost* added 50 grams and later only 30 grams of synthetically grown yeast to the regular provisions as extra "protein."[2] At the time that these experiments were under way, the camp administration made changes to the provisions of the camp population at large. Ernst Martin, a former Mauthausen prisoner and clerk for Schenck, remembers that a certain Mycel *Wurst* was distributed to prisoners throughout the camp, replacing the normal sausage allotment. "According to its appearance and smell," Martin recalls, "it was a kind of liver sausage spread."[3] This "sausage," it turned out, came from the Lenzing cellulose and paper factory.[4] Martin's secret investigations revealed that Mycel *Wurst* was produced out of the pulping waste and wastewater from the factory, enriched with liver flavoring and delivered to the Mauthausen camp as *Leberwurst* or liver sausage. Martin, an engineer by training, secretly examined a sample under the microscope, which showed an enormous amount of cellulose particles. "Dogs did not touch this sausage, not even when fried in margarine," Martin testified years after the war.[5]

This *Müllwurst* (garbage sausage) was given to prisoners at Mauthausen between 1943–1944, causing acute gastrointestinal complications in the severely malnourished inmates. The camp authorities only stopped distributing it after 70–80 percent of prisoners died of the effects of ulcers and purulent colitis.[6] Obviously, the garbage sausage failed to solve the nutrition problem in the camps and ultimately its use backfired, killing the inmates rather than extending their ability to work.[7] However, the circular thinking that spurred the *Müllwurst* experiments continued.

Empire of Rags and Bones. Anne Berg, Oxford University Press. © Oxford University Press 2024.
DOI: 10.1093/oso/9780197744000.003.0007

Part of a wider trend, these experiments illustrate the regime's increasingly fanatical approach to resource and labor exploitation. The initial idea behind them was to supplement rations for German soldiers to enhance their will to fight under conditions of extreme scarcity. Dr. Schenck reasoned that, if soldiers had to suffer from malnourishment and hunger, supplementing foodstuffs with indigestible yet filling waste might help suppress feelings of hunger and extend their fighting spirit.[8] As the experiments at Mauthausen had shown, the current state of bioengineering was unable to grow yeast cultures that could effectively replace animal protein. Schenck nonetheless advocated mixing sawdust and other indigestible extenders into bread and other provisions to extract maximal output from prisoners by masking their imminent starvation.[9]

Experiments to produce single-cell proteins using fungi, yeasts, or bacteria to metabolize agricultural or industrial waste products had been conducted as early as 1915.[10] In the context of the Third Reich, the idea of growing protein without having to sacrifice arable land energized the imaginations of SS scientists. They thought in terms of cycles. If waste-metabolizing yeast colonies could sustain prisoners who, in turn, could be forced to do society's shit work, the cycle could be squared. Plus, the utilization of otherwise polluting effluents had the benefit of cleaning industrial wastewater and recovering chemical pollutants.[11] In specific terms, the idea was as follows: Sulfide lye was a waste product of paper factories. It could be used to extract the polymer lignin, which, in turn, could be used as fuel, fertilizer, tanning agent, or for alcohol distillation, but more interestingly to SS scientists, sulfide lye supported the growth of sulfide yeasts.[12] Claus Ungewitter, the author of the Nazi garbage bible *Verwertung des Wertlosen* (Utilization of the Worthless), and head of the *Reichsstelle Chemie* or Reich Office for Chemistry, estimated in 1938 that the metabolization of sulfide waste lye could yield as much as 100,000 tons of yeast solids.[13] A few years later, when Schenck conducted experiments in Mauthausen, Oswald Pohl, the head of the SS Main Economic and Administrative Office (*SS-Wirtschafts-Verwaltungshauptamt*, SS-WVHA), dreamed about expanding them to include 100,000 prisoners.[14]

As Mauthausen demonstrated, the experiments were not scalable in the ways the SS imagined. Waste products were not able to reproduce the labor force of the Reich. It turned out that the garbage sausage not only contained significant amounts of cellulose residue but also contaminants such as arsenic and lead. The desired goal to reproduce and maximize output thus predictably failed. While the experiments with the *Müllwurst* came to a halt, the logic of processing discarded materials with minimal inputs continued, following the same principles that drove the Food Relief Works when feeding garbage to swine.[15]

The idea of feeding industrial waste to forced laborers took hold at the very moment that labor shortages and material bottlenecks hemorrhaged the war economy. On the surface, the garbage sausage resembles scientific endeavors that attempted to minimize spoilage and recover valuable material, such as the attempt to make nonperishable, canned bread (*Konservenbrot*).[16] But ultimately, these experiments were not about food per se. They were about minimizing expenditures while maximizing labor output. As such, the *Müllwurst* experiments are best understood as part of a continuum of labor exploitation that ranged from tapping prison labor for recycling old cables, to building up a slave-labor complex that churned out uniforms by processing the material remnants of the Nazi genocide, to forcing so-called *Sonderkommandos* to process the dead. If not for the debilitating and ultimately deadly effects of the garbage sausage, it might well have served as a short-term implement to make a deadly cycle more economically efficient.

In 1943, even the SS had to come to grips with the fact that labor was a finite resource. Oswald Pohl decided to release new regulations about prisoner provisions and "care" in order to preserve labor. Pohl recommended better food, not overboiling vegetables, sending meals to prisoners rather than the other way around, and providing rest time to allow for digestion.[17] The Plenipotentiary for Labor Fritz Sauckel openly argued for the necessity of extracting equivalent labor in exchange for the supply of nutrients.[18] This logic of "caloric throughput," of calculating metabolic efficiency as a function of energy input and labor output, was hardly limited to prisoner food, but the SS applied it in general terms. Camps literally became part of the regime's waste management infrastructure, processing (in the case of Mauthausen, literally metabolizing) waste and secondary materials on an industrial scale.

Prisoners and guards understood the logic of this system. Labor, even if almost exclusively waste labor, was the product. Guards would ensure it was extracted comprehensively and with the utmost ruthlessness, a feat only excessively violence could accomplish. Prisoners understood that only useful toil, no matter how futile or filthy, separated them from certain death. While the contemptuous inscription on the gates of Nazi camps invoked labor as rehabilitative, the simple truth was there was no way of working one's way out of the Nazi camps.[19] They were established for the purpose of extracting labor from individuals considered "scum." The daughter of Heinrich Himmler,

Gudrun "Püppi" Himmler, put it bluntly when defending her father's role after the war, insisting that "Hitler had only entrusted the 'most loyal,' namely her father, with 'the garbage collection of the Reich.' "[20]

Extraction Machines

The Nazi regime could look back on long histories of imperial confinement, extractive labor practice, and labor policing for inspiration. From vagrancy laws to workhouses for the poor, to prisons, modern states relied on carceral institutions to curtail the ability of workers to move in search for higher wages and utilize the labor of "unproductive" populations for "the common good."[21] New World plantations and convict labor in Australia, the most prominent colonial relatives to Nazi labor camps, certainly informed Nazi thinking.[22] The Nazi press favorably compared its own camps to British concentration camps in South Africa, while readily glossing over Germany's own colonial rule in German Southwest Africa (Namibia), which combined colonization with genocide and camp-based slave labor.[23]

The early camps, "wild," spontaneous, localized, and disorganized as they were, were not generally established as labor camps.[24] They had neither uniform characteristics nor a name. They were established in vacant storage sheds or cellars of public buildings to contain the scores of individuals rounded up by the Gestapo, the Storm Troopers (SA), and the police in the initial period of terror following the Reichstag fire and the decree for the "protection of the people and the state" of February 28, 1933.[25] It was not until 1936 that the concentration camp was reimagined as a labor camp.[26] Nonetheless, labor was at the crux of the concentration camp system from the beginning since the provisional camps were central to the destruction of organized labor and the breakup of working-class resistance by deploying random, arbitrary terror.[27] The localized nature of this emergent carceral landscape made violence immensely personal because "jailers and jailed often knew each other well. They had grown up in the same streets and shared a long history of violence and vendettas."[28] Holding pens for political opponents, these early camps contained a growing number of professionals, civil servants, labor organizers, and workers in "protective custody," and thus made possible the redistribution of jobs in line with the prerogatives of local Nazis who were doling out favors.[29] Even though numerically insignificant in comparison to later numbers of incarceration, the arbitrary, public nature of the terror combined with redistribution of highly coveted jobs had a significant psychological effect on the population in the context of mass unemployment and the political consolidation of the regime.[30]

By 1935, Hitler placed the camps under the authority of the newly created Inspectorate of the Concentration Camps (*Inspektion der Konzentrationslager*, IKL), headed by Theodor Eicke, which consolidated existing camps and expanded the entire concentration camp complex.[31] The later camps, established from 1936 onward, were aimed at extracting labor from each and every incarcerated body. For the first time since the end of World War I, Germany faced not looming unemployment but an acute and rapidly growing labor shortage further underscoring the need for forced and prison labor.[32]

Germany's overall economy thus is important for understanding the planning for and construction of the new generation of labor camps and the transformation of early camps like Dachau and Lichterburg in line with their new economic function. Dachau, shaped by Eicke's vision, served as the model for the second-generation camps: Sachsenhausen (1936), Buchenwald (1937), Mauthausen (1938), and Ravensbrück (1939). In contrast to the earlier variants, these new camps were deliberately hidden from public view and operated in secrecy.[33] The mass arrests of 1938 funneled "unproductive" and "deviant" individuals into the new camps. This so-called *Aso-Aktion* incarcerated thousands of "asocials," a category that included idleness, shirking, drunkenness, promiscuity, gambling, vagrancy, and all sorts of socially conspicuous behaviors, in order to purify society and put to work those who resisted discipline and offended Nazi ideas of order.[34] No longer intended to merely remove and contain politically suspect individuals, these camps were designed for the exploitation of prison labor in the interest of an economy increasingly geared toward war.[35]

Initially, labor details were thought up that were entirely pointless and served the sole function of instilling "camp discipline" in the inmates. At Sachsenhausen, the so-called asocials were forced to carry dirt in their jackets from one side of the camp to the other.[36] Still in 1940, "exercise" in Dachau, reported former prisoner Bravenes Zdenkék, consisted of "rolling barrels" in a tight line so that each prisoner's feet slammed into the head of the prisoner following on his heels.[37] While such cruelty didn't subside, futile labor assignments became fewer once the camps had been fully incorporated into the Nazi economy of extraction and torture was incorporated into "useful" toil.[38]

Waste-labor and recycling were key components from the beginning.[39] The directives from Göring's Four-Year Plan Authority concerning the collection of secondary materials—applied to concentration camps and the public sector more broadly.[40] The commandant of Sachsenburg concentration camp, Bernhard Schmidt, reminded his staff to collect wastepaper, textile waste, metal scrap, and bones from camp kitchens and ensure their return to the economic cycle.[41] Soon, fanatical scrapping affected the routines of prisoners in particularly violent forms. For example, in the winter of 1938–1939, Sachsenhausen camp guards forced Jewish prisoners to straighten rusty nails. Tools were not provided. Standing knee-deep in snow and wielding used bricks, prisoners hammered the bent and rusted nails back into shape—ostensibly for reuse.[42] It became the responsibility of every SS guard to ensure the "return of all valuable materials to the state," including "wire scraps, metal fragments, nails, tin cans, food cans, toothpaste tubes, light bulbs, jugs, metal cigarette boxes, etc." Extracting materials at all costs and under any circumstance simultaneously served torture and salvage, both in performative and measurable terms.[43] Humiliation and torture were integral to shit work, waste labor, and recycling; over time, they attained the status of systematic practice.[44]

Inside Nazi Germany, concentration camps were not the only institution to rediscover labor exploitation. City governments looked for essentially free labor in mental institutions and ordinary prisons.[45] The example that likely inspired imitation by the SS in a number of business ventures was a large-scale experiment between the *Reichsbahn* (Reich Railway Authority) and the Ministry of Justice at the penitentiary in Kassel-Wehlheiden. In the late fall of 1936, the technical director of the *Reichsbahn* Kassel and the head of the prison Kassel-Wehlheiden started to discuss plans to build a plant in which prisoners would dismantle old electrical cables and wirings on the prison grounds. Up until this point, the *Reichsbahn* had burned old cables in its repair workshops, which only allowed for the recovery of low-grade lead and copper.[46] In May 1937, the *Reichsbahn* provided the building materials, and thirty prisoners began constructing a massive half-timbered shed that would contain the disassembly workshops. Under the supervision of experts provided by the *Reichsbahn*, prisoners stripped electrical cables of insulation, recovering large quantities of high-quality lead and copper as well as jute, tin, cotton, aluminum, rubber, and silk. Jute had to be degreased and for this purpose the *Reichsbahn* put prisoners to work building a second shed, which contained the brand-new perchloroethylene processor.[47]

Figure 6.1 An official of the *Reichsbahn* demonstrates the process of cable recycling. Courtesy of Bundesarchiv.

Figure 6.2 Baled copper wires at Kassel-Wehlheiden. Courtesy of Bundesarchiv.

Operations at Kassel-Wehlheiden started with a small volume of waste from select railway districts; by 1938, the central railway office in Berlin transferred almost the entire volume of old cables and electrical wiring to Kassel-Wehlheiden: a total of about 800 metric tons per year. The workshops expanded rapidly, employing more and more prisoners, whose tasks expanded to include disassembling light bulbs, sealing rings, switches, small motors, batteries, and all sorts of electrical equipment. The joint venture recovered a total of 1,870,000 kilograms of secondary materials in 1940 alone. In January 1942, the Ministry for Armaments and Ammunitions under Fritz Todt contemplated the recovery of scarce metals using the joint venture between *Reichsbahn* and the Ministry of Justice as a model.[48] Initially, the penitentiary in Kassel did not charge the *Reichbahn* for the labor of prisoners, a practice that soon changed. By 1943, a prisoner's daily toil eventually earned the Justice Department a minimum of 4 RM per day.[49] This profitable venture supplemented the *Reichsbahn* raw material supply, and it funneled cash into the coffers of the Nazi state for the financing of war. More importantly, it produced strategic revenue by using prison labor to spin not straw into gold but old cables into war funding.[50] Essentially, the forced labor complex produced an economic implement that replaced the war bond.

SS Industrial Complex

The entrepreneurial frenzy that gripped private individuals, corporations, and the public sector also enthralled the SS over the course of the 1930s. What makes the SS ventures different is their scope and scale, as well as their level of independence, particularly as the SS operated very much like a state within the state after 1939.[51] Some of the earliest ventures were the prisoner workshops at Dachau.[52] They included supplemental workshops for carpentry, locksmithing, tailoring, and shoemaking. There, prisoners performed essential labor for camp maintenance, made furnishings for guards, and mended the uniforms of SS men as well as the clothing of their families.[53] In addition, Dachau maintained butcher and bakery workshops, a set-up that would be copied on a massive scale at Auschwitz and KGL Lublin (Majdanek) in 1941.[54] The organizational umbrella, the Deutsche Wirtschaftsbetriebe GmbH (German Economic Corporation), took the shape of a holding company in 1940 and brought workshops, large-scale ventures, and the pet projects of individual SS officers under the joint patronage of Oswald Pohl and Georg Lörner, who were incidentally the two highest officers in the SS-WVHA as of 1940.[55]

One of the earliest SS *Betriebe* (SS-owned and run companies) was the German Earth and Stone Works (Deutsche Erd- und Steinwerke, DESt), which was the fad of an SS officer, Arthur Ahrens.[56] Ahrens built very expensive and very deadly brickworks at Oranienburg that relied on prison labor from the Sachsenhausen camp. The location for the Mauthausen camp, adjacent to a massive quarry, was made with the DESt in mind.[57] Imagining himself as an important business magnate, Ahrens fantasized that the DESt would manufacture the granite, marble, and brick for Albert Speer's designs of Germania—the reimagined representational mega city and capital of the world, formerly known as Berlin.[58] The problem was that for all his zeal, Ahrens knew next to nothing about brickmaking.[59] The Oranienburg plant never produced a single usable brick, though granite mining at Mauthausen proceeded so long as the supply of prisoners—who were dying at alarming rates under the excruciating work conditions—could be procured.[60]

The experience with the DESt inadvertently confirmed the emerging focus of SS ventures: centering around the exploitation of inferior raw materials by utilizing forced, manual, camp-based labor.[61] War functioned as an accelerator in the key industries identified by the Four-Year Plan. The massive growth of the concentration camp population over the course of 1938 and 1939 made it possible to increase the output of concentration camp workshops.[62] In May 1939, the SS created the German Equipment Works (*Deutsche Ausrüstungswerke*, DAW), which swallowed the existing workshops at Dachau and subsequently expanded its operations across camps in Germany and Nazi-occupied Europe. The proliferating network of SS companies did not follow a particular business plan, but rather developed in an ad hoc fashion and was not consistently separated according to task or function.[63] For example, the *SS-Bekleidungswerk* (SS-Clothing Works), whose actual structures and competencies often intersected with those of the DAW, also became a catch-all distributor for products from existing camp workshops and later for the various manufacturers based in Nazi-occupied Poland and labor details that survived the dissolution of other SS companies in the occupied east.[64]

The DAW shareholders' agreement obfuscated the fact that the entire rationale of the corporation was the production of essential provisions for the SS slave-labor complex and its slave drivers.[65] With the invasion of the

Soviet Union, Hitler made it clear that raw material for "auxiliary goods for the Wehrmacht," the production of uniforms, coats, socks, underwear, and bedding for the SS and military formations, crucial for the regime's ability to fight its war, was to be economized.[66] The DAW utilized "idle manpower that cannot be used in the free economy for a variety of reasons," essentially, "inferior" human material (*Menschenmaterial*).[67]

Although the official records of the DAW obscure the slave-labor principles, the workshops established in the camps inside the Reich, as well as in camps in Nazi-occupied Poland, focused on, in the words of the Nazi expert on recycling, Claus Ungewitter, "the utilization of the worthless" both in terms of raw material and people.[68] Accordingly, the DAW became a prime venue for SS recycling.[69] In countless workshops, prisoners repaired equipment and garments or fashioned new wares from secondary materials. They disassembled metal war booty, took apart broken down military equipment and airplane junk, and turned textile wastes into cleaning supplies and new fabric for military and prisoner uniforms.[70] By 1943, the DAW recorded 16,742,296.42 RM in gross revenues inside the Reich alone.[71] A year later, a recorded 17,410 camp prisoners toiled in DAW workshops within the Reich.[72] Particularly significant were the works established in the General Government. In addition to textiles, wood and iron works dominated production in Lublin. Prisoners harvested the raw material "wood" to make wooden shoes and other items. They too disassembled metal junk and war machinery.[73] In Kraków and the Radom district, which together accounted for a total of 9,000,000 RM in turnover, over 6,000 prisoners were tasked with various sorts of textile reprocessing. Workshops and factories specialized in the recycling of rags, textile wastes, and garments stripped from victims of the Nazi killing machine.[74]

Textile and shoe manufacturing were important supplementary industries to the armaments industry. Whereas technical know-how was key in many other industries, textile factories could render reliable output with minimal technological investment by relying on low-skilled or unskilled labor.[75] In June 1940, the SS incorporated yet another venture for this purpose. The TexLed, short for *Gesellschaft für Textil und Leder Verwertung* (Textile and Leather Utilization GmbH), likely inspired by the countless textile workshops established in the ghettos in Nazi-occupied Poland, moved to streamline the recycling of old textiles to produce uniforms for prisoners and Nazi killers alike. "Rationalizing the work process" in textile sweatshops, the TexLed prided itself on productivity and congratulated company management for churning out "results with involuntary labor that are not inferior to those of civilian workers."[76] Relying almost exclusively on unskilled laborers, the TexLed became one of the most successful SS *Betriebe*.[77] It operated in two locations, Dachau and Ravenbrück, where inmates fashioned prisoner clothing and shoes from discarded goods. Soon the TexLed filled orders from the Wehrmacht as well, scaling up to industrial capacity along the lines of the DAW's ghetto economy.[78]

Large-scale expansions took place at the women's camp in Ravensbrück, where the textile works became the main industry.[79] The company's exponential growth proved to be unique.[80] At Ravensbrück, the company operated tailoring workshops, workshops for processing fur, a knitting mill, a weaving mill, a workshop making sanitary wares, mat-weaving workshops, and straw shoe–weaving workshops.[81] In 1942 and 1943, the tailoring workshops at Ravensbrück met the entire demand of jackets, pants, shirts, underwear, hats, overcoats, and mittens for the inmates in all concentration camps combined, while simultaneously churning out products for the Wehrmacht and SS formations.[82] Women prisoners worked two shifts around the clock, struggling to meet constantly rising quotas.[83] Gustav Binder, the SS supervisor on the floor of the tailoring factory, trained women to make a shirt in two and a half minutes so they could meet their quota of 180 shirts per shift. The women worked under horrendous conditions characterized by blacked out windows and constant physical abuse. Binder's excessive violence kept the 600 women in a constant state of terror. If a worker failed to meet her target, "[H]e hits her across the face and she falls off her stool." Binder would repeatedly hit her until the worker "has been battered so hard that she can barely sit up." Kicking, beating, throwing scissors at women who fell asleep or failed to meet their targets were part of Binder's regular repertoire.[84]

Former prisoner Maria Kusmierczuk, who made footwear for Wehrmacht soldiers and Waffen-SS troops on guard duty in the straw shoe workshops, remembers:

> Our entire transport was tasked with sewing straw boots. Prisoners worked three shifts on this assignment, eight hours each, also at night. The first shift started at 5.00 a.m. During our work, we were watched by guards, who were there to ensure the high quality of the product, and if they noticed any defects, they beat us around the head with a boot. In eight hours, each prisoner was supposed to make two pairs of shoes.[85]

Despite SS reports describing the TexLed works at Ravensbrück as a regular textile factory, it was envisioned as a recycling endeavor for old textiles and shoes from the beginning.[86] In all workshops, combined waste products served as the primary raw material. Workers utilized in-house textile wastes to make *Fusslappen* (foot rags), which prisoners wore instead of socks. The production of *Gefangentuch* or prisoner cloth relied on inferior materials as well, such as fluffed raffia, processed wool, and rayon, much of which was produced by slave laborers in the occupied east.[87] Even the effect bags that contained the original clothing inmates wore when arrested became raw material. Made of nettle and the like, prisoners reworked these bags into underwear and camp uniforms.

Whatever "respectable" clothing the SS robbed from women interned at Ravensbrück and from populations in the occupied territories was handed out to German bomb victims or sold. The sorting, of course, was done by prisoners as well. Less than pristine clothing was earmarked for forced laborers and allocated to the regional economic offices; other garments were recycled or worn as is onsite, particularly after shortages prevented the production of prisoner cloth. Clothes deemed "unusable" were handed out to inmates and marked to differentiate camp laborers from civilian laborers outside.[88] The remaining rags were torn and respun or cut and reused as raw materials. By 1942, large amounts of material processed in the camps were clothing from people murdered by the Nazis.[89] In order to close the cycle, the TexLed envisioned the construction of a mechanical weaving mill, a ripping mill, and a spinning mill to guarantee the industrial reprocessing of rags at Ravensbrück, but the turn of military events cut short the SS efforts to expand the "*Betrieb*."[90] Even without expansion, the TexLed forced expendable populations to process garbage for the purpose of clothing the entirety of the Reich's slave-labor complex.

The weaving workshops also transitioned toward utilizing old clothes after the masses of garments and rags stripped from Jews murdered in the General Government arrived by the truck and trainload. The flood of materials coming in did not abate, exceeding the processing capacities of the camps by a wide margin. "Bringing these things and transporting them into the camp's premises, to the sheds, or piling them up in the open went on for several months, sometimes until March 1945," Władysława Dabrowska, a former prisoner at Ravensbrück, remembers.[91] Piles of garments and shoes weathered the elements as warehouse space was running out.[92]

Dumping Grounds

As the regime waged its genocidal war, it fortified the boundaries of the people's community by concentrating waste and expendable populations behind walls and barbed wire. The camps essentially became dumping grounds for discarded people and things, serving as massive waste-processing centers. Camp designs produced conditions of squalor that provided "evidence" for the inherently filthy nature of the concentrated populations and their incorrigibility. Accordingly, the camp infrastructure focused on industrial laundries, disinfestation chambers, disinfection plants, delousing facilities, and crematoria, rather than on sanitary facilities and sewers. The Nazis were concerned with the contamination of the surrounding areas, not with life inside. Inside the camps, Nazi fantasies about purity and their obsessions with cleanliness manifested in countless labor details: slurry drivers, garbage shifter, shit squad, garbage squad, dumping command, corpse carrier, unloading command, carrying columns, barrack cleaners, and potato peelers were all tasks intended to clean and maintain the camp grounds and operations in line with Nazi exhortations, while constantly clashing with the realities of camp design.[93]

In all camps and ghettos, waste labor was ubiquitous, even where work was ostensibly in the service of strategic industries. When Heinrich Himmler visited the armaments workshops at Buchenwald in March 1943, he was appalled to learn that prisoners apparently buried the brass percussion caps from detonators, rather than recycling the brass. Himmler ordered prisoners to dig up all the previously buried percussion caps and forced "criminals fit for work" to sort the full caps from the empty ones.[94] Speer thereafter notified Himmler that 6,000 to 7,000 kilograms of valuable brass had already been recovered.[95] As this example demonstrates, even the production of armaments and munitions was focused around disassembly, sorting, and recycling. The same was true for the many ghetto workshops in the General Government engaged in war-relevant production. For Jewish slave laborers in the Starachowice munitions factory in occupied Poland, one of the most arduous tasks was the pushing of heavy carts of scrap metal used to produce new casings after the metal had been melted down in the blast furnace.[96]

Camp inmates disassembled broken war machinery; turned food scraps into sausage and sawdust into bread; sorted, cleaned, mended, and refashioned trainloads full of rags, old clothing, and soiled uniforms; and cobbled together new shoes out of filthy discards. Shoe fashioning, belt and strap making, weaving, spinning, knitting, and tailoring were strategic, war-relevant forms of labor that predominantly took place in the sweatshops of the various camps, without the "tailorist" streamlining of the TexLed.

In Bergen-Belsen, Helmut Mainz, a Dutch Jew, remembered three halls filled with old military underwear and soiled uniforms. Mainz was transported to the prisoner exchange camp in Bergen-Belsen in January 1943. He immediately understood the morbid rationale of recycling to which prisoners were damned. He described the piles of textiles that were ripped to shreds by shrapnel and gunfire, likely stripped off the bodies of the dead. With large and small shears, pocketknives, and razor blades, prisoners cut and unstitched, sorted, baled, and stuffed into burlap sacks the precious raw materials they had gathered. The materials recovered were then transported to factories and other camps and transformed into underwear and uniforms to be yet again ripped to pieces by a new round of grenades.[97]

Working as a cobbler, Mainz captured the process of shoe fashioning from discards with equal clarity:

> On tables, hardly visible in the dim light, lie mountains of dirty old shoes. Our task, to cut the vamp off the rest of the shoe with dull and flimsy knives and separate such valuables as foxing and linings utterly drenched in sweat. The youth of the Third Reich, in self-sacrificing labor, collected these mountains of shoes. We, cheap slaves that we are, are supposed to produce precious material for the production of new shoes by the sheer force of our labor. Heinz and Fritz [the supervising SS-guards] repeatedly explain the importance of our work and keep jealous watch that we don't cut up the precious leather or throw it in the trash.[98]

German youth were not the only ones collecting old shoes. As part of "Operation Reinhard," the raw materials office within the SS-WVHA systematically extracted shoes (and clothes) from victims in ghettos, transit, and death camps. Odilo Globocnik, chiefly responsible for the implementation of the Final Solution in occupied Poland, estimated that close to 4,000 train cars stuffed with shoes and textiles were transported westward for refashioning by forced and prison laborers between May 1942 and December 1943.[99] Wooden shoes were produced for forced laborers in heavy industries and mining. Refurbished leather shoes were reserved for Germans.[100]

Figure 6.3 A prisoner loads baled clothing onto lorries at Bergen-Belsen. Courtesy of Hans-Jürgen Vehse.

Here, too, the morbid, resource-fetishizing creativity of the SS knew no bounds. Cans that had contained Wehrmacht provisions were collected in the occupied eastern territories, and prisoners affixed them to wooden shoes as extra soles to save wood. The inspectorate for the concentration camps described the process as follows:

> The sheet metal sole is taken twice, as it is simply too weak. The inner sheet metal sole is cut exactly as large as the wooden sole, while the outer sheet metal sole is kept about 1 cm larger on all sides. Once these two sheet metal soles are placed on top of each other, the sole nails are now riveted in place. This product is then nailed onto the wooden sole and the 1 cm wide edge

is beaded over (folded over) and also nailed in place. The heel is enclosed in the same way. This measure significantly increases the durability of the wooden sole.[101]

Shoes were subjected to longevity tests in order to determine the effectiveness of various "improvements."[102] At Sachsenhausen camp, a special shoe-runner squad, usually for those who were punished for theft or other violations of camp rules, were forced to test the shoes fashioned in the camp for 35 kilometers a day, in summer and winter.[103] Forced to carry heavy loads on their backs, prisoners marched along a circular track on the camp grounds designed to mimic the real-life conditions the shoes would have to endure, such as quarry work, digging ditches, and draining moors. Paul Reinwald ended up in this torturous labor detail because he had allegedly removed a woolen blanket from the heap of rags to turn it into a body wrap for personal use.[104]

Like experiments with the garbage sausage, such fanatical attempts to use waste materials to power and extend the destructive logic of the camp economy hint at dynamics that were all-pervasive and lay at the core of the Nazi waste regime's most violent structures. Science, technology, administration, bureaucracy, industry, and business zeal came together in a destructive matrix that accepted the premise of the "indispensability" of forced labor and the "reality" of resource scarcity. Cruelty was not merely a side-effect but strategic in a complex designed for the root-and-branch extraction of labor and material at minimal cost.

In its most extreme, waste labor focused on processing the dead. A novel labor detail crystalized during the fall of 1941—the *Sonderkommando*, essentially a corpse-processing squad that retrieved valuables from murdered Jews and disposed of their bodies. The early versions of *Sonderkommandos* were created to process the corpses of Jews murdered by the *Einsatzgruppen* in Soviet territory. At the same time, the systematic murder of mentally ill and physically disabled people as part of the expanded T4 "euthanasia program" at Chelmno also deployed *Sonderkommandos*.[105] In the Nazi-occupied east, the *Einsatzgruppen* murdering the Jews of Kiev established a *Sonderkommando* under the guidance of Paul Blobel. In September 1941, Blobel's experienced squad had to secure the belongings and clothing of the more than 33,000 Jews murdered over the course of a few days.[106]

By the summer of 1942, the *Sonderkommando* in Auschwitz-Birkenau comprised approximate 400 people, most of them Jews. They were forced to sort the belongings of the people driven into the gas chambers, break gold teeth out of the mouths of the dead, and "secure" the hair of murdered women.[107] Besides extracting dental gold for the German state, the *Sonderkommandos* gathered the raw materials that were processed by other camp workshops before discarding the dead. In Chelmno, Bełżec, Sobibor, and Treblinka, the *Sonderkommandos* were required to burn the corpses of murdered Jews on gigantic pyres and in fire pits.[108] As the first killing centers were operational in March 1942, *Sonderkommandos* gradually became a permanent part of the camps' cleanup and recycling infrastructure. Consisting almost exclusively of Jews, the new *Sonderkommandos* would process their predecessors.[109]

Materials Recovery Facility

When the SS started to clear the ghettos in occupied Poland in February 1942 and systematically murdered Jews in newly established killing centers, the volume of accumulating materials eventually overwhelmed the camp-based recycling economy. In March 1943, the SS founded the OSTI (*Ostindustrie GmbH*) as a subsidiary of the Deutsche Wirtschaftsbetriebe DWB, combining the various ventures Odilo Globocnik had set up in the Lublin district and officially expanding the SS *Betriebe* into the General Government beyond the DAW.[110] Its official purpose was "the operation of commercial enterprises, in particular in the textile- and iron-processing industry, and the participation in such enterprises."[111] The OSTI was incorporated at the very moment that Operation Reinhard, code for the liquidation of the Jewish ghettos and the murder of the Jews in the General Government, was drawing to a close and the Nazis dismantled Bełżec, the first of the Reinhard camps, and began to cover up their crimes.[112] The OSTI, dissolved within a year, was never imagined as a permanent component of the SS industrial complex.[113] Instead, it was primarily a materials recovery facility and, as such, an integral part of Operation Reinhard. The OSTI specifically retained Jewish workers slated for annihilation and intermittently diverted them from selections and transports to the death camps so that they could process the material remnants—garments, shoes, and household goods of the Jews who had already been murdered.

The OSTI was the culmination of processes that started in the summer of 1941 and a response to the ideological tension between securitization and extraction that stood at the center of the Nazi genocide. On the one hand, the regime considered Jews and other minorities a formidable threat to internal security; on the other hand, it was trying to manage shortages of labor and materials.[114] The ad hoc nature of the development of the Final Solution can be understood, in part, as a response to these competing strategic considerations. The military success of the summer of 1941 was as important as subsequent setbacks for explaining the relationship between slave-labor industries and the rapidly escalating genocide of European Jews.[115] By the end of 1941, victory seemed within reach, making the deportation of Germany's Jews politically and logistically feasible. The millions of POWs promised an infinite supply of forced labor in Soviet territory, justifying the elimination of Jews, in the eyes of the regime at once dangerous racial others and useless eaters. The initial influx of prisoners did not last; German expansion slowed, then stalled, and was eventually reversed. Their appalling treatment at the hands of the Germans had caused the death of some 2 million POWs by January 1942.[116] In light of these deaths, the deportations from Germany, and other European countries, toward the massive labor and death camps in Nazi-occupied Poland served to intermittently replenish the slave-labor economy while continuing to "cleanse" Europe of Jews.

By early 1942, Heinrich Himmler oversaw the construction of industrial killing facilities in Sobibor, Bełżec, and Treblinka, later known as the "Reinhard camps," where Jews from the ghettos in the General Government were systematically murdered. Himmler moreover expanded the POW camp at Lublin (Majdanek) and the concentration camp at Auschwitz into killing facilities. Accordingly, he informed Richard Glücks, the chief inspector of the concentration camps, of the change in plans:

> Now that Russian POWs cannot be expected, in the coming days I will send a large number of Jews and Jewesses into the camps that are to emigrate from Germany. In the next weeks you must make appropriate arrangements in the concentration camps for 100,000 Jews and up to 50,000 Jewesses. In the next few weeks, the concentration camps will be assigned great industrial tasks.[117]

But it seems that even Himmler underestimated the magnitude of those "tasks," whether with regard to recycling or disposal. The material remainders overwhelmed existing structures. Permanent crematoria and *Sonderkommandos* were a response to the accumulating corpses and the environmental hazard that burying them invariably produced. The OSTI dealt with the recyclables, streamlining processing that was already ongoing.

The old airfield in Lublin became the prime location for the OSTI's operation and developed into a major processing hub for shoes, textiles, and other materials, robbed from the Jews killed in Bełżec, Sobibor, and Treblinka. Between February 1942, when the first killing centers became operational and the founding of the OSTI in March 1943, the SS amassed staggering amounts of clothes, shoes, and other items—all precious property of the German state—which required processing or would otherwise go to waste. Accordingly, the SS transferred Jews from the remaining camps and ghettos to Lublin, where they were forced to sort, clean, and mend the garments from murdered Jews in workshops operated by the SS-*Bekleidungswerk*, the DAW, and the OSTI.[118] Assembled in an ad hoc fashion, the overcrowded camps and workshops processed over 1,800 railcars full of textiles under the direction of a textile specialist, SS-Hauptsturmführer Josef Obermaier.[119]

The main purpose of the OSTI thus was neither to produce nor to make a profit in the free market sense of the term. It processed labor and garbage, offering short-term financial gain that funneled the value extracted from genocide into state coffers, using up (*verwerten*) Jewish labor prior to disposing of their depleted bodies. The OSTI was a genocide corporation; its success was a function of waste processing. On January 5, 1944, Odilo Globocnik sent the final secret report to Heinrich Himmler and a carbon copy of it to Oswald Pohl, in which he announced the conclusion of the operation and deemed it a success. He reiterated the fourfold purpose of the OSTI, which in Globocnik's mind was identical to the goals of Operation Reinhard itself: the "resettlement" of Jews, the root-and-branch utilization of Jewish labor power, the extraction of value from objects, and capture of all hidden assets.[120] The so-called resettlement, a euphemism for the mass murder of the Jews, has received careful and nuanced scholarly attention.[121] The waste-processing aspects have so far been overlooked.

In eighteen different camps, essentially material recovery facilities, 52,000 Jews slaved to ensure the utilization of material assets.[122] The OSTI mobilized the labor of Jews to process—to recycle—whatever valuables the victims of Operation Reinhard had owned or carried on their very bodies. The managerial staff of the OSTI at the SS-WVHA, much like prosecutors at Nuremberg and historians since, were somewhat confused about the OSTI's purpose. Maximilian Horn, assigned to Globocnik's enterprises as the OSTI's manager within the SS-WVHA, had asked his boss Oswald Pohl about the precise relationship between economic and political goals, whether the company's function was "to be regarded primarily as a political or a police matter or as an economic matter." Pohl answered unequivocally: "Both."[123]

Although most of the victims were desperately poor, the Nazis deemed the value extracted from their rags and labor essential. Their murder was a foregone conclusion. The OSTI's sole purpose was processing material remnants, squeezing value from people and things otherwise considered waste. The numbers cataloguing the profit of the OSTI make clear that textile recycling was its single most important function.[124] For the duration of its operation, the OSTI took over the workshops of the SS-*Bekleidungswerk* and DAW on the old airfield in Lublin, sited new workshops, and outsourced labor to additional companies that processed the loot on its behalf. In addition, the OSTI oversaw textile-processing workshops in the Radom district, whose function aligned with the goals of Operation Reinhard.[125]

Even if robbed currency, jewels, and gold amounted for a large portion of the recorded revenue, the returns tallied from textile processing are stunning given the state of the bedraggled ghetto population. Of the grand total of 178,745,960.59 RM reported by Globocnik, almost a fourth was derived from fabrics of various sorts.[126] The company's Jewish labor was most effectively deployed for textile recycling. The report explains:

> Textiles, clothing, linen, bed feathers, and rags were collected and sorted according to their quality. The sorted items had to be searched for hidden values and lastly disinfected. More than 1,900 wagons [of textiles] were then made available to the agencies specified by the Reich Ministry of Economic Affairs on the instructions of the SS Main Economic and Administrative Office. From these stocks not only foreign workers were clothed, but a large part was used for re-spinning. No cases of illness have been reported, even though the pieces of clothing often came from people sick with typhus, evidencing that disinfection was sufficient.[127]

Sorting squads were key, tasked with piling clothes, shoes, glasses, watches, clinical thermometers. Most of the remaining labor involved some sort of recycling. Jews repaired furniture and other household items, salvaging hinges and locks from items that were beyond repair. Thousands of prisoners cleaned fabrics, tore rags into fibers, and respun those fibers into yarn. They produced or refurbished 450,000 pairs of shoes for forced laborers in woodworking workshops and sewed various kinds of items for use by the

Wehrmacht in tailoring sweatshops. Some 1,531,000 individual pieces of clothing were thus repaired or fashioned anew, in addition to 28,100 garments containing fur. Some of the inferior textiles were recycled in a brush and broom factory, established on the site of the former Lublin airport, where Jews made 4,800,000 broomsticks and scrubbers, as well as 724,000 brushes of varying sorts for the sanitization of the empire. Tellingly, the buildings of the factory themselves had no running water.[128]

The managers in the SS-WVHA stressed the importance of the OSTI to the armaments industry. Laborers in metal workshops recycled scrap, disassembled military equipment, repaired automobiles, and fashioned millions of various kinds of screws for Wehrmacht use.[129] But the conversion of the OSTI into a pure armaments factory was never actually attempted.[130] In October 1943, Globocnik reported to Himmler that Operation Reinhard had been completed.[131]

By November, the majority of textiles robbed from the victims of the operation had been processed and the murder of the OSTI's workers commenced according to plan. As a report in early 1944 concluded: "When the OSTI was deprived of these workers in November 1943, the basis of its activity was taken away and liquidation remained the only plausible path forward."[132] Euphemistically referring to this largest German massacre of Jews, by the code name "Operation Harvest Festival," the business report just turned the facts around. On November 3, 1943, after the material was processed, Waffen-SS, *Einsatzgruppen*, and police battalions shot 42,000 Jews still remaining in the Lublin district and burned their corpses in large open pits.[133]

With the dissolution of the OSTI, the former SS-owned workshops reverted to the DAW. The Warsaw-based textile companies that had processed orders on behalf of the OSTI packed up their makeshift operations in Trawniki and Poniatowa and returned to the city.[134] DAW workshops continued to operate in the General Government until the Red Army drove the Germans out, with Auschwitz serving as the main hub for textile sorting and recycling. Labor continued in the remaining camps until the collapse of the regime. The OSTI's operations illustrate Nazi ideas about zero waste in their most extreme—the root-and-branch extraction of any and all residual value married fantasies about sanitation and cleanliness to the equally total eradication of that from which no more value could be squeezed.

In light of the regime's obsessions with zero waste and total exploitation of resources, it becomes clear that logic and excess were not mutually exclusive categories. By the end of the war, the presence of wastes (from human excrement to ordinary rubbish to piled up corpses) was an everyday feature of camp life but by design. The SS was only concerned with filth once it encroached on the guard facilities, spilled beyond the camp walls, or threatened to decimate the labor force as a result of epidemics. Cruelty underpinned and reinforced the power dynamics inside the camps; arbitrary terror ensured that inmates lived in pain and in constant fear of pain as they performed their grueling tasks.[135] The regime's fanatical obsession with material remainders of every kind offered a rational incentive for working slave laborers beyond exhaustion. The magic of recycling was supposed to close the loop; protect Germans from the experience of privations; transform waste into war material, food, and clothes; and forge lethal force out of nothing but garbage.

PART III
DESTRUCTION

7
Soap Bones

Dimitri Krewoczejew was 19 years old when the German inspectors from the *Reichsstelle* for clothing photographed him. His pants were tied around his waist with a piece of string. His coat, fashioned out of layers of disintegrating garments, was open and draped over his shoulders, revealing a makeshift shirt and a ripped sweater underneath. Standing in front of one of the wooden camp barracks, Krewoczejew squinted slightly. His posture refused to concede defeat, and there was a hint of defiance in his slightly clenched jaw. Like countless others, Dimitri Krewoczejew had been dragged off by German slave hunters. He moved dirt for a Czech company that specialized in earthwork and was one of many subcontractors used by the German mining conglomerate Sudenten Bergbau AG.

In March 1944, Krewoczejew was one of several workers scrutinized by the inspectors sent from Germany to Brüx (Most) in the Protectorate of Bohemia and Moravia to determine the conditions of clothing of *Ostarbeiter*—a derogatory term used to refer to forced foreign laborers from the east. Where Krewoczejew was from and how long he had been at the camp did not concern the inspectors. Instead, they focused on the appearance of his shoes and clothing, for words, they claimed, could not possibly convey the conditions. The inspectors noted that Krewoczejew was known as a "good worker," which is what mattered to the German inspectors.[1]

The men forced to pose for the cameras that day were barely 20 years old and most seem to have been in worse conditions than Krewoczejew. Marian Brzozowksi stood on the snow-covered camp grounds in torn pants and a flimsy shirt without buttons, chest exposed. The *Reichsstelle* identified him as an *Ostarbeiter* and a mine worker who did not own underwear. Unlike Brzozowski and Krewoczejew, many of the other men captured in the report compiled by the *Reichsstelle* remained nameless. Instead, commentary such as "terribly clad *Ostarbeiter*," "impossible footwear," "jacket and pants in dire need of repair," or "work suit is also Sunday's best" were written on the backs of their photographs, punctuated by exclamation marks. The inspectors' report mocked men wrapped in rags, their skin exposed, their bodies worn.[2]

Figure 7.1 Dimitri Krewoczejew was born on April 26, 1924. He was deported for forced labor from an unknown location and praised by the inspectors as a "good worker." He worked as an excavator. Courtesy of Bundesarchiv.

Why did the *Reichsstelle* spend money sending inspectors to compile a report on the clothing of forced laborers? It turns out they were following up on a complaint by the camp director about inadequate clothing, which kept seventy workers away from work for weeks, amounting to about 16,800 lost working hours and significantly reduced output.[3] Those complaints had reached the Regional Economic Office (*Landeswirtschaftsamt*, LWA), which sold used inferior clothing (stolen from murdered Jews or donated by diligent Germans) to forced laborers. The Sudeten Bergbau, which had a workforce of 42,000, more than half of whom were forced laborers housed in camps, had assured officials from Berlin that clothing provided for forced laborers was sufficient.[4] In March 1944, the *Reichsstelle* investigated competing claims, discovered that new provisions had already been sent, and absolved both the Sudeten Bergbau and the LWA from any implied mismanagement.[5]

Figure 7.2 Marian Brzozowksi was born in 1924. Deported for forced labor from an unknown location, Brzozowksi worked as a miner below ground. The inspectors described him as a "good worker" who "doesn't own underwear." Courtesy of Bundesarchiv.

When the representatives from the *Reichsstelle* scrutinized the disheveled appearance of Krewoczejew and Brzozowski, they concluded that the workers themselves were to blame for the conditions of their attire for they "displayed little concern for their own appearance." To underscore this point, the report included photographs of workers who had been reclothed to "prove" that the ragged appearance was a matter of personal "choice" and "carelessness." After all, as photographs like that of Dimitro Pichovicz purported to illustrate, it was possible to fashion clean and functional clothing out of the simplest of materials, such as camp blankets or old garments.[6]

Denying that laborers' destitution was part of a deliberate design, authorities insisted that the workers' race accounted for their "lack of care" and "excessive slovenliness." In the context of wartime shortages, ideas about

Figure 7.3 Dimitro Pichovicz was born in 1924. Deported for forced labor from an unknown location, Pichovicz worked as an excavator. Courtesy of Bundesarchiv.

cleanliness, hygiene, and contamination were remapped onto the bodies of Jews, forced laborers, and Soviet POWs. From the height of the war to the regime's collapse, Germans worked in close proximity to forced laborers and concentration camps prisoners, while blaming them for being contaminated and contagious. As the regime scrutinized the appearance of forced laborers, it restricted soap allocations for occupied and incarcerated populations, who were jammed together in rubbished spaces that were filthy and deadly by design.

In this morbid cycle of labor extraction, war making, and ethnic cleansing, soap was key. Soap not only underpinned German sanitization fantasies, but also played a crucial role in the regime's operations in the occupied eastern territories. While the Germans attempted to extract additional fats for soap production from the occupied lands, they continuously reduced soap allocations for Jews, forced laborers, concentration camp prisoners, and occupied civilians, producing conditions of indescribable filth in the overcrowded ghettos and camps, which they again mobilized as "evidence" for their "innate filthiness." Cleanliness served as a marker of racial purity. The Nazis comfortably operated within the familiar parameters of Western modernity that readily marked the bodies of social and racial others as unclean.[7] However, to meet the cleanliness standards for its own population, they relied on those they maligned as dirty to do society's shit work. The regime forced laborers to hunt for animal bones and mine wastewater for grease to funnel valuable glycerides into soap and detergent production.

Germans recoiled from the stink of war and the "subhuman" people they forced to clean up the German mess. When they encountered labor columns of bedraggled, exhausted, malnourished, and sometimes half-dead prisoners, who were housed in concentration camps, forced labor camps, POW camps, and so-called *Russenlager* (camps for "Russians," routinely deployed as a shorthand for Soviet citizens), Germans found their racial stereotypes confirmed. That filth and squalor were built into the living and working environments of forced laborers, prisoners, and camp inmates was most readily ignored or openly disavowed.

Marking Difference

At the height of the war, with most men at the front and Hitler unwilling to conscript women into the workforce, most labor was performed by forced laborers, most of whom had been transported to Germany from Nazi-occupied Poland and the Soviet territories.[8] To a lesser extent, though still numbering in the hundreds of thousands, other enemy nationals and POWs were forced to work inside the Reich.[9] The regime defined *Ostarbeiter* as members of those "non-German peoples, which were brought to the Reich from the Reich Commissariat Ukraine, the General Commissariat Belarus, or those territories that border on the former free-states of Lithuania, Estonia and Latvia in the east (including the Protectorate of Bohemia and Moravia)." Of the 7.6 million forced laborers in the Reich, 36 percent were Soviet civilians and POWs, and more than half of the civilian workers were women. The second largest contingent, 22 percent of all foreign workers were Polish, with 35 percent of them women.[10]

Polish and Soviet workers were not only the largest contingents of foreign workers, but were also forced into the most excruciating labor and most appalling living conditions, maligned as "dirty," "dangerous," and "subhuman."[11] In the immediate aftermath of the invasion of the Soviet Union, neither Hitler nor the Reich Ministry for Economic Affairs considered bringing Soviet POWs and civilians to Germany for work. In fact, within the first few months, between 3,000 and 4,000 Soviet POWs died daily in hastily assembled POW camps in the occupied east and the General Government from malnutrition, neglect, and disease.

From the earliest days of the invasion of the USSR, POWs and Soviet civilians in general were considered expendable. The POW camps in the German operation zone and inside the Reich indicated the inhumane conditions to which Soviet soldiers were subjected.[12] Hundreds of thousands of men were forced into rudimentary camps, fortified with barbed wire and minimal, if any, protection against the elements; open pits served as latrines. By January 1942, 2 million of the 3.9 million captured soldiers had died.[13] Only in light of the acute and rapidly growing labor shortage inside the Reich did Hitler reconsider his approach to Soviet POWs held captive by the Wehrmacht in October 1941.[14] By the end of 1941, schemes to make use of this " massive human material" were being discussed in Hitler's circle.[15]

The Wehrmacht subsequently forced endless columns of half-dead and dying POWs to march on foot into "reward" territory.[16] By March 1942, the regime started to capture large numbers of Soviet civilians and deported them to Germany for work.[17] By April, Plenipotentiary for Labor Fritz Sauckel insisted on the rapid delivery of roughly 1.5 million people fit for work. The extraction of workers from Soviet territory peaked that year. The Death's Head Units and police formations combined genocidal violence against civilians and so-called anti-partisan warfare with slave hunts, and military personnel indiscriminately grabbed people and loaded them onto trucks bound for the Reich.[18] Methods grew ever more brutal and reckless once the fortunes of the war turned. In early 1943, Sauckel set daily quotas, and the army, together with police formations, dragged off entire families of farmers and agricultural laborers. The Germans even snatched children as young as 10 and 12 years old.[19]

POWs were to be worked around the clock in two shifts, expanding the capacity of any given industrial facility while saving raw materials. When it came to foreign labor, Nazi race thinking informed the working conditions and remuneration that workers received. *Ostarbeiter* found themselves at the bottom of the racial hierarchy, together with "Gypsies" and, of course, Jews.[20] Both Soviet POWs and civilian workers were forced en masse into agriculture, road construction, mining, and earthworks.

In so-called *Russenlager*, laborers were forced to live in dugouts in the damp earth or makeshift wooden constructions. They received next to nothing in exchange for excruciating labor.[21] Yet, they had to use part of their meager compensation to pay for "accommodations" and "provisions" parceled out by the camp authorities. After deductions, which included the *Ostarbeiter* levy and expenses for housing and meals in the camps, most of the workers only had a few marks left and could not afford to purchase workclothes, sanitary products, or materials needed for repairs of clothing and equipment.[22] The *Landeswirtschaftsämter* (LWA) or regional economic offices provided companies with supplies of "*Ostarbeiter* clothing," which they, in turn, sold to their slave-labor force.[23] However, since wages were so low, workers were still not able to afford the required clothing without loans from their employers. Employers were reluctant to offer advances on wages or give credit, until workers proved their "reliability" over a 2–3 months' probationary period. If forced laborers were dismissed because of inadequate clothing, sickness, or exhaustion, they were still required to pay the camp authorities for food and lodging, and thus incurred more debt toward which subsequent wages were applied before workers could purchase clothing, medicine, or additional food.[24]

Alerted to difficulties with clothing provisions in Braunschweig by the city's minister of finance, the Brunswick Institute for Economic Research (*Braunschweigisches Institut für Wirtschaftsforschung*, BIWF) decided to survey the state of "*Ostarbeiter* clothing" and its effect on the production process in 1944. The BIWF surveyed 2,044 men and 2,175 women who worked for 15 different Braunschweiger companies. The scientists explained the retardation of production as a result of the proximity between Germans and foreign workers. Since most Germans did not want to work side by side the "disinfected but nonetheless with vermin infested [people] dressed in reeking clothes," the BIWF set out to examine the actual clothing conditions "solely under the premise of guaranteeing the greatest possible productivity," explicitly noting that the study was not undertaken out of humanitarian concern for the workers.[25] The "research" found that over 90 percent of *Ostarbeiter* did not have shoes or socks, more than 80 percent had neither coats nor jackets, and barely 10 percent owned underwear. Apparently, out of consideration for the hygienic sensibilities of German workers, companies increased the distance between German and foreign workers. Germans interpreted such reassignments as "favors" to forced laborers. They complained that they were burdened with the brunt of the workload and forced laborers were assigned to auxiliary tasks, reinforcing the stereotypes of eastern workers as lazy.[26]

The recommendations derived from this research confirmed the racist assumptions of the BIWF and their business partners, and demonstrated their willful ignorance of actual conditions. Several companies suggested that Soviet workers be instructed to have relatives send clothing, despite most having neither clothes nor relatives left back home. Internal collections of secondary textiles among employees were unsuccessful since Germans were unwilling to share with forced laborers, nor were they to be provisioned out of the clothing supplies reserved for Germans. The BIWF insisted that "the *Ostarbeiter* mustn't be measured according to German standards." Instead, the report concluded that given the harsher climatic conditions in the Soviet Union, *Ostarbeiter* had habituated to chronic want and simply needed less than their German counterparts. Germans readily invested in these fantastical justifications for neglect. Only individuals who worked in food and related industries or in close physical proximity to Germans, the BIWF insisted, should receive adequate clothing to protect the German food supply from "contamination" and to respect German standards of cleanliness and decorum in the workplace.[27] German companies, whether they could avail themselves of services such as those provided by the BIWF or not, universally decried workers from the east as lazy, dirty, and incompetent.[28]

Similarly, Oswald Pohl, recognizing the debilitating effects on output in Germany's concentration camps due to poor provisions and inadequate clothing for prisons, offered to reward ingenuity for "practical designs for all kinds of heat-protective clothing."[29] A year later, the regime conducted inspections of the major concentration camps to ensure that incidents of "excessive" use of clothing by prisoners would not proliferate, noting that prisoners wore multiple layers of clothing. In light of an "extremely critical situation in textile provisioning," the SS-WVHA investigated numerous cases at Auschwitz where prisoners were discovered wearing "two sets of underwear" and, with few exceptions, "two sets of outerwear," concluding that "the amount of clothing worn by the individual prisoner far exceeds the normal target."[30] Inspectors reported both instances of "excess" as well as cases in which prisoners were unable to report for work due to inadequate shoes and clothing. Unwilling to address shortages in any meaningful way, the SS zeroed in on instances of "sabotage," alleging that prisoners treated their clothing carelessly or deliberately destroyed them to be excused from work.[31]

Ordinary Germans likewise felt little sympathy for Soviet POWs and civilian forced laborers. In response to measures that extended additional rations for heavy labor to eastern workers, official reports noted that Germans not only objected but also expressed bewilderment and rage over measures that "fatten Russians inside the Reich, while our own racial comrades are maimed and murdered in battle."[32] In reality, the opposite was the case.[33] The Wehrmacht subjected captives to deliberate policies of starvation, neglect, and abuse. When German citizens argued that "Russians should only be fed just enough so as not to starve," they were, in fact, expressing a desire that had long been official policy toward forced laborers in the Reich.[34]

Standing in line for basic items, clamoring for extra sugar rations, harvesting tobacco from cigarette butts, and fantasizing about pork roast while waiting out air raid sirens in the bomb shelter, Germans failed to appreciate the structural differences between their own experiences of wartime deprivation and the hollowed out existence of the forced laborers and concentration camp prisoners in their midst. Priding themselves on their maintenance of standards of respectability and immaculate cleanliness, they read the disheveled appearance of forced laborers and camp inmates through the lens afforded by Nazi racism.

Proximity to forced laborers did not turn ordinary Germans into genocidal killers, but it hardened their resentment and sense of superiority, shoring up implicit support for Hitler's war of extermination.[35] To most Germans, whether military personnel, administrators, or ordinary citizens, it did not matter whether forced laborers were civilians or POWs, male or female. In their eyes, Jews crammed into ghettos and workers interned in forced labor and POW camps merged into an expanding category of "subhumans," regardless of Nazi doctrine belaboring the differing racial characteristics of Jews and Slavs. Access to soap and clean clothing coded racial hierarchies as unmistakably as if marked by color.

Imperial Soap Economy

Soap was crucial to both distance and proximity, grounding German performances of superiority in rituals of cleanliness. But soap was in exceedingly short supply. Prior to the war, Germany had imported large amounts of oils and fats to produce machine grease, industrial lubricants, technical fats, soap, and detergents, but increasingly stressed the need for internal fat recovery from waste and wastewater. Peacetime efforts focused first on bones, which long played a role in soap production, and the regime incentivized the processing of bones from slaughterhouses and industrial kitchens.[36] Quantities of technical fats extracted from bones increased moderately but consistently over the first few years after the Nazis took power, peaking at 13,830 tons in 1938. Over the course of the war, the production of bone fat declined as meat consumption decreased and labor shortages grew.[37] Nonetheless, fats extracted from bones continued to play an important role even after 1940 and the regime incentivized bone collections in schools, despite the complaints by parents and teachers about the insufferable stench, vermin, and possible adverse health effects.[38] Campaigns only intensified due to wartime import-related difficulties and foreign currency shortages. As with other collections, the zeal of students and Hitler Youths was greater than the regime's ability to transport and process the material. Accordingly, particularly in rural areas, locals complained about "the unbearable stench" with which rotting matter, particularly decaying bones, "polluted the surroundings."[39]

In parallel to ramping up bone collections, the Germans targeted other sources for the recovery of fats. Starting in 1936, the regime embarked on a more comprehensive mission of extracting oils and fats from waste products. Until then, fats recovered from drain grease, sieve grease, grease sludge, sewage sludge, food scraps, and kitchen grease from food-processing establishments such as hotels, restaurants, military barracks and hospitals, and other grease-containing wastes remained negligible. In 1936, only 260 tons of fats were recovered in this fashion, but by the end of 1939, the Reich extracted almost 10 times the amount of fats from wastes, sludge, and wastewater. In 1940, the regime decreed the mandatory installation of fat skimmers in slaughterhouses; meat-processing facilities; and industrial kitchens in hotels, restaurants, hospitals, military barracks, sanatoria, orphanages, prisons, and concentration camps.[40]

Up until this point, the installation of fat skimmers had been part of general efforts to remove animal products from the wastewater of cadaver-processing plants and slaughterhouses to prevent the contamination of rivers and streams and the clogging of drains with grease and animal parts.[41] The main concern had pertained to the immense stench that emanated from untreated wastewater, containing large amounts of blood, skin, intestines, feces, and animal proteins. With growing wartime shortages, the focus shifted toward the liquid gold captured by skimmers in the form of sludge. Legislators also expressed concerns for the proper and timely cleaning of the fat skimmers since sludge blackened over time, leaving grease unusable for the recovery of fats.[42]

Territorial expansion immediately caused a soap problem. The *Reichsstelle* for industrial fats (*Reichsstelle für industrielle Fettversorgung*, RIF) centrally managed the fat economy and determined the resources allocated for soap and detergent production.[43] Questions of soap allocations for occupied Poland was a concern even before the Nazi authorities had decided on administrative structures. Prior to the war, independent Poland had imported roughly 70 percent of technical and industrial fats; by mid-September 1939, planners were already insisting that the Poles could not receive more than the Germans inside the Reich.[44] Estimating that 35 million inhabitants had used roughly 55,000 tons of soap and detergents in 1938, the Reich's local soap expert, Hermann Rigele from the Schicht-Lever AG in Warsaw, suggested the launch of a uniform house laundry soap, rather than the separate toilet soap and laundry detergent customary in Germany.[45] The "backward" rural population, the experts reasoned, were not accustomed to washing their laundry with powdered detergents but soaped it in rivers and streams.[46] Rigele, presumably an ethnic German, estimated a much lower overall use of soap products by the Polish population, venturing "that they would barely notice a difference" if they received slightly higher allocations of less potent soap with a lower fat content.[47]

By the end of 1939, western Polish territories had been incorporated into the Reich, and racial categories were being used to reconfigure soap allocations for the General Government. On February 1, 1940, the Reich released the Soap Ordinance for the General Government.[48] Soap allocations followed medical-police minimums for the roughly 13 million Poles and Jews, whereas the German military administration and the remaining ethnic German population, together roughly 1 million people, received soap rations comparable to those existing within the Reich.[49] Occupied Poland, again, was a testing ground. Local administrators justified their requests for fat subsidies from Germany because of "the significant risk of epidemics due to the infestation of the population with lice and bugs."[50] At the same time, the Reich made it illegal for Polish and Jewish households to produce their own soap from grease and tallow extracted from kitchen scraps and soup bones.[51]

Similarly, the ordinance forbade the use of any fats for soap making that could be used for human nutrition, establishing a clear hierarchy of needs that privileged labor power over hygiene.[52]

Initial calculations estimated that 14,000 tons of fats and oils would have to be imported from Germany for soap and detergent production in the seven existing soap factories to prevent the outbreak of epidemics.[53] To mitigate the pressures on supply, the governor-general diminished allocations for Jews and Poles, by calculating and distributing soap rations not per head but per family. More drastic cuts, Governor Hans Frank argued, would constitute a public health emergency since "only an adequate supply of soap can reduce the risk of typhus and dysentery caused by the filth contamination and lice infestation of the population."[54] The following month, however, the Reich minister for economic affairs insisted that fat allocations could be further reduced, ignoring the cautionary remarks about the constant increases in population of the General Government as the Germans forcibly resettled Jews, Roma, and Poles there.[55] Nonetheless, soap allotments continued to drop. Within the first three years of the war, the imperial overlords slashed fat allocations for soap production to just over 20 percent of the already stingy initial allotments of 1939.[56]

At the same time, planners inside the General Government ramped up the hunt for fats and grease from waste products. The suggested venues were labor-intensive and dirty, and the expected yield limited. Nonetheless, fats were actively recovered from the stewing of dead animals in animal cadaver–processing plants; the extraction of oils from animal claws; the comprehensive collection of all animal bones from households and industrial kitchens, slaughterhouses, meat-processing plants, and garbage dumps; and the mining of wastewater.[57] By the end of October 1941, the yield from waste and animal cadavers was 81 tons of fats. The representatives of the *Reichsstelle* speculated that perhaps production could be increased if soap bonuses were handed out to the manufacturers directly.[58]

In Latvia, the recovery of fats from waste products had been undertaken before the war. Paul Kore, who founded a company for the "utilization of the worthless" based on German principles, offered his services to the Germans once they occupied the country in 1941. He managed fifteen different locations where workers mined garbage dumps for bones and other recyclables. Kore rejected the Nazi suggestion of forcing Jews to do this kind of work because he felt an obligation to keep his current staff employed.[59] The report to the *Reichsstelle* noted that 50 tons of old rubber shoes, roughly 500 tons of sorted and unsorted rags, 200 tons of wastepaper, and 50 tons of fresh bones were "immediately available." But transport from rural areas could not be secured, and the railway authorities refused to accept bone shipments.[60]

A report for the *Ostland* from August 1941 insisted on the necessity of exploiting wastes to the fullest extent. The soap expert for Latvia estimated that carcass and bone processing alone could "cover 50 percent of the soap industry's demand for fats."[61] In Ukraine, too, German industrial scouts found that "Ukrainians are very resourceful when it comes to innovating raw materials for soap production." They further reported that small enterprises extracted fats from all kinds of substances, including used machine oil, rancid nutritional fats like cooking oil and kitchen grease, and even rotten eggs and cheese.[62] Whatever local ingenuity the Reich's representatives discovered in Soviet territory, the fact remained that it was impossible to satisfy even the most rudimentary needs using fats extracted and reclaimed locally. The regime didn't bother calculating soap allocations for the occupied Soviet territories. For the General Government, the Reich opted for further reductions and transitioned to powdered detergents, which required less fat content to be effective. However, the *Reichsstelle* for paper and packaging refused to deliver the necessary packaging material. In the end, the only feasible solution was to further cut soap and detergent allocations for Jews and Poles.[63]

In 1942, the *Reichsstelle* for chemical industries estimated that a total of 540,000 tons of bones accrued from animal processing inside Germany. But more than half of this amount was used as animal feed or otherwise escaped the Reich's recycling efforts for fat recovery. In December 1943, the Reich's bone collections amassed almost 5.5 million kilos of bones in all of the territories controlled by the Nazi regime, 1.2 million kilos of which were extracted from the eastern territories.[64] This kind of collection frenzy did not stop at bones. Over the course of the war, the RIF began to extract fats from skins, wool, claws, and already processed animal matter.[65] The RIF had looked toward *Hautkratzfett* (literally, "skin-scratch fat") from pigskins used for leather manufacturing as early as 1940, but started to aggressively expand its targets as the war progressed.[66] By 1942, the RIF began to work with a number of carcass-processing companies in the General Government and the Reich to retroactively extract the remaining fats from carcass meal and cake after research determined those products still contained 8–12 percent of fats.[67] By 1944, the matter suddenly became urgent according to the *Reichsstelle*.[68] In July 1944, a total of almost 105 tons of fat extracted in this way was shipped to soap and detergent manufacturers, but this amount was a mere drop in the bucket.[69]

The extraction of fats from animal claws followed a similar trajectory. While secondary materials traders in Germany refused to collect various kinds of animal wastes such as claws and horns as uneconomical, the pressures of war shifted priorities to include those wastes.[70] By the end of 1942, the guild association of butchers issued a circular calling for the collection of *Knochensägespäne* (literally, "bone saw dust").[71] Such ludicrous suggestions illustrate the urgency with which Ungewitter's principle of the "utilization of the worthless" was making the rounds. In 1943, the Reich harvested 2,236,689 kilograms of *Klauenöl* (oil extracted from animal claws and hooves) in a desperate attempt to recover fats needed for soap production.[72] Ultimately, the accumulation of decaying matter from sewage sludge to animal parts and kitchen bones only heightened the urgency with which Nazi purification fantasies spurred on the mining of wastes.

Alongside stepped up campaigns for fat recovery, the RIF, which was renamed the *Reichsstelle* for industrial fats and detergents (Reichsstelle für industrielle Fette und Waschmittel) in 1942, conducted a number of experiments with leaders in the detergent industry and the German Women's Work (*Deutsches Frauenwerk*, DFW) to lower the fat content in soap and laundry detergent without sacrificing potency.[73] By 1943, detergent consumption was astronomical. Calculating production on the basis of 110 million detergent users—a number that included the public sector; the Wehrmacht; forced laborers and POWs; and individual consumers inside the so-called old Reich, East Prussia, the *Ostmark* (formerly Austria), and the Protectorate of Bohemia and Moravia—the Reich needed to produce 31,800 tons of RIF detergent per month to satisfy the most basic demands.[74] At 20 percent fat content, detergent manufacturing alone required 6,360 metric tons of fats per month. By comparison, the combined yield of fat recovery from wastewater and bones amounted to 7,939 metric tons of fats over the course of the entire year of 1942.[75]

Fat was not the only raw material that was in short supply. Severe shortages of soda as well as packaging material for the 30,300 metric tons of detergent budgeted monthly only caused further headaches for the RIF.[76] As transports of Jews to killing centers in Nazi-occupied Poland from central and western European countries increased dramatically over the course of 1942 and expanded to include deportations from within the occupied east and states within the German sphere of influence, the demand for detergent escalated because the clothes of the murdered Jews all needed to be washed.[77]

Rubbished Spaces

While the Nazi regime hunted after fats in order to maintain its standards for cleanliness, it actively forged squalid environments for the very people on whose labor it depended. At the height of the war, dearth, filth, and death marked environments in Germany and across Nazi-occupied Europe. Nowhere was this more pronounced than in the many camps and ghettos operated by the SS. The Nazi camps were designed as rubbished spaces. People were crammed into crowded conditions. Occupancy was determined by the dual desire for labor extraction and the removal of unwanted populations, not by the limits of capacity.

In a regime obsessed with cleansing and cleanliness, one would assume that waste and sanitation infrastructure would have figured centrally in the planning of camps, but this was not the case. The surviving records make little mention of sanitary and waste infrastructures, and even the records of the Central Building Office of the Waffen-SS do not reflect concerns about sanitation until much later in the war.[78] Official plans as well as reconstructions by survivors merely note the locations of latrines and washrooms.[79] Even camps designed to hold tens of thousands of prisoners had insufficient facilities that were rudimentary pits housed in makeshift structures. Most camps were not connected to sewer systems or only retroactively.[80] Instead, they relied on penal labor details, such as *Scheisskommandos* (shit squads) or *Jauchefahrer* (cesspool drivers) to empty the overflowing latrines and pits, cart excrement beyond the camp walls, or dig rudimentary drainage systems that discharged into adjacent watersheds.[81]

In Dachau, the very first camp established in March 1933, a dysentery outbreak triggered the process for the replacement of the open pit that served the roughly 500 inmates who worked in the SS sweatshops in April 1934.[82] By January 1937, the Bavarian Ministry of the Interior approved 20,000 RM for the construction of a lavatory and disinfecting facility. Instead of connecting the new facilities to the sewer system, the designer envisioned a cement-coded cesspool into which water closets and urinals flushed excrement, to be emptied by the usual *Scheisskommandos*.[83]

As if to make up for the absence of sanitation infrastructure, the SS plastered camps and ghettos with exhortations about personal hygiene and cleanliness. Coping with an acute water shortage almost immediately after the establishment of Buchenwald concentration camp in 1937, the camp administration rationed drinking water for prisoners and made personal hygiene all but impossible.[84] Regardless of lack of available water or sanitary facilities, guards ensured that cleaning tasks performed by prisoners were executed with the utmost care, leaving not a particle of dust behind.[85]

At times, fanaticism about cleanliness took on murderous forms. Jan Pstross, a former prisoner at Mauthausen, detailed the tortures endured by sick prisoners who accidentally soiled their beds as typhus and other epidemics raged. As punishment, such prisoners were placed naked on the concrete floor and hosed off with ice-cold water or placed in barrels filled with ice water, which often resulted in immediate death.[86] The camp doctor at Buchenwald wrote to the commandant and demanded that Kapos force those inmates who wet their beds to sleep in the outhouses.[87]

Bergen-Belsen's outhouses were in a wooden shack behind the cobbler's barracks. In spite of the "cleverly designed ventilation" in the form of a horizontal opening along the length of the shack and the absence of doors, the stench was mind-numbing, according to Alexander Roseboom, who worked for the *Latrinenkommando* (latrine squad) as a de-clogging specialist. With the aid of a hook on a long wooden pole and a bucket, Roseboom was opening up the small drainage channel.[88] Waste removal was equally makeshift. Josef Klatt, who worked for the garbage collection commando at Mauthausen, was charged with "stacking the rubbish" on a number of disposal sites beyond the camp walls. Klatt recalled that the garbage heaps were continuously ablaze.[89]

As wartime mortality dramatically increased in Germany's concentration camps, questions about the removal of corpses were chief among the commandants' infrastructural concerns. Convenience, efficiency, and cleanliness was important when designing cremation furnaces for the crematoria. For 7,753 RM, Mauthausen could purchase a "coke-fired pot cremation furnace with double muffle and compressed air system" that included two "wrought iron ash pans" and a "wrought iron corpse introduction device."[90] During the war, the infrastructure for the removal of corpses rapidly reached capacity, even with such state-of-the-art equipment. As part of his job, Klatt had to make a stop at the crematorium, where the workers put out the bones that had not properly burned:

Sometimes we ground them. There was a bone mill. Because they had—when there was a big rush, they burned five, six corpses at once and then only the flesh burned and the bones remained. And there was a little mill, just a small mill, I don't know what it was for, grain or I don't know. But it spit out little pieces, approximately a centimeter by a centimeter.[91]

Prisoners then loaded the ground-up bones onto a cart and dumped them with the rest of the rubbish onto the smoldering piles.

As camp populations exploded, the sanitary conditions, especially in hastily constructed, makeshift subsidiary camps, only worsened. In a satellite camp of Buchenwald at Tröglitz, the SS doctor described the facilities for even the SS troops as "primitive":

> The large lavatory rests under the open skies; corrugated iron serves as a privacy fence. However, the outflow of this lavatory is unsatisfactory. [The lavatory] finds itself on a slope, at the bottom of which an approximately 100 square meter large pond has formed, which was expected to gradually seep into the ground. The depth of this pond could not be determined. Another malady results from the fact that initially kitchen garbage such as potato peelings, vegetable scraps and so forth were also poured into or around this pond. The commanding officer's attention was urgently drawn to this nuisance, which could quickly lead to outbreaks of epidemics and must be remedied.[92]

The doctor bemoaned the fact that vermin and an insufferable stench disturbed the SS troops, whose quarters were located near the pond, but they were less affected by the outhouses for prisoners since those were located on the other end of the camp. Despite being regularly doused with chlorinated lime, the cleanliness of the latrines, in the doctor's opinion, "left much to be desired."[93] However, the most pressing problem, which apparently prompted the inspection in the first place, was the fuel shortage that hindered the regular transport of corpses and their incineration at the crematoria in Gleina, a town more than 50 kilometers from the camp.[94]

In the Nazi-occupied east, conditions were infinitely worse. In addition to the existing ghettos, labor, and concentration camps, the Wehrmacht channeled hundreds of thousands of Soviet POWs into General Government, 100,000 of whom the army agreed to surrender to Himmler's authority in September 1941.[95] Essentially, the arrival of POWs shifted the existing pressures from "too few laborers" to "too many eaters," prompting the deliberate neglect and even starvation of POWs and the systematic evacuation of Jews from ghettos to killing centers constructed in the late fall of 1941 and throughout the spring of 1942.[96] Neither the initial extermination camps (Bełżec, Sobibor, and Treblinka) nor the *Durchgangslager* (transit camps) nor POW camps were built to last; they were sites of disposal and temporary containment—hence, the haste in their planning and the makeshift character of their construction.

Given the horrendous conditions in POW camps and the deliberate mass murder in the Reinhard camps, the main concern was not the proper drainage of excrement, soap provisions, or clean drinking water, but the disposal of corpses.[97] Initially, even at killing centers such as Chelmno, Bełżec, Sobibor, Treblinka, and Auschwitz, the bodies of the murdered victims (whether killed by bullet or gas) were buried in large mass graves. The "hygiene problem" first manifested in Chelmno in the spring of 1942, causing panic about the potential outbreak of epidemics.[98] Accordingly, the Nazis began to experiment with the mass burning of previously buried and "unearthed" corpses, a practice that spread to other camps.[99] By the fall of 1942, *Sonderkommandos* were forced to dig up previously buried corpses and burn them atop giant pyres.[100] Bodies continued to be burned in open pits or pyres constructed of railroad sleepers at Bełżec, Sobibor, and Treblinka, even as the SS moved toward installing permanent crematoria at Auschwitz-Birkenau and Kriegsgefangenenlager Lublin or KGL Lublin (POW Camp Lublin, also known as Majdanek).[101]

By the late fall 1941, the SS had pushed the construction of a POW camp in Lublin and began the expansion of the concentration camp Auschwitz at Birkenau, as the Wehrmacht captured millions of Soviet POWs.[102] Envisioned as more permanent structures, both camps served strategic purposes before they were transformed into combined labor and death camps. Auschwitz farmed out inmates to work in agriculture, mining, or manufacturing. German companies, like Krupp and the chemical conglomerate I.G. Farben, sited factories there. At Auschwitz Monowitz, I.G. Farben's Buna plant drew on camp labor to produce synthetic rubber.[103] After Himmler resolved in the summer of 1942 that the existing killing centers did not have the capacity to accomplish the destruction of Jews envisioned on a European scale, Auschwitz-Birkenau and KGL Lublin were expanded into killing facilities.[104]

KGL Lublin was supposed to be built by POWs, but the arriving prisoners were in such "catastrophic physical condition that effective labor is out of the question, at least initially" the authorities conceded.[105] The construction therefore had to draw on concentration camp prisoners, mainly Jews, along with civilian forced laborers.[106] Since the camp was envisioned to eventually accommodate 50,000 to 150,000 prisoners but located only 2 kilometers from the city of Lublin proper, the SS planners negotiated with city administrators to tap into existing infrastructures—particularly for electricity, freshwater supply, and storm- and wastewater drainage.[107] In exchange, they offered to expand the existing wastewater treatment plant and build a *Faulgasverwertungsanlage*, a sewage sludge gasification plant with energy recovery to provide the electricity for the expansion of the wastewater treatment plant and allow for experimentation with *Faulgas* (literally "rotten gas," chemical methane) as fuel for trucks.[108] The SS envisioned the camp operating for at least five to ten years, at which point the sewage gasification plant would become the property of the city of Lublin.[109]

However, little of these plans came to pass. Himmler overrode Governor Hans Frank's objection to the construction of the camp, but the scheme was foiled by shortages of important building materials.[110] The storm-and wastewater drainage was eventually completed and connected to the city's sewer system, but the misaligned diameters of the pipes led to flooding of factory basements in 1943.[111] Neither the expansion of the wastewater treatment plant nor the sewage gasification plant were ever completed.

These ambitious infrastructural projects were never conceived with the camp inmates in mind. Instead, the SS intended for them to benefit a postwar SS housing development supported by a constant population of 50,000 camp inmates that would staff larger SS workshops.[112] Himmler's fantastical ideas about the "New Order" of settler colonialism German-style included settlements ranging from farmsteads to towns that utilized modern technology to cultivate the land and support large numbers of racially valuable German families.[113] Lublin was supposed to provide the slave-labor reservoir on the edges of the Reich's "defensive frontier" from where the processes of SS-style colonization of the east were to commence.[114]

The facilities at the Lublin camp were anything but modern, however. Concrete pits served as latrines. The construction of a drainage system that would allow for the wastewater to be treated and emptied into the Weichsel River was halted due to freezing temperatures. Initially, no provisions were made for cleaning prisoner clothing, and later authorities had to vie for soap and detergent allocations.[115] The building plans for KGL Lublin focused on a disinfection facility and an industrial laundry to sanitize and wash clothing to be recycled in the SS textile workshops, delousing facilities, a mortuary, crematoria, and various workshops and storage facilities for reworked goods.[116] In addition, horse stables were to be repurposed as accommodations for prisoners. While there was talk of flush toilets and wash basins inside those barracks, they never materialized and were not intended to replace the "emergency latrines." The "emergency latrines"—large barracks containing four continuous communal pit toilets with a total of eighty-four back-to-back "seat holes" divided among four wooden benches—served roughly 5,000 Jews.[117]

Instead of running water, three shallow bore holes provided the only water supply for thousands of inmates. Only one was designated as a source of drinking water, which, in turn, had to be carried to the barracks in buckets. When the Hygienic Institute of the Waffen-SS took water samples and assembled its report, it found "intestinal bacteria," particularly *E. coli*, as well as other pathogens and contaminants, among them ammonia.[118] By February 1943, the shortage of potable water had still not been resolved.[119] The rudimentary washrooms, mere troughs for washing, were still under construction, too. Commandant Herman Florsted took the delay as an occasion to speculate about the sense of locating the washrooms as planned. Since they were supposed to be roughly 300 meters from the barrack, Florsted argued, "[G]iven that the camp inmates already had an innate aversion to water, this solution would not achieve the desired goal of keeping the prisoners clean." He therefore urged for latrines with simple washbasins to be designed within the barracks.[120] In fact, there was neither clean water nor soap nor detergent, and the only hygiene process for both prisoners at KGL Lublin and their clothing was to funnel fully dressed prisoners through the disinfection barrack.[121] In addition to raw material shortages, KGL Lublin had to grapple with the effects that chronic malnutrition, exertion, and epidemics had on the slave-labor force not yet slated for extermination.

Warnings about lice and admonitions about handwashing graced the walls of the washroom at Auschwitz. Himmler repeatedly reminded SS personnel that "it is strictly forbidden to take water from the water pipes and wells" in the *Lager*. The camp administration was well aware that the water was unsafe to drink unless boiled.[122] The placards displayed in the camp nonetheless insisted that washing saved inmates from certain death, while those who were unclean were doomed.[123] As Primo Levi wrote:

> The rites to be carried out were infinite and senseless: every morning one had to make the "bed" perfectly flat and smooth; smear one's muddy and repellent wooden shoes with the appropriate machine grease, scrape the mud stains off one's clothes (paint, grease, and rust-stains were, however, permitted); in the evening one had to undergo the control for lice and the control of washing one's feet; on Saturday, have one's beard and hair shaved; mend or have mended one's rags; on Sunday undergo the general control for skin diseases and the control of buttons on one's jacket, which had to be five.[124]

Illustrating the ludicrousness of these rules, Levi causally refers to an additional cleanliness requirement that Himmler decreed in August 1942, for Jews specifically—namely, "the daily washing of feet." In Himmler's "experience," the washing of feet had apparently resulted in fewer cases of illness and in increased performance. Himmler failed to elaborate whether or not such benefits would accrue to non-Jews as well.[125] Clearly, these rules were instruments of torture and humiliation, rather than hygienic measures.

Thinking the Soap Cycle

In the context of industrial mass murder, the squalid conditions in ghettos and camps, and the simultaneous German fanaticism about cleanliness, congealed into assumptions that were both mistaken and yet made "sense" within the parameters established by the Nazi waste regime. Given the exorbitant amount of textiles that were harvested from the bodies of the victims, the factories for labor extraction and mass murder further increased the Reich's voracious need for soap and detergents. It is perhaps unsurprising that survivors and liberating Allies readily misinterpreted the RIF abbreviation printed on the standardized soap bars (*Einheitsseife*) and detergent packages as *reines Judenfett* or "pure Jew fat."[126] Survivor testimonies illustrate that prisoners believed the Nazis used bones and tallow seeping from corpses for the production of soap. By 1942, Rabbi Stephen S. Wise suspected that the corpses of those dragged off from the Warsaw ghetto would be processed, factory-style, into soap and fertilizer.[127] Even SS personnel thought in terms of a soap cycle.[128] The doctor onsite in Stutthof, Siegfried Schwela, gave a lot of thought to "the 'better' utilization of the 'material' [corpses] that had been accumulating since the spring of 1942" and apparently shared his musings with Rudolf Höss, the Auschwitz commandant.[129] Höss, however, showed no interest. Nonetheless, such rumors prompted Himmler to insist on guarantees "that in every place the bodies of these deceased Jews be either burned or buried" and prohibited any form of "abuse."[130]

Starting in the spring of 1942, the regime decided to obliterate all physical traces of the mass extermination of Europe's Jews and other vilified groups.[131] The Reinhard camps, together with the countless sites of mass murder of entire communities, villages, and towns, and even Auschwitz, the iconic symbol of Holocaust, all started with the crudest methods of disposal. The SS apparently had not given much thought to the matter. Initially, the bodies of the victims were dumped, sometimes meticulously stacked into mass graves. In the killing centers, these mass graves were often adjacent to or even on the grounds of the camp complex itself. By the end of the summer of 1942, the killing centers switched to a system of burning corpses, initially on stakes constructed from railroads sleepers and in dugouts in the ground, and eventually in professionally constructed crematoria. The SS further forced the *Sonderkommandos* to grind up bones and disperse the ashes.[132]

This shift toward secrecy and erasure was partially the result of an increasingly global war and its turning fortunes.[133] But at least as important were the environmental effects of tens of thousands, sometimes hundreds of thousands, rotting corpses. The contamination explains the urgency with which changes to the disposal mechanisms and technologies were implemented in those areas where the Nazis' murdering presence continued or even attempted "development." It forced the killers to realize that burying the dead didn't mean they were gone, not even temporarily. A mere change in the seasons spread a revolting stench that penetrated the air for miles.[134] Warmer temperatures further optimized the bacterial growth required for decomposition. As the corpses heated up and swelled, the earth cracked and spit out the dead. Erko Hejblom, a survivor of Auschwitz, explained, "We would have needed gas masks. The corpses seemed to rise out of the ground, it was as if the earth itself was rejecting them."[135] The decomposing bodies poisoned groundwater, attracted vermin, and destabilized the area's ability to withstand heavy rains, erosion, and soil settlement.[136] The fly and vermin infestation was so grave that Himmler instituted regular garbage collection at Auschwitz in February 1943.[137]

Most survivors had smelled the smells of rotting and burning flesh and lived in environments saturated by smoke and ash, but few had intimate experience with the processing of the dead. Those were tasks exclusively assigned to the *Sonderkommandos*. Prisoners were, however, all too familiar with the exhortations about "utilization" of any and all waste materials. Accordingly, they could readily imagine the stewing of human corpses in large vats as a means to extract fat for soap production as a logical solution to the extreme shortages of fats. But Nazism did not cross the species boundaries in the ways the dehumanizing language of propaganda would suggest. In fact, in the summer of 1942, just when the SS began to exhume mass graves at the extermination camps and burn the decomposing corpses, the Reich forbid the burning of animal bones.[138] The *Knochenvernichtungsverbot* (prohibition on the destruction of bones) was decreed in the interest of increasing fat recovery; however, it did not apply to human bones.[139] No matter the hateful speech of Hitler likening Jews to pests or the propaganda tracts produced by Fritz Hippler comparing Jews to rats, neither the army, nor the SS and the police forces who perpetrated the Nazi genocide, saw the Jews as anything other than human.[140] The Nazis willfully and deliberately murdered people, and they buried and burned their bones.

8
Bombed Out and Trashed In

In April 1944, the Experimental and Research Institute and Technical University for Horticulture in Pillnitz, a small town southeast of Dresden, conducted experiments on the odor-blocking effects of rock powder. Utilizing "fecal matter from the office" that contained "solid and liquid components and constituted a papescent mass, rather than liquid," the Institute tested the effects of various kinds of materials that might be used to cover the human waste accumulating in dry outhouses. In its initial experiment, the Institute compared two types of rock powder derived from basalt and phonolite, respectively. Mixing the rock powder with fecal matter revealed that alkaloid powder enhanced rather than blocked the odor of fecal matter, an anticipated result. Since the experiment demonstrated that basalt-meal did not have the same odor-enhancing properties, a second round of experiments compared the effect of rock powder to peat moss. This time, the powder was scattered on top of the fecal matter rather than mixed in. After two days, the containers were examined and the emitted odors recorded and compared. Unsurprisingly, the uncovered feces emitted a "very strong, revolting odor." The feces layered with peat moss alone still emitted a "faint, cloying odor," whereas one could "hardly detect an odor" when the fecal matter had been layered with either basalt-meal or with the mixture of peat moss and basalt-meal.[1]

The experiment was then repeated, testing four additional covers in comparison to the initial experimental groups: soil, phonolite, a mixture of soil and phonolite, and a mixture of soil and peat moss. The results again confirmed that uncovered fecal matter emitted a "nauseating" stench, whereas various covers all had a beneficial, odor-mitigating effect, with regular dirt (soil) being the most effective and pure rock powder still allowing a "faint smell" to escape. The nature of the material used for cover mattered little, with the exception of regular soil, which trapped odor most effectively. Accordingly, the Institute made the recommendation "to add peat moss to absorb the liquid parts and to cover them with dry, crumbly soil to prevent

Empire of Rags and Bones. Anne Berg, Oxford University Press. © Oxford University Press 2024.
DOI: 10.1093/oso/9780197744000.003.0009

the odor from escaping" from dry lavatories that contained both liquid and solid fecal matter.[2]

Herbert Backe, as Reich minister without portfolio, had commissioned these experiments and promptly forwarded the results to the office of the Reich Commissioner for Tenements Robert Ley.[3] Ley, the head the German Labor Front (DAF), assumed this additional post when Hitler created the German Tenements Relief Works (*Deutsches Wohnungshilfswerk*, DWH) in September 1943.[4] By 1944, the DWH had to cope with the rapid accumulation of human excrement in the countless makeshift shelters constructed as temporary encampments for the ever-growing number of bombed out citizens and the masses of refugees arriving from the east.[5] Whether for the homeless survivors of the bombing raids or for the ethnic Germans fleeing from the Red Army, these camps shared with concentration and prison camps the same kind of hastily erected wooden barracks and makeshift toilets.[6]

The German authorities were less concerned with the plight of the refugees than with the inevitable filth they carried on their bodies into the Reich. The *Reichsstelle* for industrial fats and detergents (RIF) put it bluntly when commenting on the shortfall of 560 metric tons of detergent in East Prussia. The RIF attributed the increased demand "to the fact that about 100,000 refugees from Ukraine have arrived in the Bialystok region." If a solution to provide the requisite amount of detergent could not be found, "the outbreak of epidemics and other diseases is to be expected, since the Ukrainian refugees are practically caked in dirt."[7] As access to most basic goods broke down, the pillars of order and cleanliness that had fortified the racial hierarchies also collapsed. But as the above experiment illustrates, even in the face of near total destruction and utter provisioning chaos, the regime continued its perverse focus on simply improving waste management as the ultimate panacea.

Over the course of 1944, waste matter accumulated in the Reich in unprecedented quantities. Feces and sewage, garbage, rubbish and recyclables, rubble, junk and debris, and corpses proliferated at a time marked by wide-ranging scarcity. By the end of the year, the Nazi war against waste only exacerbated the conditions on the ground, keeping pace with the implosion of the Reich.[8] Research institutes, corporations, and the Reich's planning offices focused on abstract technical experiments, rather than the realities of impending collapse. As infrastructures crumbled in the face of the air war, the managers of the war economy continued to uphold the logic of the waste regime, seeing resource extension and recycling as the only solutions. Clogged railways and glutted stations were filled with decommissioned barracks, metal junk, textile waste, and materials of all sorts "evacuated" from hostile territories, competing with the constantly growing number of corpses for the limited transport capacities of the regime. Rather than alleviating shortages, obsessive hoarding contributed to bottlenecks and logjams that paralyzed the distribution of essential goods.

Desperate Ingenuity

In the context of food scarcity, production bottlenecks, shrinking imperial borders, and massive labor shortages, industry and the Reich Ministry for Food and Agriculture bet on garbage technology. Alerted to the DANO system, a garbage-processing plant designed by the Danish company Dano Ingenørforretning OG Maskinfabrik in 1941, the Reich invested in this technology just as the air war intensified and eventually paralyzed the war economy. The DANO system promised to turn fresh garbage as well as the contents of existing dumps into fertile soil, yielding nutrient-rich, composted *Müllerde* (garbage soil) that could overcome the shortage of chemical fertilizers and boost agricultural output. The concept was sound and so was the technology. However, given the extent of raw material shortages and infrastructural destruction, the idea that compost was going to deliver a decisive boost to German production was illusory. Both business proposals and the Reich's plans ignored a simple fact: the only materials available in abundance were waste products that could not overcome endemic shortages. The regime's investment in garbage technologies merely reiterated fantasies of closed-loop cycles and final victories.

The case of Hamburg best illustrates the disconnect between extravagant plans to overcome the raw material crisis and dire everyday reality. In the summer of 1943, the city was largely obliterated in a series of air raids, as British and American bombers dropped 8,500 tons of explosives and incendiaries over the course of ten days. The worst destruction came on the evening of July 28th when the densely populated working-class districts of Hamm, Hammerbrook, and Borgefelde, brimming with refugees from previous raids, were flattened within three hours.[9] The summer heat compounded by the immense pressure generated by the explosions spawned a tornadolike firestorm that raged at 800°C and sucked the oxygen out of air.

Approximately, 35,000 people died from the blasts, fire, suffocation, and heat exposure. Within days, rumors spread that 100,000 people had died in the raids. The general chaos made it impossible to obtain reliable information.[10]

Over the next several months, the city struggled to restore the most rudimentary infrastructure. Basic utilities were disrupted, leaving the population without safe drinking water and electricity; food distributions were entirely chaotic; fires smoldered in the rubble for weeks; garbage piled up in the ruins; and debris-filled roads impeded rescue efforts and provisioning. Nonetheless, the planning for a high-tech plant that would metabolize municipal garbage and convert it to valuable compost was quickly revived. Germany's second DANO plant was to be located in Hammerbrook, one of the districts flattened in the raids. How this would address the pressing issues of the battered city the planners did not explain, but they were certainly not planning to grow crops there.[11]

Discussions of the DANO process began in 1941, when the Düsseldorf-based company Karrenberg & Co. Feuerungsbau, a furnace construction company, alerted Hermann Göring to a new idea concerning the utilization of garbage developed by a company in Copenhagen and sought his support

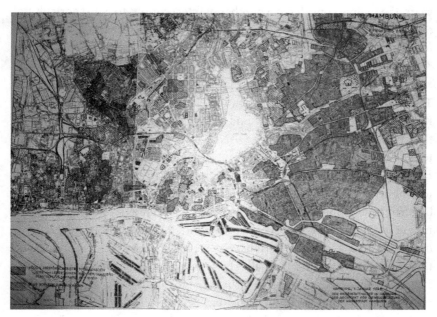

Figure 8.1 Map of bomb damage in Hamburg. Courtesy of Staatsarchiv Hamburg.

for the development of this technology in Germany.[12] Karrenberg & Co. was hoping to obtain the distribution license for this technology and carefully explained to Göring the inner workings of a garbage conversion plant that would turn municipal solid waste into valuable *Müllerde*. To prove the efficacy of the plant, Karrenberg had shipped a container filled with 15,000 kilograms of Berlin garbage to Copenhagen, where the Dano Ingenørforretning OG Maskinfabrik (DANO Works) processed the garbage earlier that summer. Karrenberg eagerly relayed the results to Göring, highlighting the technological advantages of the DANO process: its actual elimination of garbage, the utilization of the resulting compost for vegetable crops and agricultural purposes, and the root-and-branch recovery of secondary materials contained in the garbage. The 15,000 kilograms of war garbage from Berlin impressively isolated 356 kilograms of tin, 41 kilograms of iron, 15 kilograms of other metals, 8 kilograms of slag, 3 kilograms of rubber, 31 kilograms of bones, 39 kilograms of glass bottles, and 70 kilograms of rags.[13]

When the letter introducing the DANO process arrived, the Reich's authorities were pondering plans to guarantee future food security.[14] Meat rations had been cut in 1941, and bread rations could only be maintained by cutting deep into the Reich's grain reserves.[15] Over the next couple of years, the regime considered a number of interventions to boost agricultural output. The DANO process promised relief. Following a visit to Copenhagen in early June, the Reich Food Estate and the Reich Ministry for Food and Agriculture agreed that fall to build a trial DANO plant in Berlin.[16]

In the spring of 1942, the Reich imposed further cuts to food rations.[17] The following November, in anticipation of more severe food shortages, Karl Kaufmann, the *Reichsstatthalter* and governor of Hamburg, commissioned the immediate procurement of a DANO plant, which would convert 25,000 tons of city garbage into soil-meliorating *Müllerde*.[18] The strategic importance of this plant notwithstanding, Hamburg had to wait until May 1943 for confirmation that the request for an exemption from the construction ban had been granted.[19] After the Sixth Army became trapped at Stalingrad in late 1942, the regime accelerated its efforts to increase agricultural production across Germany. Various experts weighed in on how to address this need, reconsidering the value of sewage, manure, and city garbage.[20] *Landwirtschaftsrat* Henkel argued that the most valuable of all urban waste products was "doubtlessly fecal matter." Second, Henkel stressed the importance of the 14 million cubic meters of garbage Germans produced annually, which could be exploited together with the already decomposed garbage in existing dumps. Simple technologies such as conveyor belts and drum strainers were able to produce significant amounts of *Müllerde,* Henkel argued, invoking the experiments with DANO technology planned in Berlin and Hamburg.[21] Such reports in trade journals increased the interest in DANO technology across different cities. Construction started in Berlin Spindlersfeld in February 1943, though shortages of building materials delayed construction in Hamburg.[22]

As Hamburg emerged from the smoldering rubble, the plans for the DANO plant took a back seat to rescue and repair work. Of course, the destruction of the city only heightened concerns over the accumulation of garbage. In several districts, municipal garbage collection did not resume until September and, even then, much of it remained irregular. Accordingly, trash piled up in the streets and on people's doorsteps. Increasingly, the population began to appropriate bombed out buildings and ruins as makeshift garbage dumps.[23] In March 1944, planning for the garbage plant in Hammberbrook resumed, and the assembly of machinery moved forward after iron allocations arrived.[24] As additional cities expressed interest in DANO technology, Henkel told them that reserves of construction material would not become available in 1944.[25] Since he was unable to grant requests for metal allocations, Henkel advised the mayors of Linz and Graz to resort to simpler methods of manually sorting secondary materials.[26]

Berlin considered dismantling existing dumps since construction of the DANO plant proceeded so slowly.[27] There, too, the city's garbage collection company ran into difficulties since the *Reichsbahn* refused to allocate railcars to transport the recovered garbage soil to the countryside. Fuel, metal, and building material shortages compounded transportation bottlenecks and impeded the utilization of garbage and garbage soil alike.[28] The DANO plants in Berlin and Hamburg, each of which cost around 300,000 RM to construct, were never completed and neither metabolized a single kilogram of garbage. The precious *Müllerde* retrieved from existing dumps piled up next to equally precious recyclables as the regime imploded.[29]

The problem was not with the technology or the idea of composting per se, but its timing. By 1943 and 1944, the idea that compost derived from urban garbage would achieve German food security was absurd. None of the planners considered whether the diversion of resources for the construction of DANO plants in either Berlin or Hamburg could be offset by agricultural yield enhanced due to the plants' eventual output. It was evident that the regime was unable to manage the growing chaos, let alone build up resilient structures to ensure a bare-bones continuation of daily life. Hitler himself fostered such magical thinking by announcing the "Fritz Todt Prize" to reward the strategic ingenuity of citizens who invented technologies that saved or extended raw materials.[30]

The Stench of Defeat

As planners in the Ministry for Food and Agriculture and the Four-Year Plan Authority strategized about how to best funnel the nourishing properties of garbage and sewage into agricultural production, these substances "fertilized" basements and nourished populations of rats and flies. Yet, attempts to address the growing local crises of waste accumulation were confined to correspondence acknowledging the gravity of the situation and the simultaneous lack of resources and manpower to effectively intervene.

In January 1944, the Hygienic Institute of Kiel University conducted a water survey in the Husum harbor, detecting typhus bacilli in enormous quantities. Husum, a maritime town close to the Danish border located on tidal flats and surrounded by salty marshes, was only partially connected to an underground sewerage system. Work connecting the northern areas to the sewer had to be placed on hold due to labor shortages. Accordingly, the city organized the collection of fecal matter and supervised the disinfection of the 2,500 to 2,700 buckets that were carted off each week. City officials nonetheless questioned the report about the contaminated coastal waters, wondering whether test results might have been affected by the dredging of the harbor currently under way.[31] Until the matter was resolved, a police ordinance forbade bathing in the entire harbor area and banned the use of harbor water for personal and industrial uses.[32] The test results never arrived. A bombing raid destroyed the samples and the lab.[33]

Problems with sewage were not limited to small towns like Husum; they affected the villas of Berlin politicians and lawyers in Wannsee as well. When Dr. Werner, a senior medical officer at the Ministry of the Interior, who had been involved in the investigations in Husum, visited the villa of the attorney and notary Dr. Gustav Schwarz in October, he observed firsthand that its septic tank was filled to the brim. Since the soil was already saturated, the heavy fall rains pushed contaminated sewage water through the basement walls into the house. Regular emptying of the septic tank would have solved the problem, but the hauling company nearby was unable to secure the necessary fuel allocations to be able to drive its truck to empty the cesspool or deliver a small pump to spread its contents more evenly across the property. Dr. Werner appealed to his colleague, senior counselor Dr. Haack, to intervene on behalf of Dr. Schwarz.[34] The only result, however, was to raise the hopes of Schwarz who started fantasizing about the possibility of forced labor allocations for the construction of an entirely new septic tank.[35]

In the context of the imploding regime, the septic tanks of Berlin's villa owners were minor problems, even if such scenarios multiplied in countless instances across Germany. The Reich Ministry of Armaments and War Production headed by Albert Speer, which was in charge of allocating raw materials for all construction projects, focused instead on emergency measures to regain basic functioning in destroyed urban centers. Construction firms were allocated to clear the main roads, participate in the rescuing of people trapped in the rubble, and repair essential infrastructure.[36] Beyond immediate rescue efforts, cities adjusted and administered devastation, rather than overcoming it.

In recognition of the catastrophic conditions, Hermann Göring tried to ease the administrative burdens on cities. In August 1944, he revoked the obligation of cities to sort municipal garbage for the duration of the war, at the very moment that Berlin and Hamburg invested hundreds of thousands of Reichsmark in facilities for the mechanical sorting of municipal garbage.[37] The garbage-sorting mandate, which had been in place since August 1937, had required cities with a population of 20,000 or higher to sort out secondary materials from the collected city trash.[38]

The problem with garbage sorting was one of labor allocation, given that it employed at least 3,000 full-time workers.[39] Nonetheless, a number of municipalities opted to continue the practice, likely as an additional source of income.[40] More importantly, garbage practices had developed into key mechanisms of maintaining the social order, of exercising social and political control, of binding citizens to the state and its local, regional, and national manifestations. Similarly, garbage practices and waste-utilization innovations had created a fertile space for entrepreneurs and corporations that were able to retool their operations for an economy of scarcity. Therefore, administrators and citizens alike had vested interests in the practices of waste collection and utilization.

Many cash-strapped municipalities fielded questions about municipal services as property owners and tenants complained about having to pay for street maintenance, garbage collection, and sewage in partially or totally destroyed buildings. By the end of 1944, practices varied widely from city to city, even though some municipalities lobbied for Reich-wide legislation so as to not have to respond to the countless queries and complaints.[41] Almost all cities waived collection fees for destroyed properties because the city no longer collected garbage at those locations. In fact, garbage collection had become insufficient and irregular in most cities.

By contrast, municipalities argued that street maintenance and sewage were an entirely different matter since cities had to maintain sewers and remove ice and snow from sidewalks regardless of houses being occupied and inhabitable.[42] Municipalities appealed to "all German *Volksgenossen* to volunteer their labor for the cleaning of streets and sidewalks."[43] The official records imply that cities were mainly concerned with dust, leaves, and snow removal. In areas that suffered heavy bomb damage, entire city blocks were covered in rubble and debris so the very notion of sweeping sidewalks or shoveling snow bordered on the grotesque.

The real problem was' clearing city streets from rubble and repairing damage to the sewer system in order to maintain basic infrastructural functioning, all of which required funds, raw materials, and labor, none of which was available while destruction continued to visit at nightly intervals.[44] Air raids not merely destroyed dwellings, they decimated warehouses, food-processing facilities, and shops, liberating all sorts of organic matter from their places of containment. Air raids caused death. And while survivors did appropriate the ruins as garbage dumps, the decaying flesh of charred and mangled corpses that remained trapped in the rubble caused "the sudden and alarming increase in the parasitical creatures thriving on the unburied bodies."[45] W. G. Sebald notes the uncanny silence about such matters in available records, the impenetrable stench and the growing populations of vermin—from finger-length maggots to oversized rats—that were fattening themselves on the rot of the Reich.[46]

Vermin

Prior to the war, fly infestations were common in agricultural settings, breeding in dung heaps and attracted by livestock. While flies were omnipresent in urban areas, infestations of the kinds observed during the war were limited to garbage dumps, slaughterhouses, cesspools, and the like. In households and stores, paper-based fly traps were used to trap flies attracted by the smell of food. but in light of the growing paper shortage, the production of those products slowed.[47]

Processing municipal waste and utilizing organic scraps were fetid endeavors that drew the presence of flies and other vermin. Obviously, certain industries, such as slaughterhouses and waste-processing plants, combatted flies prior to the war, relying on remedies created by the chemical industry.[48] The wholesale collection of waste materials to boost Germany's resource base had expanded the habitats for flies. In 1938, the Department of Public Health had informed the Regional Office for Water, Soil, and Air Hygiene about the conditions they encountered during an inspection of the extraction plant and bone mill Fritz Schulz in Velten. The health department had been tipped off because Schulz's workers refused to report for work due to the nauseating conditions at the plant. The bones collected from slaughterhouses and butchers were piled high in the hall and moved by workers with shovels and pitchforks onto a large conveyor belt that then fed them into the crusher. They teemed with maggots, which feasted on the pieces of tissue, skin, and fur still attached to the bones.

Normally, bones were processed right away but the factory simply could not manage the resulting volume; bones amassed too quickly. On average, bones awaited processing for about two to two and a half days and began to decay, enabling maggots to travel along the conveyer and up the walls. The health department made it clear that bones had to be processed as quickly as possible and that the floors, walls, and conveyor must be thoroughly cleaned with hot lye. Experts at the Regional Office for Water, Soil, and Air Hygiene recommended mechanical methods to separate the maggots from the bones, such as collecting the bones in wire mesh over a pit filled with lye into which the creatures would fall.[49] During the war, forced laborers and maggots worked side by side, processing the bones that consumers dutifully collected.

Ingenious citizens invented and promoted their insect-repelling solutions to the Reich Food Estate or directly to Hermann Göring. Carl Greiner in Konstanz devised a smoke-generating device that, unfortunately, only targeted mosquitoes and could not be deployed in the war against flies.[50] Hugo Thöle built a fly trap and sent descriptions, sketches, and a photograph to the attention of Göring, suggesting that such a trap be mounted at every farm and slaughterhouse.[51] Such zeal and creativity notwithstanding, the proposed contraptions were hardly able to tackle a problem of the scale produced by wartime destruction.

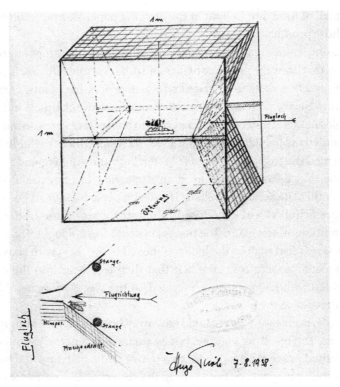

Figure 8.2 Drawing of Hugo Thöle's fly trap. Courtesy of Bundesarchiv.

The problem only intensified as recyclables piled up at collection points; the garbage designated for NSV piggeries reeked and spoiled; and decomposing bones accumulated in school yards and storage rooms.[52] With the turning fortunes of war, order was breaking down and it manifested in the accumulation of reeking, rotting matter. The aerial annihilation experienced by German cities only exacerbated the already pervasive encroachment of vermin. Hans Erich Nossack, a Hamburg-based writer, called attention to the spread of vermin after the 1943 bombing:

> Rats and flies were the lords of the city. Insolent and fat, the rats disported themselves on the streets. Even more nauseating were the flies. They were large and of a shimmering green; no one had ever seen flies like this. They wallowed in swarming clumps on the pavement, sat, copulating, on top of the ruined walls, warmed themselves, bloated and tired, on splinters of window glass. When they could no longer fly, they would crawl after us

through the narrowest crevices, soiling everything, and their rustling and buzzing was the first thing one heard in the morning. This didn't stop till October.[53]

The conditions in Hamburg, "where fly infestation is growing continuously," inspired Gerolf Steiner to write to the Department of Public Health in Berlin, in the hopes of preventing the same conditions elsewhere. Steiner had spent five years researching zoological solutions to fly infestations and suggested breeding large quantities of ichneumon wasps that attacked the fly pupae. Steiner maintained that in "cases where corpses lie under rubble" the ability of wasps to identify breeding and pupation sites might be useful, particularly since "chemical control is impossible for spatial reasons."[54] The Department of Public Health sent a short response. It no longer concerned itself with such matters, especially "since the gentlemen have all been drafted and the zoological department had to be shut down as a result of bomb damage." The remaining staff was preoccupied with the constant testing of insecticides against lice and bedbugs.[55]

The SS and camp guards delt with these infestations only when they reached crisis proportions. As temperatures warmed, the rotting flesh of thousands upon thousands of hastily buried corpses attracted flies and rats in unprecedented proportions. From Lublin, Odilo Globocnik sent to the Regional Office for Water, Soil, and Air Hygiene an urgent request for reading materials about flies in 1942, noting that "I need this literature for combatting fly infestations and want to learn about the lifespan and habits of fly species."[56] The leading doctor of the SS settlement in Lublin wrote to the Robert Koch Institute in the spring of 1943 to again request whatever literature was available about insecticides effective against flies.[57] The problem plagued SS murder facilities and camps with high mortality rates elsewhere. In July 1943, the public health department in Katowice inquired about the most effective means "to combat fly infestations in the staff and service rooms of the *Ostarbeiter* camps and other labor camps."[58] In August, Himmler appointed Heinrich Josten as the fly control officer for the entire Auschwitz complex and surrounding areas.[59] Josten's responsibility broadened over the following months when he became entrusted with the war against vermin of all sorts, until he was removed from his post the following May, presumably for losing the battle against the flies.[60]

By the spring of 1944, the German Labor Front faced similar conditions in the camps for forced and foreign laborers inside Germany. Having concerned themselves primarily with the battle against lice and bedbugs, camp administrations found themselves overwhelmed by fly populations that threatened their already meager food supply. The experts at the Regional Office for Water, Soil, and Air Hygiene recommended the I.G. Farben product "Gix," which they speculated "should be available in two to three months."[61]

The Nazi regime had perfected and reproduced at mind-boggling speed the structures that "proved" the filthy nature of people forced into ghettos and camps, drawing clear boundaries between clean and rubbished spaces. By the end of the war, these boundaries were breaking down, as more and more Germans "who had proposed to cleanse and sanitize all Europe, now had to contend with a rising fear that they themselves were the rat people."[62]

Glut

The air war against German cities reached its peak in 1944 and continued apace throughout April 1945.[63] Amidst this chaos of bombs and death, the regime choreographed its retreat. The Greater German Reich was rapidly shrinking. The Red Army pushed into Poland over the summer, liberating the camp in Lublin (Majdanek) in July.[64] The Allies liberated Paris in August and Brussels in September.[65] Hitler summoned the *Volkssturm*, a people's army consisting of men and boys ages 16–60 that was to rise up in total mobilization to repel the enemy by the sheer force of their determination. Underequipped and largely without uniforms, the people in arms lacked arms and training.[66] Behind the military machinations of the crumbling regime were the frantic efforts of economic managers to secure and organize the return of the loot, glutting Germany with mind-boggling quantities of junk. In July and August of 1944, the *Reichsstelle* for textiles was still putting together plans for raw-material allocations for Belgium and Holland. A month later, they were feverishly trying to freight rags and textile waste to safety.[67] Evacuated materials, ranging from office stationery to the contents of warehouses, was shipped eastward from France, Belgium, and the Netherlands. Ovens, kettles, pumps, cooking equipment, tubs, and buckets piled up at train stations, competing for storage facilities with railcars stuffed with rayon wastes, textiles of various sorts, shoes, and female sanitary products.[68] Even restaurants and inns were turned into storage facilities for evacuated loot and waste products.[69]

The situation was overwhelming but not entirely surprising. Already in the fall of 1942, Reich Minister of Justice Georg Thierack considered it necessary to designate select prisons, detention centers, and penitentiaries as central warehousing facilities for the storage of secondary materials from the recycling centers, where prisoners reworked the textiles and shoes.[70] Between 1942 and the end of the war, shipments of clothing and personal items, stolen from the Jews and others murdered in the Nazi-occupied east, arrived in the Reich at ever-increasing volumes. Once the Red Army forced the retreat of the Wehrmacht, tons of robbed and hoarded materials were freighted back to the Reich, in addition to decommissioned and "rescued" infrastructure and military equipment. The volume of evacuated property was staggering. Forced laborers tasked with unloading trains and storing loot could not keep up.

By the end of the war, the reliance on carceral labor was not just common knowledge but widely accepted within the business community. For example, Dr. Ernst Scheld wrote to the Reich Ministry of Justice in 1944 to offer his critique as a board member of the Lohmann-Werke in Bielefeld. Before the war, the company had specialized in the manufacturing of bicycle saddles, bags, suitcases, and other leather goods, but pivoted its production line to include equipment belts and machine straps as well as other leather, rubber, and textile-based implements relevant for the armaments industry.[71] Noting "everyone's approval" of the comprehensive efforts to allocate inmates from the Reich's prisons for war production, Scheld faulted prison directors and the Reich Department of Justice more generally for prioritizing metalworks and not allocating sufficient prison laborers for businesses like his.[72]

Scheld was no expert on criminology, yet he invoked the language of prison reform, stressing the disciplinary benefits of cell-based labor for the prisoner, particularly for juveniles.[73] To his mind, the shortages and backlogs, the forcible movement of prisoners and equipment, were evidence not of a dying system, but of poor planning and execution. As Scheld observed, there were still people one could coerce to do work and there was still raw material that could be fashioned into war-relevant equipment. Yet, the Nazi economic managers moved people and things, without creating functional pairs. While Scheld's perspective was admittedly narrow, he exemplified attitudes that characterized the regime more broadly amidst the growing chaos.

Of course, not all materials reached their destinations. Trucks went up in flames and railcars suffered bomb damage, moths and mold damaged improperly stored materials, so the Reich's logistics company, ROGES (Rohstoff und Handelsgesellschaft mbH), informed the *Reichsstelle* for textiles that it refused to insure the rearward freight.[74] What material did arrive at factories frequently was neither requested nor had any use once it reached their facilities.[75] For example, the company of Rudolf Näser, specializing in felts and felt goods, received two railcars of felts and unwoven materials on November 20, 1944. Näser insisted that "since we were not aware of anything and a question or discussion did not precede [the shipment], acceptance should be refused." But because he noticed that the material had been sent on behalf of the *Reichsstelle* for textiles and because "the *Reichsbahn* demanded that the boxcars be emptied on the same day," he grudgingly decided to take the material into consignment but refused to accept any responsibility for potential damage to it. Näser noted right away that the processing of this material was out of the question since he had neither space nor manpower available.[76] In January 1945, the Soviet offensive unleashed the same sort of shipping frenzy in the east that characterized the evacuation of the western territories in the fall of 1944.[77]

As the Wehrmacht faced "a time of utmost military crisis," those declared indispensable to the war economy were counting garbage.[78] The estimated quantities of rags and textile wastes east of the Elbe River stored at sorting and processing facilities amounted to 9,475 metric tons in February. The *Reichsstelle* for textiles frantically tried to place all of this loot either in storage or with factories that could still process material. When the *Reichsstelle* informed the Vienna-based cement factory that it would shortly draw on its service, the owner Ludwig Hatschek explained that he would be unable to warehouse or sort the various kinds of textiles, informing the authorities that his company had "nothing to do with textiles and this has been true for over 40 years."[79] In response to the same request, the Hitiac AG in Vienna explained that because the three-month-long moratorium on shipments, "[W]e have accumulated immense quantities of finished products which we cannot ship due to the lack of railcars, so that we are only able to take on very limited quantities."[80] In other situations, company managers and owners had been drafted into the *Volkssturm*, leaving no one to receive shipments or process materials.[81] While the army rescued an additional 12–14 railcars of textiles, including 2,000 blankets, shipping them to Chemnitz from Krakow, 40,000 blankets and a large quantity of underwear had to remain in Łódź as neither the army nor the public sector could allocate any means of transportation.[82] Hitler's attempts to command the chaos proved fruitless.[83]

Hitler had made it clear that the evacuation of strategic material, fuel, and food took precedence over human lives, insisting that "even refugees can only be transported after this need has been met completely."[84] There were no general provisions in the defense of the Reich for whether or when the population would be evacuated from active military territory—Hitler reserved that decision for himself. The population was the responsibility of the party; the army was responsible for POWs; and the SS for all forced and foreign laborers. The most important task was to secure all strategic assets and prevent them from falling into the hands of the enemy, if necessary by destroying all remaining industrial facilities and machinery.[85] Aachen was the first German city to be evacuated in September 1944. Railcars were shot up and large numbers of railway workers deserted, so much of the evacuation had to rely solely on the labor power extracted from *Ostarbeiter*. Much of the German staff did not report to work, and instead searched for their families or tried to board the evacuation trains. The evacuation of goods preceded the evacuation of people, but many did not wait for the order that arrived on September 12, 1944, and left of their own accord.[86]

The situation was similar in the east. As the Red Army advanced, millions of people were on the run. The "Albert Kommission" designated to deal with foreign refugees funneled them into camps, separated by nationality, and allocated them for work through Plenipotentiary for Labor Fritz Sauckel. The Coordination Center for Ethnic Germans (*Volksdeutsche Mittelstelle*, VoMi) was in charge of ethnic Germans and the NSV for German citizens.[87] Increasingly, refugees, whether leaving German cities destroyed in the air war or frantically evacuating the lost territories in the east and west, arrived in Germany on foot. While some clung to a near desperate hope for miracle weapons and secret offensives, many Germans, who had adopted Hitler's apocalyptic vision, braced themselves for "annihilation" once victory no longer seemed within reach.[88] In Hamburg, where the end times had arrived almost two years earlier than elsewhere in the Reich, many citizens just wished "the Tommy" would come.[89]

The Death of Piety

Throughout 1944 and over the first months of 1945, Allied bombing was relentless. More than half of the civilians killed by Allied airstrikes died after August 1944.[90] Following Hamburg, many cities such as Berlin, Cologne,

Hamburg, Nuremberg, Darmstadt, Kassel, Heilbronn, Stuttgart, Essen, and Düsseldorf were bombed, many repeatedly. In February 1945, Dresden was obliterated.[91] The overwhelming number of corpses further stretched the capacity of the *Reichsbahn*.

Starting in the summer 1944, the dead were transported to municipal crematoria in open railcars, which understandably caused consternation among the population.[92] To address the matter, Friedrich Weber of the Ministry of the Interior called a meeting with representatives from the professional group for funeral services, the Department of Public Health, the Department of Transportation, and the Reich Security Main Office. Weber had grave reservations about the "open car" transport for medical and hygienic reasons. During the meeting, it became clear that raw material shortages affected the delivery and the allocation of coffins, which needed to be transported both empty from the factories and full to the crematoria, taking up considerable space both ways, but the carpenters guild objected to the assembly onsite rather than in the factory. In any case, raw material shortages, particularly wood, were the problem, not boxcars, the representative from the funeral services insisted. The official in charge of *Ersatz* (or replacement) coffins, Mr. Hampf, explained that he was currently producing substitute coffins, "which required no raw materials since they are constructed out of waste products from the aviation industry." Hampf demonstrated through a model of the *Ersatz* coffin that "no carpenters but only unskilled workers (prisoners) would be required to assemble the components of his coffins." Accordingly, 1,000 *Ersatz* coffins could fit in one railcar and be assembled at the place of need.[93]

Whether made of airplane junk or wood, the coffin problem only intensified. In September, the Reich Minister of Traffic ordered limits on *Leichenpässe*, essentially permits to transport corpses by rail, because such transports increasingly competed with railcars designated for the Wehrmacht's purposes, armaments shipments, transporting the harvest, and evacuations. From September 1944 onward, the rail transport of corpses to crematoria was forbidden, except for cases in which a state or party funeral had been ordered.[94] These limitations applied to those interned in various camps and subsidiary outposts as well as military training facilities and other geographically isolated institutions that did not have their own internal crematoria.

In urban centers, the transport of the dead, whether they died of natural causes or during an air raid, was usually accomplished by truck or carriage. But the transport of corpses to morgues and crematoria posed immense difficulties even in urban centers. In September 1944, Wolf-Heinrich Graf von Helldorf, the police commissioner in Berlin, changed the cremation ordinance to simplify the process and allow the surrender of urns to relatives directly.[95] The Greater-German Cremation Association filed bitter complaints about the "impious" treatment of the dead. But the two vehicles that normally transported urns to the respective cemeteries in Berlin were out of commission due to repairs and fuel shortages. Accordingly, impious or not, the police commissioner allowed relatives to pick up the ashes of their loved ones from the crematoria directly until the transport of urns could resume in the usual manner.

The collection of the dead from their dwellings also gave cause for concern since the usual funeral cars only transported the bodies around the corner, where they were loaded onto *Tempowagen* (speed trucks), onto which numerous coffins were piled and thus delivered to the morgue.[96] In order to assuage popular outrage, the regional professional group for funeral services recommended that at least the vehicles be painted in pious black and the panel trucks covered with blankets or tarps to disguise their purpose. However, in February 1945, there was neither fuel left for the transport of corpses nor blankets that could be allocated to the living, let alone the dead. In Berlin, the authorities contemplated the use of electrical streetcars and trollies for the transport of corpses.[97] The problem was simple: there were too many dead and not nearly enough fuel to conform to standards of purity and piety.

The smell of death was everywhere. Mayor Ludwig Steeg of Berlin suggested further simplifications to speed up the process of dealing with dead bodies. He considered cremation the only reasonable approach and advocated the cremation of bomb victims, refugees, and forced laborers, even without wills or relatives to give permission. He decided to save paper by ceasing to keep death records in duplicate and suggested suspending the forensic coroner's inquest for the duration of the war, arguing that no case of criminal death had been discovered for years.[98] The police commissioner admitted that the current state of mass inquest couldn't possibly deliver any meaningful information. There was not enough light in the hallways and storage rooms of Berlin's morgues where corpses were laid out for mass inspection, "many in a state of advanced decomposition, most of them rotting." Personnel was short, too, so the bodies were neither undressed nor removed from their coffins.[99] Nonetheless, the industrial-style processing of bodies in

Berlin's morgues and crematoria suggested by Mayor Steeg did not receive the endorsement of the police chief who, along with Dr. Friedrich Weber, insisted on privileging the increasingly unrealistic desires of relatives for a dignified funeral.[100] Such desires notwithstanding, neither burial nor cremation was able to keep up with the dying.

By January 1945, as most Germans resigned themselves to total defeat, the regime stepped up repression against its own citizenry, including incarceration and execution of shirkers, saboteurs, military "stragglers," and deserters.[101] Military losses were staggering; half of the German soldiers who died in the war, died in the last ten months. In addition, as the Allied bombing campaigns reached their peak, many more German civilians died between June 1944 and the end of the war than in all previous years of the war combined.[102] All German cities and towns reeked to the heavens, communicating the imminence of defeat in the most revolting ways possible; yet in Germany, the masses did not revolt.[103]

9
Piles

In January 1945, SS Obergruppenführer Oswald Pohl, the head of the SS Main Economic and Administrative Office (*SS-Wirtschafts-Verwaltungshauptamt*, SS-WVHA) and one of the main architects of the Nazi genocide, informed his boss Heinrich Himmler that 200 wagons of loot from Warsaw had arrived at Ravensbrück concentration camp for sorting. Noting that the material varied drastically in kind and quality, Pohl ventured that "a significant portion can only be used for recycling [*kann nur der Altmaterialverwertung zugeführt werden*]."[1] Oswald Pohl was well aware of the human cost of the Reich's mission to rescue textile waste and metal junk from the formerly occupied territories. Yet, he was only concerned with the logistical impasse the parallel arrival of *Menschenmaterial* (human labor) and *Altmaterial* (recyclables) spelled, when, in fact, they were supposed to augment their respective use value and relieve the pressures on raw material and labor shortages.[2]

Pohl tried to paint an optimistic picture for Himmler, but was unable to conceal the dysfunction that characterized the entire process. "The sorting and inventorying has been on-going for weeks; but it is, of course, very difficult in the unprecedented chaos," he explained. The freight volume overwhelmed the infrastructural capacity of the Reich's sorting and recycling complex. Of course, the SS guards deployed their usual brutality to ensure that the work proceeded with precision, allegedly attempting to prevent squander and carelessness, and to avoid misdirected shipments or the shipping of useless stuff. Among those forced to do the work, "reliable specialists" were lacking. To Pohl's mind, concentration camp prisoners could hardly be trusted to undertake these gargantuan tasks with the necessary diligence and care. Matters were further complicated by the fact that for most of the materials piling into the Reich in these final months, "a purpose has yet to be found."[3] Nonetheless, the shipments continued unabated, containing "mostly old textiles"; in other words, rags and other rubbish—that were piled high next to crematoria and hospital barracks. The sorting of these precious raw materials continued even though there was neither detergent left to clean them, nor fuel to transport them, nor factories to process them.

Concentration and prison camps swelled with prisoners and forced laborers from the east who, alternatively described as dangerous parasites and an essential reservoir of labor, were forced to march back to the Reich by their masters.[4] Abandoned belongings, broken down vehicles, dead horses, and corpses lay alongside roads and railroad tracks that the treks of prisoners and slave laborers were forced along to their next deadly destination. They also littered roads traveled by evacuees and refugees who ran from bombs or armies or both.[5] Rubble and craters had become signature features of abandoned towns and surrendering cities alike. Where people remained or were concentrated under threat of imminent death, precious raw materials became part of the proliferating landscape of collapse. Nowhere was the mountainous accumulation of matter more egregious than in the Nazi camps, where "human material" was just left to rot, while the Germans clung to a fantasy according to which hundreds of thousands of dying prisoners would turn junk into weapons and turn the tides of war in Germany's favor.

Bergen-Belsen's piles not only transformed the natural landscape, they also upended prisoners' strategies of survival. For years, work, though never a path toward freedom, had held the promise of at least intermittent potential for survival. The fanatical resource fetishism of the regime reimagined prisoners as the raw material: *Mensch*.[6] As long as some use value could be gained from their labor, prisoners knew they might ward off death a bit longer. With the implosion of the necropolitical regime, labor and its faint promise for survival were eviscerated, too.[7] The piles posed questions of survival in terms of environmental determinism: to either live among them or to become them.

The Germans pitted their own piles of rubbled cities and shattered lives against the piles amidst which the surviving victims of the Nazi system eked out their existence. The German population failed to understand the structural difference of this overwhelming architecture of death that their hoarding and sorting of rubbish and secondary materials had shored up. The comprehensive cleanup that commenced under the guidance of the Allies proved for them not a reckoning but an erasure. As the piles were cleaned up, leveled, buried, burned, they were planted with trees and shrubs and built over with bus stops and elementary schools. The infrastructure of normal life erased the "violence work" of the killers and the waste labor of the victims.[8] This chapter forces our attention on this man-made landscape of piles and the dismantled architecture of the imploding Nazi waste regime.

Dirty White Hell

In late March 1945, there was still some snow on the ground, but most of the melted countryside had turned to mud. Born in Poland, Moshe Oster had passed through various ghettos and camps since the beginning of the war. After surviving Auschwitz, Mauthausen, and Gusen, he ended up near Hannover, where he worked at Hanomag.[9] In March 1945, Oster was part of a group of prisoners forced to travel on foot from Hannover to the hellscape of Bergen-Belsen. Sometimes, they traveled on roads; at other times during this three-day march, they trudged across fields pulling heavy wooden carts loaded with the possessions of their SS wardens. The carts sank into the mud. The SS men screamed and shouted, beating the prisoners who tried unsuccessfully to move carts that would not budge. Only after the prisoners removed the cargo, dug the carts out of the sodden ground, and logged the parcels and bundles to the road could the trek continue. Oster had neither a sense of location nor direction except that the SS man, whom he knew as Rex, was behind him shooting in the head those who stumbled or collapsed from exhaustion. The prisoners had to move the dead to the side of the road before continuing.[10]

The group spent one night in a barn on some field, piled on top of each other for lack of space, crying and moaning until the SS started shooting in order to stop their wailing. The journey continued the next morning. After the trek passed through the small town of Celle, Oster felt he was barely able to set one foot in front of the other. A friend was finished off by Rex; Oster continued on, delirious. When Oster finally reached the gate of Bergen-Belsen, he did not quite know how to make sense of what he saw:

> It seemed strange to us, the whole camp was somehow white, as if the environment itself was white. We didn't understand what was going on. Only when we were inside the camp did we understand. The whole area was littered with corpses, there were thousands of them. All over the camp there were mountains [of corpses]. We entered the camp. On the left side were the men, on the right side was the women's camp. It was as if everything had been painted white. We just couldn't understand in what sort of place we had ended up.[11]

Bergen-Belsen did not make sense to anyone. When new arrivals like Oster asked what was going on in this hellish place, people told them something about Russian POWs, that people were being concentrated here from everywhere, and that nobody knew what was going to happen next.[12]

Mendel Gur, who arrived in Bergen-Belsen in March, tells a similar tale. A secular Jew from Transylvania, Gur had been imprisoned in Budapest for "anti-Nazi activities" and "communist agitation." He arrived in Bergen-Belsen by train from Auschwitz, via Groß-Rosen and Breslau (Wrocław), and then marched on foot from the station to the camp. He, too, trudged through the snow "in a certain direction," watching carefully "not to step on anyone, who couldn't walk anymore." Gur told the interviewer: "Everywhere, corpses were scattered, mountains, mountains. We asked about them, and we were told it was because of the hunger and typhus epidemic."[13] He didn't remember much of the first few days besides being piled into a barrack and standing for rollcall the next day, finding those who had fallen on the march from the train station laid out on the ice next to the barracks; they "were as good as dead" to the Germans. "But for us, they still had plans."[14]

Established in 1940 for POWs, Bergen-Belsen was an unusual camp. During the winter of 1941–1942, most of the interned POW's had died of disease, hunger, and exhaustion, and the remaining prisoners were deployed in work details around the countryside, leaving the original camp almost completely empty.[15] In early 1943, when the fortunes of war turned and Operation Reinhard was drawing to a close, Himmler sited a prisoner-exchange camp on the existing grounds of the POW camp in Bergen-Belsen to preserve foreign national Jews as "valuable hostages" for leverage in eventual negotiations between the German Foreign Office and enemy nations.[16] The prisoner-exchange camp, the so-called *Sternlager* (star camp), was subordinated to the Inspectorate of the Concentration Camps (*Inspektion der Konzentrationslager*, IKL) in Oranienburg, which ensured that, unlike other internment camps, Bergen-Belsen was incorporated into the machinations of the SS-WVHA.[17] *Austauschjuden* or exchange Jews arrived in Bergen-Belsen in July 1943 from all across the Europe, many diverted from transports to the death camps.[18]

In the fall of 1944, Oswald Pohl determined that Bergen-Belsen was underutilized. The camp's location far from industry did not allow for the usual deployment of prisoner labor in surrounding factories.[19] Moreover, sick and dying prisoners took up space in the existing labor camps and impeded smooth operation there.[20] On the one hand, Pohl reconsidered providing rations and medical care for camp inmates to preserve labor, a mere theoretical exercise.[21] On the other hand, Himmler started to device schemes beyond liquidation transports and reimagined the prisoner-exchange camp as a convalescence camp to which sick and dying prisoners were sent to recover or die, alleviating the pressures on labor camps. Bergen-Belsen became a *Sterbelager*, a camp of slow death.[22]

In a camp designated for dying, counting was more important than work.[23] Accordingly, the rollcall was mandatory for all, whether sick, old, frail, or merely on the verge of starvation. Often this took hours, and prisoners were forced to stand in front of the barracks until the counting was completed to the satisfaction of the guards.[24] Some prisoners were assigned to labor details, others volunteered, most were too sick and weak to move.[25] Prisoners were deployed for the usual camp maintenance functions, from potato peeling to the declogging of drains, from servicing the crematoria to carting off the rubbish.[26] Bergen-Belsen also had a weaving mill, where prisoners wove together various sorts of waste products—cellophane, paper, fats, rags, and rubber—to make straps supposedly for munitions manufacturing.[27] And, of course, prisoners sorted and recycled shoes and garments.[28]

Many prisoners worked "in the shoes." When Manfred Rosenbaum started there in late February 1944, the work at first did not appear that difficult. He just noticed the dirt and dust.[29] He and other men separated the uppers and the heels from the soles, while the women cut the upper leather to preserve reusable pieces in a separate pile.[30] Irvin Juda Van Gelder described the oven that stood in the center of the work shed as well as a tent, the size of a circus tent, bursting with old shoes. Millions of shoes, old and worn out, women's and men's shoes.[31] As one of the younger workers, Van Gelder had to climb the mountain of shoes with a wheelbarrow or a jute sack and collect the next batch of shoes to be dissected inside one of the sheds. Verbal abuse was constant. "You made us poor and now you must make us rich again," the SS men yelled, using whips and batons to drive prisoners to work faster and meet their quotas.[32] The guards knew that Germany was losing the war and compensated for growing German impotence by reinforcing the fiction that their current plight was the work of Jewish string-pullers the world over who unleashed "violence without moral limit" against German civilians.[33]

The piles of leather scrap outside the shoe sheds grew so large that one day they appeared in danger of collapsing and crushing the two sheds. The guards mobilized the entire shoe squad to dismantle the existing mountains of shoes and rebuild them with broader bases. This action, Alexander Roseboom remembers, was a festival for SS Oberscharführer Heinz, a festival that lasted several weeks. Heinz supervised the work of the prisoners,

Figure 9.1 Mountains of shoes at Bergen-Belsen, post liberation. Courtesy of the United States Holocaust Memorial Museum.

swinging his whip. The leather mountains had been outfitted with running boards on which prisoners traveled to reorder the piles. The solid ground

> could only be reached by a particularly long running board. Everyone had to walk over it. Guess, who was standing next to it at the end of this board? Life-size! Heinz, the cattleman. Like in a circus, the whistle in his mouth, the whip in hand. "Go . . . go . . . go *Judenzeug* [Jew junk] down!!!! Faster, damnit, faster . . . go!" The first pitiful backs were already receiving their portion of "the Heinz special."[34]

By late 1944, however, the cycle by which valuable raw material was created through the labor extracted from "Jew junk" was breaking down. No matter the level of brutality deployed, the SS proved unable to reverse-engineer rubbish into war equipment.

Late that fall, more and more prisoners arrived as the Germans evacuated camps further east. Many of the new arrivals were sick and dying. Trash piled up inside the barracks and across the camp. The same was true for excrement since facilities were nonexistent or defunct. Technically, the same number of washrooms and latrines served the approximately 20,000 inmates in January 1945 that had been used by 2,000 people the previous year, except that by January 1945 the water supply had been cut off from many lavatories.[35] Most of the latrines were overflowing and unusable, and prisoners were too weak to dig new ones. Many prisoners were in such terrible physical condition that they could barely walk, and were forced to defecate close to the barracks. Those weaker still urinated and defecated where they were lying, especially at night when they were crammed into barracks so tightly that they could not move, let alone get up to relieve themselves.[36] Dr. Fritz Leo, a physician prisoner, testified that "the camp soon resembled a cesspool in its entirety."[37]

Piles were the defining topographical feature of Bergen-Belsen. Rosi Simon, a Jewish woman originally from Hungary, arrived in Bergen-Belsen from Auschwitz. She noted mountains of corpses and the overcrowded conditions with 500 women packed so closely into the barracks they were unable to move. "We slept on the bare ground without taking off our clothes; they had turned off the water, we were supposed to perish quicker."[38] The British POW Hugh Jenkins described Bergen-Belsen as "a dumping ground for discarded humanity" where "the process of dealing with the dead was simple."[39] Some barracks functioned as mortuaries and into those the dead were stacked up to the ceiling, in a space-saving manner. Those half-dead and dying were placed in front of the morgue barracks to minimize their transport, and those "so ill that they would soon be in this condition were laid in front of them."[40] Such "simplicity" notwithstanding, the system devised to manage death was collapsing. People, reduced to walking skeletons, wandered among puddles of excrement; "lice, which covered the inmates like moving blankets" spread the typhoid epidemic across the camp.[41] Excessive hunger, overcrowding, lack of sanitation, disease, and epidemics were compounded by the unavoidable proximity to the toxicity of death. There was no space to hide, no strategy for escape. Slowly but surely, it seemed, the piles would amalgamate those who still moved among them.

Implosion

Forced to march through Germany on foot, prisoners and their SS guards alike knew that Germany was losing the war. They traversed "a drab Spartan country, moldering and destitute, the predominant landscape of its towns and cities now consisting of heaps of debris."[42] On the move were refugees, soldiers either deserting or cut off from their regiment, the flying court-martials who hunted after absconders and saboteurs, escaped prisoners, and, of course, the continuous treks of concentration camp prisoners and forced laborers.[43] SS guards and regular citizens alike had internalized Nazi propaganda and accordingly saw in the columns of dying prisoners dangerous bands of violent criminals.[44] When Rudolf Höss, the commandant of Auschwitz, traveled by car through Upper Silesia, he saw

> columns of prisoners who struggled through the deep snow. Without rations. The Unterführer who led these walking corpse trains usually did not even know where they were going. They knew only the final destination, Groß-Rosen. But how they would ever get there was a mystery to everyone. . . . Overnight stays in barns or schools were out of the question, everything was crammed with refugees. The paths of the trains of suffering were easy to reconstruct; every few hundred meters there was a collapsed prisoner or someone who had been shot.[45]

Even Höss, who had prided himself on the various "improvements" he oversaw in the Auschwitz killing machinery, found these treks discombobulating, so much so that he shouted at one of the SS men who had just murdered a prisoner for resting against a tree. When the SS guard told Höss to mind his own business, Höss lost his cool and opened fire.[46] Rather than demonstrating Höss' newfound conscience, the scene reveals the level of random, excessive violence and the breakdown of the structures of order and command. In the face of such random violence and chaos, even professional killers like Höss became unhinged as they watched the order they had built and enforced with such diligence crumble in front of their very eyes.

When Allied planes dropped bombs on towns like Celle and Hildesheim, they struck panic and kindled rage in the local population. Prisoners and forced laborers were often the first targets when panic turned violent.[47] When Mendel Gur arrived in Hildesheim in mid-March 1945 as part of a labor detail dispatched from Bergen-Belsen, he still marveled at the beauty of the town. Housed in a concert hall filled with straw for "comfort," Gur and his fellow prisoners from Bergen-Belsen as well as scores of POWs were tasked with cleanup work around the train station that Americans bombers had just flattened. Prisoners had been directed to "fill-in the huge bomb craters and then take apart the bent railroad tracks and straighten them again to lay new rails" when they suddenly discovered a boxcar filled with sugar. The sugar had melted and burned during the blast and later congealed into sweet, delicious clumps. The prisoners ate the sugar clumps, but they did not dare touch the cans of Wehrmacht provisions scattered about for fear of being put to death by their guards. Gur had watched as a German supervisor shot a man in cold blood: a POW, a boy of 17, shot in front of his own father after picking up a can of food. The German civilians didn't flinch; they just continued on with their business.[48]

Random violence characterized society at large, but it attained entirely grotesque proportions inside the camps. When Mendel Gur returned to Bergen-Belsen in early April, he barely recognized the place from a few weeks earlier. "Everything was full of corpses," Gur remembers, and "the barracks were full to the top with dirt." It was nighttime when they returned from Hildesheim. They were assigned to a barrack: "Obviously we did not all fit." The Kapos addressed this problem with cold brutality. Equipped with whips and weighted leather straps, they "beat us so that people even tried to climb up the walls. In this way they crammed twice the amount [of people] as usual into the barracks. The next morning the lowest layer was dead, they had been trampled" to death.[49]

Mosche Oster and a fellow prisoner Katalin Frisch, who had arrived from Auschwitz, both volunteered for work.[50] Oster joined a group of other people whose job it was to collect "garbage." The interviewer who recorded Oster's testimony noted explicitly that "garbage" was the exact word that he used as it became clear over the course of his testimony that Oster was referring to corpses. His task was to collect the dead. "We had carts onto which we loaded the garbage and took it to some place where it was dumped and burned."[51] Oster carted the dead to the crematorium, where he saw "people who were busy with the burning of garbage. They took the corpses and burned them. They cut up the meat and ate it." Noting that he had nothing in his stomach to vomit up, Oster just ran, leaving his cart behind, and decided, "I will go nowhere no more. This sight, to see how they butchered the dead."[52] Isolated cases of cannibalism did occur as provisioning was breaking down.[53] Little is known about the extent of cannibalism but, pointing out such horror, Oster and survivors like him announced their resistance against a landscape of death that threatened to devour them. Whether or not prisoners witnessed or partook in those acts, reporting on them, even after the fact, was an act of self-affirmation by articulating the refusal to be reduced to this level of desperation.

People suffered incredible hunger, which further exacerbated their vulnerability to typhus that ripped through the camp. In February 1945, the camp administration still passed out bread rations, two slices of bread per prisoner a day. Soup was occasionally distributed from massive wooden barrels that were difficult to move and often violently attacked by hungry prisoners.[54] Prisoners used the time not working or standing for rollcall to scavenge for food, digging up roots, rummaging through garbage piles, or scouting to find stashed provisions. Most of the kitchens had been closed, and SS men were guarding whatever stockpiles there were and routinely shot at prisoners digging through the garbage heaps.[55] In the eyes of the Germans, neither the materials nor the people retained any value. The waste regime had become unhinged.

The Grand Cleanup

Valentina Bobina, originally from Ukraine, had been deported to Germany for forced labor. In 1942, at the age of 16, she ended up working at the crematoria at Auschwitz. In October 1944, she was transferred to Bergen-Belsen. Although she had seen it all, Bergen-Belsen, "a corpse camp," made no sense since even mass murder was chaotic. Bobina didn't just seem perplexed by the sheer numbers of the dead, but by the fact that "the crematorium didn't work. It was a small crematorium. It either couldn't manage to burn everyone or it wasn't operating. I don't know. There were innumerable corpses. Even the wastewater drainage was filled with the corpses."[56] Prisoners had become accustomed to recognizing the morbid order of the Nazi camps. Not so the SS. Overwhelmed by the amount of corpses to be stacked up on pyres and burned and bothered by the stench of burnt flesh, the SS ordered a comprehensive cleanup operation, forcing all prisoners still able to walk to participate.[57]

Between April 11th and 14th, everyone who was not dead or imminently dying was tasked with moving corpses into mass graves beyond the barbed wire.[58] Teams of four prisoners dragged or carried one corpse, sometimes with the help of blankets or pieces of cloth because corpses were slippery from oozing fluids, to designated pits "like a trail of ants."[59] Moshe Oster, his legs swollen and his body ridden with lice, was among those who transported the dead. He felt himself breaking down and was terrified for his own life since the SS guards kicked corpse-carriers who seemed too weak into the mass grave along with the dead. Oster eventually retreated to one of the barracks into which they had stacked the corpses up to the ceiling and lay there with the dead during the day, returning to his barrack at night, where he learned of rumors that the Germans planned to incinerate these morgue barracks together with their decomposing contents. From then on, Oster and his team decided to leave the dead by the road to shorten the distance and avoid being kicked into the mass grave themselves.[60] But the Germans caught on. Oster's squad was hardly the only one trying to evade the last-minute cleanup operations that mobilized the barely living to "disappear" those who had already died. Within days, the British continued the process of cleaning up the camp. But with bulldozers.[61]

On April 15th, Bergen-Belsen was liberated. The British were entirely unprepared for what they found when they entered the camp, even though the Red Army had reported on the discovery of death camps after they liberated Majdanek in July 1944 and Auschwitz in January 1945. But the camps in the east were practically devoid of people.[62] Instead of piles of corpses, which the Nazis had burned on stakes and in pits as well as in crematoria, the Red Army liberated piles of stuff and a few thousand emaciated prisoners who had been left behind when the Germans hastily evacuated the last of the killing centers. The Soviets found "Zyklon B cylinders, the interior of 'gas cells', the interior of barracks 'showing remnants of rope used to hang victims' and the exterior of the 'torture chamber', piles of shoes and boots, ashes of human remains in the crematoria and a pile of identity cards" that documented the industrial scale of the killing.[63] Starting in the summer of 1944, the Germans "evacuated" most of the prisoners to Germany in infamous death marches and, as a result, most of the survivors of the Nazi genocide were, in fact, liberated by American and British forces. The western Allies did not understand the difference between death camps, concentration camps, POW camps, and the countless subsidiary camps and, accordingly, failed to appreciate the central place the Nazi genocide of the Jews occupied in this landscape of death.[64]

With liberation the abuse stopped, but the dying continued. When the British arrived at Bergen-Belsen, the official estimate of the dead was 10,000. Roughly 60,000 people were in the camp when the British army arrived, horrified and utterly overwhelmed by the humanitarian disaster.[65] Faced with mass starvation, British authorities brought provisions into the camp. However, the emaciated prisoners' stomachs could not handle the heavy food. Those who survived stayed. Although they were technically free, they

Figure 9.2 British soldiers survey mountains of rags. Courtesy of the United States Holocaust Memorial Museum.

were forbidden from leaving the camp to contain the typhus epidemic. Most had no place to go anyway and on top of that were much too weak to travel.

Lieutenant-Colonel M. W. Gonin described the horrid scenes that the British encountered. They were entirely unprepared for the

> piles of corpses, naked and obscene, with a woman too weak to stand propping herself against them as she cooked the food we had given her over an open fire; men and women crouching down just anywhere in the open, relieving themselves of the dysentery, which was scouring their bowels; a woman standing stark naked washing herself with some issue soap in the water from a tank in which the remains of a child floated.[66]

Understandably such scenes were not only shocking, they also inspired rage. Josef Kramer, the camp commandant, spent 24 hours stuffed into a refrigerator at low temperature before Sergeant Norman Turgel let him out, interrogated, and arrested him. Of the 160 remaining SS personnel, about half escaped into the forest. British soldiers readily "emptied their machine guns" into the absconding criminals, Turgel recalled.[67]

Over the next month, the remaining SS guards, roughly 50 men and 30 women, were forced to clean up the corpses that had amassed inside the camp over the prior months and not been removed in the desperate cleanup operation they had orchestrated.[68] They were assigned to burial squads and for eight hours a day they loaded the thousands of corpses in varying stages of decomposition onto trucks and transported them to mass graves.[69] Some died of sepsis, some of typhus, some committed suicide with rope left in their cells by the British guards.[70]

The British military authorities were desperately understaffed, underresourced, and overwhelmed, and their primary concern was to contain Bergen-Belsen's raging typhus epidemic. They requisitioned the abandoned Wehrmacht barracks a few kilometers from the camp and turned them into a hospital.[71] Second Army Brigadier H. L. Glyn-Hughes, who was in charge of the relief operation, noted: "The task of cleansing the area seemed at first insuperable." The British relied largely on the Hungarian guards whom the Nazis had installed to secure the camp. British medical students, who were flown in to help with the humanitarian disaster, supervised the cleanup work done by the "Hungies" (Hungarians), whom they ordered to clear the filth and rubbish, the feces and soiled rags out of the huts and barracks.[72] Upon taking over the camp, the British army had to source medical supplies, clothes, linens, dressings, doctors, and nurses from the local population. They eventually managed to outfit the hospital barracks with 14,000 beds. They subsequently informed the mayor of Celle that every citizen of the town was required "to hand in one blanket" to outfit the hospital with the most rudimentary necessities.[73] German women from the surrounding countryside were called in to mop the floors.[74] Medical personnel had to decide who to first remove and transfer to the hospital, identifying those whom they thought were most likely to survive. Those selected were marked with an X on their forehead, subsequently stripped naked, wrapped in blankets, and carried to the "human laundry," a disinfecting station located in the former cavalry staples, where German nurses shaved, washed, and DDT-ed the emaciated survivors before they were admitted to the military hospital.[75] The military officers had to prevent prisoners not yet selected for care from forcing their way into the vehicles, often by force.[76]

Even though the British army established feeding stations inside the camp to alleviate the suffering, 500 people died each day.[77] Over the next several weeks, the barracks were evacuated and demolished, many of the structures and the surrounding piles of accumulated shoes and rags were burned. It took over a month to remove all prisoners from their filthy and infested barracks. The camp remained. Bergen-Belsen became a displaced persons camp. A militarized medical regime took over.[78]

The stigma, however, stuck to the prisoners, even as the United Nations Relief and Rehabilitation Administration (UNRRA) took over the administration of refugee and displaced persons' camps in Germany. UNRRA took its responsibility for "rehabilitation" at least as serious as the "relief" part of its operation. Surveillance was key. Humanitarian relief was both medicalized and militarized.[79] The dismal conditions of displaced persons (DPs), from the ethnic German expellees and refugees from Eastern Europe, to the millions of forced laborers and POWs, to the liberated concentration camp populations, only hardened the conviction of humanitarians that these masses of people needed to be recivilized into "free, independent, and self-sufficient human beings."[80] The populations liberated from concentration camps hardly evoked universal compassion or empathy. This was doubly true for Jewish survivors, whose unique plight the Allies failed to grasp. According to U.S. Army General George Patton, "The 'Jewish type of DP is, in the majority of cases, a sub-human species,' . . . 'lower than animals.'"[81] Only after the Harrison Report of August 1945, which highlighted the particular victimization of Jews and called for a better treatment of Jewish DPs, at least the American administrators adjusted relief operations and attitudes.[82]

A year after the liberation of Bergen-Belsen camp, the German civilian authorities complained about the contaminating filth and garbage from the DP camp. The mayor of Belsen reported to district authorities that inmates of the former concentration camp deposited all kinds of garbage along the country road between Belsen and Winsen, creating an unauthorized dump, which, so the mayor claimed, impeded access to agricultural fields. Finally, the garbage gave off revolting odors wafting into the makeshift emergency housing for Germans, which "could lead to epidemics" the mayor asserted.[83]

No amount of "relief" and "rehabilitation" could dissociate the survivors from filth and disease in the eyes of the surrounding German population. A "penetrating odour" of death, of rotting matter, of garbage and decomposing corpses had hung over the camps and saturated the air for miles beyond their walls in the spring of 1945.[84] As the Germans cleaned up the mess of war, they looked with suspicion upon the survivors and DPs administered by UNRRA. The Belsen mayor and the district director refused to shoulder the cost for the removal of the garbage, insisting that this mess was UNRA's responsibility.[85] The mayor proposed that the garbage be used to "fill the many depressions in the soil" within the rubbished space of the DP camp.[86] In the name of health and food security, the Germans reaffirmed the racial hierarchies in the language of cleanliness, using a rhetoric that outlived the collapse of the Nazi regime.

Rubble People

Over the course of the Allied military occupation, German self-understanding morphed from the utter impotence of a vanquished people to a nation of master cleaners, rubble clearers, and rebuilders. German views of Jews and Poles as incorrigibly filthy, dirty, and lazy, in turn, were slow to change.[87] The rubble women or *Trümmerfrauen* emerged as the unlikely heroes of the nation's indestructible spirit and resilience, of orderliness and hard work—an army of widows and mothers who selflessly cleaned up the mess of war. This myth obscured the fact that, in all cities, the occupying Allies had to mandate rubble clearance and force Germans to do this kind of work.[88]

U.S. and British military leadership had, in part, justified the indiscriminate bombings of civilians with the hope that Germans would rise up against the "Nazi oppressors" and end the war. When such a revolt did not materialize, they braced for the suicidal resistance of Germans defending their cities and towns to the end.[89] Yet, when the Allies encountered Germans, they did not find themselves confronted with fanatical killers but with an apathetic people looking after their own affairs.[90]

There were few exceptions, such as when Hannover erupted in an orgy of violent looting. In early April 1945, as Allied troops entered Hannover, the *Volkssturm* and the police, instead of defending the city or maintaining "order," joined thousands of ordinary citizens who ransacked the city's depots and warehouses in search for food, clothing, and other essentials. In a city reduced to rubble, "There was no regard for sex or age. Men struck women down with fists, and even barrel staves. Boys robbed aged women and men carrying [sic] off sacks of meal and flour." Apparently, people did not care that they were still in an active war zone. "[T]hey clawed and beat one another savagely while troops of the 84th Division completed the occupation."[91] The American observers were shocked at this sudden breakdown of discipline and order, noting that "[i]n previous instances of this kind, liberated slave workers have smashed into the food depots, but although 25,000 [forced laborers] were freed today in Hannover, they remained for the most part on the sidelines, watching the Germans fight over their own loot."[92]

While such incidents of wanton pillage were rare, they illustrate the fundamental shift in self-perception. The roles were reversed now. The Germans had to see themselves through the eyes of the occupiers—they were now the agents of disorder, being observed, evaluated, and judged. Walter Lippmann explained this phenomenon to American readers at the time: "What we are witnessing now is a spectacle which the word defeat no longer describes. It is the disintegration of Germany as a national state."[93]

As they passed through obliterated cities and towns, the Allies struggled to make sense of the destruction they had wielded; they were shocked by the devastation and havoc they had wrought. At once in awe and terrified of their own annihilative capacity, observers struggled with the fact that thousands of refugees were returning to cities without plumbing, and to cities where no house seemed to be intact.[94] Allies curiously observed the Germans as they defiantly organized their lives in this rubblescape, noting the mobs of children and adults who chased after American garbage trucks. German civilians dug through the trash of the victors, scavenging for food in the dumps and searching the ruins for firewood.[95] In many cities, most houses were mere silhouettes, skeletons rising above the rubble, "and most of the streets were so badly damaged that rubble piled six feet high closed them off to traffic. Grass growing in the ruins gave evidence of old bombings and there also were scattered signs stuck in the debris indicating that 'Dr.Schmidt' was forced to move his office elsewhere in the city."[96] Since 1943, 10 million people had been evacuated from German cities, most of them women and children, who tried to find their way back home to see what, if anything, still remained.[97] Even small towns and villages had suffered bomb damage. "Bulldozers, steam shovels, and tractors began a systematic leveling of sections of the villages to obtain brick, pieces of cement and other rubble," filler that was used by British combat engineers to patch impassable roads.[98] The Germans had a word for this kind of practice—*Trümmerverwertung* (rubble recycling).[99]

National discussions about how to combat the rubble had been under way since 1944. The Nazis had bulldozed the rubble into cellars and basements and piled larger amounts of rubble into the parts of cities and towns completely destroyed.[100] Thinking of their many uses for garbage, mayors wondered whether the rubble could not be put to some useful purpose, such as using the charred remains of buildings to produce charcoal or utilizing the debris for moor cultivation.[101] By the end of 1944, Nazi administrators envisioned a consortium that would operate under the joint leadership of the *Hauptring Steine und Erden* (industry representatives for mining and

Figure 9.3 Rubble mountain in Berlin, June 1949. Courtesy of Landesarchiv Berlin.

quarrying), the department for demolition, and the construction industry. The Reich Ministry of Labor invested in research for rubble recycling, inviting scientists and engineers to join the long list of innovators in the Nazi waste regime. [102]

Initially compelled to carry out hard and dirty labor in all occupation zones, Germans soon learned to place their garbage credentials and technological ingenuity at the service of the occupying authorities.[103] Eugen Berck, an engineer from Frankfurt, caught the attention of the international press after he invented "a process for transforming rubble into bricks and building blocks" that were allegedly even harder than kiln bricks, and raised hopes "to shorten the clearing of ruins and the rebuilding of German cities."[104]

Meanwhile, the metal industry quickly recognized that the rubble held the only remaining reservoir of metal scrap with which to restart the production of tools, machinery, and new construction. Accordingly, metal workers in Berlin organized to make the production of farming tools and agricultural implements a priority to enable the cultivation of farmland. A congress of 500 representatives of metal workers in Berlin drew up "an emergency program" that fashioned "hoes, scythes, sickles, spades, wheelbarrows, and trailers" out of the metal debris retrieved from the Berlin rubble.[105]

Harvesting reusable bricks and metal scrap from the rubble thus became an important component of the cleanup project. By November 1945, "The process of sorting this trash has been going on steadily for six months." but it was nonetheless a slow, labor-intensive process.[106] After a survey concluded that "it would take daily trains of fifty cars each sixteen years to cart all the rubble out of" Berlin, German architects involved in the planning for reconstruction suggested instead that the trees in the Tiergarten, Berlin's largest inner-city park, "be chopped down for firewood and the park will be used as a dump for bomb-created rubble."[107] Germans continued to use trees for firewood due to coal shortages without permission. They effectively razed the Tiergarten and turned it first into a barren wasteland and then into garden plots to grow potatoes and other vegetables to supplement their meager rations.[108]

Figure 9.4 Rubble recycling apparatuses. Courtesy of Historisches Museum Hannover.

Figure 9.5 Rubble recycling plant, September 1949. Courtesy of Landesarchiv Berlin.

The rubble had to find a different home. Roughly 30–50 percent of the rubble could be recycled into new building material; some cities, like Hamburg and Cologne, had special rubble removal offices and most cities maintained organizations for rubble recycling.[109] However, rubble recycling produced new problems and disruptions. In Berlin, Max Gross built a rubble-processing plant, which soon caused the authorities to worry about its health effects, particularly since it operated under the open skies and was located next to a secondary school, exposing students to constant dust pollution.[110] Over the next several years, a consensus emerged in Berlin that the clouds of fine dust, churned up by the constant removal of rubble, posed a serious danger to citizens' health.[111]

Figure 9.6 Speer's military academy, December 1951. Courtesy of Landesarchiv Berlin.

Ultimately, the long history of dumping garbage onto badlands determined the fate of Berlin's rubble. Albert Speer's *Wehrtechnische Fakultät* (military academy) in the heart of the Grunewald, one of the few representational buildings the Nazis actually completed and that proved indestructible, inspired landscape architect Reinhold Lingner. Lingner, who served as the head of the Berlin Office for Landscaping, presented his plan for the "dumping of rubble away from Berlin's residential quarters in sites outside the city where the rubble could be integrated with the existing natural geography" to Berlin planning authorities in 1950.[112] Near the Devil's Lake in the Grunewald, some 17 kilometers outside of the city center, Lingner oversaw the construction of a 26 million cubic meter rubble mountain that

Figure 9.7 Rubble milestone at Teufelsberg, 1968. Courtesy of Landesarchiv Berlin.

fully entombed Speer's indestructible military academy in Berlin's greatest garbage melioration project to date. It took 25 years to build this 120-meter-high tomb, which fittingly was replanted with trees and incorporated into the Grunewald forest.[113]

Cleaning up the mess of war constituted countless individual acts of erasure that engaged Germans in a national project of renewal. In the national imagination, rubble recycling and the hard physical labor it entailed not only cleared German cities and towns of rubble and debris, but also scrubbed clean the stains of war and genocide without acknowledging the crime. Cleanup, frugality, and thrift, and the meticulous utilization of scarce raw materials, were ideals that had served the Nazi regime and its genocidal war. Not only did these ideals survive the war unscathed, Germans readily redeployed them in the service of their own redemption. Unlike concentration camp prisoners and slave laborers, whose daily toil sanitized the Reich's murderous loot, the rubble women were not maligned as dirty and filthy. Instead, they anchored fantasies of national renewal in collective performances of cleanup. The back-breaking labor of resource extension and recycling, of cleanup and sanitation, forced on Jews and other populations marked as scum, left barely any traces in the memories of the Germans who fashioned themselves into a society of order, hard work, and reconstruction.[114] As they mastered the rubble and cleared the heaps of debris, Germans turned their backs on the piles of rags and bones.

Conclusion

Hidden in Plain Sight

Waste is supposed to be invisible.[1] Its invisibility is readily taken as a primary indicator of civilization, modernity, development, and progress. Civility is a function of distance from waste and rubbished spaces; garbage is invariably taken "outside."[2] The clean polity is demarcated and fortified against waste's intrusions by infrastructural implements that increase in complexity the further the noxious stuff travels from its original owner. As long as waste finds itself on one of these pathways toward disposal (or recycling), it might as well be invisible, even when in plain sight. Such, in short, is the modern logic of garbage.[3]

The Nazi waste regime ensured that most Germans did not see garbage when they lugged wastepaper, bones, and other rubbish to local collection points for secondary materials. They saw wheat fields when garbage was flushed onto marshes and bacon when it was fed to hogs. They saw precious resources when concentration camp inmates sorted through rags, woolens, and textile waste, when forced laborers scrapped airplane junk and military equipment. As waste encroached on German cities and towns, citizens approached it from the perspective that everything, even rubble, could be recycled.[4]

Initially, most Germans remained comfortably removed from the destructive inner workings of the garbage economy. Over the course of the war, wastes intruded into the lives of ordinary Germans and hardened their resolve to combat disorder. Allied victory "robbed" Germany of its waste labor force, leaving Germany itself laid to waste. In the face of defeat, cleaning up this mess was paramount. Germans and Allies alike interpreted the mountainous accumulation of matter, of corpses and junk, as by-products of war without appreciating the connection between resource extraction, war, and genocide. Germans, moreover, associated the amassed loot and rubbish with defeat and collapse without recognizing them as central components of the order the Nazi regime and its citizens had forged.

The Allies, who entered German territory in the spring of 1945, encountered shocking scenes of chaos and destruction. Yet, nothing prepared them for the topography of death and decay they encountered when entering Nazi camps. Teams of photographers took still and moving images of the conditions that according to Lieutenant Colonel Richard Taylor, the British officer who took over as commandant of Bergen-Belsen, "defy description."[5] Without instruction and minimal training, soldier-photographers from the British Army Film and Photography Unit produced most of the images documenting the liberation of Bergen-Belsen in April 1945.[6] Drawn to piles of dead bodies and groups of the living dead scavenging around the camp grounds, photographers arranged "this pitiful human flotsam as if it were some gigantic still-life," recording their own horror and shock as they attempted to make sense of the humanitarian disaster that engulfed them.[7]

Susan Sontag reminds us that "ever since cameras were invented in 1839, photography has kept company with death." She insists that the "very notion of atrocity, of a war crime" required the existence of photographic evidence.[8] Photographs have long since served as superior evidence because they manage to both objectively record reality and explicitly bear witness.[9] Nonetheless, at the height of the war, the camera's objective authority was challenged by the West's growing ideological distrust of the Soviet Union and lingering memories of World War I's (false) atrocity stories.[10] The initial reports on the liberations of Auschwitz and Majdanek by Soviet war reporters were willfully ignored by Western democracies and readily dismissed as Soviet propaganda.[11]

After entering camps like Bergen-Belsen, Dachau, and Buchenwald, the Western Allies used photography to combat the disbelief they had previously fostered in response to survivor testimony from Nazi-occupied Poland and reports from Soviet sources.[12] The discovery of gas chambers in camps liberated by the Western Allies not only confirmed the reports about Nazi death factories that had initially been dismissed as Soviet propaganda, but also hardened their convictions that the Nazi crimes constituted a category of their own.

The Allies were shocked by what they saw, heard, and smelled, and could find no apparent logic to this landscape of death. Their cameras set out to capture the absence of logic and thus fundamentally shaped subsequent understanding of the Nazi regime and its crimes. The "confusing representation of slaughter" foreclosed questions about the nature of Nazi policies and intentions, the identity and origin of the victims, the connection between war

CONCLUSION 227

and genocide, the development and proliferation of carceral landscapes and the concentration camp complex, the technologies of killing, and the context of retreat and implosion. However, without providing an immediate understanding of these larger dynamics, the photographs "simply didn't make sense."[13] They were nonetheless crucial, if not foundational, to the initial sense-making process. In the absence of gold mines and cotton plantations, still and moving images of orchestrated mass starvation and murderous destruction of human lives through slave labor in the most industrialized country of Europe lacked the familiar frame that had contained such imagery in the context of colonial slaughter and orchestrated famine.[14] However, the Allies' professed speechlessness betrayed their knowledge of and participation in a longer history of imperial extraction, on which the Nazi regime explicitly modeled its own operations.[15] Contemporaries such as Aimé Césaire called out the hypocrisy of Europeans and Americans and objected to their refusal to recognize the Nazi crimes as akin to the crimes of colonialism. Césaire argued that

> at bottom, what he [the European] cannot forgive Hitler for is not *the crime in itself, the crime against man*, it is not *the humiliation of man as such*, it is the crime against the white man, the humiliation of the white man, and the fact that he applied to Europe colonialist procedures which until then had been reserved exclusively for the Arabs of Algeria, the "coolies" of India and the "niggers" of Africa.[16]

Césaire's critique fell on deaf ears and continues to do so. The images of the liberated camps and the human debris they contained function as a visual wall, separating monsters from men.

The images taken at Bergen-Belsen of piled, sprawled, dumped, and orderly stacked corpses provided the frame for understanding the photographs of mountains of shoes and garments, the bales of hair, and crates of teeth and dentures taken by the Red Army upon entering Majdanek in July 1944 and Auschwitz in January 1945. The Soviets encountered largely depopulated camps, plus the Nazis had dismantled and destroyed much of the evidence of the so-called Reinhard camps before the territory was captured.[17] Underequipped and without the technological advantages available to Western war journalists, Soviet war photographers tried to document the industrial scale of the killing after discovering the remnants of the infrastructures of destruction.[18] Instead of piles of corpses, they photographed piles of stuff, mountains of shoes and garments, warehouses filled with junk, personal items, secondary materials of all sorts, and finished goods. After the liberation of the camps inside Germany, these images became a proxy for millions of victims already buried and burned in Chelmno, Bełżec, Sobibor, Treblinka, Majdanek, Auschwitz, and the countless killing fields across Eastern Europe. Understandably, the explanations for these objects focused on the crimes rather than the logic behind them, inadvertently erasing the history of imperial extraction.

The visual record translated rags into bones. Each pair of shoes, each pair of glasses, each piece of clothing denoted a victim. As such, the images, together with the preserved materials, attested to the lives and deaths of millions of people. But as the camera zeroed in on the destruction, it also captured traces of the morbid logic of the Nazi waste regime, showing the spoils of empire that had been meticulously sorted into separate piles by the very people whose murder they came to denote.

The Nazis had notoriously recorded, with scientific precision, the nature of their own operations in film, photography, charts, and statistics to provide "evidence" for the "racial inferiority" of Jews and other victims.[19] When they amassed mountains of stuff, they did not do so to illustrate their lack of rationality or the magnitude of their crimes. They intended to recycle these materials by forcibly extracting the labor power of the remaining "expendable" populations. Criminal investigators and historians subsequently have described the piles of materials as "possessions" of the victims.[20] In addition to illustrating the perfidy of the Nazi regime, these material objects were used to approximate the number of victims.[21] But in the eyes of the regime, they were secondary materials, extracted for reuse and processing. As Obergruppenführer Pohl made explicit in August 1942, human hair made "hair yarn booties for U-boat crews and hair felt stockings for the *Reichsbahn*."[22] The warehouses and storage facilities uncovered by the Allies contained mountains of rubbish and orderly stacked garments, but the labor that went into sorting and making them remained hidden.

The piles of stuff that were discovered and photographed by the Allies were the material record of the toil of millions of people fighting for their survival. They were more than just a shorthand for senseless mass murder. They represented the comprehensive efforts of the Nazi regime to extract value from waste and secondary materials by metabolizing the labor power of those they purged as unclean and dangerous and condemned to death. However, the photographs of the mountains of shoes, clothing, and rags soon attained the status of superior evidence that enshrined Nazi irrationality at its most extreme and, inadvertently, overshadowed the logic of the Nazi waste regime.

The Third Reich was premised on an economic rationality driven by ideals of total resource exploitation and remainder-less extraction, rather than by profit in the conventional sense. Individual and collective zeal underwrote an economy of designed scarcity that subsequently radicalized the structures of imperial extraction and genocide in the context of war. Waste avoidance and resource-thinking suffused all aspects of life and death in Nazi Germany and its occupied lands. This everyday experience of the mundane, reeking, and intimately personal aspects of war and genocide has been sidelined by a focus on industrial killing.

Waste thinking and garbage practices, this book has argued, were at the very center of the Nazi system and pervaded every aspect of it. Initially, the rhetoric around cleanliness and resource scarcity opened up venues for participation that made the Nazi waste regime a truly collective project. In its maturation, the collective performance of frugality and thrift cemented the political importance of resource extension and waste reclamation in everyday practice, forcing grudging compliance with the proliferating regulations for material substances. Wartime scarcity and destruction readily obscured the political nature of practices that had become habits, and most Germans understood their participation in the Nazi garbage economy as selfless acts of unquestioned necessity and examples of good, orderly behavior, rather than recognizing them as part of the engine of destruction. For the Nazi managers of the war economy, anticipated scarcity and destruction justified the absolute ruthlessness of resource and labor extraction and eventually even rendered the destruction of human lives a "necessary" resource-saving measure. In this way, both the deliberate starvation of Soviet POWs and the systematic mass murder of Europe's Jews figured in the economic calculations of Himmler, Göring, and Backe, as they weighed labor extraction and caloric input.

In this system of extraction and destruction, food, sanitation, and medical care were lacking by design, cruelty and brutality attained the status of labor-extending technologies, squeezing every last calorie out of workers who had no intrinsic value beyond their output. Inside Germany, camps became reservoirs for slave labor to metabolize inferior and secondary materials, to process the loot and turn it into war material as crude as linens, towels, underwear, straw shoes, and uniforms for the killers and their prisoners. In the occupied east, the Nazi overlords condemned civilians to physical labor and collected Jews "fit" for work in special camps and "self-administered" ghettos, where they slaved for the war economy, making screws, wooden shoes, cloth out of processed rags, and felt boots out of human hair. In its most extreme, the recycling frenzy forced Jews slated for annihilation to process the hair, rags, shoes, and personal belongings stripped from those who had already been murdered.

The Nazi camps were part of the regime's waste management infrastructure. The death factories disposed of millions of people, whom the Nazis valued less than the rags they wore on their skins. The remaining camps were machines for labor extraction; accordingly, resource-thinking and waste avoidance shaped food and clothing provisioning for prisoners as well as the makeshift, rudimentary infrastructure of the camps themselves. Squalidness, dearth, and disease characterized the dismal living and working conditions of the populations jammed together in this fashion. But Germans readily took the dirt, grime, and filth as evidence for the racial inferiority and innate uncleanliness of those condemned to do society's shit work.

As the regime imploded and looted materials threatened to suffocate the Reich, Germans focused on their own affairs. Yet, the frantic hoarding and killing fundamentally structured the environment in ways that could not have escaped anyone. German civilians nonetheless claimed to know nothing about it and cast themselves as victims thrice over.[23] Abdicating responsibility, Germans understood themselves as having been seduced by Hitler, then suffering through a brutal and inhumane war, only to find themselves occupied by vengeful victors who confronted them with atrocity propaganda and administered suffering in a worse fashion than the Nazis.[24] In the months and years after the war, Germans fashioned themselves into a society of cleanup and reconstruction.[25]

Waste management practices, such as extending resources and squeezing value from inferior or old materials, did not present a rupture with the past, nor did the strategies devised to disappear waste or mine it for residual value introduce novel technologies. The Nazis dumped, burned, and recycled. While zealous citizens and SS fanatics entertained outlandish ideas such as pressing potato extract into pills or producing sausage from garbage, for the most part, the extraction of value from wastes used familiar techniques and targeted materials such as textiles, metal, paper, bones, and wastewater that had long histories of reuse and recycling. It was the fanaticism that set Nazism apart from other waste utilization endeavors; it was their political ideology that turned resource extension and waste management into instruments of war, destruction, and genocide intended to extend the lifespan of a murderous regime. Yet, the limits within which the waste regime's logic was applied also indicate that "dehumanization," often invoked as an explanatory framework, did not actually work. Irrespective of the dehumanizing language deployed and the inhumane conditions under which Jews and other targets of the regime were forced to live, the Nazis remained fully conscious of the fact that they were deliberately and recklessly exploiting and murdering members of their own species.

Garbage practices, this book suggests, are practices of systematic maintenance. They demarcate what is clean and make the materials that offend public sensibility disappear. In the case of Nazi Germany, they were used to sort humans and inanimate matter according to arbitrarily fixed value and to cast useless matter aside. Throughout, garbage practices were fundamental to the appearance of order. Such practices function in this way beyond the admittedly special case of Nazi Germany. The structures that render order a function of cleanliness and productivity keep waste management at the center of contemporary societies.[26] Today, racial capitalism has an eerie green tinge, enforced by a not-so-thin blue line. Recycling's recent glorification as the panacea to the climate crisis lets us easily forget the economic rationales that drive it. Garbage practices fortify the order that is routinely invoked to legitimate systems of governance and their violent enforcements.[27] This convergence between waste management and violent governance poses complicated questions about long-term continuities, about shared histories, and about possible futures of violent systems of resource extraction, of labor exploitation and policing, of the destruction of human and nonhuman lives and environments. *Empire of Rags and Bones* does not purport to answer these questions. It seeks instead to make visible waste and the central role its management plays in the perpetuation of systems that rubbish on an industrial scale.

Notes

Introduction

1. BArch R3-1919, M. A. Rothe an Reichsministerium für Rüstung und Kriegsproduktion, May 13, 1944.
2. BArch R3-1919, Aktenvermerk, October 31, 1944.
3. BArch R8II-46, Reichsstelle für Kleidung und verwandte Gebiete an Firma Biechteler & Co., September 8, 1943.
4. BArch R8II-46, Reichsstelle für Kleidung und verwandte Gebiete an Firma Biechteler & Co., September 8, 1943.
5. BArch R3-1919, M. A. Rothe an Reichswirtschaftsministerium Abt II Min.Öl 3, September 9, 1943.
6. BArch R3-1919, M. A. Rothe Anlage zur Ausnahme vom Bauverbot, January 19, 1945.
7. BArch R3-1919, M. A. Rothe Ausnahme vom Bauverbot, January 19, 1945.
8. Blatman, *The Death Marches*.
9. For a detailed account on the implosion of the Nazi regime, see Kershaw, *The End*.
10. Denton, "'Récupérez!' The German Origins of French Wartime Salvage Drives, 1939–1945" and "Steel of Victory, Scrap of Defeat: Mobilizing the French Home Front, 1939–1940"; Denton and Weber, "Bones of Contention," 119–139; Thorsheim, *Waste Into Weapons*; Strasser, *Waste and Want*; Stokes and Köster, *The Business of Waste*.
11. Walker, *Nazi Science*.
12. I borrow the concept from sociologist Zsuzsa Gille, who argues that waste regimes "are delineated according to how--that is, through what economic, political and material dynamics--waste is produced, how it is conceptualized and how it is politicized." Gille, *From the Cult of Waste*, 9. Simply put, waste regimes are political systems in which waste making and waste management are central to the maintenance and perpetuation of the existing order. Most modern societies are waste regimes in the broadest sense, but rarely do we think of them in such terms. Yet, in modern societies the presence of unmanaged or unregulated wastes is generally interpreted as a sign of social disruption or infrastructural breakdown. Accordingly, their regulation and disappearance (different as they may be across ideological divides) are foundational to the understanding of order in the abstract. Shanks, Platt, and Rathje, "The Perfume of Garbage: Modernity and the Archeaological," 71.
13. Tooze, *The Wages of Destruction*, 203–243; Corni and Gies, *Brot. Butter. Kanonen*; Petzina, *Autarkiepolitik*; Backe, *Um die Nahrungsfreiheit Europas*.
14. Berg, "The Nazi Rag-Pickers and Their Wine."
15. Aly and Heim, *Architects of Annihilation*, 3; Stargardt, *The German War*; Fritzsche, *Life and Death in the Third Reich*; Kershaw, *The End*.

16. "Altmaterialerfassung und Verwertung im Vierjahresplan," November 27, 1936, in *Der Reichskommissar für Altmaterialverwertung*. See also Weber, "Nazi German Waste Recovery and the Vision of a Circle Economy," and Weber, "'Total' Recycling."
17. Allen, *The Business of Genocide*, 245.
18. Browning, "The Nazi Decision to Commit Mass Murder"; on Nazi "security" thinking regarding the Jews, see Moses, *The Problems of Genocide*, 327.
19. Browning, *Origins of the Final Solution*, 19.
20. Quoted in Tooze, *The Wages of Destruction*, 540.
21. Allen, *The Business of Genocide*; Tooze, *The Wages of Destruction*; Müller, *Der Manager der Kriegswirtschaft*.
22. Hayes, ed., *How was it possible?*; Neumann, *Shifting Memories*. For the exact use of the phrase, see https://www.berlinstory.de/hitler-dokumentation as well as Fechner, *Wie konnte es geschehen?* For a more conceptual approach, see Smith, "The Vanishing Point of German History: An Essay on Perspective."
23. See, in particular, the pioneering study by Raul Hilberg first published in 1961 as the first comprehensive study on the subject. Hilberg, *The Destruction of the European Jews*. Most important for my own work are Longerich, *Holocaust*; Browning, *Ordinary Men*; Cesarani, *Final Solution*; Blatman, *The Death Marches*; Bloxham, *The Final Solution*; Confino, *A World Without Jews*; Snyder, *Black Earth*; Stone, ed., *The Historiography of the Holocaust*.
24. For an excellent summary of the controversy over Hitler's role and intention, see Kershaw "Hitler: 'Master in the Third Reich' or 'Weak Dictator'?"
25. See Detlev Peukert's seminal essay "The Genesis of the 'Final Solution' from the Spirit of Science"; also Bauman, *Modernity and the Holocaust*; Herf, *Reactionary Modernism*. Mark Roseman offers incisive commentary and a very useful summary of the different positions. Roseman, "National Socialism and the End of Modernity."
26. Friedländer, *Nazi Germany and the Jews, 1933–1939*; Diner, *Beyond the Conceivable*; Bauer, *Rethinking the Holocaust*. Daniel Jonah Goldhagen described German antisemitism as "eliminationist" to distinguish it from less virulent forms. Goldhagen, *Hitler's Willing Executioners*. Incidentally, Goldhagen's controversial work is relying on the same corpus of evidence that informs Christopher Browning's seminal study *Ordinary Men*, which demonstrates that antisemitism, though central to Hitler's mind, was often ancillary to the motivations of the killers of Police Battalion 101. A useful summary and juxtaposition of these opposing views can be found in *The "Willing Executioners/"Ordinary Men" Debate*.
27. Rothberg, *Multidirectional Memory*; Zimmerer, *Von Windhuk mach Auschwitz?*; Moses, *The Problems of Genocide*. Following the publication of Achille Mmembe's essay "The Society of Enmity" in *Radical Philosophy*, German intellectuals accused Mbembe of antisemitism after he suggested linkages between South Africa's apartheid system, the Holocaust, and the brutalization of Palestinians in the occupied territories. See also "Achille Mbembe Accused of anti-Semitism: The German controversy," *The Africa Report* (May 31, 2020); Assmann, "A Specter Is Haunting Germany." The debate subsequently intensified with the publication of Moses, "The German Catechism," and morphed into a *Feuilletonkrieg* in German newspapers. Biller,

"Die neuen Relativierer"; Friedländer, Frei, and Steinbacher, eds., *Ein Verbrechen ohne Namen*. For an overview of the revived debates regarding the comparability and imperial nature of the Nazi genocide, see the contributions to "Discussion Forum: Holocaust Memory and Postcolonialism," in *Central European History*.
28. Tooze, *Wages of Destruction*; Aly, *Hitler's Volkstaat*; Allen, *The Business of Genocide*; Bajohr, *Arisierung in Hamburg*; Kaienburg, *Die Wirtschaft der SS*; Georg, *Die Wirtschaftlichen Unternehmungen der SS*; see also Petzina, *Autarkiepolitik im Dritten Reich*.
29. Kehr, *Der Primat der Innenpolitik*.
30. Robinson, *Black Marxism*; Leroy and Jenkins, eds., *Histories of Racial Capitalism*. See also the foundational text by Williams, *Capitalism and Slavery*.
31. Ferdinand, *Decolonial Ecology*; Mills, *The Racial Contract*.
32. Melamed, *Represent and Destroy*.
33. Historians disagree on whether antisemitism and other racisms are conceptually linked or constitute distinct historical phenomena. While historians like Bloxham and Moses fall firmly in the first camp, Friedländer, Herf, Burleigh, and Wipperman firmly belong to the other. Specifically on the role of racism as a means to exact consent, see Roseman, "Racial Discourse," and Pendas, Roseman, and Wetzell, *Beyond the Racial State*. In addition, Kershaw, "Working Toward the Führer"; Gellately, *Backing Hitler*; Eley, *Nazism as Fascism*; Wildt, *Volksgemeinschaft als Selbstermächtigung*; Bloxham, *The Final Solution*; Moses, *The Problems of Genocide*; Friedländer, *Nazi Germany and the Jews*; Friedländer, "Introduction," in *Probing the Limits*; Burleigh and Wipperman, *The Racial State*; Friedländer, "A Fundamentally Singular Crime"; Herf, *The Jewish Enemy*.
34. Roseman, "Racial Discourse," 31.
35. Stargardt, *The German War*, 377.
36. Stargardt, "Legitimacy Through War," in *Beyond the Racial State*, 402–428, 406.
37. See Moses' discussion of "permanent security" in *The Problems of Genocide*, 35–37, 315, 319, 323–30.
38. Berg, "The Nazi Rag-Pickers and Their Wine."
39. Aly and Heim, *Architects of Annihilation*, 234–236; also Davis, *Homefires Burning*; Chickering, *Imperial Germany and the Great War*; Cox, *Hunger in War and Peace*; Kocka, *Facing Total War*; Daniel, *The War From Within*; Vincent, *The Politics of Hunger*.
40. Tooze, 135–165; Corni and Gies, *Brot, Butter, Kanonen*; König. *Volkswagen, Volksempfänger, Volksgemeinschaft*; Schanetzky, *Kanonen statt Butter*.
41. See Herbert, "'Die guten und die schlechten Zeiten.' Überlegungen."
42. For a global history of empire, see Burbank and Cooper, *Empires in World History*, which provides an excellent overview of imperial projects from antiquity to the present that illustrates the importance of resource extraction without making it its central theme. In contrast, the following monographs engage with specific instances of empire building and imperial extraction from a range of different of perspectives: Mintz, *Sweetness and Power*; Mitchell, *Carbon Democracy*; Headrick, *The Tools of Empire*; Arboleda, *Planetary Mine*; Beckert, *Empire of Cotton*; Mitman, *Empire of Rubber*.

43. Mazower, *Hitler's Empire*; Lower, *Nazi Empire-Building*; Baranowksi, *Nazi Empire*; Lumans, *Himmler's Auxiliaries*; Eley, *Nazism as Fascism*; Tooze, *The Wages of Destruction*, 461–485.
44. Mazower, *Hitler's Empire*; Snyder, *Black Earth*; Aly, *Hitler's Volkstaat*.
45. Scholars have engaged in heated debates over the relationship between Germany's colonial past and Nazi eastward expansion. Three main positions have emerged in response to the "Windhoek to Auschwitz" thesis advanced by Jürgen Zimmerer, "Krieg, KZ und Völkermord. Der erste deutsche Genozid," in *Völkermord in Deutsch-Südwestafrika*, 45–63. Zimmerer not only argues that German colonial genocides made the Holocaust possible but sees direct lines of continuity. A second position, summarized and evidenced by Robert Gerwarth and Stephan Malinowski, "Der Holocaust als 'kolonialer Genozid'?," insists on the fundamental disparity between the Holocaust on the one hand and the German genocide of the Nama and Herero peoples on the other, opting to refer to the latter as a "colonial massacre" and insisting that Nazi Germany's war in the east cannot be integrated into a history of Western imperialism. The third position, which also displays greater internal variation than either of the other two, sits somewhere in the middle, recognizing the imperial character of the Nazi regime, but stressing knowledge transfers, borrowings, and shared imaginaries instead of direct continuities or causal connections. See, for example, Baranowski, *Nazi Empire*; Naranch and Eley, *German Colonialism in a Global Age*; Kundrus, "From the Herero to the Holocaust?" For the nuances setting different positions apart, see "Forum: The German Colonial Imagination," in *German History*.
46. Traverso, *The Origins of Nazi Violence*.
47. BArch R121-587, Band 1, Wirtschaftsführungstab Ost "Richtlinien für die Führung der Wirtschaft in den neubesetzten Ostgebieten (Grüne Mappe) Teil 1 (2.Auflage) Aufgaben und Organisation der Wirtschaft" (Berlin, July 1941); LOC NT Vol. XXXVI Document 347-EC. For additional detail, see Document 126-EC in the same volume.
48. Davis, *Late Victorian Holocausts*.
49. Extractivism is the name given to the violent and destructive imperial and neo-imperial processes of resource and labor extraction. Grounded in postcolonial theory, political ecology, eco-feminism, and a materialist critique of capitalism, extractivism understands empires as capitalist extraction machines, rather than merely political entities whose territorial expansion extends dominion. In world history, this concept has become key in explaining the north–south wealth gap as the result of colonial and neo-imperial regimes of violent extraction that destroyed and continue to destroy societies, cultures, and ecosystems. See Ferdinand, *A Decolonial Ecology*; Burchardt and Dietz, "(Neo-) extractivism—A New Challenge for Development Theory from Latin America"; McKay, "Agrarian Extractivism in Bolivia"; Kröger, *Iron Will*; Svampa, *Neo-Extractivism in Latin America*; Arboleda, *Planetary Mine*; Becerril, *Resisting Extractivism*.
50. Bernstein, *Radical Evil*; Diner, ed., *Zivilisationsbruch*; Diner, *Beyond the Conceivable*; Benzler, "Auschwitz als Zivilisationsbruch"; Adorno, "Kulturkritik und Gesellschaft"; Arendt, *The Origins of Totalitarianism*.
51. I owe this insight to a conversation with Andrew Needham.

52. Agamben, *Homo Sacer*. Interestingly, Hermann Göring uses the same formulation "nacktes Leben." BArch R144-842, Ministerpräsident Generalfeldmarschall Göring, December 19, 1939.
53. The term *Ostarbeiter* literally translates as "eastern worker" but is loaded with Nazi racist assumptions and at the same time a euphemism masking the structural violence that shaped the experiences of people forcibly deported from their homes in Eastern Europe and across Soviet territory to work inside Germany under horrendous conditions. In its everyday use, *Ostarbeiter* lumped together POWs and civilian workers forcibly deported. Benz, "Zwangsarbeit im Nationalsozialistischen Staat"; Keller, *Sowjetische Kriegsgefangene im Deutschen*; Herbert, *Hitler's Foreign Workers*; Herbert, ed., *Europa und der 'Reichseinsatz'*; Pohl and Sebta, *Zwangsarbeit in Hitler's Europa*; Pohl, *Die Wirtschaft der Wehrmacht*; Dick, *Builders of the Third Reich*.
54. Buggeln, "Were Concentration Camp Prisoners Slaves?"
55. Mills, "Black Trash"; Anderson, "Excremental Colonialism"; Zimring, *Clean and White*; Aguiar and Herod, *The Dirty Work of Neoliberalism*.
56. Medina, *The World's Scavengers*; Lewis, *Scammer's Yard*; Newell, *Histories of Dirt*; Pellow, *Garbage Wars*.
57. Müller, *Der Feind steht im Osten*; Heim, *Plant Breeding and Agrarian Research*; Rössler and Schleiermacher, eds., *Der 'Generalplan Ost.'*
58. Bernhard, "Hitler's Africa in the East"; Zimmerer, "The Birth of the Ostland"; and Zimmerer, "Colonialism and the Holocaust."
59. Aly, *Hitler's Volksstaat*; Bajohr, *Arisierung in Hamburg*; Aly, *Hitler's Beneficiaries*; Aalders, *Nazi Looting*.
60. Earlier claims by Anna Bramwell in *Blood and Soil: Walther Darré and Hitler's Green Party* (Abbotsbrook, UK: Kensal Press, 1985) about a supposedly "green wing" of the Nazi party led by the *Reichsbauernführer* (Reich Peasant Leader) Richard Walther Darré have been thoroughly refuted. Historian Frank Uekoetter suggests that even while German conservationists sought the favor of the regime and were able to push through some of their agenda, "There is no way we can speak about a Nazi permeation of the conservation movement," or of a coherent environmental policy. Uekoetter, *The Greenest Nation?*, 52; Brüggemeier, Cioc, and Zeller, eds., *How Green Were the Nazis?*; Uekoetter, *The Green and the Brown*; as well as Köstering, "Müllspülung im Golmer Luch." See also Williams, "Protecting Nature between Democracy and Dictatorship"; Koshar, "Organic Machines"; Lekan, *Imagining the Nation in Nature*.
61. As historian Etienne Benson suggests, it is useful to look beyond the conservationist movements of the early twentieth century or the progressive environmental movements that originated in the 1960s and has proliferated since when trying to explain how people understood the "environment" or practiced "environmentalisms" in the past. See Benson's *Surroundings*, specifically, p. 14.
62. Krüger, "Der Raum als Gestalter der Innen- und Aussenpolitik," 110. Lamenting the "increasing despatialization [*Enträumlichung*] of human life since the beginning of the 19th Century" as a result of urbanization, densification, and speed of travel, Krüger stresses the "natural" qualities of particular "spaces" and their effect on "human feeling and wishing [*menschliches Fühlen und Wollen*] which can be

vividly captured with the concept of 'rootedness in soil [Bodenständigkeit].'" Based on this notion of Bodenständigkeit, Krüger insists on a particularly layered ordering of space: describing the Erbhof (ancestral estate) as the smallest spatial unit on which the forces of the soil could be brought to bear, Krüger outlines the subsequent units of space always containing the former as the Gemeinde (municipality) in the form of a local congregation (Ortsgemeinde), the countryside (Landschaft), the state, and ultimately the Reich as the geographical boundary of the autarch race.

63. Hiller, Deutscher Kampf um Lebensraum, 2. Hiller argues that "as long as a people is rooted in the soil of the homeland, it remains healthy; as soon as it disengages therefrom, it will fall sick and die." Also Daitz, Lebensraum und gerechte Weltordnung, 10. Vastness of territory was associated with an abundance of resources and possibilities. Compare Tooze, The Wages of Destruction, xxiii.
64. Beyond the canonical works, of particular relevance for my engagement with the field are Demuth, Floating Coast; Benson, Surroundings; Saraiva, Fascist Pigs; Needham, Power Lines; Samalin, The Masses Are Revolting; Davis, Ecology of Fear; Davis, Late Victorian Holocausts; Mitchell, Carbon Democracy.
65. Blackbourn, The Conquest of Nature; Uekötter, Turning Points in Environmental History; Uekötter, The Age of Smoke; Radkau, Natur und Macht.
66. Snyder, Black Earth, 241, 321.
67. Schmitt, Der Nomos der Erde; Schmitt, Staat, Großraum, Nomos; Kapp, Weltkrieg um Grossräume.
68. Sudrow, Der Schuh im Nationalsozialismus; Weber, "Towards 'Total' Recycling: Women, Waste and Food Waste Recovery in Germany, 1914–1939"; Denton and Weber, "Bones of Contention"; Köstering, "Müllspülung im Golmer Luch"; Köstering, "'Pioniere der Rohstoffbeschaffung' Lumpensammler im Nationalsozialismus 1934–1939"; Zeller, Consuming Landscapes; Zeller, Driving in Germany; Weber, "Nazi German Waste Recovery and the Vision of a Circle Economy."
69. Muscolosi, The Ecology of War in China; Brady, War Upon the Land; Briggs, Footprints of War; Russell, War and Nature; Tucker, At War: The Military and American Culture; Tucker and Russell, eds., Natural Enemy, Natural Ally; Brantz, "Environments of Death."
70. Schmitt, Staat, Großraum, Nomos; Eulenburg, Grossraumwirtschaft und Autarkie; Overy, "Business in the Grossraumwirtschaft"; Volkmann and Chiari, Ökonomie und Expansion. The concept "environments of destruction" is informed by Brantz, "Environments of Death."
71. Zimring, Clean and White; Washington, "Ball of Confusion"; Montrie, The Myth of Silent Spring; Andreson, The Cultivation of Whiteness; Newell, Histories of Dirt.
72. See, for example, MacBride, Recycling Reconsidered; Zimring, Cash for Your Trash; Hecht, "Human Crap: The Idea of Disposability is a New and Noxious Fiction"; Simons, "Waste Not. Want Not: Excrement and Economy."
73. Reno, "Toward a New Theory of Waste," 7–8; Gille, From the Cult of Waste, 23; Samalin, The Masses Are Revolting. Also see O'Brien, A Crisis of Waste.
74. Boudia et al., Residue.

75. Reid, *Paris Sewers and Sewermen*; Anderson, "Excremental Colonialism: Public Health and Poetics of Pollution"; Martin, "Sewage and the City."
76. Douglas, *Purity and Danger*, 44.
77. Ungewitter, *Die Verwertung des Wertlosen*.
78. Samalin's analysis of disgust is useful here. Waste similarly appears as an important "driving force of social change, fueled by the call for its own repudiation. Like a broom made out of dust, the more it swept up after itself, the more of itself it left behind." See Samalin, *The Masses Are Revolting*, 12.
79. Webster, *Aftermath: The Remnants of War*, 112–113.
80. In a letter to the Reich's regulatory agency for water and air, the Waffen-SS explicitly opts out of having the air tested for fly ash in preparation for the planning of a heating plant. BArch R154-48, Zentral-Bauleitung der Waffen-SS an die Reichsanstalt für Wasser und Luftgüte. Betr. KL Auschwitz, May 26, 1944.
81. Diner, *Beyond the Conceivable*, 130–137; Bauer, *Rethinking the Holocaust*, 45.
82. While the relevance of metals to the war effort is intuitive, textiles were the largest import-based industry and thus the regime anticipated shortages already in peacetime. Apelt, "Gegenwartsfragen der deutschen Textilwirtschaft," 682; Tooze, *Wages of Destruction*, 76–79.

Chapter 1

1. Kershaw, *Hitler, 1889–1936: Hubris*, 52.
2. Hitler, *Mein Kampf*, 61.
3. Anderson, *The Cultivation of Whiteness*; Anderson, "Excremental Colonialism: Public Health and Poetics of Pollution"; Mills, "Black Trash." See also Russell, *War and Nature*; Zimring, *Clean and White*.
4. See Mills, *The Racial Contract*; Zimmerer, *Von Windhuk mach Auschwitz*; Zimmerman, *Anthropology and Antihumanism in Imperial Germany*; Bruns, "Toward a Transnational History of Racism"; Chin et al., *After the Nazi Racial State*; Traverso, *The Origins of Nazi Violence*.
5. While scholars of racial capitalism have demonstrated the economic logic of racism and racial oppression for decades, scholarship on Nazi Germany has too often understood Nazi racism as separate from and fundamentally different from other racisms. Thus, few scholars have examined the economic logic of Nazi racism. Notable exceptions are Kaienburg, *Die Wirtschaft der SS*; Allen, *The Business of Genocide*; Tooze, *The Wages of Destruction*; Kaienburg, ed., *Konzentrationslager und deutsche Wirtschaft*. For important works on racial capitalism, see Robinson, *Black Marxism*; Leroy and Jenkins, eds., *Histories of Racial Capitalism*; Melamed, *Represent and Destroy*.
6. The concept of the racial state was originally popularized by Burleigh and Wippermann, *The Racial State*. For a more recent nuanced and critical engagement with the concept and its reach, see Pendas, Roseman, and Wetzell, eds., *Beyond the Racial State: Rethinking Nazi Germany*.

7. Elsewhere, I have illustrated how the presence of waste and garbage increased the urgency of moving toward social policing and law and order politics. Berg, "A Rubbished World." See also Wilkerson, *Caste: The Origins of Our Discontents*; Osterweil, *In Defense of Looting*.
8. Lebzelter, "Die 'Schwarze Schmach.' Vorurteile Propaganda Mythos," 55.
9. Fischer, *Bündnis der Eliten*; Stähler, *Zionism, the German Empire, and Africa*.
10. Zantop, *Colonial Fantasies*; Zantop, *The Imperialist Imagination*; Pugach, Pizzo, and Blackler, *After the Imperialist Imagination*; Sandler, *Empire in the Heimat*; Conrad and Osterhammel, *Das Kaiserreich transnational*; Hull, *Absolute Destruction*.
11. On the relationship between German colonialists and the Nazi regime, see Sandler, *Empire in the Heimat*.
12. Lebzelter, "Die 'Schwarze Schmach.' Vorurteile Propaganda Mythos," 43. It serves to note that imperial Germany also forced Africans into military service, deploying them in the spaces of empire because they were supposedly better able to withstand the climatic and environmental conditions. See Moyd, "Color Lines, Front Lines."
13. Arendt, "Race-Thinking Before Racism"; Evans, *Anthropology at War*.
14. Evans, *Anthropology at War*, 138.
15. The most famous example constitutes Oswald Spengler's pessimistic bestseller *The Decline of the West* from 1918.
16. Melosi, *Garbage in the City*, 17, 28, 42ff.
17. Foucault, *Discipline and Punish*. The importance of Jeremy Bentham for both urban development and planning and prison and disease is key. Also Porter, *Health, Civilization and the State*; Gilmore, *Golden Gulag*; Davis, *Are Prisons Obsolete ?*; Garland, *The Culture of Control*; Brodeur, *The Policing Web*; Rawlings, *Policing: A Short History*.
18. Brodeur, *The Policing Web*, 18; for connections between public health and social order in other contexts, see Bashford, *Imperial Hygiene*; Porter, *Health, Civilization and the State*; Barnes, *Intimate Communities*; Heynen and Van der Meulen, *Making Surveillance States*; Rosen, *A History of Public Health*.
19. Brodeur, *The Policing Web*, 60–64; Rawlings, *Policing*, 97ff.
20. Spengler, *The Decline of the West*.
21. Cocks, *The State of Health in Nazi Germany*, 34–35; Kershaw, *Hitler, Hubris*, 78–79; on the nineteenth-century origins of this discourse, see Evans, *Death in Hamburg*, 394, 477–478. Also, Weindling, *Epidemics and Genocide in Eastern Europe*; Proctor, *The Nazi War on Cancer*; Bashford, *Imperial Hygiene*, 5; Lyon, *Surveillance as Social Sorting*.
22. In Hamburg, Andreas Walther applied this biosocial logic to the study of the city referring to malignant individuals who infect healthy parts of the city like a cancer. Walther, *Neue Wege zur Großstadtsanierung*. Racial science, however, was an international, collaborative endeavor, undergirding the equally international project of eugenics. See Traverso, *The Origins of Nazi Violence*, 48–49, 54–63; Stern, *Eugenic Nation*; also the contributions in Berg and Wendt, *Racism in the Modern World*; Goldberg, *Racist Culture*; Jacobson, *Whiteness of a Different Color*; Weiss-Wendt and Yeomans, eds., *Racial Science in Hitler's New Europe, 1938–1945*.

23. Nazi urban planners revived the garden city model, proposing the concentration of healthy members of the *Volksgemeinschaft* in urban areas as a proactive response to squalor, overcrowding, prostitution, disease, and social unrest. The Garden City Association was founded on June 10, 1899, based on concepts developed by Ebenezer Howard, who is credited with the urban utopia of the Garden City in reaction to the rapid growth of nineteenth-century cities and the overcrowded, filthy living conditions that characterized the working classes and urban poor. See Sennett, *Garden Cities in Theory and Practice*; Parsons and Schuyler, eds., *From Garden City to Green City*; Buder, *Visionaries and Planners*; Unwin, *Nothing Gained by Overcrowding*. For Germany in the 1920, see Migge, *Deutsche Binnenkolonisation*.
24. Stern, *Eugenic Nation*.
25. Lemke, *Biopolitics: An Advanced Introduction*.
26. Benson, *Suroundings*, 71, 89–93; Amato, *Dust: A History of the Small*, 74–80; also Ried, *Paris Sewers and Sewermen*; Worboys, *Spreading Germs*; Tomes, *The Gospel of Germs*.
27. As Etienne Benson has shown, "environment" and its German translation "*Umwelt*" meant something different in the first half of the twentieth century than the "environment" activists discovered as beleaguered nature since the 1960s. Benson, *Surroundings*, 118–119.
28. Zeller, *Driving Germany*.
29. Lohalm, "Für eine leistungsbereite und 'erbgesunde' Volksgemeinschaft."
30. Köstering, "Müllspülung im Golmer Luch." On the history of these tensions in prior imperial Germany, see Uetkötter, *City Meets Country*.
31. Köstering, "Müllspülung im Golmer Luch," 76–89.
32. BArch R154-509, Studiengesellschaft für Feldberegnung an die Landesanstalt für Wasser-Boden-und Lufthygiene, November 18, 1935.
33. Walther, *Neue Wege zur Großstadtsanierung*, 4.
34. Wachsmann, *KL: A History of the Nazi Concentration Camps*; Aly, *Aussonderung und Tod*.
35. Walther, *Neue Wege zur Großstadtsanierung*, 9.
36. Walther, 7; Lidbetter. *Heredity and The Social Problem Group*. Lidbetter entered the service of the poor law authority in 1898 and had been intimately involved in relief for the poor in London until the publication of his book in which he advanced arguments about the hereditary inferiority of social problem groups. While not negating negative environmental effects, he insisted on the heredity of certain defects.
37. Benson, *Surroundings*, 93.
38. Benson, *Surroundings*, 94.
39. Benson, *Surroundings*, 113–117.
40. Uexküll, *Staatsbiologie*, 20.
41. Benson, *Surroundings*, 118–119.
42. Uexküll, *Staatsbiologie*, 25.
43. Uexküll, *Staatsbiologie*, 18.
44. Uexküll, *Staatsbiologie*, 32. Here, he argues, "Surely a Hottentot who worships his fetish is a hundred times closer to reality than a professor who declares the universe to

be a haphazard atomic dance" [Sicher ist ein Hottentotte, der seinen Fetisch anbetet, der Wirklichkeit hundertmal näher als ein Professor, der das Universum für einen planlosen Atomtanz erklärt].
45. Mildenberger and Herrmann, "Nachwort" in *Umwelt und Innenwelt der Tiere*, 307.
46. Uexküll, *Staatsbiologie*, 42–48. On the importance of biology for lay people's understanding of social organization, see Nyhardt, *Modern Nature: The Rise of the Biological Perspective in Germany* (Chicago: University of Chicago Press, 2009), 7.
47. Nyhardt, *Modern Nature*.
48. Hitler, *Mein Kampf*, 311, 312, 330.
49. Herbert, "Die guten und die schlechten Zeiten." A shorter version of the article was published as "Good Times, Bad Times."
50. Tooze, *The Wages of Destruction*, 142.
51. Tooze, *The Wages*, 190–193.
52. Tooze, *The Wages*, 193; also Petzina, *Autarkiepolitik im Dritten Reich*.
53. Tooze, *The Wages*, 79.
54. Tooze, *The Wages*, 197.
55. Tooze, *The Wages*, xxiii–xxv, 4.
56. Mazower, *Hitler's Empire*; Lower, *Nazi Empire-Building*; Baranowski, *The Nazi Empire*; Eley, *Nazism as Fascism*; Bernhard "Hitler's Africa in the East."
57. The colonial novel by Hans Grimm *Volk ohne Raum* fantasizes about Africa. The title however captured the ideological imagination of the Nazi regime that pushed the novel and remained generally favorably disposed to Grimm, but the ideology of *Lebensraum* clearly envisioned eastward expansion. On Grimm, see Smith, "The Colonial Novel as Political Propaganda." Also Daitz, *Lebensraum und gerechte Weltordnung*; Hiller, *Deutscher Kampf um Lebensraum*; Krüger, "Der Raum als Gestalter der Innen- und Aussenpolitik": Meyer, ed., *Volk und Lebensraum*. For the ideas held by some of the most important ideologues, see Cecil, *The Myth of the Master Race*; Piper, *Alfred Rosenberg: Hitler's Chef Ideologe*; Longerich, *Heinrich Himmler*. For a vision of empire, see Müller, *Hitlers Krieg im Osten*; Baranowski, *Nazi Empire*; Giaccaria and Minca, *Hitler's Geographies*.
58. See Epstein, *Model Nazi*; Aly and Roth, *Die restlose Erfassung*; Aly and Heim, *Architects of Annihilation*; Hayes, *Industry and Ideology*; Klee, *Auschwitz, die NS-Medizin und ihre Opfer*; Wildt, *Generation des Unbedingten*; Schmuhl, *The Kaiser Wilhelm Institute for Anthropology*; Schafft, *From Racism to Genocide*.
59. The administrative chaos of the Nazi state has been carefully outlined in a number of studies. For a summary of the debates on Nazi administrative (in)efficiency, see Kershaw "Hiter: 'Master in the Third Reich' or 'Weak Dictator'?" Particularly useful in understanding the interplay between structural and ideological parameters is Kershaw, "'Working Toward the Führer.'" In addition, Hüttenberger, "Nationalsozialistische Polykratie"; Rebentisch, *Führerstaat und Verwaltung im Zweiten Weltkrieg*. See contributions to *Der "Führerstaat": Mythos und Realität*.
60. Ungewitter, *Verwertung des Wertlosen*, 165.
61. Tooze, *The Wages of Destruction*, 222–225.

62. Volkmann and Chiari, *Ökonomie und Expansion*.
63. During the Depression, as Susan Strasser illustrates, Americans in contrast to their German counterparts were encouraged as consumers to save by spending money, to buy on credit in order to jump-start the economy. Only during the war did the United States develop a scrap economy that in many ways resembled the efforts undertaken in Nazi Germany. While the Third Reich extracted from all *Volksgenosse n* their "bit" as soon as it put the German economy on a war footing, in the United States, the constriction of consumer society and the ethics of scrap were phenomena particular to the war. See Strasser, *Waste and Want*, 203–263.
64. Tooze, *The Wages of Destruction*, 64.
65. The Nazi press drew attention to the wastefulness of British and American women. See 'So wirtschaftet die Hausfrau in England' in *Hamburger Tageblatt*, February 19, 1939. 'Macht der Zucker dick?' in *Hamburger Tageblatt*, February 10, 1939. The *Hamburger Tageblatt* regularly printed recipes and instructions to German women as prewar food rationing became a fact of everyday life. See "Speisequark und Milcheiweisspulver: Zwei wichtige 'Rohstoffe' der modernen Ernährung in vielfältiger Verwendung" in *Hamburger Tageblatt*, February 11, 1939.
66. Ungewitter, *Die Verwertung des Wertlosen*.
67. Armstrong. "Introduction" in *Science and Salvage*, 7.
68. Denton, "'Récupérez!' The German Origins of French Wartime Salvage Drives, 1939–1945" and "Steel of Victory, Scrap of Defeat: Mobilizing the French Home Front, 1939–1940"; Thorsheim, *Waste Into Weapons*; Strasser, *Waste and Want*; Stokes and Köster, *The Business of Waste*.
69. Ungewitter draws on a list allegedly provided by Joseph Goebbels to detail the collection effort of Germany during World War I. Among other items, imperial Germany collected kitchen waste, pits and stones from fruits, acorns and chestnuts, wastepaper, rubber waste, gramophone records, cork and cork waste, human hair, scrap metals, lamp sockets, bones, bottles, celluloid, and rags. Claus Ungewitter, *Science and Salvage*, 100.
70. Ungewitter, *Science and Salvage*, 101. He notes that the production from reused materials was significant. In 1929, the U.S. produced 999 metric tons of copper from virgin materials and more than half this amount by means of reclamation. The percentages were similar for lead and rubber, and somewhat lower for zinc.
71. Ungewitter, *Science and Salvage*, 176.
72. Darré, *Neuland aus Blut und Boden*; Gies, *Richard Walther Darré*; Gerhard. "Food as a Weapon: Agricultural Sciences and the Building of a Greater German Empire"; Uekoetter, *The Green and the Brown*.
73. Tooze, *The Wages of Destruction*, 186–188; on the deteriorating relationship between Darré and Backe, see Corni and Gies, *Brot, Butter, Kanonen*, 133, 185, 192–197, 206. See also Gies, *Richard Walther Darré*.
74. Tooze, 173, Corni and Gies, *Brot, Butter, Kanonen*, 247.
75. Corni and Gies, *Brot, Butter, Kanonen*, 206–207, 245.
76. For the replacement of existing recycling infrastructure, see Köstering, "'Pioniere der Rohstoffbeschaffung.'"

77. Dahlman and Hirschfeld, eds., *Lager, Zwangsarbeit, Vertreibung und Deportation*; Benz, "Zwangsarbeit im Nationalsozialistischen Staat"; Keller, *Sowjetische Kriegsgefangene im Deutschen Reich*; Herbert, *Hitler's Foreign Workers*; Herbert, ed., *Europa und der 'Reichseinsatz'*; Pohl and Sebta. *Zwangsarbeit in Hitlers Europa*; Pohl, *Die Wirtschaft der Wehrmacht*; Dick, *Builders of the Third Reich*. For the transition of early camps into labor camps, see Wachsmann, *KL*, 79–118.
78. BArch R2-21423, Reichskommissar für Altmaterialverwertung. Bedeutung der Altstoffwirtschaft, November 1940.
79. The General Building Plans of 1940–1941 and 1944 are particularly revealing in this respect. They attained concrete form first in light of the impressive military victories, and later in the context of already cleared spaces. See Bose et al., "*Ein neues Hamburg entsteht.*" Revealing in this context are also Mächler, "Die Großstadt als Kultur- und Raumproblem und die Grenzen ihrer Größe"; Killus, "Der Totalitätsgedanke im Neuen Städtebau": Fleige, "Städtebau--Gestern und Heute"; Krüger, "Der Raum als Gestalter der Innen-und Aussenpolitik." The bombed out cities a few years later provided a rubble littered blank slate for the exaggerated revival of planning efforts at the very moment that the Reich spiraled toward implosion.
80. BArch R2-21423, Reichskommissar für Altmaterialverwertung. Bedeutung der Altstoffwirtschaft, November 1940.
81. BArch R2-21423, Hans Heck, "Die Bedeutung der Altstoffwirtschaft," November 1940. Reichswirtschaftminister and Reichsmarschall Göring, December 23, 1940.
82. Longerich, *Holocaust*; Aly, Chroust, and Pross, *Cleansing the Fatherland*; Peukert. "The Genesis of the Final Solution from the Spirit of Science"; Burleigh and Wippermann, *The Racial State*; Cocks, *The State of Health*.
83. See, in particular, *Ewiger Wald* [The Eternal Forest] (1936), and for a careful reading of the film by Sabine Wilke: "'Verrottet, verkommen, von fremder Rasse durchsetzt': The Colonial Trope in the 'Nazi Kulturfilm' 'Ewiger Wald.'"
84. German art in the National Socialist spirit was postulated against both its Weimar predecessors and its American contemporaries. See Lauder et al., eds., *Degenerate Art*; Petropoulos, *Artists Under Hitler*; Clinefelder, *Artists for the Reich*. For defamations of U.S. culture, see, for example, Dresler, *Deutsche Kunst und entartete "Kunst,"* and later examples such as "Unverschämt, Schamlos, Albern" in *SS Das Schwarze Korps*, January 5, 1939, and "Lasset die Kindlein" in *SS Das Schwarze Korps,* February 16, 1939, with particular attention to the negative influence of racial mixing in U.S. culture.
85. Again, Tooze's arguments in *The Wages of Destruction* are pivotal in this case.
86. Ungewitter, *Die Verwertung des Wertlosen*.
87. Simmons, "Waste Not, Want Not: Excrement and Economy in Nineteenth-Century France," 73.
88. Munns and Nickelsen, *Far Beyond the Moon*; Munns, *A Single Sky*.
89. A number of excellent studies draw attention to the processes of exclusion in Nazi Germany. In particular, note Wildt, *Volksgemeinschaft als Selbstermächtigung*; Kaplan, *Between Dignity and Despair*; Aly, *Aussonderung und Tod*; Bergerson, *Ordinary Germans in Extraordinary Times*; Peukert, *Inside Nazi Germany*;

Connelly, "The Uses of Volksgemeinschaft"; Gellately and Stoltzfus, eds., *Social Outsiders in Nazi Germany*; Proctor, *Racial Hygiene*; Fritzsche, *Life and Death in the Third Reich.*

90. Scholars have carefully explicated the importance of othering to the formation of social cohesion. In the case of Nazism, such othering was justified primarily in biological terms. See, in particular, Aly and Roth, *Die restlose Erfassung.* On the use of *restlos*, see Allen, *The Business of Genocide*, 30.
91. Allen, *The Business of Genocide*, 30.
92. Ungewitter, *Die Verwertung des Wertlosen*, 46–50.
93. "Roh- und Werkstoffwirtschaft" *Vierjahresplan* 6 (1938): 351–353.
94. BArch R5-20585, Vordruck für "Die Umschau in Wissenschaft und Technik," 23 Heft vom 5 June 1938.
95. Levi, *Survival in Auschwitz,* 34.
96. BArch Plak 003-035-100, "Anordnung," November 7, 1941.
97. For the concept of "shit work," see Mills, "Black Trash." For the "abuse" of German labor, see Hitler, *Monologe im FührerHauptquartier 1941–45* (Hamburg: Albert Knaus Verlag, 1980), 166. I should note here that the while the tenor of the "monologues" certainly rings plausible or true, they are compilations from memory by more than one observer. For a careful analysis of the source, see Nilsson, "Hitler Redivivus: 'Hitler's Tischgespräche' und 'Monologue im Führerhauptquartier'—eine kritische Untersuchung."
98. Hitler, *Monologe*, 76.
99. BArch NS5-VI-8279, "Vom Adel der Schweren Berufe," *Völkischer Beobachter*, October 25, 1936.
100. Russell, *War and Nature*, 73. Emphasis in the original.
101. Gräbe, "Description of a Mass Execution," Browning, *Ordinary Men*, 61.
102. Frank, *Das Diensttagebuch*, 52, 152, 258, 330. See also Angrich, *Aktion 1005.*
103. Arendt, *Eichmann in Jerusalem*, 85–86.
104. Kershaw, "Working Toward the Führer"; Browning, "The Nazi Decision to Commit Mass Murder."
105. Weber, "Towards 'Total' Recycling: Women, Waste and Food Waste Recovery in Germany, 1914–1939"; Köstering, "Müllspülung im Golmer Luch"; Köstering, "'Pioniere der Rohstoffbeschaffung' Lumpensammler im Nationalsozialismus 1934–1939."
106. Köstering, "'Pioniere der Rohstoffbeschaffung' Lumpensammler im Nationalsozialismus 1934–1939," 45.
107. Quoted in Ungewitter, *Verwertung des Wertlosen*, 160.
108. Huchting, "Abfallwirtschaft im Dritten Reich," 258.
109. "Zum Reichskommissar für Altmaterialverwertung wird SA-Brigadeführer Ziegler ernannt," July 12, 1938, in Heck, *Der Reichskomissar für Altmaterialverwertung*, 44.
110. "Die ersten Richtlinien für die Erfassung in den Haushaltungen," November 27, 1936. See also Huchting, Abfallwirtschaft, 260. "Der Reichskommissar nimmt seine Tätigkeit auf," August 6, 1937, in Heck, *Der Reichskommissar für Altmaterialverwertung*, 45.

111. "Die ersten Richtlinien für die Erfassung in den Haushaltungen," November 27, 1936.
112. Huchting, "Abfallwirtschaft im Dritten Reich," 268, also Köstering, "'Pioniere der Rohstoffbeschaffung' Lumpensammler im Nationalsozialismus 1934–1939."
113. "Die Partei, ihre Gliederungen und angeschlossene Verbände arbeiten mit," September 3, 1937, in Heck, *Der Reichskommissar für Altmaterialverwertung*, 46. Heck, "Die Bedeutung der Altstoffwirtschaft," November 1940, in BArch R2-21423.
114. Köstering, "'Pioniere der Rohstoffbeschaffung' Lumpensammler im Nationalsozialismus 1934–1939," 55–58.
115. "Schreiben betreffend Erfolgskontrolle an sämtliche Gaubeauftragten für Almaterialerfassung," January 9, 1939, in Heck, *Der Reichskommissar für Altmaterialverwertung*, 32. Here, NSV, the National Socialist Women's League, the Hitler Youth, the League of German Girls, the Reich's Air Raid Protection League, and local cell, block, and district leaders, all played a crucial role. Weber, "Nazi German Waste Recovery and the Vision of a Circle Economy", 6.
116. BArch R2-21423, Der Reichswirtschaftsminister an den Herrn Reichsmarschall des Großdeutschen Reiches, Minsterpräsident Hermann Göring, December 23, 1940.
117. Ungewitter, *Verwertung des Wertlosen*, 169.
118. Ungewitter, *Verwertung des Wertlosen*, 168.
119. Ungewitter, *Verwertung des Wertlosen*, 165.
120. BArch NS18-1041, Vorlage. Betrifft Löffelsammlung durch die NS-Frauenschaft, January 14, 1943.
121. "Erfassung in der Gewerblichen Wirtschaft," November 25, 1936, in Heck, *Der Reichskommissar für Altmaterialverwertung*.
122. "Die ersten Richtlinien für die Erfassung in den Betrieben!," February 8, 1937, in Heck, *Der Reichskommissar für Altmaterialverwertung*.
123. BArch R144-817, Fragebogen für Textilindustrie, Lederindustrie, Textilhandel, Lederhandel, September 23, 1939.
124. BArch NS3-551, WVHA Verteiler, Betr. Verwertung des anfallenden Abwasserfettes in den Unterkünften der Waffen-SS und Konzentrationslager, November 14, 1942. For instructions regarding the cleaning of skimmers, see BArch R8II-19, Reichsstelle für Industrielle Fette und Waschmittel, December 10, 1942.
125. BArch R8II-19, Reichsstelle für Industrielle Fette und Waschmittel, November 10, 1942.
126. BArch R8II-19, Reichsstelle für Industrielle Fette und Waschmittel, Aussnahmen von der Stromkürzung, February 6, 1943.
127. BArch R8II-19, Reichsstelle Industrielle Fett und Waschmittel [handschriftlich in Bleistift], Bericht von Herrn Hermann, Berlin. Anlage 4, December 1, 1944.

Chapter 2

1. BArch R154-535, A. Pütter an Dr. Krohn, December 20, 1935.
2. BArch R154-538, Dr. Sanders and die Maschinenefabrik Pills, December 14, 1937; on how to recover protein from dairy plant effluents, R154-534, Verordnungen

der Deutschen Milchwirtschaft, April 17, 1936 (RGBl I, p. 374). See Frauenholz, "'Verwertung des Wertlosen:' Biotechnologische Surrogate aus unkonventionellen Eiweissquellen im Nationalsozialismus"; Pelzer-Reith and Reith, "Fischkonsum und 'Eiweisslücke' im Nationalsozialismus"; Adam Tooze, *The Wages of Destruction*, 193.
3. BArch R154-535, Landesanstalt für Wasser-, Boden-und Lufthygiene. Aktenvermerk, February 12, 1938.
4. Weinreb, *Modern Hungers*; Davis, *Home Fires Burning*; Corni and Gies, *Brot. Butter. Kanonen*; Cox, *Hunger in War and Peace*.
5. For popular adjustments to the new parameters implemented by the Nazi regime, see in particular Fritzsche, *Life and Death in the Third Reich*; Bergerson, *Ordinary Germans in Extraordinary Times*; Koonz, *The Nazi Conscience*.
6. Kershaw, "'Working Towards the Führer.' Reflections on the Nature of the Hitler Dictatorship."
7. Köstering, "'Pioniere der Rohstoffbeschaffung.'"
8. Fritzsche in *Life and Death in the Third Reich* shows how Germans integrated National Socialism into their own personal lives and details how they reasoned through dissonance that some of the regime's policies produced. Stargardt's *The German War* illustrates how Germans adapted to the war and how war, in turn, shaped German understanding both of their own crimes and their defeat. Peukert's *Inside Nazi Germany* serves as an excellent example of the turn away from superstructures to the everyday practices of National Socialism. Furthermore, Mallmann and Paul, in "Omniscient, Omnipotent, Omnipresent? Gestapo, Society and Resistance," destabilize the image of the "omnipotent supermen in black" and instead argue that repression depended "upon a system of insinuation and suspicion" of cooperation of Germans that makes the view of the Gestapo as a "foreign institution imposed upon the population" impossible. For a more comprehensive approach to popular consent, see Gellately, *Backing Hitler*, and an excellent review of these questions appears in Eley's "Hitler's Silent Majority? Conformity and Resistance."
9. Denton, "'Récupérez!' The German Origins of French Wartime Salvage Drives, 1939–1945." Also Denton, "Steel of Victory, Scrap of Defeat: Mobilizing the French Home Front, 1939–1940"; Zimring, *Cash for Your Trash*; Strasser, *Waste and Want*.
10. Simmons, "Waste Not, Want Not: Excrement and Economy in Nineteenth-Century France," 73.
11. See Evans, *Death in Hamburg*, 129–132. Also Melosi, *Garbage and the City*; Samalin, *The Masses Are Revolting*; Porter, *Health, Civilization and the State*.
12. Evans, *Death in Hamburg*, 132.
13. Samalin, *The Masses Are Revolting*, 44–58; Melosi, *Garbage and the City*, 20–22; Porter, *Health, Civilization and the State*, 107.
14. Melosi, *Garbage and the City*, 34; Rüb, "Müll und Städtehygiene um 1900," 19–29.
15. Evans, *Death in Hamburg*, 132–133. See also Haug, *Von der Kloake zur Kanalisation*; Reid, *Paris Sewers and Sewermen*.
16. See Porter, *Health, Civilization and the State*, whose focus on collective action offers important correctives to George Rosen, *From Medical Police to Social Medicine*.

17. Melosi, *Garbage in the Cities*, 9; Köster, *Müll*, 137–141.
18. For a comprehensive overview of Berlin's garbage history, see Flachowsky, *Saubere Stadt. Saubere Weste?*
19. Schmidt, "Der lange Weg zur Kommunalisierung der Berliner Müllabfuhr"; Park, "Von der Müllkippe zur Abfallwirtschaft: Die Entwicklung der Hausmüllentsorgung in Berlin (West) von 1945–1990," 19.
20. Park, "Von der Müllkippe zur Abfallwirtschaft: Die Entwicklung der Hausmüllentsorgung in Berlin (West) von 1945–1990."
21. BArch R8127-8761, Die Stadt deckt auf: Unregelmässigkeiten bei der Müllabfuhr. Amtsenthebung bei der Müllabfuhr A.G., October 28, 1929. See Flachowsky, *Saubere Stadt*, 232ff.
22. Schmidt, 32–37; see also Flachowsky, *Saubere Stadt*.
23. Melosi, *Garbage in the Cities*, 84–85.
24. Rüb, "Müll und Städtehygiene um 1900."
25. LhaP Rep. 27 C Potsdam 296, Verein zur Förderung der Moorkultur im Deutschen Reich, April 18, 1934; Neulandgewinnung durch Müllspühlung im nördlichen Teil des Golmer Bruches, June 20, 1938; LhaP Rep. 2A1 Pol 2584, Der Magistrat, Betrifft Zuschütten von Erdlöchern mit Berliner Müll, December 10, 1924; and Regierungspräsident, Betr. Müllschüttungsgenehmigung, August 14, 1928.
26. LhaP Rep. 2A1 Pol 2584. Hellmut Späth, who owned and operated Europe's largest tree nursery in Ketzin, had purchased a lavish villa a few years before Berlin haulers were licensed to deposit stinking garbage into the peat pits and cavities in proximity to his property. In a letter of complaint to the district president of Potsdam, Späth noted how wind carried garbage all the way to the villa, attracting vermin—particularly flies and rats, and producing a nauseating stench. See Dr. Helmut Späth an Regierungspräsidenten, November 11, 1929.
27. LhaP Rep. 2A1 Pol 2584, Bürgermeister Karl Reumschüssel an Beigeordneten Menzel, February 5, 1930.
28. LhaP Rep. 2A1 Pol 2584, Der Kreisarzt des Osthavelland an den Landrat des Kreises Osthavelland, July 7, 1930. After the doctor inspected the property, he reported that "a significant nuisance due to odor near human settlements cannot be determined." The report further insisted that "a moderate aggregation of vermin was evident only near the dump sites" and not one single rat could be spotted during a 90-minute-long inspection of the property.
29. LaB A.Pr.Br.Rep. 057.1756, Oberbürgermeister. Vorlage, November 4, 1935. For an overview, see Flachowsky, *Saubere Stadt*, 441f.
30. LhaP Rep. 27 C Potsdam 296, Neulandgewinnung durch Müllspülung im nördlichen Teil des Golmer Bruches, June 30, 1938; see also Flachowsky, 445; Köstering, "Müllspülung im Golmer Luch."
31. LaB A.Pr.Br.Rep. 05.1758, Niederschrift über die Sitzung der Berliner Müllabfuhr A.G., November 15, 1933.
32. LaB A.Pr.Br.Rep. 057.1756, "Aus Luchboden wird Weizen-Acker," *Berliner Morgenpost*, April 3, 1936; "Luchboden wird durch Müll zu Weizenacker," *Deutsche Allgemeine Zeitung*, April 3, 1936.

33. LhaP Rep. 27 C Potsdam 296, Neulandgewinnung durch Müllspühlung im nördlichen Teil des Golmer Bruches.Vermerk über die Besprechung im Landeswirtschaftsministeriums, June 22, 1938; LhaP Rep. 57 WSD 4600, Preussisches Wasserbauamt, June 22, 1935.
34. LaB A.Pr.Br.Rep. 057.1756, Vorlage an die Ratsherren, June 12, 1935.
35. LhaP Rep. 2A1 Pol 2584, Dr. Med. L. Conti an Regierungspräsidenten in Potsdam, April 22, 1936.
36. LhaP Rep. 27B Potsdam 950, Regierungspräsidenten Potsdam an Wasserbaudirektion, October 7, 1938.
37. LhaP Rep. 27B Potsdam 950, Regierungspräsidenten Potsdam an Wasserbaudirektion, October 7, 1938.
38. LhaP Rep. 57 WSD 4600, Fischereischutzgenossenschaft an Wasserbaudirektion, May 31, 1937; Preussisches Wasserbauamt, June 22, 1935.
39. Köstering, "Müllspühlung im Golmer Luch," 84.
40. LhaP Rep. 57 WSD 4600, Regierungspräsident Potsdam. Betr. Amtsenthebung des Deichhauptmanns des Golmer Deichverbandes Kraatz, September 26, 1938. Oberpräsident der Provinz Brandenburg. Aktenvermerk, December 7, 1937; LhaP Rep. 27C Potsdam 150, Kraatz is removed effective February 11, 1938; Rep. 27 B Potsdam 950, discussion about the necessity for improvements commence immediately and by end of June a plan is in place. Erläuterungsbericht, March 17, 1939.
41. Flachowsky, *Saubere Stadt*, 457–458.
42. LhaP Rep. 27C 308, Erläuterungsbericht, March 17, 1939; LhaP Rep. 27C Pdm 150, Nachtragsentwurf zur Entwässerung der Nierung Grube-Nattwerder-Golm unter besonderer Berücksichtigung der Müllspülung.
43. LaB A.Pr.Br.Rep. 057.1756, Berliner Morgenpost, April 3, 1936, "Aus Luchboden wird Weizen-Acker"; "Luchboden wird durch Müll zu Weizenacker," *Deutsche Allgemeine Zeitung*, April 3, 1936.
44. Here too, historical precursors set the stage. As early as April 1933, civil engineer Karl Dierkes wrote to the Regional Office for Water, Soil, and Air Hygiene to draw attention to this sewage irrigation system, reporting that between 1925 and 1933, a total of ten sewage irrigation systems had been installed successfully. Regime change in 1933 inspired Dierkes to offer his technological know-how in the service of the national economy. See BArch R154-509, Dierkes an Landesanstalt für Wasser, Boden und Lufthygiene, April 21, 1933.
45. Landwirtschaftsrat Henkel, Berlin. "Einsatz städtischer Abfallstoffe zur Bodenverbesserung und Düngung," *Mittleilungen für die Landwirtschaft* 58, no. 3 (January 16, 1943): 50.
46. LhaP Rep. 57 WSD 4153, Gutachtliche Stellungnahme, January 8, 1941; LhaP Rep. 208 4039, Der Kulturbaubeamte an Regierungspräsidenten Potsdam, December 12, 1939; LhaP Rep. 208 3939, Reichsanstalt für Wasser und Luftgüte an den Bürgermeister Abt Nr. I. Perleberg, August 19, 1944.
47. BArch R154-509, Dierkes an Landesanstalt für Wasser, Boden und Lufthygiene, April 21, 1933. See also "Steigerung der Erzeugung durch Feldberegnung," *Der Vierjahresplan* (July 1938), 399.

48. BArch R154-509, Studiengesellschaft für Feldberegnung an die Landesanstalt für Wasser,-Boden,- und Lufthygiene, November 18, 1935, which advocated for the use of wastewater from hospitals and asylums, arguing that "the hygienic concerns that were often raised against this measure in the beginning seem to have been exaggerated in light of experiences made so far. . . . During the sewage irrigation in Beeskow/Mark we even found out this year that it was common practice there to sprinkle forage grass with fecal water in the early morning, to cut it late morning and feed it at noon." See also BArch R154-509, Hygienisches Institut der Universität Breslau an Landbau Aussenstelle der Landesbauernschaft, January 5, 1942; Kanzelei, March 20, 1936. Also Landwirtschaftsrat Henkel, Berlin. "Einsatz städtischer Abfallstoffe zur Bodenverbesserung und Düngung," *Mitteilungen für die Landwirtschaft* 58, no. 3 (January 16, 1943), 50.
49. BArch 154–509, Landesanstalt für Wasser,-Boden- und Lufthygiene an Reichsminister des Innern, October 8, 1944.
50. König, *Volkswagen, Volksempfänger, Volksgemeinschaft*, Tooze, *The Wages of Destruction*, 147–165.
51. LaB A.Pr.Br. Rep. 057 1756, Harry John an Staatskommissar Lippert, October 22, 1935. For the clarification of an illegible name in the original source, see Flachowsky, *Saubere Stadt*, 487–488.
52. LaB A.Pr.Br.Rep. 057 1756, Harry John an Staatskommissar Lippert, October 22, 1935.
53. BArch R2-19516, Brief von Göring and Reichminister der Finanzen, November 4, 1936. For Lippert's biography, see https://www.deutsche-biographie.de/sfz51823.html; for the decree that makes the collection of kitchen garbage mandatory, see Mitwirkung der Gemeinden bei Verwertung der Küchenabfälle zur Schweinemast. RdErl. b. RuPrMdJ v 3.11.1937.
54. After all, Lippert owed his position as the right-hand man of the Berlin's lord mayor Sahm to Göring and soon became the trusted man in charge of cleansing the administration of Jewish and other "corrupt elements."
55. Flachowsky, *Saubere Stadt*, 488.
56. Landesarchiv Berlin A.Pr.Br.Rep. 057 1756, Harry John an Staatskommissar Lippert, October 22, 1935; see also Flachowsky, *Saubere Stadt*, 487ff.
57. Tooze, *The Wages*, 193.
58. BArch R2-19516, Letter from Backe to Finance Minister, November 4, 1936.
59. Ungewitter, *Verwertung des Wertlosen*, 195. Up to this point, the United States had been the uncontested leader in the field of utilizing household garbage among industrial nations. Reduction, stewing garbage in large vets to separate oils and glycerine, from the "residuum" was a household recipe for candle production that Henry Ford implemented on an industrial scale during the Depression. Ford used up to 9 tons of garbage daily to produce a new kind of hyper-potent fertilizer and distilled commercial alcohol as well as various oils from organic refuse. In Los Angeles, industrial solutions to waste were slow in coming; instead, garbage was carted to massive hog farms in LA county. See Berg, "Waste Streams and Garbage Publics."
60. Ungewitter, *Verwertung des Wertlosen*, 186.

61. BArch R2-19516, Letter from Backe to NSV leadership, November 5, 1936.
62. BArch R2-19516, Der Reichsbeauftragte für die Erfassung und Verwertung von Küchen u. Nahrungsmittelabfällen an den Herrn Staatssekretär Reinhardt, Reichsfinanzministerum, January 28, 1938.
63. BArch R2-19516, Reichsministerium der Finanzen an Hilgenfeld, March 31, 1938.
64. BArch R2-19516, Mittwirkung der Gemeinden bei der Verwertung der Küchenabfälle zur Schweinemast. Runderlass, August 20, 1940; Reichsleitung NSDAP, Bekanntmachung, October 1, 1940; Reichsminister des Innern an Oberbürgermeister, August 28, 1940.
65. BArch R2-19516, Göring and Reichsminister Todt an die Gaubeauftragten, August 20, 1940; Auszug aus dem Erlass des Reichsarbeitsministers über den Einsatz von Kriegsgefangenen in der Bauwirtschaft, July 10, 1940.
66. BArch R2-19516, Bericht über die wirtschaftliche Entwicklung des Ernährungshilfswerks, June 27, 1941.
67. BArch R2-19516, Bericht über die wirtschaftliche Entwicklung des Ernährungshilfswerkes, June 27, 1941.
68. BArch R2-19516, Abschlussbericht, January 23, 1942. *Merkblatt über Verfütterung von Küchenabfällen* (Bulletin for the Feeding of Kitchen Garbage), April 1942. As part of the normal operations, the garbage used as feed was heated to 90°C to prevent epidemics.
69. BArch R2-19516, Backe an Reichsminister der Finanzen, January 25, 1941.
70. BArch R2-19516, Reichsleitung NSDAP an Gauleiter, May 6, 1942.
71. BArch R2-19516, Der Beauftragte für den Vierjahresplan an Reichsminister der Finanzen, March 15, 1941; Der Beauftragte für den Vierjahresplan an Reichsminister der Finanzen, May 23, 1941; Übersicht betreffend die Finanz-und Betriebswirtschafts-Stände bez. Entwicklung im Ernährungshilfswerk in den Jahren 1937–1942.
72. BArch R2-19516, Reichsministerum der Finanzen. Vermerk, October 12, 1944.
73. Ungewitter, *Verwertung des Wertlosen*.
74. Peukert, *Inside Nazi Germany*, 208.
75. Peukert, "The Genesis of the 'Final Solution' from the Spirit of Science"; Ayass, *Asoziale im Nationalsozialismus*; Gellately and Stoltzfus, *Social Outsiders in Nazi Germany*; Burleigh, *Death and Deliverance*.
76. Historian Detlev Peukert documents the change in scientific understanding of physical and mental illness, criminology, and the pathologization of social deviance during the Weimar period. Peukert, *Grenzen der Sozialdisziplinierung*; Peukert, "The Genesis of the 'Final Solution' from the Spirit of Science"; Bridenthal, Grossmann, and Kaplan, eds., *When Biology Became Destiny*.
77. Schürmann and Dilling, *Schicksale Psychiatrischer Patienten*; Ebbinghaus, Kaupen-Hass, and Roth, eds., *Heilen und Vernichten im Mustergau Hamburg*; Frewer and Siedbürger, eds., *Medizin und Zwangsarbeit im Nationalsozialismus*; Wolff and Kalinich, *Zur Geschichte der Krankenanstalten in Berlin-Buch*.
78. See Ankele, "The Patient's View of Work Therapy"; Wachsmann, "Between Reform and Repression: Imprisonment in Weimar Germany"; Wolff and Kalinich, *Zur*

Geschichte der Krankenanstalten in Berlin-Buch; Schürmann and Dilling, *Schicksale psychiatrischer Patienten*; Crouthamel, "War Neurosis versus Savings Psychosis"; Killen, "From Shock to Schreck"; Winter, "Shell-Shock and the Cultural History of the Great War"; Deborah Cohen, *The War Come Home*; Müller, "Between Therapeutic Instrument and Exploitation of Labor Force."

79. Burleigh and Wippermann, *The Racial State*, 154.
80. Ungewitter, *Verwertung des Wertlosen*, 167.
81. LaB A Rep. 003 04 01 175 various.
82. LaB A Rep. 003 04 01 175, Oberbürgermeister bezgl. Verwertung von Zahnersatzstücken, November 16, 1933, Anlagen.
83. LaB A Rep. 003 04 01 175, Oberbürgermeister bezgl. Verwertung von Zahnersatzstücken, November 16, 1933, Anlagen.
84. LaB A Rep. 003 04 01 175, Oberbürgermeister bezgl. Verwertung von Zahnersatzstücken, November 16, 1933, Anlagen.
85. LaB A Rep. 003 04 01 175, Oberbürgermeister bezgl. Verwertung von Zahnersatzstücken, November 16, 1933.
86. Wolff and Kalinich, *Zur Geschichte der Krankenanstalten in Berlin-Buch*, 98–99.
87. LaB A Rep. 003 04 01 175, Städtische Heil und Pflegeanstalt Buch, November 29, 1933.
88. LaB A Rep. 003 04 01 175, Hugo Rollert, Berlin an Städtische Heil-und Pflegeanstalt Buch, December 13, 1933.
89. LaB A Rep. 003 04 01 175, Oberbürgermeister. Betr. Verwertung von Abfällen, October 2, 1934.
90. LaB A Rep. 003 04 01 175, Wilhelm Schumann an Heil-und Pflegeanstalt Buch, November 30, 1934.
91. LaB A Rep. 003 04 01177, Oberbürgermeister Berlin, Betr. Verwertung von Altmaterialien, July 12, 1935.
92. LaB A Rep. 003 04 01177, Oberbürgermeister an die zentralen Dienststellen, Betr. Verwertung von Alt-Materialien, July 12, 1935.
93. LaB A Rep. 003 04 01177, Oberbürgermeister an Dienststellen der Hauptverwaltung, September 28, 1935.
94. LaB A Rep. 003 04 01177, Verschiedene Eingänge.
95. LaB A Rep. 003 04 01177, Walter Holzinger an Städtische Heil-und Pflegeanstalt Buch, January 9, 1936.
96. LaB A Rep. 003 04 01177, Oberbürgermeister an Heil-und Pflegeanstalt Buch, May 24, 1937. Here, the clerical assistant Schulze emphasizes that the quantities of interest are only those materials that are actually discarded, not the food scraps that are puréed and dispensed as liquid food.
97. LaB A Rep. 003 04 01177, Max Gottesmann and Heil-und Pflegeanstalt Buch, September 2, 1936.
98. LaB A Rep. 003 04 01177, Oberbürgermeister an Entzinnungswerk Karl Beinhard, October 4, 1938.
99. LaB A Rep. 003 04 01177, Mitteldeutsche Seifenfabrik GmbH an Heil-und Pflegeanstalt Buch, January 1, 1938.
100. LaB A Rep. 003 04 01177, Erfassung und Verwertung von Altmaterialien.

101. LaB A Rep. 001 06 34487, Müllbeseitigungsanstalt an die Allgemeine Hauptverwaltung, May 5, 1937.
102. LaB A Rep. 003 04 01177, Oberbürgermeister and Bezirksbürgermeister, November 16, 1936.
103. Köstering, "Die Müllspülung im Golmer Luch," 108.
104. Ungewitter, *Verwertung des Wertlosen*, 167–168.
105. LaB A Rep. 003 04 01177, Der Oberbürgermeister an die Heil-und Pflegeanstalt Buch, January 14, 1937.
106. LaB A Rep. 003 04 01177, Dr. Conti in Vertretung für Oberbürgermeister an Bezirksbürgermeister, December 24, 1936. For Conti's ascension to Reich physicians leader, see Kater, "Dr. Leonardo Conti and His Nemesis," 306. For the *Aktion Kampf dem Verderb*, see Chapter 3 in this book.
107. Wachsmann, *Hitler's Prisons*, 96–97.
108. LaB A Rep. 003 04 01177, Oberbürgermeister an Bezirksbürgermeister Pankow, November 15, 1938.
109. LaB A Rep. 003 04 01177, Gesundheitsamt an Heil-und Pflegeanstalt Buch, November 19, 1937.
110. LaB A Rep. 003 04 01177.
111. Wachsmann, *Hitler's Prisons*, 99–100, Wachsmann, *KL: A History of Nazi Concentration Camps*, 627.
112. Wachsmann, *Hitler's Prisons*, 198.
113. Wolff and Kalinich, *Zur Geschichte der Krankenanstalten in Berlin-Buch*, 111.
114. Benedict and Shields, *Nurses and Midwives in Nazi Germany*; Greve, *Die Organisierte Vernichtung 'lebensunwerten Lebens' im Rahmen der Aktion T4*.

Chapter 3

1. "Rede des Ministerpräsidenten Generaloberst Göring am 28 September 1936 im Sportpalast," *Der Vierjahresplan* 1 (1937), 31.
2. "Rede des Ministerpräsidenten Generaloberst Göring," 33.
3. Tooze, *The Wages of Destruction*, 193. In 1936, a discreet system of rationing only affected butter and meat, introduced in the fall of 1935 to counteract shortages that resulted from rapid increases in popular demand. During the first weeks of war, rationing was extended to food and clothing on a comprehensive scale but that was hardly in view of the Germans who listened to Görings weight-loss confessions in 1936.
4. Ungewitter, *Verwertung des Wertlosen*, 170.
5. Strasser, *Waste and Want*, 229–263.
6. Norbert Frei describes Nazi Germany as a career-state in "German Zeitgeschichte und Generation, or How to Explain the Belated Career of the Nazi *Volksgemeinschaft*." For an exploration of *Volksgemeinschaft* as a vehicle for Nazi citizenship, also see Schiechen-Ackermann, ed., *"Volksgemeinschaft": Mythos, wirkunsmächtige soziale*

Verheißung oder soziale Realität im "Dritten Reich?"; Keller, *Volksgemeinschaft am Ende*; Wildt, *Volksgemeinschaft als Selbstermächtigung*; and Connelley, "The Uses and Abuses of the Volksgemeinschaft." For the local forms of Nazi citizenship, see Berg, *On Screen and Off*.

7. Fritzsche, *Life and Death*, 23.
8. For the precise dates of the National Socialist subsistence battle, see Degler, "Die Verlorene Erzeugungsschlacht."
9. The Nazi regime was particularly worried about food security in light of the experience of World War I when severe scarcity and hunger drove women into the streets, contributing in important ways to the revolutionary pressures after 1916. See Davis, *Home Fires Burning*; Corni and Gies, *Brot. Butter. Kanonen*; Weinreb, *Modern Hungers*. and Collingham, *The Taste of War*.
10. Reagin, "Marktordnung and Autarkic Housekeeping."
11. Stibbe, *Women in the Third Reich*; Koonz, *Mothers in the Fatherland*.
12. See Internationale Grüne Woche Berlin at https://www.gruenewoche.de/de/auf-einen-blick/daten-und-fakten/. The second Green Week in Nazi Germany took place January 26 to February 3, 1935. It was completely devoted to celebrating German Bauernstand. See BArch R16-2112, Berliner Nachrichtendienst, "Die Grüne Woche Berlin wird vorbereitet," November 2, 1934.
13. BArch R16-26 and R16-2015.
14. BArch R16-2015, 10 Gebote, "Kampf dem Verderb."
15. BArch R16-2015, 10 Gebote, "Kampf dem Verderb."
16. Rathje and Murphy, *Rubbish: The Archaeology of Garbage*, 60. On the *Volkskühlschrank*, see König, *Volkswagen, Volksempfänger, Volksgemeinschaft*.
17. BArch R16-2015, "Kampf dem Verderb" Teil V [Film treatment].
18. See Reagin, "Marktordnung and Autarkic Housekeeping," 174. For the use of the rhetoric around the people's community as a bludgeon to stigmatize neighbors and insist on one's own credentials, see Connelly, "The Uses and Abuses of Volksgemeinschaft." On Nazi film propaganda, see Welch. *Propaganda and the German*.
19. BArch R16-2015, Georg Reichart an den Reichsnährstand, July 18, 1936.
20. BArch R16-2015, Aktenvermerk: Es gelangen zur Vorführung, 16.
21. See, in particular, Tooze's chapter, "1936: Four Years to War" in *The Wages of Destruction*, 203–243. Tooze notably points to the constriction due to shortages in foreign currency shortages and the "steel squeeze" that, in Hitler's mind, could only be solved by the acquisition of *Lebensraum*.
22. Heck, *Der Reichskommissar für Altmaterialverwertung*, 5.
23. Köstering, "'Pioniere der Rohstoffbeschaffung,'" 45.
24. Heck, *Der Reichskommissar für Altmaterialverwertung*, 5. Köstering's research confirms that a significant number of businesses were owned by Jews and explains the difficulties the branch experienced in response to the regime's exclusionary interventions. Köstering, "Pioniere der Rohstoffbeschaffung," 47.
25. Tooze, *The Wages of Destruction*, 93–94.
26. Zolling, *Zwischen Integration und Segregation*.

27. Köstering, '"Pioniere der Rohstoffbeschaffung,"' 57.
28. Since mandatory membership in the industry-specific *Fachgruppe* remained unenforceable and individual peddlers resisted the state's attempts at interference and regulation, the regime reorganized the trade over the course of 1937 and 1938. "Im Rohproduktengewerbe wird eine Bezirkseinteilung geschaffen," December 13, 1937, in Heck, *Der Reichskommissar für Altmaterialverwertung*, 64; "Den Sammlern oder Händlern werden Pflichtsammelbezirke zugewiesen. Sie werden mit Ausweiskarten, Armbinden und Metallmarken versehen. Die Begriffe Mittelhändler, Kleinhändler, Platzhändler und Sammler werden festgelegt," March 5, 1938, in Heck, *Der Reichskommissar für Altmaterialverwertung*, 71.
29. Otto and Houwink ten Cate, eds., *Das organisierte Chaos: 'Ämterdarwinismus' und 'Gesinnungsethik'*; Rebentisch, *Führerstaat und Verwaltung*. A notable exception that extends the investigation of systemic competition to the level of the municipal administration is Gotto, *Nationalsozialistische Kommunalpolitik*.
30. "Der Reichsführer SS und Chef der Deutschen Polizei setzt die Polizei zur Sammelkontrolle ein," September 15, 1937, in Heck, *Der Reichskommissar für Altmaterialverwertung*, 52.
31. Bajohr, *"Arisierung" In Hamburg*; Biggeleben, Schreiber and Steiner, eds., *Arisierung in*; Genschel, *Die Verdrängung der Juden aus der Wirtschaft im Dritten Reich*; Wojak and Peter Hayes, eds., *"Arisierung" Im Nationalsozialismus*.
32. A Rep 003 04 01 175, Städtische Heil- und Pflegeanstalt Buch, November 29, 1933.
33. "Die Ersten Richtlinien für die Erfassung in den Haushaltungen," November 27, 1936, in Heck, *Der Reichskommissar für Altmaterialverwertung*, 5
34. RGBL 1938, Teil I 1580, cited in Bajohr, *Arisierung in Hamburg*, 277.
35. Köstering, '"Pioniere der Rohstoffbeschaffung,"' 51.
36. Köstering, '"Pioniere der Rohstoffbeschaffung,"' 50.
37. Köstering, "'Pioniere der Rohstoffbeschaffung,"' 61.
38. See "Entrümpelung von Landschaft und Dorf" February 3, 1937, in Heck, *Der Reichskommissar für Altmaterialverwertung*, 160.
39. "Rede des Ministerpräsidenten Generaloberst Göring am 28. September 1936," 35.
40. See "Entrümpelung von Landschaft und Dorf," February 3, 1937, in Heck, *Der Reichskommissar für Altmaterialverwertung*, 160. For Köhler's role within the Four-Year Plan Authority, see Huchting, "Abfallwirtschaft im Dritten Reich," 254.
41. See "Entrümpelung von Landschaft und Dorf," 161-162. Also Weber, "Nazi German Waste Recovery and the Vision of a Circle Economy," 6.
42. Erste Schrottaktion in den gewerblichen Betrieben (Reichswirtschaftskammer), June 23, 1937, Heck, *Der Reichskommissar für Altmaterialverwertung*, 163.
43. Entrümpelung von Landschaft und Dorf is mentioned in "Aktionen im 'westlichen Entfallgebiet,'" June 27, 1938, and "Aktionen im 'östlichen Entfallgebiet,'" August 12, 1938, in Heck, *Der Reichskommissar für Altmaterialverwertung*, 164.
44. "Aktionen im 'westlichen Entfallgebiet,'" June 27, 1938, and "Aktionen im östlichen Entfallgebiet, August 12, 1938, in Heck, *Der Reichskommissar für Altmaterialverwertung*, 164, 169.

45. "Entfernung eiserner Vorgartenzäune und Einfriedungen (Eisengitter-Aktion). Bildung von Schrott-Einsatzstäben," August 11, 1938, in Heck, *Der Reichskommissar für Altmaterialverwertung*, 173ff.
46. "Entfernung eiserner Vorgartenzäune und Einfriedungen (Eisengitter-Aktion). Bildung von Schrott-Einsatzstäben," August 11, 1938, in Heck, *Der Reichskommissar für Altmaterialverwertung*, 176–177.
47. Ministerpräsident Generalfedmarschall Göring, II L-726/38, September 17, 1938, in Heck, *Der Reichskommissar für Altmaterialverwertung*, 193.
48. Schrott-Sammelaktion, August 31, 1939, in Heck, *Der Reichskommissar für Altmaterialverwertung*, 237–238.
49. BArch NS18-1037, Göring an Reichsminister, February 23, 1940. See also Aktennotiz für Pg Hoffmann, March 7, 1940.
50. BArch NS18-1037, Anordnung A42/40, April 11, 1940.
51. BArch NS18-1037, Vorlage für den Stabsleiter, April 19, 1940.
52. See BArch Bild 183-H26751.
53. BArch NS18-1037, Rundschreiben an die Gauleiter, March 1940.
54. BArch NS18-1039, Rundschreiben Nr. 19/41 GBA. Anlage AE.NR.2308/41. Christopher Browning repeatedly notes the massive consumption of alcohol by the Reserve Police Battalion during mass shootings in Poland in 1942, modeled after the actions by *Einsatzgruppen*, police battalions, and Waffen-SS in Soviet territory in the summer and fall of 1941. Browning, *Ordinary Men*, 61, 69, 80, 82, 83, 85, 100, 108.
55. It should be noted that the date set for the bottle collection coincided with the wave of deportations of Jews from the Reich. Browning thus illustrates this: "From mid-October 1941 to late February 1942, 59 transports carried more than 53,000 Jews and 5,000 Roma from the Third Reich 'to the east.'" The second of four transports from Hamburg, with 990 Jews, left for Minsk on November 8th. Browning, *Ordinary Men*, 42.
56. BArch NS18-1039, Fernschreiben. Tiessler and Pg Witt, Führerbau, November 11, 1941.
57. BArch NS18-1039, Rundschreiben Nr. 144/41. Reichspropagandaleitung, November 1, 1941. Here, the Propaganda Ministry "insists that the collection bears the name 'Bottle Collection for Our Army,' Reich's Collection on November 8, 1941. Designations such as '*Reichsflaschensammlung* [Reich's bottle collection]' or '*Reichsflaschentag* [Reich's bottle day],' '*Reichsflaschenaktion* [Reich's bottle action]' and the like are not permitted. Only the shortened version 'Reich's Collection: Bottles for Our Army' may be used instead.'"
58. On "language rules," see Arendt, *Eichmann in Jerusalem*, 85–86. The *Hamburger Tageblatt* avoided naming the bottle drive explicitly. Instead, the Hamburg-based paper informed the population that "on November 8, there will be a Reich's wide collection of bottles for our Wehrmacht." See "Die Front im Osten wird sich sehr freuen," *Hamburger Tageblatt*, November 6, 1941.
59. BArch NS18-1039, Reichskommissar für Altmaterialverwertung und Reichsbeauftragter der NSDAP für Altmaterialerfassung, Hans Heck and Pg Tiessler,

Leiter des Reichsrings für nationalsozialistische Propaganda und Volksaufklärung, October 28, 1941.
60. Browning, *Ordinary Men*, 61, 68.
61. Browning, *Ordinary Men*, 42.
62. Fritzsche, *Life and Death*, 250–255.
63. BArch NS18-1039, Rundschreiben Nr. 20/41 GBA, "Flaschen für unsere Wehrmacht," October 28, 1941.
64. Nonetheless, a mixed model was implemented in large cities such as Berlin and Hamburg, where door-to-door collection and drop-off stations operated in parallel, as Tiessler's observations and the advertisement in the *Hamburger Tageblatt* reveal. See BArch NS18-1039, Fernschreiben. "Die Front im Osten wird sich sehr freuen."
65. BArch NS18-1039. The list of bottling companies spans thirteen pages.
66. BArch NS18-1039, Rundschreiben Nr. 144/41. Reichspropagandaleitung, November 1, 1941.
67. Ungewitter, *Verwertung des Wertlosen*, 128. See also Kollmeier, *Ordnung und Ausgrenzung*, 205.
68. The *Hamburger Tageblatt* attempted to explain the failure of the regime to pick up and transport the bottles filling centers as follows: "The success of the collection conducted on November 8, "Bottles for Our Army" exceeded all expectations. The German housewives' willingness to donate was so tremendous that the vehicles and volunteers requisitioned for transport simply could not handle the volume, particularly in the big cities." See "Viel mehr Flaschen als erwartet," *Hamburger Tageblatt*, November 12, 1941.
69. BArch NS18-1040, Führerinformation: Woll- und Wintersammlung für die Front, December 19, 1941."Damit nicht wie bei der Flaschensammlung der grössere Teil der Sammlung wegen Fehlens von Transportmitteln liegen bleibt."
70. BArch NS18-1040, Geheim. Wollsachensammlung durch die Partei, December 15, 1941.
71. The *Reichsbahn* worried that collections would compete with regular mail transport, but the postal service and the OKW agreed to manage the retention of mail out of public view. BArch NS18-1040, Vorlage für den Herrn Minister, December 16, 1941.
72. BArch NS18-1040, Reichspropagandaleitung an alle Gaupropagandaleiter, December 18, 1941.
73. BArch NS18-1040, Führerinformation, December 19, 1941.
74. BArch NS18-1040, Ausführungsbestimmungen zur Verfügung des Reichspropagandaleiters der NSDAP, December 20, 1941.
75. BArch NS18-1040, Notizen für die Ministerbesprechung, December 21, 1941, Vorlage für Reichsleiter Bormann, December 24, 1941. BArch NS18-1040, Aktzennotiz, December 30, 1941.
76. BArch NS18-1040, Reichspropagandaleitung der NSDAP an Reichsfrauenführung, December 22, 1941.
77. BArch NS18-1040, Einsatz der Wehrmacht bei der Sammlung, December 19, 1941. Ausführungsbestimmungen zur Verfügung des Reichsorganisationsleiters

der NSDAP über die Woll- und Wintersachensammlung für die Front, December 20, 1941.
78. BArch NS18-1040, Vorlage für den Herrn Minister: Betrifft Sammlung von Skiern und Skistiefeln, December 23, 1941.
79. BArch NS18-1040, Gauleiter Sauckel an Reichsleiter Borman, Führerhauptquartier, December 28, 1941.
80. BArch NS18-1040, Teilergebnisse Übersicht, December 30, 1941; Reichspropagandaleitung. Woll-, Pelz- und Wintersachen-Sammlung für die Front. Ergebnis, December 31, 1941.
81. BArch NS18-1040, Vorlage für den Herrn Minister: Betrifft Sammlung von Skiern und Skistiefeln, December 23, 1941.
82. BArch NS18-1040, Vorlage, January 2, 1942.
83. BArch NS18-1040, Fernschreiben an alle Gauleiter, January 2, 1942. For collection results, a total of 18,530,046 items, see BArch NS18-1040; Reichspropagandaleitung, January 2, 1942. By January 3rd, the yield had increased to 23,459,430; by January 4th, to 32,144,201 items. For information on the secrecy surrounding the results, see NS18-1040, January 2, 1942.
84. BArch NS18-1040, Brief an Hitler, January 4, 1942. By January 7th, the numbers had already increased to 49,532,251 items. The final results, tallied on January 21, 1941, amounted to 69,659,688 items. See NS18-1040, Reichspropagandaleitung, January 21, 1942.
85. BArch NS18-1040, Propagandaparole Nr. 12, December 23, 1941.
86. BArch NS18-1040, Albrecht-Krankenhaus an Reichskanzlei, December 29, 1941; NS18-1040, Reichspropagndaleitung an alle Gauleiter, January 2, 1942.
87. BArch NS18-1041, Gauleitung: Bayer. Ostmark: Aus dem Monatsbericht November 1941, December 8, 1941.
88. BArch NS18-1040, Propagandaparole Nr. 12, December 23, 1941.
89. BArch NS18-1040, Rundschreiben 47/41 RGBA, December 22, 1941.
90. "Erfassung und Verwertung von Altmaterial," September 13, 1936, in Heck, *Der Reichskommissar für Altmaterialverwertung*, 245.
91. StAHH 354-5, Jugendbehörde I 343b. Auszug aus Berichten der Kreisdienststellen und Obefürsorgerinnen. Kreisstelle 4a, December 1, 1939.
92. "Knochensammlung in Schulen," January 28, 1937, in Heck, *Der Reichskommissar für Altmaterialverwertung*, 245–246.
93. Weber, "Nazi German Waste Recovery and the Vision of a Circular Economy," 5.
94. LaB A.Rep. 001-06-34487, Schulsammlungen, January 25, 1940.
95. LaB A.Rep. 001-06-34487, Abt. Altmaterialverfassung. App. 337.
96. LaB A.Rep. 001-06-34487, Oberbürgermeister. Betrifft: Erfassung von Alt-und Abfallstoffen, October 12, 1941.
97. LaB A.Rep. 001-06-34487, Oberbürgermeister der Reichshauptstadt Berlin, June 30, 1943.
98. LaB A.Rep. 001-06-34487, Schulrat des Schulaufsichtskreises, Berlin - Neukölln II, September 9, 1943.

99. BArch NS18-1041, Vorlage. Betrifft Löffelsammlung durch die NS-Frauenschaft, January 14, 1943.
100. BArch NS18-1041, Notiz. Schutzbrillensammlung, July 3, 1943.
101. BArch NS18-1041, Reichsministerium für Volksaufklärung und Propaganda an Korspführung des NSKK, June 28, 1943.
102. BArch NS18-1041, Parteikanzelei an Prosagandaministerium, June 12, 1943.
103. BArch NS18-1041, Parteikanzelei an Pg Hittinger und Pg Tiessler, June 16, 1943.
104. BArch NS18-1041, Reichsbeauftragte für Altmaterialerfassung an Reichspropagandaleitung NSDAP, September 6, 1943.

Chapter 4

1. BArch NS19-0285, Erfahrungsbericht., G. Hörrmann, March 8, 1942.
2. BArch NS19-0285, Erfahrungsbericht., G. Hörrmann, March 8, 1942.
3. BArch R3112-99, Bericht über die Sitzung beim Herrn Reichsmarschall, August 8, 1941.
4. BArch R3112-99, Bericht über die Sitzung beim Herrn Reichsmarschall, August 8, 1941.
5. Baranowski, *Nazi Empire*; Mazower, *Hitler's Empire*; Housden, *Hans Frank: Lebensraum and the Holocaust*; Kamenetsky, *Secret Nazi Plans for Eastern Europe*; Hiller, *Deutscher Kampf um Lebensraum*.
6. It should be noted that the large-scale attempt to salvage material, particularly metal, was not unique to Germany and characterized war economies more generally. See Thorsheim, *Waste into Weapons*.
7. Kershaw, *The Hitler Myth*, 145. See also Rossino, *Hitler Strikes Poland*.
8. Archiwum Instytutu Pamieci Narodowej (AIPN), Dzienniki H. Frank. IPN Głowna Komisja (GK), 95/8 "Wirtschaftstagung," June 6–7, 1940.
9. Schenk, *Hans Frank: Hitler's Kronjurist und Generalgouverneur*; Housden, *Hans Frank, Lebensraum and the Holocaust*; Alberti, *Die Verfolgung und Vernichtung der Juden im Reichsgau Wartheland*.
10. Aly, *Endlösung*, 103.
11. Aly, *Endlösung*, 112.
12. Longerich, *Holocaust*, 159, 149.
13. Longerich, *Holocaust*, 157; Aly, *Endlösung*, 107–110.
14. Aly, *Endlösung*, 111; Schenk, *Hans Frank*, 160.
15. Fröhlich, *Die Tagebücher von Joseph Goebbels: Sämtliche Fragmente*, 387.
16. Browning, *The Origins of the Final Solution*, 19; Kershaw, *Hitler: 1936–1945*, 240–249.
17. AIPN IPN GK 95/8, "Wirtschaftsbesprechung," June 6–7, 1940.
18. Cited in Schenk, *Hans Frank*, 148.
19. Browning, *The Origins of the Final Solution*, 19–20. Longerich, *Holocaust*, 148–150, 161ff.

20. AIPN IPN GK 95/8, "Wirtschaftsbesprechung," June 6–7, 1940.
21. BArch R144-842, Göring to Reichsminister Frank, Gauleiter Forster, Koch, Wagner and Senatspräsident Greiser, October 19, 1939. On the history of the HTO, see Jeanne Dingell, *Zur Tätigkeit der Haupttreuhandstelle Ost, Treunhandstelle Posen 1939–1945* (Frankfurt: Peter Lang, 2003).
22. Schenk, *Hans Frank*, 158.
23. BArch R144-842, Göring an die Obersten Reichsbehörden, November 28, 1939.
24. Apparently, Hans Frank was determined to limit the HTO's competences in the General Government, securing his own power over the economic administration of the colony. See "Einleitung" in *Dienstagebuch des deutschen Generalgouverneurs in Polen 1939–1945*, edited by Werner Präg and Wolfgang Jacobmeyer (Stuttgart: DeutscheVerlagsanstalt, 1975), 25.
25. Schenk, *Hans Frank*, 255–280.
26. BArch R144-842, Grundzüge für die Errichtung der Treuhand- und Verwertungs G.m.b.H, undated. The Wifo provided the 500,000 RM seed money for the VVG in the form of a loan, which the latter was to repay with 5 percent interest. The managing director of the Wifo, Ernst Ranis, served as one of three managing directors of the VVG. His colleagues Erich Bauwerker and Erich Marschner were selected for their expertise as a metal specialist and a banker, respectively.
27. BArch R144-842, Erfahrungsbericht, November 24, 1939.
28. BArch R144-842, Wifo an Bührmann, November 21, 1939.
29. AIPN IPN GK 95/8, "Wirtschaftstagung," June 6–7, 1940.
30. AIPN IPN GK 95/8, "Arbeitssitzung," September 20, 1940.
31. AIPN IPN GK 95/8, "Wirtschaftstagung," June 6–7, 1940.
32. On April 23, 1940, Hans Frank laid out his logic about the different racial categories and German responsibilities toward occupied populations with respect to rations. Hans Frank, *Das Diensttagebuch*, edited by Werner Präg and Wolfgang Jacobmeyer (Stuttgart: Deutsche Verlags-Anstalt, 1975), 186–187.
33. Frank, *Das Diensttagebuch*, 186–187.
34. Longerich, *Holocaust*, 157.
35. BArch R144-842, Göring to Reichsminister Frank, Gauleiter Forster, Koch, Wanger and Senatspräsident Greiser, October 19, 1939.
36. BArch R144-842, Arbeitsplan (Entwurf), undated.
37. AIPN IPN GK 95/1, Dzienniki H. Franka, November 1, 1939.
38. AIPN IPN GK 95/4, Dzienniki H. Franka, April 11, 1940.
39. Tooze, *The Wages of Destruction*, 334, 337; for ammunitions, see 340–347.
40. On Hitler's wavering orders for war with France, see Tooze, *The Wages of Destruction*, 330.
41. BArch NS18-1037, Göring an die Herren Reichsminister, February 23, 1940, and Richtlinien über die Metallsammlung in den Behörden, February 23, 1940.
42. BArch R58-184, May 6, 1940, 44.
43. AIPN IPN GK 95/4, Dzienniki H. Frank, "Besprechung," May 9, 1940.
44. Frank, *Das Dienstaggebuch*, 195.

NOTES TO PAGES 94-97   261

45. BArch R121-484, Schreiben von Schu an das Oberkommando des Heeres, August 23, 1941.
46. In just the first quarter of 1940, steel requirements amounted to 566,000 tons of steel and more than 8,000 tons of copper for Hitler's ammunitions plan, not to mention the required amount of explosives to fill the shells, which otherwise, too, would pile up in storage facilities, empty. See Tooze, *The Wages of Destruction*, 345.
47. Tooze, *The Wages of Destruction*, 343. On transport issues related to the *Ostbahn*, see AIPN IPN GK 95/8, "Wirtschaftstagung," June 6-7, 1940.
48. BArch R121-830, Gesamt-Leistung des Beauftragten für Schrott und Altmetallerfassung in den gesamten besetzten Gebieten, Stab Major Schu von October 15, 1939-June 30, 1944.
49. BArch R121-1539, Bericht der Deutschen Revisions- und Treuhand-Aktiengesellschaft Berlin (1941), 3-5.
50. BArch R121-1539, Bericht der Deutschen Revisions- und Treuhand-Aktiengesellschaft Berlin über die bei dem Beauftragten für Schrott- und Altmetallerfassung in den gesamten besetzten Gebieten, Rittmeister Schu, vorgenommene Prüfung über die Verwendung der von der Roges gegebene Mittel bis zum 30. Juni 1941. It becomes clear that Schu refuses to reveal information about his operation, claiming records and numbers of military relevance and classified. The report thus acknowledges its preliminary and incomplete nature.
51. BArch R121-1356, RW19-3201.
52. BArch R121-1539, Bericht der Deutschen Revisions- und Treuhand-Aktiengesellschaft Berlin über die bei dem Beauftragten für Schrott- und Altmetallerfassung in den gesamten besetzten Gebieten, Rittmeister Schu, vorgenommene Prüfung über die Verwendung der von der Roges gegebene Mittel bis zum 30. Juni 1941.
53. BArch R121-484, Bewirtschaftungstelle für Metalle im Generalgouvernement an die Wirtschaftliche Forschung GmbH., April 13, 1942.
54. BArch R121-484, Bericht: Erfassung Südost, September 12, 1942.
55. BArch R121-484, Roges Hausmitteilung, August 28, 1941.
56. BArch R12-484, Liste der Altmetallgrosshändler, nach Bezirken, November 1, 1941.
57. BArch R121-1539, Bericht der Deutschen Revisions- und Treuhand-Aktiengesellschaft Berlin (1941), 8.
58. BArch R121-1539, Bericht der Deutschen Revisions-und Treuhand-Aktiengesellschaft Berlin (1941), 27.
59. BArch R121-484, Mansfeldschwer Kupferschieferbergbau Aktiengesellschaft an Roges, September 21, 1942.
60. BArch R121-484, Reichsminister für Luftfahrt an Leiter des Arbeitsringes Umschmelzaluminium, August 21, 1944.
61. BArch R121-484, Oberkommando des Heeres an den Beauftragten für Schrott und Altmetallerfassung, August 20, 1943.
62. BArch R121-484, Schu an Oberkommando des Heeres, August 23, 1943.
63. The ROGES was formed out of the department "Acquisition West" of the Wifo and the department "West" of the VVG, the two *Ostgesellschaften* that organized the systematic

gutting of Poland. BArch R121-1066, Zusammenlegung der Abteilung "Erfassung West" und der Abteilung "West" der Verwaltung-und Verwertungsgesellschaft der Haupttreuhandstelle Ost, February 15, 1941.
64. See BArch R121-2043, BArch R121-1539, BArch R121-1436, BArch R121-1066, Band I.
65. BArch R121-2043, "Art und Abwicklung der Geschäfte," October 18, 1947, and "Abschrift aus Bericht Nr. 1 an Herrn Kotelmann," July 5, 1945.
66. BArch R121-599. In Sachen Roges/Budich, November 15, 1952. The lawyer representing the ROGES argued that the group's assets were not subject to the control of the military government and reminded the courts that the plaintiff had not been viewed as compromised and was not charged or implicated by the Nuremberg Trials.
67. Müller, *Der Feind steht im Osten*, 174; Mazower, *Hitler's Empire*, 67–72; Kershaw, *Hitler: 1936–1945 Nemesis*, 252. See also Hartmann, *Wehrmacht im Ostkrieg*.
68. Müller, *Der Feind steht im Osten*, 186; Mazower, *Hitler's Empire*, 80–89.
69. Müller, *Der Feind steht im Osten*; Hartmann, *Wehrmacht im Ostkrieg*; Glantz, *Barbarossa*.
70. Pohl, *Die Herrschaft der Wehrmacht*, 98, 101.
71. Pohl, *Die Herrschaft der Wehrmacht*, 110.
72. BArch 121-587, Band 1, Wirtschaftsführungstab Ost, "Richtlinien für die Führung der Wirtschaft in den neubesetzten Ostgebieten (Grüne Mappe) Teil 1 (2.Auflage) Aufgaben und Organisation der Wirtschaft" (Berlin, July 1941); LOC NT Vol. XXXVI, Document 347-EC; for additional detail, see Document 126-EC in the same volume. Rolf-Dieter Müller, *Der Feind steht im Osten*; Mechthild Rössler and Sabine Schleiermacher, eds., *Der "Generalplan Ost": Hauptlinien der nationalsozialistischen Planungs- und Vernichtungspolitik* (Berlin: Akademie Verlag, 1993).
73. Eichholtz, *War for Oil*; Auzanneau, *Oil, Power, and War*.
74. LOC NT Vol. XXXVI, Document 347-EC, p. 40.
75. On the importance of the war against the Soviet Union for the concretization of the Nazi genocide of the Jews, see Longerich, *Holocaust*, 179f.
76. LOC NT Vol. XXXVI, Document 347-EC, p. 41.
77. BArch R121-587, Band 1, Wirtschaftsführungstab Ost, "Richtlinien für die Führung der Wirtschaft in den neubesetzten Ostgebieten (Grüne Mappe) Teil 1 (2.Auflage) Aufgaben und Organisation der Wirtschaft" (Berlin, July 1941). See also Snyder, *Black Earth*.
78. LOC NT Vol. XXXVI, Document 126-EC.
79. LOC NT Vol. XXXVI, Document 126-EC, p. 3.
80. LOC NT Vol. XXXVI, Document 126-EC, p. 4.
81. See Pohl, *Die Herrschaft der Wehrmacht*, 68; Snyder, *Black Earth*.
82. LOC NT Vol. XXXVI, Document 126-EC, p. 18.
83. LOC NT Vol. XXXVI, Document 126-EC, p. 6 ff.
84. LOC NT Vol. XXXVI, Document 003-EC. "Wirtschaftsaufzeichnungen für die Berichtszeit vom 15.8. bis 16.9.1941," p. 2. "Grundsätzlich sollen in den besetzten Gebieten nur diejenigen in der entsprechenden Ernährung gesichert werden, die für uns arbeiten."

85. Tooze, *The Wages of Destruction*, 481.
86. Pohl, *Die Herrschaft der Wehrmacht*, 185–194.
87. Pohl, *Die Herrschaft der Wehrmacht*, 178.
88. Pohl, *Die Herrschaft der Wehrmacht*, 158–159.
89. LOC NT Vol. XXXVI, Document 003-EC, "Wirtschaftsaufzeichnungen für die Berichtszeit vom 15.8. bis 16.9.1941," p. 3.
90. LOC NT Vol. XXXVI, Document 338-EC, pp. 1–2.
91. Tooze, *The Wages of Destruction*, 482–483; Mazower, *Hitler's Empire*, 160–164.
92. Pohl, *Die Herrschaft der Wehrmacht*, 166.
93. LOC NT Vol. XXXVI, Document 126-EC, p. 17.
94. BArch NS19-285, Oberkommando des Heeres, betreffs Groß-Schrottaktion, May 31, 1943.
95. BArch NS19-285, Oberkommando des Heeres. Abschrift. Betr. Gross-Schrottaktion, May 31, 1943.
96. BArch NS19-285, Heinrich Himmler an SS Obergruppsenführer von dem Bach, an die Höheren SS und Polizeiführer in den Ostgebieten, July 11, 1943.
97. BArch NS19-285, Rohstoffamt. Aktenvermerk, August 30, 1943.
98. BArch NS19-285, Himmler Order, September 8, 1943.
99. BArch R3-1657, Leiter des Planungsamtes an Herrn Generalleutant Waeger, March 14, 1944.
100. Susanne Heim illustrates how the desperate need for synthetic rubber prompted the regime to plan for large scale farming of the "rubber plant" kok sagyz, a dandelion-like plant, in Nazi-occupied Poland, most notably at Auschwitz, and in the occupied Soviet territories. See Heim, *Plant Breeding and Agrarian Research*, 118–153.
101. LOC NT Vol. XXXVI, Document 003-EC, p. 4.
102. AIPN IPN GK 95/8, "Wirtschaftstagung," June 6–7, 1940.
103. BArch R5-ANH.I-151, Hans Peter Hagedorn, Geschichte des Stabes des Feldeisenbahnkommandos 2, undated; BArch R5-ANH.I-162, Berichte des Feldeisenbahnkommando 3. According to Hagedorn, there were five separate FEKdo; according to the report of FEKdo 2, there were only four.
104. BArch R5-ANH.I-162, Berichte des Feldeisenbahnkommandos 3, undated.
105. BArch R5-ANH.I-154, Einsatzbefehl für Erkundungstrupps des F.B.A. 6, Merkblatt für die Erkundungsmeldung, June 20, 1941. See also Davie, "The Influence of Railways on Military Operations."
106. BArch R5-ANH.I-154, Einsatz Brest-Litwosk, June 22, 1941–August 9, 1942.
107. BArch R5-ANH.I-154, Einsatz Brest-Litwosk, June 22, 1941–August 9, 1942.
108. BArch R5-ANH.I-151, Hans Peter Hagedorn, Geschichte des Stabes des Feldeisenbahnkommandos 2, undated.
109. BArch R5-ANH.I-162, Berichte des Feldeisenbahnkommandos 3, undated.
110. BArch R5-ANH.I-162, Berichte des Feldeisenbahnkommandos 3, undated.
111. BArch R5-ANH.I-151, Hans Peter Hagedorn, Geschichte des Stabes des Feldeisenbahnkommandos 2, undated.
112. BArch R5-ANH.I-151, Hans Peter Hagedorn, Geschichte des Stabes des Feldeisenbahnkommandos 2, undated.

113. The invocation of people as material or *Menschenmaterial* is recurrent in the correspondence of administrators and was part of Hitler's regular parlance. The use sometimes had "positive" connotations, but was more often used to refer to people being exploited for their labor. See Klüger, *Still Alive*, 106.
114. Gedenkstätte Celle, Niedersächsisches Staatsarchiv Wolfenbüttel 12 Neu 18 Nr. 783 Arbeitseinsatz in Niedersachsen, Band 1. 1940–1942. "Das Programm des Generalbevollmächtigten für den Arbeitseinsatz," herausgegeben am Geburtstag des Führers 1942.
115. Pohl, *Die Herrschaft der Wehrmacht*, 131. At times, 50,000 Germans resided in Smolensk, in comparison to the remaining 37,000 Soviet residents.
116. BArch R5-ANH.I-151, Hans Peter Hagedorn, Geschichte des Stabes des Feldeisenbahnkommandos 2, undated.
117. BArch R5-ANH.I-154, "2.Tätigkeitsbericht des Feldeisenbahn-Betriebsamtes 6," August 10, 1941–December 31, 1942.
118. BArch R5-ANH.I-151, Hans Peter Hagedorn, Geschichte des Stabes des Feldeisenbahnkommandos 2, undated.
119. BArch R5-ANH.I-154, "2.Tätigkeitsbericht des Feldeisenbahn-Betriebsamtes 6," August 10, 1941–December 31, 1942.
120. BArch R5-ANH.I-157, Bildbericht zum Tätigkeitsbericht über den Eisenbahndienst. Monat, August 1943.
121. BArch R5-ANH.I-156, Richtlinen für die Unterhaltung und Verbesserung des Oberbaues im Sommer 1942, June 1, 1942.
122. BArch R5-ANH.I-154, "2.Tätigkeitsbericht des Feldeisenbahn-Betriebsamtes 6," August 10, 1941–December 31, 1942.
123. BArch R5-ANH.I-162, Berichte des Feldeisenbahkommandos 3, undated.
124. BArch R5-ANH.I-150; R5-ANH.I-165.
125. Pohl, *Die Herrschaft der Wehrmacht*, 322.
126. BArch R5-ANH.I-157.
127. BAF RW19-3213, "5 Jahres Bericht der Organisation Schu, 1939–1944," Anlage October 30, 1944.
128. Hayes, *From Cooperation to Complicity*; Hayes, *Industry and Ideology*; Koop, *Das Schmutzige Vermögen*; Lindner, *Hoechst. Ein I.G. Farben Werk*.

Chapter 5

1. BArch R8I-194, Advertisements.
2. BArch R8I-194, Das Otto-Ansohlverfahren im Dienste der Bewirtschaftung von Textilien. Emil Otto, 1942.
3. BArch R8I-194, Das Otto-Ansohlverfahren im Dienste der Bewirtschaftung von Textilien. Emil Otto, 1942.
4. BArch R8I-194, Das Otto-Ansohlverfahren im Dienste der Bewirtschaftung von Textilien. Emil Otto, 1942.

5. BArch R8I-194, Das Otto-Ansohlverfahren im Dienste der Bewirtschaftung von Textilien. Emil Otto, 1942.
6. BArch R8I-194, Das Otto-Ansohlverfahren im Dienste der Bewirtschaftung von Textilien. Emil Otto, 1942.
7. Tooze, *The Wages of Destruction*, 69. This was the result, in part, of an accelerating trade deficit; German exports in 1933 and 1934, compared to 1932; German debt diplomacy; and the international dynamics of protectionism or what Tooze calls "a cycle tit-for-tat trade restriction" (p. 73) accounted for the fact that by the summer of 1934 the total foreign currency reserves of the Reichbank barely covered the cost of one month's worth of imports.
8. Tooze, *The Wages of Destruction*, 76–79; Barkai, *Das Wirtschaftssystem des Nationalsozialismus*; Petzina, *Autarkiepolitik im Dritten Reich*.
9. Apelt, "Gegenwartsfragen der deutschen Textilwirtschaft," 682. Almost 20 percent of Germans were employed in textile- or clothing-related industries, trade or retail. See Tooze, *The Wages of Destruction*, 94.
10. Apelt, "Gegenwartsfragen der deutschen Textilwirtschaft," 682.
11. Apelt, "Gegenwartsfragen der deutschen Textilwirtschaft," 683. BArch R8I-41, Überwachungstelle für Wolle und andere Tierhaare. Anordnung: Verbot des Sammelns von Lumpen durch den Einzelhandel, January 19, 1937. See mention there of the "Verordnung über die Errichtung von Überwachungstellen vom 4. September 1934."
12. Tooze, *The Wages of Destruction*, 81.
13. Apelt, "Gegenwartsfragen der deutschen Textilwirtschaft," 683.
14. Apelt, "Gegenwartsfragen der deutschen Textilwirtschaft," 684.
15. Mackenroth, "Bericht über den Vierjahresplan," 699.
16. Rags were classified by fabric (wool, cotton, etc.) but generally already constituted processed textiles that were either produced as rags (cleaning rags) or that were now raggedy clothing and other fabric. Textile wastes conversely refer to fibrous material and trimmings that accrue during production.
17. BArch R8I-41, Überwachungstelle für Wolle und andere Tierhaare. Anordnung über die Lumpenwirtschaft, February 27, 1937.
18. Köstering, "'Pioniere der Rohstoffbeschaffung,'" 45.
19. BArch R81-1227, Das Hadernaufkommen im Deutschen Reich nach Erfassungsstellen.
20. Competencies of the six *Reichsstellen* was organized around raw materials; they included one for wool and other animal hair, one for cotton, one for cotton yarn and other netting, one for silk and rayon, one for clothing and related areas, and one for bast fibers. The initial monitoring agencies (*Überwachungsstellen*) were transformed into *Reichsstellen* with expanded competences in August 1939, meticulously regulating the movement of goods pre- and post-production. Apelt, "Die Textilwirtschaft im Krieg," 42.
21. BArch R8I-59, Bewirtschaftung und Verbrauchsregelung in der Spinnstoffwirtschaft in den eingegliederten Ostgebieten, June 26, 1940.
22. BArch R8I-59, Bewirtschaftung und Verbrauchsregelung in der Spinnstoffwirtschaft in den eingegliederten Ostgebieten, June 26, 1940; see also Apelt, "Die Textilwirtschaft im Krieg," 42.

23. BArch R8I-59, Bewirtschaftung und Verbrauchsregelung in der Spinnstoffwirtschaft in den eingegliederten Ostgebieten, June 26, 1940. For a summary of the development of the regulatory apparatus of the *Reichsstelle* for textiles, see EHRI Project, "Reichsstelle für Textilwirtschaft. Archival Description," at https://portal.ehri-proj ect.eu/units/de-002429-r_8_i.
24. For the built-in competition and institutional doubling, see Otto and Houwink ten Cate, eds., *Das organisierte Chaos: 'Ämterdarwinismus' und 'Gesinnungsethik'*; Broszat, *The Hitler State*; Hüttenberger, "Nationalsozialistische Polykratie."
25. In 1939, almost 97 percent of all rags processed were obtained through the secondary materials trade. By 1943, that number declined to 53 percent, which must be explained by the massive influx of textiles extracted in the east and robbed from murdered Jews. The production of raw materials from industrial textile waste inside the Reich remained relatively constant during the same period. BArch R8I-1227, Erzeugung und Bestände an Reißspinnstoff und sonstigem Reißmaterial; Hadernaufkommen im Deutschen Reich nach Erfassungsstellen, 1933–1944. See also Köstering, " 'Pioniere der Rohstoffbeschaffung,' " 60.
26. BArch R8I-239, Aktenvermerk, August 18, 1944.
27. Zysiak et al., *From Cotton and Smoke*: Łódź.
28. Horowitz, *Ghettostadt*, 25; Gutman, "Introduction" in Isaiah Trunk, *Łódź Ghetto*, xxix–lvii. The name was chosen in honor of German General Karl Litzmann who died there in battle in 1915. Dobroszycki, "Introduction," in *The Chronicle of the Łódź Ghetto*, xxiii. BArch R144-842, "Innerdienstliche Anweisung Nr 30," January 6, 1940.
29. Horowitz, *Ghettostadt*, 62; Gutman, "Introduction," xxxi; Horowitz, *Ghettostadt*, 33, 60; also Müller, *Der Manager der Kriegswirtschaft*.
30. Quoted in Horowitz, *Ghettostadt*, 59.
31. The category of "*andere Tierhaare*" (other animal hair) generally comprised hair from animals other than sheep (wool) including horsehair, pig birstles, and so forth. As of 1943, the category also came to include human hair in some records, which had been listed as a subcategory in prior years and was absorbed into *andere Tierhaare* when its industrial use skyrocketed for the production of industrial felts, as described at the end of this chapter.
32. BArch R144-846, Der Oberbefehlshaber Ost. Innerdienstliche Anweisung Nr. 16, December 13, 1939.
33. BArch R144-819, Verordnung des Chefs der Zivilverwaltung vom 13. 10. 39 über die Erfassung von Textil-Rohstoffen, October 13, 1939. The order required all owners of warehouses to register their inventory in textile raw materials (cotton, cotton wastes, wool, woolen waste, rags, silk, rayon, etc.) with the trustee for textile raw materials, including location, lot number, number of bales and bale numbers, weight and quality descriptions.
34. BArch R144-817, Fragebogen für Textilindustrie, Lederindustrie, Textilhandel, Lederhandel, September 23, 1939.
35. BArch R144-842, Arbeitsplan der Haupttreuhandsetelle-Ost (Entwurf), October 19, 1939; BArch R144-842, Abschrift. Erlass des Vorsitzenden des Ministerrats für die Reichsverteidigung über die Rohstofferfassung in den ehemals polnischen Gebieten, November 28, 1939.

36. BArch R144-846, Verwaltungs- und Verwertungsgesellschaft m.b.H. an den Beauftragten für die Rohstofferfassung beim Oberbefehlshaber Ost, Herrn Generalmajor Bührmann, December 4, 1939.
37. BArch R144-818, Schreiben von Lang, Mass & Co Stuttgart-Zuffenhausen an Beauftragten für die Rohstofferfassung, January 12, 1940.
38. BArch R144-818, Der Beauftragte für Rohstofferfassung an Herrn Kampf, Alexandrow, January 18, 1940.
39. BArch R144-818, Abt. 6 an den Polizeipräsidenten des Oberschlesischen Industriegebietes, November 28, 1939; BArch R144-818, Der Beauftragte für Rohstofferfassung an Firma Bracia Kaszub, Lodsch, February 14, 1940.
40. Browning, *The Origins of the Final Solution*, 25–35.
41. BArch R144-818, Kartonfabrik Laakman an Oberbefehlshaber Ost, Beauftragter für die Rohstofferfassung, May 27, 1940.
42. AIPN IPN GK 95/8, "Wirtschaftsbesprechung," June 6–7, 1940.
43. R144-824, Einzelbericht über die durchgeführte Prüfung des Zustandes der ehemaligen polnischen Baumwollwebereien in Lodsch und Umgegend, undated.
44. BArch R144-818, Lodscher Warenhandelsgesellschaft an den Beauftragten für Rohstofferfassung, February 20, 1940. In addition, Jews required a special permit to leave the ghetto and enter the "aryan" sectors of Łódź. BArch R144-832, Reichskommissar für Altmaterialverwertung an Verein der Kaufleute von Textilrohstoffen und Halbfabrikaten z Hd. Treuhänder Palinski, January 10, 1940.
45. Browning describes Poland as the Nazis' laboratory for genocide. See *The Origins of the Final Solution*, 12ff.
46. Browning, *The Origins of the Final Solution*, 18–20.
47. BArch R144-832, Abteilung 6 Wegener, Aktenvermerk, February 6, 1940.
48. BArch R144-846, Sitzung am 30, November 1939. Protokoll, December 5, 1939.
49. BArch R144-818, Lodscher Warengesellschaft an den Beauftragten für die Rohstofferfassung, February 14, 1940. See also Aktenvermerk, January 27, 1939.
50. BArch R144-819, Abteilung 6 an den Herrn Polizeipräsidenten, Lodsch, November 28, 1939.
51. BArch R144-818, Abteilung 6 an Strafanstalt Warthestadt, February 8, 1940; Abteilung 6 an Lodscher Warenanstalt, February 8, 1940.
52. BArch R144-820, Centrala Sanitarna an den Chef der Zivilverwaltung in Łódź, November 15, 1939.
53. BArch R144-824, Nr. 45 Firma Spinnerei & Reiterei Hugo Flaker & Co. Arisches Unternehmen, undated.
54. BArch R144-820, Der Reichsführer SS und Chef der deutschen Polizei; Der Chef des Hauptamtes Haushalt und Bauten an den Beauftragten für die Rohstofferfassung in den ehemals polnischen Gebieten, April 30, 1940.
55. Reichsführer SS und Chef der Deutschen Polizei, Hauptamt Haushalt und Bauten an Befehlshaber Ost, Beauftragter für die Rohstoff-Erfassung, z.Hd Pg. Wegener, February 3, 1940.
56. BArch R144-820, Der Reichsführer SS, Schnellbrief, February 14, 1940.

57. Longerich, *Holocaust*, 147; Browning, *Ordinary Men*, 5. While the initial numbers of the regular *Einsatzgruppen* of roughly 3,000 men were relatively small in comparison to their later strength, the Order Police were allowed to recruit 26,000 additional volunteers consisting of Germans and ethnic Germans to supplement the 8,000 men of the Order Police that were already assisting the army. On the original numbers of the *Einsatzgruppen*, see Browning, *Origins of the Final Solution*, 16, 225, 482n51. Browning estimates that "the number of men recruited from native populations into auxiliary units under the Order Police increased nearly tenfold in 1942, from 33,000 to 300,00," to whom the task of shooting Jews were increasingly assigned in order to "shift the psychological burden of German police to their collaborators." See Browning, *Ordinary Men*, 24-5.
58. BArch R144-832, Ackerman an Abteilung 6 z.Hd Wegener, March 7, 1940.
59. BArch R144-832, Abteilung 6 an Ackerman, March 13, 1940; Abteilung 6. Aktenvermerk, February 19, 1940.
60. Adelson, ed., *The Diary of Dawid Sierakowiak*, 62.
61. The SS mandated the self-administration of Jewish ghettos in Nazi-occupied Poland, installing Jewish councils that were mandated to manage labor, provision, policing, and eventually had to provide lists of names for deportations. See Longerich, *Holocaust*, 128, 291, 296, 336.
62. "Introduction," in *The Chronicle of the Łódź Ghetto*, xlviii.
63. "Introduction," in *The Chronicle of the Łódź Ghetto*, xlvii.
64. Trunk, *Łódź Ghetto*, 53, 148.
65. Trunk, *Łódź Ghetto*, 100–103.
66. Trunk, *Łódź Ghetto*, 151. *The Chronicle of the Łódź Ghetto*, 54.
67. Adelson, *The Diary of Dawid Sierakowiak*, 121.
68. Trunk, *Łódź Ghetto*, 148, 151, 153–157.
69. *The Chronicle of the Łódź Ghetto*, 85.
70. AIPN IPN GK 95/8, "Arbeitssitzung," September 20, 1940.
71. Adelson, *The Diary of Dawid Sierakowiak*, 210–211.
72. Trunk, *Łódź Ghetto*, 171.
73. Adelons, *The Diary of Dawid Sierakowiak*, 198.
74. Trunk, *Łódź Ghetto*, 170.
75. Adelons, *The Diary of Dawid Sierakowiak*, 176, 201.
76. Adelons, *The Diary of Dawid Sierakowiak*, 268, vii.
77. Krüger, *Deutsche Grossraumwirtschaft*; Teichert, *Autarkie und Grossraumwirtschaft*; Frommelt, *Paneuropa oder Mitteleuropa*; Voigt, ed., *Großraum-Denken*.
78. Pohl, *Die Herrschaft der Wehrmacht*, 179–181.
79. Müller, *Der Manager der Kriegswirtschaft*, 75.
80. BArch R3101-34177, Tätigkeitsbericht der Ost-Faser-Gesellschaft m.b.H und ihrer Tochtergesellschaften für das Geschäftsjahr 1941/42 (1943).
81. BArch R3101-34177, "Tätigkeitsbericht der Ost-Faser-Gesellschaft m.b.H und ihrer Tochtergesellschaften für das Geschäftsjahr 1941/42 (1943).
82. Kehrl, *Krisenmanager*, 227.
83. Müller, *Der Manager der Kriegswirtschaft*, 89.

84. In 1947, Kehrl was tried for his own involvement in the armaments ministry and sentenced to fifteen years in prison. Müller, *Der Manager der Kriegswirtschaft*, 161–164.
85. Kehrl, *Krisenmanager*, 228.
86. BArch R3-480, Zahlen aus der Arbeit der Ost-Faser, 1945.
87. BArch R3101-34177, Tätigkeitsbericht der Ost-Faser-Gesellschaft m.b.H und ihrer Tochtergesellschaften für das Geschäftsjahr 1941/42 (1943).
88. Pohl, *Die Herrschaft der Wehrmacht*, 122, 214, 322, 172–173.
89. BArch R3101-34177, Tätigkeitsbericht der Ost-Faser-Gesellschaft m.b.H und ihrer Tochtergesellschaften für das Geschäftsjahr 1941/42 (1943).
90. BArch R3101-34177, Tätigkeitsbericht der Ost-Faser-Gesellschaft m.b.H und ihrer Tochtergesellschaften für das Geschäftsjahr 1941/42 (1943).
91. BArch R3101-34177, Tätigkeitsbericht der Ost-Faser-Gesellschaft m.b.H und ihrer Tochtergesellschaften für das Geschäftsjahr 1941/42 (1943).
92. BArch R3101-34177, Tätigkeitsbericht der Ost-Faser-Gesellschaft m.b.H und ihrer Tochtergesellschaften für das Geschäftsjahr 1941/42 (1943).
93. BArch R3-480, Friedrich Dorn an Dr. Toepfer, December 2, 1944, "Zusammenfassung und Folgerungen."
94. BArch R3101-34177, Tätigkeitsbericht der Ost-Faser-Gesellschaft m.b.H und ihrer Tochtergesellschaften für das Geschäftsjahr 1941/42 (1943).
95. BArch R3-480, Friedrich Dorn an Dr. Toepfer, December 2, 1944, "Zusammenfassung und Folgerungen."
96. BArch R3-480, Friedrich Dorn an Dr. Toepfer, December 2, 1944, "Zusammenfassung und Folgerungen."
97. Pohl, *Die Herrschaft der Wehrmacht*, 184.
98. Most of the English- and German-language literature on *Ostarbeiter* or eastern workers focuses on the experience of those whom the Nazis dragged off to the Reich as slaves. See Herbert, *Hitler's Foreign Workers*; Benz, "Zwangsarbeit im Nationalsozialistischen Staat"; Binner *"Ostarbeiter" und Deutsche im Zweiten Weltkrieg* (Munich: M-Verlag, 2008). For forced labor in the occupied territories, see Pohl, *Die Herrschaft der Wehrmacht*; Pohl and Sebta, *Zwangsarbeit In Hitlers Europa*; Dahlmann and Hirschfeld, *Lager, Zwangsarbeit, Vertreibung und Deportation*.
99. Pohl, *Die Herrschaft der Wehrmacht*, 185.
100. Müller, *Der Manager der Kriegswirtscahft*, 94, 162–163.
101. Pohl, *Die Herrschaft der Wehrmacht*, 187, 124, 197.
102. Pohl, *Die Herrschaft der Wehrmacht*, 194.
103. Pohl, *Die Herrschaft der Wehrmacht*, 195, 190, 298.
104. Pohl, *Die Herrschaft der Wehrmacht*, 309.
105. BArch R26I-47, Reichsmarschall des Grossdeutschen Reiches. Vermerk. Betrifft: Bandenunwesen in der Ukraine, September 1943.
106. Pohl, *Die Herrschaft der Wehrmacht*, 285–297.
107. BArch R3101-34177, Tätigkeitsbericht der Ost-Faser-Gesellschaft m.b.H und ihrer Tochtergesellschaften für das Geschäftsjahr 1941/42 (1943); German Textile Industries during 1939–1945.

108. BArch R8I-215, Bezirksgruppe M. Gladbach der Fachgruppe Tuch und Kleiderstoff-Industrie an Herrn Hermann Reichsstelle für Wolle u. Andere Tierhaare, December 23, 1942.
109. Heim, *Plant Breeding and Agrarian Research*.
110. BArch R90-1, Der Reichskommissar für das Ostland an Adolf Hitler, Führerhauptquartier, November 1, 1943.
111. BArch R8I-214, Verarbeitete Mengen in den Monaten January bis Mai 1943 bei den Betrieben die zur Wollfilzindustrie gehören.
112. Andrzej Strzelecki, "The Plunder of Victims and Their Corpses," in *Anatomy of the Auschwitz Death Camp*, 260–261; Steinbacher, *Auschwitz*, 128; Gedenkstätte Sachsenhausen Archiv, JSU 1 Bd 11 Teil 2; also LOC NT Vol. XXVI, 998-PS references the industrial use of human hair.
113. DaA 4093, SS in KL Dachau. SS eigene Industriebetriebe. Verwendung von Haaren. Frauenhaare aus Vernichtungslagern für U-Boot Besatzungen. SS Wirtschafts-Verwaltungshauptamt Oranienburg, August 6, 1942.
114. BArch R8I-181 Überblick über die Versorgung mit Tierhaaren und Menschenhaaren, undated. Numbers are given for 1937, 1938 and 1939. All human hair used between 1937 and 1939 is imported. Prior to the late 1930s, human hair was used by wig-makers only. "Haargewirre von Menschenhaare, zu Perückenmacher- oder anderer Haararbeiten nicht verwendbar." R8I-40. Der Reichswirtschaftsminister. Bekanntmachung, August 1, 1938.
115. BArch R8I-1218, Rohstoff Vorräte. See also R8I-41, Reichsstelle für Wolle, Aufstellung der verarbeiteten Mengen und Bestände an Tierhaaren und Menschenhaaren in den Jahren 1937 und 1938.
116. BArch R8I-214, Anordnung der Reichsstelle für die Textilwirtschaft betreffend Herstellung von technischen (nicht gewebten) Filzen, April 5, 1943.
117. BArch R8I-214, Anlage 1 (Positive Liste) Filze für technische (nicht gewebte) Zwecke, April 5, 1943.
118. BArch R8I-214, Reichsstelle für Wolle und andere Tierhaare an Fachgruppe Heeres und sonstige Filzindustrie, March 19, 1943.
119. The earliest mention of human hair lists them as a separate category of *Menschenhaare*. As the stock movements at horsehair spinning mills made clear, human hair was listed as a subcategory of "other animal hair" and eventually subsumed into that category. Record-keeping was not always uniform. The Industry Group Textiles, for example, kept lists of textile raw materials that recorded only wool, noil, woolen waste, processed rags, tiolan (a textile fiber made from animal protein), and a catch-all category of "other," of which the Filzfabrik Gear Frejmark & Co in Łódź used between 0.8 and 3.2 tons per month between January and May 1943. See BArch R8I-1218; BArch R8I-214 Verarbeitete Mengen in t in den Monaten January bis Mai 1943 bei den Betrieben die zur Wollfilzindustrie gehören.
120. BArch R8I-214, Verarbeitete Mengen in t in den Monaten January bis Mai 1943 bei den Betrieben die zur Wollfilzindustrie gehören.
121. Hair from Flossenbürg, Mauthausen, Neuengamme, Ravensbrück, and Mauthausen were sold at 1 RM per 0.50 kilogram to Alex Zink Pelzfabrik AG in Roth near

Nuremberg. BArch NS3-386, Wirtschaftverwaltungshauptamt an Amtsgruppe D Konzentrationslager, January 4, 1943; see also BArch NS4-FL-384.

122. BArch R8I-214, Verarbeitete Mengen in t in den Monaten January bis Mai 1943 bei den Betrieben die zur Wollfilzindustrie gehören. Ukrainian Filzstifel Fabrik is mentioned in BArch R3101-34177, Tätigkeitsbericht der Ost-Faser-Gesellschaft m.b.H und ihrer Tochtergesellschaften für das Geschäftsjahr 1941/42 (1943).
123. BArch R90-4, Der Generalkommissar für Litauen. Bericht über Ablauf der wirtschaftlichen Räumung des Generalbezirkes Litauen, September 1, 1944; BArch 91-27, Bericht über Auflockerung und Räumung in Kauen, July 2–29, 1944.
124. BArch R3-480, Friedrich Dorn an Dr. Toepfer, December 2, 1944. "Zusammenfassung und Folgerungen."
125. Ukrainian Filzstifel Fabrik is mentioned in BArch R3101-34177, Tätigkeitsbericht der Ost-Faser-Gesellschaft m.b.H und ihrer Tochtergesellschaften für das Geschäftsjahr 1941/42 (1943)
126. Pohl, *Die Herrschaft der Wehrmacht*, 322.

Chapter 6

1. To this day, Schenck is better known for his "medical biography" of Hitler whom Schenck observed by accident in the *Führerbunker* a few days before Hitler's suicide, rather than for the nutritional experiments Schenck conducted on prisoners in Mauthausen concentration camp. Schenck later claimed these were designed to improve the lives of prisoners and he was acquitted in 1968. On the role of Schenck at Mauthausen and afterwards, see Klee, *Auschwitz, die NS-Medizin und ihre Opfer*, 185–189. As Uwe Frauenholz asserts, "In the postwar period, this doctor was able to stylize himself as a benefactor in various publications; his portrayal in the feature film *Der Untergang* (Downfall) invites positive identification." See Frauenholz, "'Verwertung des Wertlosen': Biotechnologische Surrogate aus unkonventionellen Eiweissquellen im Nationalsozialismus," 107. For Schenck's own writing on Hitler's last days, see Schenck, *Das Notlazarett unter der Reichskanzlei* and *Patient: Hitler*.
2. MaA MM_H_7a_27, "Ernährungsversuche im KL Mauthausen vom Frühjahr 1943 bis 31.7.1943." See Frauenholz, "Verwertung des Wertlosen," 107–108; Klee, *Auschwitz, die NS-Medizin und ihre Opfer*, 185–186.
3. MaA MM_H_7a_27, Ernst Martin an Staatsanwalt, February 28, 1966.
4. The Lenzinger Zellwolle, a cellulose and paper factory based in Lenzing, Austria, then, Ostmark, was founded in 1938 and by 1943 operated "an der Rentabilitätsschwelle [at the break-even point]." Given the hype around the total exploitation of chemical and organic residue, the company's venture with the garbage-sausage endeavor illustrates the extent to which resource consciousness and *Verwertungswut* (recycling mania) suffused private businesses. The company, now Lenzing Group, continues to pride itself on its sustainable business practices. For the history of Lenzinger Zellwolle, see "Lenzinger Zellwolle an der Rentabilitätsschwelle," *Die Deutsche Volkswirtschaft* 7 (1943), 236. For the

practice of mining the wastewater of cellulose manufacturers, see "Abwässer der Zellstoffindustrie," *Die Deutsche Volkswirtschaft* 2 (1942), 778. For the Lenzing Group's current self-presentation, see https://www.lenzing.com.
5. MaA MM_H_7a_27, Ernst Martin an Staatsanwalt, February 28, 1966.
6. MaA MM_H_7a_27, Ernst Martin an Staatsanwalt, February 28, 1966.
7. For SS scientists, though, the sausage fiasco was not a complete failure since it produced scientific "insights" about the necessary purity of artificially grown protein and the effects of excessive amounts of cellulose on already stressed digestive tracts. See Frauenholz, "Verwertung des Wertlosen,"109. Frauenholz draws attention to subsequent shifts in experimentation, using mold (fungus) that was easier to filter out of the wastewater.
8. Klee, *Auschwitz, die NS -Medizin und ihre Opfer*, 187.
9. Klee, *Auschwitz*, 187. The industrial bakeries in Oranienburg, Auschwitz, Lubin, and Herzogenbusch utilized thousands of kilograms each of *Holzstreumehl* (sawdust) in 1943. See BArch NS3-333, Geschäftsbericht der Deutsche Lebensmittel GmbH für das Jahr 1943.
10. BArch NS3-1373, Vermerk, August 15, 1944. Authorities wondered "whether the consumption of the bread containing lime additions mentioned in the report" would cause damage. They deferred, however, to the experts, insisting that this question could only be answered "when the discussion with SS-Sturmbannführer Professor Dr. Schenk has taken place." See also Frauenholz, "Verwertung des Wertlosen," 96.
11. Frauenholz, "Verwertung des Wertlosen," 109.
12. "Abwässer der Zellstoffindustrie," *Die Deutsche Volkswirtschaft* 2 (1942), 778.
13. Ungewitter, *Verwertung des Wertlosen*, 120; Frauenholz, "Verwertung des Wertlosen," 101.
14. Frauenholz, "Verwertung des Wertlosen," 100–101, 108.
15. For a detailed discussion of garbage as hog feed, see Chapter 2. See also Weber, "Towards 'Total' Recycling."
16. BArch NS3-333, Geschäftsbvericht der Deutsche Lebensmittel GmbH für das Jahr 1943.
17. BArch NS3-386, Chef des Wirtschafts-Verwaltunghauptamt Pohl an alle Lagerkommandanten. Geheim, October 26, 1943.
18. Quoted in Tooze, *The Wages of Destruction*, 540.
19. Drobisch, "Hinter Der Torinschrift 'Arbeit macht frei.'"
20. Cited in Himmler and Wildt, *Himmler privat*, 350.
21. In the sixteenth and seventeenth centuries, vagrancy laws in Great Britain attempted to tie agricultural laborers down and prevent their movement, casting them as spreaders of disease and associating them with idleness and sin. Rawlings, *Policing*, 46–47. Poor laws up until the nineteenth century were structured to disincentivize the poor from seeking relief. At the same time and even more so after the organization of labor in the second half of the nineteenth century, policing focused on mob control and property protection. See Rawlings, *Policing*, 62, 110; Brodeur, *The Policing Web*s, 66–67.
22. Burnard and Garrigus, *The Plantation Machine*; Madley, "From Terror to Genocide." Nazi ideas about responsibility with regard to forced labor drew explicitly on his

knowledge of plantations. In a collection of plausible and alleged utterings, the following has been attributed to Hitler: "Sure, a plantation owner has an interest in ensuring that disease doesn't break out among his workers, but would rather have slightly lower profits than upset the natural order of the world." Hitler, *Monologe*, 360. On the problematic nature of this particular source, see Nilsson, "Hitler redivivus."
23. Zimmerer, *Von Windhuk nach Auschwitz?*, 57–61; Pitzer, *One Long Night*, 81–87; Kiernan, *Blood and Soil*, 385–386; Dan Stone, *Concentration Camps*. Paul Moore further notes that the German press held up the example of camps in South Africa in the early 1930s to argue for the humanity of German camps. Moore, "'And What Concentration Camps Those Were!'" Also Forth and Kreienbaum, "A Shared Malady"; Hull, *Absolute Destruction*.
24. Wachsmann, *KL: A History of the Nazi Concentration Camps*, 23–78.
25. Orth, *Das System der nationalsozialistischen Konzentrationslager*, 24.
26. Orth, 33; Wachsmann, *KL*, 93, 96.
27. Mason, *Social Policy in the Third Reich*; Lüdtke, *Eigen-Sinn: Fabrikalltag, Arbeitererfahrungen und Politik*.
28. Wachsman, *KL*, 41.
29. Wachsman, *KL*, 46.
30. Wachsmann, *KL*, 63–64, 68.
31. There were exceptions to this rule. For example, the so-called Emsland camps were not established in existing facilities but purposefully built with prison labor. What is more, labor here was central from the beginning. Prisoners worked in land-reclamation projections, draining moors and swamps, and worked in agriculture. See Wachsmann, *KL*, 49–50.
32. See Allen, *The Invention of the White Race*, which illustrates that problems with labor lay at the root of colonial administration in North and Central America driving the slave trade and justifying the brutal exploitation of slave and indentured labor. In French, Spanish, and Portuguese colonies, labor shortages explain why the Iberians turned to African labor (p. 8); England instead used colonization "as a means of 'venting' the nation's surplus of 'necessitous people' into new world plantations" (p. 11).
33. Wachsmann, *KL*, 99, 149, 159.
34. SaA, P3 Bringmann, Fritz, September 21, 2006.
35. Wachsmann, *KL*, 149, 159.
36. SaA, P3 Bringmann, Fritz, September 21, 2006.
37. DaA 3502, NL München. Parteikanzlei. Protokoll Bravenes Zdenkék, June 21, 1975.
38. For example, when the Waffen-SS suddenly required 65,000 camouflage jackets, only 15,000 could be procured from ordinary suppliers, meaning that 50,000 had to be produced at Ravensbrück in just five weeks. The TexLed workshop had a day to adjust its schedule, and the output of 1,500 jackets per day could only be achieved by draconian discipline. See DaA 4089, SS in den KL Dachau. SS eigene Industriebetriebe, Gesellschaft für Textil und Lederverwertung. Similarly, at the end of the war, prisoners from Bergen-Belsen were forced to fill bomb craters and disassemble and straighten rails before railways could be repaired. See BeA 0.3/10510 Mendel Gur, undated.

39. Most scholarship on camp labor has focused on the exploitation of prisoners by corporations such as Daimler-Benz, Volkswagen, the Herman-Göring Works, Siemens Works, the chemical giant I.G. Farben, and the like, and how it otherwise privileged the more successful SS industries that were established in the camps in later part of the 1930s. Kaienburg, *Die Wirtschaft der SS*; Kaienburg, ed., *Konzentrationslager und deutsche Wirtschaft*. See also Hayes, *From Cooperation to Complicity*; Hayes, *Industry and Ideology*; James, *Krupp*; Koop, *Das Schmutzige Vermögen*; Lindner, *Hoechst*; Georg, *Die Wirtschaftlichen Unternehmungen der SS*.

40. BArch NS4-BU-289, Kommandantur, Konzentrationslager Sachsenburg, Kommandantur Befehl Nr. 240, October 23, 1936.

41. BArch NS4-BU-288, Sachsenburg, Sturmbannbefehlt Nr. 170, September 17, 1936.

42. SaA, D30/A/8/3, Michalius, M.S. Slaza, Michel, June 11, 1946.

43. BArch NS4 289, Kommandantur, Konzentrationslager Sachsenburg, Kommandantur Befehl Nr. 240, October 23, 1936.

44. Prisoner testimony is, in fact, filled with details clarifying that both labor and torture were intertwined. See, for example, MaA, Archive MM 5.2.0813 Josef Klat; SaA, P3 Finn Kleppe, P3 Fritz Bringmann; DaA 436, Krematurium. Baracke X; DaA 3486, NL München. Freimann, Pawel Antoni Respondek (Bericht), to mention only a few examples.

45. Wachsmann, *Hitler's Prisons*, 96–97, 99-100; LaB. A Rep. 003 04 01177. Oberbürgermeister an Bezirksbürgermeister Pankow, November 15, 1938; LaB. A Rep. 003 04 01177. Gesundheitsamt an Heil-und Pflegeanstalt Buch, November 19, 1937. See also Wachsmann, *KL*, 627.

46. BArch R3001-21396, Generalstaatsanwalt an den Herrn Reichsminister der Justiz, August 27, 1937.

47. BArch R3001-21396, Generalstaatsanwalt an den Herrn Reichsminister der Justiz, August 27, 1937.

48. BArch R3001-21396, Reichsminister für Bewaffnung und Munition, January 23, 1942.

49. BArch R3001-21396, Staatsanwalt an den Reichsminister der Justice, May 18, 1943.

50. BArch R3001-21396. Generalstaatsanwalt an Reichsminister der Justiz, betrifft Massnahmen zur Verwertung von Altmaterial im Zuchthaus Kassel-Wehlheiden, August 31, 1937.

51. Wildt, *Generation des Unbedingten*; Longerich, *Heinich Himmler*.

52. Kaienburg, *Die Wirtschaft der SS,* 139ff; Georg, *Die Wirtschaftlichen Unternehmungen der SS*, 12–13. In 1943, the Auschwitz bakery produced 28,354 loafs of bread. The bakery in KGL Lublin had different production runs; they made *Truppenbrot* (bread for the SS and Wehrmacht) and *Häftlingsbrot* (bread for prisoners), close to 8,000 loafs each. BArch NS3-333, Geschäftsbericht der Deutsche Lebensmittel GmbH für das Jahr 1943.

53. BArch NS4-BU-289, Kommandantur, Konzentrationslager Sachsenburg, April 22, 1936. "SS men and leaders may have their personal boots soled and repaired in the camp workshop. When delivering items for repair, they are to bring the necessary material with them."

54. BArch NS3-333, Geschäftsbericht der Deutsche Lebensmittel GmbH für das Jahr 1943.
55. Kaienburg, *Die Wirtschaft der SS*, 416–422; Georg, *Die Wirtschaftlichen Unternehmungen der SS*, 70–71. See also Oswald Pohl's testimony in Nuremberg LOC NT_war-criminals_Vol. V, 559–560.
56. Oswald Pohl's testimony in Nuremberg LOC NT war-criminals_Vol. V, 559–560.
57. Allen, *The Business of Genocide*, 60–61.
58. Allen, *The Business of Genocide*, 58. See also Jaskot, *The Architecture of Oppression*.
59. Allen, *The Business of Genocide*, 70–71.
60. For a comprehensive overview of the DESt activities, see Kaienburg, *Die Wirtschaft der SS*, 603–770. Compare also Allen, *The Business*, 58ff, and Wachsman, *KL*, 166–168. In addition, see Ma A MM_A_06_01, Verpachtung des Wienergraben an das Reich; Ma A MM_F_1_8, Bericht über die Todesstiege, Dr. Helmut Fierender.
61. Kaienburg, *Die Wirtschaft der SS*, 937, 942; Georg, *Die Wirtschaftlichen Unternehmungen der SS*, 59.
62. On the explosive growth of concentration camp population, see Wachsmann, *KL*, 139, 145, 148–149; Oswald Pohl's testimony in Nuremberg LOC NT_war-criminals_Vol. V, 559.
63. By 1940, all SS ventures were subsumed under the newly founded holding company, the German Economic Works (*Deutsche Wirtschaftsbetriebe*, DWB), representing an attempt to get an administrative handle on the mushrooming endeavors. Kaienburg, *Die Wirtschaft der SS*, 21, 27.
64. Kaienburg, *Die Wirtschaft der SS*, 546, 561, 942.
65. Da A 4266, Bericht über die bei der "Deutschen Ausrüstungwerke GmbH, Werk Dachau" vorgenommene Kurzprüfung. 18–14.1.1944. NS3-783, Deutsche Ausrüstungswerke. Aktenvermerk, July 10, 1944.
66. "Befehl des Führers 14 July 1939" in *Führer-Erlasse*, 184.
67. Cited in Georg, *Die Wirtschaftlichen Unternehmungen der SS*, 59.
68. The term *Menschenmaterial* (human material) appears ubiquitously in Nazi correspondence and was used in a variety of different contexts, sometimes referring to excellent *Menschenmaterial* available to the army or the Hitler Youth, for example, but also in reference to the exploitation of humans as laborers or for scientific experiments. A particularly egregious example appears in a letter to Himmler from Dr. Sigmund Rascher requesting access to felons for dangerous altitude experiments. LOC_NT_Vol. XXVII, Document 1602-PS, Letter from Dr. Sigmund Rascher to Reichsführer SS, May 15, 1941. For corpses used as *Menschenmaterial* for scientific purposes, see further R3001-2147. Also Hitler, *Monologe*, 161.
69. Translation of Document NO-1270, Prosecution Exhibit 61 LOC NT_war-criminals_Vol. V, 505.
70. Gedenkstätte Dachau Archiv DaA 4266, DAW Jahresbericht 194; BArch NS3-783; Translation of Document NO-555, Prosecution Exhibit 451a LOC NT_war-criminals_Vol. V, 537; see also Georg, *Die Wirtschaftlichen Unternehmungen der SS*, 62.

71. BArch NS3-783, Aktenvermerk, July 10, 1944.
72. BArch NS3-783, Deutsche Ausrüstungswerke GmbH ohne GG-Betriebe. Umlage der Hauptverwaltungskonnten ab 1. Juni 1944.
73. Translation of Document NO1036, Prosecution Exhibit 66 LOC NT_war-criminals_ Vol. V, 545–546.
74. BArch NS3-783, Umlage der Hauptverwaltungskosten ab 1. Juni 1944. See also Kaienburg, *Die Wirtschaft der SS*, 546–547.
75. Kaienburg, *Die Wirtschaft der SS*, 966–967.
76. BArch NS3-1252, Bericht über Prüfung der Jahresabschlüsse, July 10, 1944.
77. Unlike historian Hermann Kaienburg, who attests to the failure of the TexLed and other SS companies, arguing that the respective "inefficiency" of their operations accounts for the fact that "on the whole the SS-economy never became a strategic factor," I urge us to move beyond market-based profit-and-loss calculations when evaluating the respective success or failure of an SS venture.
78. "Introduction," in *The Chronicle of the Lodz Ghetto 1941–1944*, xlviii; Adelson, ed., *The Diary of Dawid Sierakowiak*, 121; Kaienburg, *Die Wirtschaft der SS*, 947–948, 965; Strebel, *Das KZ Ravensbrück*, 213ff.
79. Helm, *Ravensbrück*, 199.
80. The company maximized profit *and* labor exploitation by introducing output-increasing machines (which increased the output of each person), rather than labor-saving machines such as power looms (which allowed one person to operate numerous machines). See Allen, "Flexible Production in Ravensbrück Concentration Camp," 182–217.
81. Kaienburg, *Die Wirtschaft der SS*, 951.
82. Kaienburg, *Die Wirtschaft der SS*, 946.
83. ZapisyTerroru, Halina Piotrowska, Lublin, October 11, 1945, and Jadwiga Bielska, Lublin October 9, 1945, at https://www.zapisyterroru.pl/dlibra.
84. Helm, *Ravensbrück*, 199–201; Strebel, *Das KZ Ravensbrück*, 219.
85. ZapisyTerroru, Maria Kusmierczuk Warsaw, September 14, 1945, at https://www.zapisyterroru.pl/dlibra.
86. Kaienburg, *Die Wirtschaft der SS*, 942.
87. BArch NS3-125, Tex-Led Geschäftsbericht Berlin, May 21, 1943; LOC NT_Vol. XXXIV 4024-PS Odilo Globocnik, "Bericht über Abwicklung."
88. BArch NS3-386, Bekleidung und Ausrüstung der Häftlinge, December 16, 1943.
89. BArch NS3-125, Tex-Led Geschäftsbericht Berlin, May 21, 1943.
90. BArch NS3-125, Tex-Led Geschäftsbericht Berlin, May 21, 194; NS3-1161, Prüfung der Ostindustrie GmbH Berlin über die Zeit seit der Gründung der Gesellschaft bis zum 29.2.1944.
91. ZapisyTerroru, Władysława Dabrowska, Puławy, January 18, 1946, at https://www.zapisyterroru.pl/dlibra.
92. Kaienburg, *Die Wirtschaft der SS*, 958–960.
93. For labor details, see, for example, BArch NS4 BU 160 (1941-1943), NS4 BU 149 (1944), NS4 BU 148 (1943), NS4 BU 140 (1939); MaA MM F 2 2 2 (1943).

94. BArch NS19-181, Reichsführer SS an Reichsminister für Rüstung und Kriegsproduktion Betr. Gewinnung von Messing aus Sprengkapseln im Konzentrationslager Buchenwald, March 5, 1943.
95. BArch NS19-181, Reichsminister für Reichsminister für Rüstung und Kriegsproduktion an RF-SS Himmler, March 26, 1943.
96. Browning, *Remembering Survival*, 155.
97. BeA, BT 159 Mainz, Helmut, September 1944.
98. BeA, BT 159 Mainz, Helmut, September 1944.
99. LOC NT_Vol. XXXIV Document 4024-PS, Heinrich Himmler, Reichsführer-SS an Odilo Globocnik, November 30, 1943. Himmler also expressed support for exoneration in a letter to Pohl, January 21, 1944.
100. Sudrow, *Der Schuh im Nationalsozialismus*, 487, 606, 607.
101. SaA XXIV/28 Der RFSS der Inspekteur der Konzentrationslagerverwaltung, May 10, 1941.
102. See Sudrow, *Der Schuh*, 526ff. SaA Archiv XXIV/28 Der RFSS der Inspekteur der Konzentrationslagerverwaltung, May 10, 1941; AuA. Abteilung IV Rozne akta Oddzialu Administracji KL Auschwitz wplywy bizace 1. Der Reichsführer SS an Inspekteur der Konzentrationslager Verwaltung; Oranienburg, May 10, 1941.
103. SaA Archiv D30/A/8/3 Michalius, M.S. Slaza, Michel, June 11, 1946.
104. SaA D25 A7 T.2 Reinwald, Paul (2577), June 19, 1944.
105. Angrick, *Aktion 1005*, 35, 37, 193.
106. Angrick, *Aktion 1005*, 41.
107. Angrick, *Aktion 1005*, 172; Venezia, *Meine Arbeit im Sonderkommando Auschwitz*, 110–114.
108. Angrick, *Aktion 1005*, 251.
109. Angrick, *Aktion 1005*, 173. As a result of the gruesome dynamic, flight and organized resistance often originated with and enjoyed large support from members of the *Sonderkommandos*. Angrick, *Aktion 1005*, 113, 270–271.
110. BArch NS3-618, Gründung der Ost-Industrie, March 12, 1943; NS3-1161 Bericht, June 21, 1944. Also LOC NT_Vol. XXXIV Document 4024-PS. See, too, Longerich, *Holocaust*, 292–296; Browning, *The Origins of the Final Solution*; Musial, ed., *"Aktion Reinhardt" Völkermord*; Lehnstaedt and Traba, eds., *Die "Aktion Reinhardt."*
111. BArch NS3-618, Gründung der Ost-Industrie, March 12, 1943; NS3-1161 Bericht, June 21, 1944.
112. Angrick, *Aktion 1005*, 242.
113. Scholars have either ignored the OSTI or written it off as a failure. Kaienburg, who offers the most comprehensive history of its operation, and Allen both question its economic logic, following its main critic inside the SS-WVHA, Maximilian Horn, who seemed confused by the seeming contradiction between labor and genocide when the company purposefully eliminated its entire workforce in November 1943. Kaienburg, *Die Wirtschaft der SS*, 560–561; Allen, *The Business of Genocide*, 246f; Nasser, *SS-Wirtschaft und SS-Verwaltung*, 184ff.; Longerich, *Holocaust*, 377. Eichholtz, whose *Geschichte der Deutschen Kriegswirtschaft* gives the most

comprehensive and authoritative history of the war economy, does not mention the OSTI at all.

114. The concept of "permanent security" developed by historian Dirk Moses is crucial in this regard. See Moses, *The Problems of Genocide*.
115. Longerich, *Holocaust*, 277–304.
116. Mazower, *Hitler's Empire*, 163; Allen, *The Business of Genocide*, 2.
117. Cited in Allen, *The Business of Genocide*, 151.
118. Kaienburg, *Die Wirtschaft der SS*, 542–545.
119. Kaienburg, *Die Wirtschaft der SS*, 544.
120. LOC NT_Vol. XXXIV Document 4024-PS.
121. Longerich, *Holocaust*; Browning, *Ordinary Men*; Browning, *The Origins of the Final Solution*; Blatman, *The Death Marches*; Bloxham, *The Final Solution*; Bauman, *Modernity and the Holocaust*; Confino, *A World Without Jew*; Snyder, *Black Earth*; Stone, ed., *The Historiography of the Holocaust*; Friedländer, *Nazi Germany and the Jews*; Hilberg, *The Destruction of the European Jews*.
122. LOC NT_Vol. XXXIV Document 4024-PS.
123. LOC NT_war_criminals_Vol. V, "Extracts from Testimony of Defendant Pohl," 556.
124. Kaienburg, *Die Wirtschaft der SS*, 555, 557.
125. The OSTI acquired some additional ventures that seemed to have served solely to legitimize its status as a corporation, as those ventures, including a peat factory, served neither to recycle materials nor to primarily exploit the labor of Jews. Kaienburg, *Die Wirtschaft der SS*, 551.
126. LOC NT_Vol. XXXIV Document 4024-PS Odilo Globocnik, "Bericht über Abwicklung."
127. LOC NT_Vol. XXXIV Document 4024-PS Odilo Globocnik, "Bericht über Abwicklung."
128. USHMM RG-15.056M, Reel 11, Ostindustrie GmbH an den Chef der SS-Verwaltung, June 9, 1943.
129. LOC NT_Vol. XXXIV Document 4024-PS Odilo Globocnik, "Bericht über Abwicklung." See also Christopher Browning, *Ordinary Men*, 138.
130. LOC NT_Vol. XXXIV Document 4024-PS Odilo Globocnik, "Wirtschaftlicher Teil der Aktion Reinhard."
131. LOC NT_Vol. XXXIV Document 4024-PS, Odilo Globocnik an Reichsführer SS, Heinrich Himmler, November 4, 1943.
132. BArch NS3-1161, Prüfung der Ostindustrie GmbH Berlin über die Zeit seit der Gründung der Gesellschaft bis zum 29.21944 und Geschäftsbericht Ostindustrie GMBH für das Geschäftsjahr 1943.
133. For the massacres code-named "Erntefest" or "Harvest Festival," see Browning, *Ordinary Men*, 135–139. Also Angrick, *Aktion 1005*, 289; Grabitz and Scheffler, *Letzte Spuren*, 328–333.
134. Kaienburg, *Die Wirtschaft der SS*, 558–559; on the operations and labor at Schultz & Co., see Grabitz and Scheffler, *Letzte Spuren*, which presents the company's history through primary sources and photographs. On the relocation of the company to Trawniki, 179ff.
135. Scarry, *The Body in Pain*, 13, 27.

Chapter 7

1. BArch R8II-47, Bericht über die Bestands- und Bedarfserhebung an Spinnstoffen bei den Gefolgschaftsmitgliedern der Schächte und der Fremdfirmen der Sudetenberg Brüx, undated.
2. BArch R8II-47, Bericht über die Bestands- und Bedarfserhebung an Spinnstoffen bei den Gefolgschaftsmitgliedern der Schächte und der Fremdfirmen der Sudetenberg Brüx, undated.
3. BArch R8II-47, Vermerk, March 23, 1944.
4. Barch R8II-47, Bericht über die Bestands- und Bedarfserhebung an Spinnstoffen bei den Gefolgschaftsmitgliedern der Schächte und der Fremdfirmen der Sudetenberg Brüx, undated.
5. BArch R8II-47, Bericht über die Bestands- und Bedarfserhebung an Spinnstoffen bei den Gefolgschaftsmitgliedern der Schächte und der Fremdfirmen der Sudetenberg Brüx, undated.
6. BArch R8II-47, Bericht über die Bestands- und Bedarfserhebung an Spinnstoffen bei den Gefolgschaftsmitgliedern der Schächte und der Fremdfirmen der Sudetenberg Brüx, undated.
7. Burke, *Lifebuoy Men, Lux Women*; Kelley, *Soap and Water*; Ward, *The Clean Body*; Anderson, *The Cultivation of Whiteness*; Anderson, *Colonial Pathologies*; Zimring, *Clean and White*; Feiter and Boy, *90 Jahre Persil*.
8. Tooze, *The Wages of Destruction*, 359–366; on Hitler's decision not to conscript women into the workforce, see Herbert, *Hitler's Foreign Workers*, 39–40.
9. Herbert, *Hitler's Foreign Workers*, 298. Also Benz, "Zwangsarbeit im Nationalsozialistischen Staat"; Binner, *"Ostarbeiter" und Deutsche*; Keller, *Sowjetische Kriegsgefangene im Deutschen*; Herbert, ed., *Europa und der 'Reichseinsatz'*; Pohl and Sebta, *Zwangsarbeit In Hitlers Europa*; Pohl, *Die Herrschaft der Wehrmacht*; Dick, *Builders of the Third Reich*.
10. BArch R10VI-59, Secret Report. Braunschweigisches Institut für Wirtschaftsforschung, March 1943. See also Herbert, *Hitler's Foreign Workers*, 298, 462; Benz, "Zwangsarbeit im Nationalsozialistischen Staat," 4.
11. Binner, *"Ostarbeiter" und Deutsche im Zweiten Weltkrieg*, 98.
12. Keller, *Sowjetische Kriegsgefangene im Deutschen Reich 1941/42*, 72ff.
13. Mazower, *Hitler's Empire*, 162–163.
14. Benz, "Zwangsarbeit im Nationalsozialistischen Staat"; Herbert, *Hitler's Foreign Workers*.
15. Hitler, *Monologe*, 162.
16. Pohl, *Die Herrschaft der Wehrmacht*, 172–173, 207.
17. Pohl, *Die Herrschaft der Wehrmacht*, 181.
18. In October 1944, German police were charged with the procurement of 4,000 workers for a cement factory. They indiscriminately grabbed all male passers-by on the street without checking identity papers, abducting a number of German trustees whom German administrators later insisted be released, while the rest of the men were shipped to west Prussia. See R90-4, Bericht über eine Reise in das

Reichskommissariat Ostland in der Zeit vom 10.-26, October 1944. Also Benz, "Zwangsarbeit im Nationalsozialistischen Staat," 7.
19. Pohl, *Die Herrschaft der Wehrmacht*, 312–316.
20. Over the course of the war, the different categories of "subhuman" seemed to more readily flow into each other, providing different variants of the same theme of a mortal enemy trying to destroy the German "race." On the merging of antisemitism and anti-Bolshevik ideas in Europe since World War and its intensification during World War II in Nazi ideology, see Hanebrink, *A Specter Haunting Europe*. Hanebrink notes that the "fusion of Jewish Power and eastern savagery resonated powerfully with well-worn stereotypes of Eastern Europe as a backward and barbarous region dependent on Germans for modeling civilized culture and honorable conduct" (p. 128).
21. Keller, *Sowjetische Kriegsgefangene im Deutschen Reich*, 85–109. See also Herbert, *Hitler's Foreign Workers*.
22. BArch R8II-47, Bericht über die Bestands- und Bedarfserhebung an Spinnstoffen bei den Gefolgschaftsmitgliedern der Schächte und der Fremdfirmen der Sudetenberg Brüx, undated.
23. BArch R8II-123, An alle Landwirtschaftsaämter Richtlinien 3/44 LWA der Reichsstelle für Kleidung und verwandte Gebiete (Verwertung zugeteilter Altkleidung), April 29, 1944.
24. BArch R8II-47, Bericht über die Bestands- und Bedarfserhebung an Spinnstoffen bei den Gefolgschaftsmitgliedern der Schächte und der Fremdfirmen der Sudetenberg Brüx, undated.
25. BArch R10VI-59, Secret Report, Braunschweigisches Institut für Wirtschaftsforschung, March 1943.
26. BArch R10VI-59, Secret Report, Braunschweigisches Institut für Wirtschaftsforschung, March 1943.
27. BArch R10VI-59, Secret Report, Braunschweigisches Institut für Wirtschaftsforschung, March 1943.
28. BArch 121–484, Mansfeldscher Kumpferschieferbergbau AG an Roges, September 19, 1942; Schrott Schu and Overkommando des Heeres, August 10, 1943; BArch 121-1066, Band 1, Woll-Wäscherei und Kämmerei in Döhren bei Hannover an Roges, April 19, 1943. See also "Bericht des Reigerungsforstamtes in Stade über Arbeitsleistung sowjetischer Kriegsgefangener in der Forstwirtschaft" in *Sowjetische Kriegsgefangene im Arbeitseinsatz*, 269, 273.
29. BArch NS3-386, Reichsführer SS, Chef des SS Wirtschafts-Verwaltungshauptamtes, Pohl an alle Lagerkommandanten. Geheim, October 26, 1943.
30. BArch NS3-380, SS Wirtschafts-Verwaltungshauptamt Amtsgruppe B, Bericht über Prüfung des Bekleidungszustandes der Häftlinge und der Bekleidungswirtschaft im KL Auschwitz, November 27, 1944.
31. BArch NS3-380, SS Wirtschaftws-Verwaltungshauptamt. Bericht über Prüfung des Bekleidungszustandes der Häftling und der Bekleidungswirtschaft im KL Buchenwald und KL Mittelbau, December 19, 1944.
32. BArch R58-164, Stimmungsbericht, September 25, 1941.

33. Hartmann, *Wehrmacht im Ostkrieg*.
34. BArch R58-164, Stimmungsbericht, September 25, 1941. See also "Bereich des Landrates des Kreises Grafschaft Diepholz user die Folgen der unzureichenden Verpflegungsätze für die sowjetischen Kriegsgefangenen," in *Sowjetische Kriegsgefangene im Arbeitseinsatz*, 158–159.
35. Fritzsche, *Life and Death in the Third Reich*, 184, 186.
36. Ward, *The Clean Body*, 108ff.
37. BArch R8V-17, Übersicht technische Knochenfett-Erzeugung. March 29, 1943. Fats extracted from bones amounted to 5,800 metric tons in 1933, 7,843 metric tons in 1936, 13,830 metric tons in 1938, 11,733 metric tons in 1939, 7,262 metric tons in 1940, 4,682 metric tons in 1942, and 3,804.5 metric tons in 1944. BArch R58-164, Zur Altmaterialsammlung der Schulen, September 5, 1941. See also Kathrin Kollmeier, *Ordnung und Ausgrenzung*, 205–206; Vaupel and Preiß, "Kinder, sammelt Knochen!"; Susanne Köstering, "'Pioniereder Rohstoffbeschaffung'"; Denton and Weber, "Bones of Contention," 119–139.
38. BArch R58-164, Zur Altmaterialsammlung der Schulen, September 5, 1941; Vaupel and Preiß, "Kinder, sammelt Knochen!," 159.
39. BArch R58-164, Zur Altmaterialsammlung der Schulen, September 5, 1941.
40. BArch R43II-1170a. Einbau von Fettabscheidern zur Sammlung und Verwertung fetthaltiger Abwässer in gemeindlichen Betrieben, Runderlass, February 26, 1940.
41. BArch R154-531, Deutsche Landwirtschafts-Gesellschaft an Preuss. Landesanstalt für Wasser-, Boden-und Lufthygiene, December 3, 1926; Landesanstalt für Wasser-, Boden-und Lufthygiene an den Herrn Regierungspräsidenten Minden, August 8, 1928; Gewerbeamt an Landesanstalt für Wasser-, Boden-und Lufthygiene, October 24, 1929.
42. BArch R8II-19, Reichsstelle industrielle Fett und Waschmittel. [handschriftlich in Bleistift:] Bericht von Herrn Hermann, Berlin. Anlage 4, December 1, 1944.
43. BArch R8II-19, Reichsstelle für industrielle Fettversorgung becomes the Reichsstelle für industrielle Fette und Waschmittel in June 1942.
44. BArch R8V-47, Hermann Rigele an Chef der Zivilverwaltung, October 19, 1939;
45. BArch R8V-47, Hermann Rigele, Schicht-Lever AG an den Chef der Zivilverwaltung, Regierungsrat Dr. Coelln, Warschau, September 19, 1939.
46. BArch R8V-47, Aktenvermerk, March 8, 1940.
47. BArch R8V-47, Hermann Rigele, Schicht-Lever AG an den Chef der Zivilverwaltung, Regierungsrat Dr. Coelln, Warschau, September 19, 1939.
48. BArch R8V-47, Verodnung über die Herstellung und Vertrieb von Seifen aller Art, February 1, 1940.
49. BArch R8V-47, Amt des Generalgouverneurs, der Leiter der Abteilung Wirtschaft and den Reichswirtschaftsminister, April 13, 1940.
50. BArch R8V-47, Aktenvermerk, March 8, 1940.
51. Recipes for soap making as well as other tips for the efficient housewife were still included in American cookbooks in the early twentieth century. Cooke, *Three Meals a Day*.
52. BArch R8V-47, Verordnung über die Herstellung und Vertrieb von Seifen aller Art, February 1, 1940.

53. BArch R8V-47, Aktenvermerk, March 8, 1940.
54. BArch R8V-47, Amt des Generalgouverneurs, der Leiter der Abteilung Wirtschaft and den Reichswirtschaftsminister, April 13, 1940.
55. BArch R8V-47, Reichswirtschaftsminister. Vermerk, May 9, 1940.
56. BArch R8V-47, Besprechungsnotiz, October 31, 1941.
57. BArch R8V-47, Reichswirtschaftsminister. Vermerk, May 9, 1940.
58. BArch R8V-47, Besprechungsnotiz, October 31, 1941.
59. BArch R8V-45, Bericht, August 11, 1941.
60. BArch R8V-45, Bericht, August 11, 1941.
61. BArch R8V-45, Bericht. August 11, 1941.
62. BArch R8V-45, Bericht über die Seifenindustrie im Bereich der Wi. In. Süd, July 1, 1942.
63. BArch R8V-47, Besprechungsnotiz, October 31, 1941.
64. BArch R8V-17. Knochen, March 29, 1943; Aktennotiz: Knochensammlung für Dezember 1943, February 16, 1944.
65. See BArch R8V-17. Reichsstelle für industrielle Fettversorgung, Rundschreiben, Betrifft Hautkratzfett, October 11, 1940; Reichsstelle für industrielle Fette und Waschmittel, Rundschreiben, Betreff: Schweinekratzfett aus Scweinehäuten, June 11, 1943; Produktionsliste, undated; Reichsstelle für industrielle Fette und Waschmittel, Rundschreiben, Betreff: Rohklauenöl, December 20, 1944; R8V-18 Reichsstelle für industrielle Fette und Waschmittel, Rundschreiben, Betreff: Wollfett, January 18, 1943.
66. BArch R8V-17, Reichsbeauftragte für industrielle Fettversorgung. Hautkratzfett, October 11, 1940.
67. BArch R8V-40, Reichsstelle für industrielle Fette und Waschmittel, "Extraktion von Tiermehl," December 10, 1942; BArch R8V-40, Aktennotiz. Besprechung mit den Extrationsfirmen wegen Nachentfettung von Tiermehl, August 27, 1943.
68. BArch R8V-40, Reichsstelle für industrielle Fette und Waschmittel. Nachentfettung von Tierkörpermehl, October 16, 1944; BArch R8V-40, Nachentfettung von Tierkörpermehl. Bestandsliste, July 1944.
69. BArch R8V-40, Nachentfettung von Tierkörpermehl. Bestandsliste, July 1944.
70. BArch R58-164, Klagen der Schlächter über die Nichtabnahme von Abfällen, wie Hörner, Klauen und Abfallknochen durch den Altmaterialhandel, September 25, 1941.
71. BArch R8II-19, Reichsstelle für industrielle Fette und Waschmittel, October 20, 1942.
72. BArch R8V-17, Klauenölproduktion 1943, November 2, 1943.
73. BArch R8V-39, Dr. Kurt Lindner, Chemisches Laboratorium. Aktenotiz, December 14, 1939; Sunlicht Gesellschaft AG. Bericht, June 24, 1940; Entwurf. An den Herrn Reichswirtschaftsminister. Verwendung von Netz-und Streckungsmitteln in den Einheitsseifenerzeugnissen, July 22, 1940; Bericht über die Waschversuche mit RIF Pulver, September 29, 1941.
74. BArch R8V-39, Zahl der Waschmittelverbraucher, February 3, 1943.
75. BArch R8II-19, Reichsstelle für industrielle Fette und Waschmittel, Fettrückgewinnung, November 15, 1943; BArch R8V-17, Knochen, March 29, 1943.

76. BArch R8V-40, Sodaverteilung für Reinigungsmittel I Quartal 1943, December 11, 1942.
77. Longerich, *Holocaust* 320ff., 387ff. See also Gottwald and Schulle, *Die 'Judendeportationen' aus dem Deutschen Reich*.
78. The building records of the Waffen-SS illustrate that such considerations played a role on paper, after the camps were already established and sanitary pressures mounted. Remaining records of the SS building office are located at USHMM RG-15.056M Zentralbauamt der Waffen-SS.
79. MaA MN_A_03_05, Skizze vom KL Mauthausen von 1939–1942. MM_B_49_01, Bericht über den Aufbau, Tätigkeit und Auflösung des KZ-Wr.Neudorf mit Dokumentenabschriften 1943–45 v. Dr. Rolf Busch-Waddeck.
80. AuA, Arbeitseinsatz 1 Vol. 1 Zentralbauleitung der Waffen SS und Polizei Auschwitz, Betrifft: Häftlingseinsatz für Entwässerunganlagen, October 26, 1942.
81. BArch NS4-BU-290, Kommandanturbefehl Sachsenburg, May 28, 1937.
82. DaA 4202, Kostenanschlag über Erstellung einer Abort-Anlage Zwischen Gebäude Nr. 211-213/Schreinereibetrieb, unter Verwendung von Gefangenen, April 13, 1934.
83. DaA 4202, Staatsministerium des Innern an die Regierung von Oberbayern, January 30, 1937. Cesspools remained common in urban areas until long after World War II, but since the 1910s vacuum excreta, or motorized shit-suckers, were available to urban sanitation forces and aided in the emptying of underground cesspools and sewage pits. See Haug, *Von der Kloake zur Kanalisation*; Reid, *Paris Sewers and Sewermen*; Melosi, *Effluent America*.
84. Löffelsender, *Das KZ Buchenwald 1937–1945*, 14.
85. MaA MM_5.2.0813, Zeugenaussage Josef Klatt, March 1, 2003.
86. MaA MM_V_3_19, Zeugenaussage Jan Pstross, May 9, 1945.
87. BArch NS4-BU-31, K.L. Buchenwald, Lagerarzt and Kommandanten, October 21, 1939.
88. BeA, BT 581 Alexander Roseboom, 27. January 15, 1989.
89. MaA MM_5.2.0813, Zeugenaussage Josef Klatt, March 1, 2003.
90. MaA MN_N_07_07, Kostenanschlag für Einäscherungsofen, November 20, 1940.
91. MaA MM_5.2.0813, Zeugenaussage Josef Klatt, March 1, 2003.
92. BArch NS4-BU-54, Der Standortarzt der Waffen-SS. Aktennotiz, August 4, 1944.
93. BArch NS4-BU-54, Der Standortarzt der Waffen-SS. Aktennotiz, August 4, 1944.
94. BArch NS4-BU-54, Der Standortarzt der Waffen-SS an den Herrn Landrat, July 20, 1944.
95. Wachsmann, *KL*, 278.
96. Historians meanwhile agree that the Wannsee Conference implemented and disseminated instructions about the Final Solution that had been made sometime in the late fall of 1941. No Führer order survived, the decision was likely passed down verbally, or the Aktion 1005 ensured that the original documents were destroyed, if there was a Führer order at all. On the decision-making process, see Angrick, *Aktion 1005*; Browning, *The Origins of the Final Solution*; Roseman, *The Villa, the Lake, the Meeting*.
97. The extermination camps Bełżec, Sobibor, and Treblinka were termed "Reinhard camps" after the assassination of Reinhard Heydrich, the chief architect of the

Final Solution in Poland. See Lehnstaedt and Traba, "Die 'Aktion Reinhardt'—Wissenschaft und Gedenken" in *Die 'Aktion Reinhardt'*, p. 9, note 1. "The name was chosen in memory of Reinhard Heydrich, killed in Prague on June 4, 1942, whose first name even Heinrich Himmler usually wrote as 'Reinhardt.'"

98. Angrick, *Aktion 1005*, 93.
99. Angrick, *Aktion 1005*, 205.
100. Angrick, *Aktion 1005*, 237.
101. Bełżec was dismantled in the spring of 1943, Sobibor later that summer. and Treblinka hastily evacuated as the Red Army arrived in July 1944.
102. Wachsmann, *KL*, 278–279.
103. Wagner, *IG Auschwitz*; James, *Krupp*. See also Heim, *Plant Breeding and Agrarian Research*.
104. Angrick, *Aktion 1005*, 180.
105. BArch NS3-1639, Hauptamt Haushalt und Bauten, Amt II/3 an Reichsführer SS, December 19, 1941.
106. Angrick, *Aktion 1005*, 161, 166–167.
107. USHMM RG 15.056M, Zentralbauamt der Waffen-SS, Reel 9. Aktenvermerk, January 17, 1942.
108. USHMM RG 15.056M, Zentralbauamt der Waffen-SS, Reel 9. Aktenvermerk, January 17, 1942; Aktenvermerk, February 12, 1942.
109. USHMM RG 15.056M, Zentralbauamt der Waffen-SS, Reel 9. Aktenvermerk, February 12, 1942.
110. USHMM RG 15.056M, Zentralbauamt der Waffen-SS, Reel 9. Aktenvermerk, March 3, 1942.
111. USHMM RG 15.056M, Zentralbauamt der Waffen-SS, Reel 9. Aktenvermerk, February 16, 1943.
112. BArch NS3-1639, Waffen-SS, Kriegsgefangenenlager Lublin an Führungshauptamt Inspekteur der KL Lublin, February 9, 1942.
113. Allen, *The Business of Genocide*, 98.
114. Allen, *The Business of Genocide*, 98, 135; Longerich, *Holocaust*, 283.
115. BArch NS3-1639, Hauptamt Haushalt und Bauten and Zentralbauleitung der Waffen-SS, November 8, 1941.
116. BArch NS3-1639, Hauptamt Haushalt und Bauten, Amt II/3 an Zentralbauleitung der Waffen-SS, December 8, 1941. und The planned incinerator and power plant (*Heizkraftwerk*) were never completed.
117. BArch NS3-1639, Hauptamt Haushalt und Bauten an Zentralbauleitung der Waffen-SS und Polizei, December 8, 1941; USHMM RG 15.056M, Zentralbauamt der Waffen-SS, Reel 8, Plan für Grosswaschanlage, May 1942; Sonderbauwerke (undated), Notabortanlage, July 1942.
118. USHMM RG 15.056M, Zentralbauamt der Waffen-SS, Reel 9, Hygiene Institut der Waffen-SS, Kurzbericht, May 11, 1942.
119. USHMM RG 15.056M, Zentralbauamt der Waffen-SS, Reel 9, Wasserversorgung Lublin, February 17, 1943.

120. USHMM RG 15.056M, Zentralbauamt der Waffen-SS, Reel 9, Waffen-SS Gefangenlager Lublin, Kommandantur an Zentralbauleitung der Waffen-SS, January 12, 1943.
121. Angrick, *Aktion 1005*, 287.
122. Kommandanturbefehl Nr. 10/42, Auschwitz, June 6, 1942; Komandanturbefehl Nr. 1/40, Auschwitz, June 6, 1940, in *Standort und Kommandanturbefehle des Konzentrationslagers Auschwitz*, 141, 3.
123. Primo Levi describes the "covered by curious didactic frescoes: for example, there's the good Häftling, portrayed stripped to the waist, about to diligently soap his sheared and rosy cranium, and the bad Häftling, with a strong Semitic nose and a greenish colour, bundled up in his ostentatiously stained clothes with a beret on his head, who cautiously dips a finger into the water of the washbasin. Under the first is written: '*So bist du rein*' (like this you are clean), and under the second: '*So gehst du ein*' (like this you come to a bad end); and lower down in doubtful French but in Gothic script: '*La propreté, chest la santé.*'" Levi, *Survival in Auschwitz*, 39.
124. Levi, *Survival in Auschwitz*, 34.
125. BArch NS3-425, Wirtschafts-Verwaltungshauptamt an Lagerkommandanten der KL, August 19, 1942.
126. Neander, "The Danzig Soap Case," On rumors in Germany, see Stargardt, *The German War*, 259
127. Angrick, *Aktion 1005*, 332. With "abuse," Angrick concludes, Himmler likely meant to prohibit the use of bodies for soap manufacturing.
128. Angrick, *Aktion 1005*, 1078–1080.
129. Angrick, *Aktion 1005*, 1078.
130. Cited in Angrick, *Aktion 1005*, 333.
131. Angrick, *Aktion 1005*, 95, 237–238, 247–248, 265.
132. Angrick, *Aktion 1005*, 269. The Reinhardt camps were dismantled, the area bulldozed and planted, so as to conceal all traces the murder facilities and the remnants of corpses, 243, 273–274.
133. Angrick, *Aktion 1005*, 30.
134. Angrick, *Aktion 1005*, 218–219.
135. Cited in Angrick, *Aktion 1005*, 208.
136. Angrick, *Aktion 1005*, 197, 214. Compare Webster, *Aftermath: The Remnants of War*, 84, 104, 107–109, 112.
137. Kommandanturbefehl Nr. 5/43, Auschwitz, February 18, 1943; Sonderbefehl Nr. 33/43, Auschwitz, August 21, 1943; Standortbefehl Nr. 38/43, Auschwitz, September 9, 1943; Sonderbefehl Nr. 7/44, Auschwitz, February 14, 1944, in *Standort-und Kommandanturbefehle*, 224–225.
138. BArch R8V-17, "Nachtrag Nr. 299 zum 'Recht der Öl - und Fettwirtschaft," August 8, 1942.
139. Except for the soap experiments by Professor Dr. Rudolf Spanner in the Danzig Anatomic Institute, isolated instances of SS trophy making, and the occasional mixing of ash with soil in camp adjacent vegetable gardens, human bodies were not

recycled. Neander, "The Danzig Soap Case," 63–86; Angrick, *Aktion 1005*, 1081. See also Berlage. "Der Anatom. Prof. Dr. Rudolf Spanner in der Zeit von 1939 bis 1945."

140. Schulte-Sasse, "The Jew as Other under National Socialism: Veit Harlan's Jud Süss": Hansen, "The Art and Science of Reading Faces: Strategies of Racist Cinema in the Third Reich": Heinz, "Fritz Hippler": Haggith and Newman, *Holocaust and the Moving Image*.

Chapter 8

1. BArch R1501-3157, Versuchs- und Forschungsanstalt für Gartenbau und höhere Gartenbauschule zu Pillnitz an Ministerialrat Dr. Görlach, Reichsministerium für Ernährung und Landwirtschaft, April 18, 1944.
2. BArch R1501-3157, Versuchs- und Forschungsanstalt für Gartenbau und höhere Gartenbauschule zu Pillnitz an Ministerialrat Dr. Görlach, Reichsministerium für Ernährung und Landwirtschaft, April 18, 1944.
3. BArch R1501-3157, Reichsminister für Ernährung und Landwirtschaft and Herrn Reichswohnungskommissar, June 7, 1944.
4. Erlass des Führers über die Errichtung des Deutschen Wohnungshilsfwerkes vom 9. September 1943. Reichsgesetzblatt 84, September 14, 1943.
5. BArch R1501-3175, Reichsminister des Innern an Reichsminister für Ernährung und Landwirtschaft, December 20, 1944.
6. Gabriel, "Nationalsozialistische Biopolitik und die Architektur der Konzentrationslager," 201–219.
7. BArch R8 V 39, Aktennotiz. Herrn Ahlmann, January 27, 1944.
8. Bataille, *The Accursed Share*.
9. Büttner, "'Gomorrha' und die Folgen. Der Bombenkrieg," 613–632. See also Stargardt, *The German War*, 366–372.
10. Büttner, "'Gomorrha' und die Folgen. Der Bombenkrieg," 616. Nossack, *Der Untergang*. Valuable description in an otherwise controversial and problematically decontextualized book, Friedrich, *The Fire*.
11. BArch R3601-2485, Der Beauftragte für den Vierjahresplan an Baubevollmächtigten des Reichsministeriums Speer, July 2, 1943; Dano Ingenørforretning OG Maskinfabrik an Landwirtschaftsrat Henkel, Reichsernährungsministerium, March 7, 1944.
12. BArch R3601-2485, Karrenberg & Co. Feuerungsbau, Düsseldorf an Reichsmarschall Göring, September 22, 1941.
13. BArch R3601-2485, Karrenberg & Co. Feuerungsbau, Düsseldorf an Reichsmarschall Göring, September 22, 1941.
14. Tooze, *The Wages of Destruction*, 540.
15. Tooze, *The Wages of Destruction*, 539.
16. BArch 3601-2485, Aktennotiz über eine Besprechung im Anschluss an die Besichtigung Müllverwertungsanalage DANO-Kopenhagen, June 17, 1941; Forschungsdienst an Beauftragten für den Vierjahresplan, October 14, 1941.

17. Tooze, *The Wages of Destruction*, 541.
18. BArch R3601-2485, Errichtung einer Aufbereitungslanlage für Müllkompost nach dem Dano-Verfahren, November 30, 1942.
19. BArch R3601-2485, Der Reichsminister für Ernährung und Landwirtschaft an Rohstoffstelle für ernährungswirtschaftlichen Ausbau, May 13, 1943.
20. Böhme, "Wie Lässt sich im 4 Kriegsjahr ein Absinken der Erzeugung verhindern?," 37–38.
21. BArch R3601-2485, Landwirtschaftsrat Henkel, "Einsatz städtischer Abfallstoffe zur Bodenverbesserung und Düngung," 50–51.
22. BArch R3601-2485, Henkel, "Einsatz städtischer Abfallstoffe zur Bodenverbesserung und Düngung," 50–51; Der Reichsminister für Ernährung und Landwirtschaft an die Reichshauptstadt Berlin, Hochbauamt, February 2, 1943; Der Beauftragte für den Vierjahresplan an Baubevollmächtigten für die Regelung der Bauwirtschaft Reichsminister Speer, July 2, 1943.
23. StAHH 351-10 Sozialbehörde I VG30.70, Lagebericht der Familienfürsorge im Stadtteil Eimsbüttel, September 1943.
24. BArch 3601-2485, Dano Ingenørforretning OG Maskinfabrik an Henkel, Reichsministerium für Ernährung und Landwirtschaft, March 7, 1944; Aktennotiz, Reichsministerium für Ernährung und Landwirtschaft, June 10, 1944.
25. BArch 3601-2485, Dano Ingenørforretning OG Maskinfabrik an Henkel, March 7, 1944.
26. BArch 3601-2485, Der Reichsminister für Ernährung und Landwirtschaft an Oberbürgermeister der Stadt der Volkserhebung, Graz, August 25, 1944.
27. BArch 3601-2485, Reichskommissar für Altmaterialverwertung an Oberbürgermeister der Gauhauptstadt Linz, July 12, 1944.
28. BArch 3601-2485, Oberbürgermeister Berlin an Reichsminister für Ernährung und Landwirtschaft, September 16, 1944.
29. BArch 3601-2485, Reichsminister für Ernährung und Landwirtschaft an die Firma Riehle u. Kleinecke, January 2, 1945.
30. Verfügung über "Dr.-Fritz-Todt-Preis," February 8, 1944, in *Führer-Erlasse*, 392. Hitler explained the criteria for selection as follows: "Consideration is given primarily to the extent of the inventive achievement, the personal commitment of the person to be awarded the prize, and the value of the invention to the armed forces and the economy."
31. BArch R1501-3158, Der Regierungspräsident Schleswig an den Herrn Reichsminister des Innern, February 15, 1944.
32. BArch R1501-3158, Der Regierungspräsident Schleswig an den Herrn Reichsminister des Innern, February 15, 1944; Reichsanstalt für Wasser und Luftgüte an den Herrn Reichsminister des Inneren, June 17, 1944.
33. BArch R1501-3158, Der Regierungspäsident Schleswig an den Herrn Reichsminister des Innern, October 14, 1944.
34. BArch R1501-3157, Obermedizinalrat Dr. Werner an Herrn Oberregierungsrat Dr. Haack, October 3, 1944.
35. BArch R1501-3158, Rechstanwalt Dr. Gustav Schwarz an Obermedizinalrat Dr. Werner, Berlin, October 6, 1944.

36. BArch R1501-908, Erläuterungen zum Antrag betr. Bezahlung des 'Bergungs- und Räumungseinsatzes' der Bauwirtschaft, undated; BArch R1501-949, Der Chef des Oberkommandos der Wehrmacht: Wehrmachtseinsatz bei Notständen, July 30, 1944.
37. BArch R1501-1545, Der Reichsmarschall des Grossdeutschen Reiches an Reichsministerium des Innern, August 15, 1944; BArch 3601-2485, Dano Ingenørforretning OG Maskinfabrik an Henkel, Reichsministerium für Ernährung und Landwirtschaft, March 7, 1944; Aktennotiz, Reichsministerium für Ernährung und Landwirtschaft, June 10, 1944.
38. BArch R1501-1545, Der Reichsmarschall des Grossdeutschen Reiches an Reichsministerium des Innern, August 15, 1944; Vereinfachung der Verwaltung; hier; Aufhebung der Verpflichtung der Gemeinden zur Müllauswertung für die Dauer des Krieges. RdErl d.RMdI, August 29, 1944.
39. BArch R1501-1545, Der Beauftragte für den Vierjahresplan, Generalbevollmächtigter für den Arbeitseinsatz an Reichsminister des Innern, September 9, 1944; BArch R1501-1545, Reichskommissar für Altmaterial an alle müllsortierenden Gemeinden, September 11, 1944.
40. BArch R1501-1545, Reichsminister des Innern. Vermerk, October 6, 1944.
41. BArch R1501-1062, Deutscher Gemeindetag an den Herrn Reichsminister des Innern, May 11, 1944; BArch 1501-1545, Der Reichsminister des Innern an die Reichsstatthalter, August 21, 1944; Deutscher Gemeindetag an Reichsminister des Innern, April 6, 1944.
42. BArch R1501-1062, Rechtsanwälte Potthast, Weimann, Dr. Bernicken, Dr. Peters an Reichsminister des Innern, September 12, 1944.
43. BArch R1501-1545, Senatspräsident an Kammergericht Dr. Conrad Weber, Berlin "Abschrift: Die Haftung des Haus- und Grundbesitzers für Schäden Dritter nach Voll- oder Teilbeschädigung des Hauses infolge Kriegssachschadens," undated.
44. BArch R1501-1062, Deutscher Gemeindetag an den Herrn Reichsminister des Innern, May 11, 1944.
45. Sebald, *On the Natural History of Destruction*, 34.
46. Sebald, *On the Natural History of Destruction*, 35.
47. BArch 154-1084, An die Verteilungsstelle für Packpapier der Reichsstelle für Papier und Verpackungswesen, May 18, 1940.
48. BArch 154-1038, Leipziger Vereinigung für Talg und Fellverwertung an Preussische Landesanstalt für Wasser, -Boden und Lufthygiene, June 6, 1934; Preussische Landesanstalt für Wasser, -Boden und Lufthygiene an die Leipziger Vereinigung für Talg und Fellverwertung, June 13, 1934. The Institute recommended the purchasing of insecticide directly from producers such as I.D. Riedel in Berlin.
49. BArch R154-1038, Gesundheitsamt an Landesanstalt für Boden-, Wasser- und Lufthygiene, November 14, 1938.
50. BArch 154-1038, Landesamt für Boden-, Wasser- und Luft-Hygiene an Reichsnährstand, May 17, 1938.
51. BArch 154-1038, Hugo Thöle an General-Feldmarschall Hermann Göring, August 9, 1938.
52. "Knochensammlung in Schulen," January 28, 1937, in Hans Heck, *Der Reichskommissar für Altmaterialverwertung*, 245–246; A. Rep. 001-06-34487,

Oberbürgermeister. Betrifft: Erfassung von Alt-und Abfallstoffen, October 12, 1941; A. Rep. 001-06-34487, Oberbürgermeister der Reichshauptstadt Berlin, June 30, 1943. See also Denton and Weber, "Bones of Contention"; Weber, "Nazi German Waste Recovery and the Vision of a Circle Economy."

53. Nossack, *The End*, 44.
54. BArch R154-1084, Gerolf Steiner an Reichsgesundheitsamt Berlin, August 11, 1943.
55. BArch R154-1084, Prof. Dr. A Hase and Gerolf Steiner, August 28, 1943.
56. BArch R154-1084, Polizeiführer Lublin an Preussische Landesanstalt für Wasser, Boden- und Lufthygiene, October 9, 1942.
57. BArch R154-1084, Der leitende Ansiedlungsarzt an Institut für Seuchbekämpfung, March 24, 1943.
58. BArch 154-1084, Staatliches Gesundheitsamt, Landkreis Kattowitz an Reichsanstalt für Wasser- und Luftgüte, July 21, 1943. See also Kommandanturbefehl Nr. 5/43 Auschwitz, February 18, 1943, and Kommandanturbefehl Nr. 7/43 Auschwitz, April 2, 1943, in *Standort- und Kommandanturbefehle des Konzentrationslagers Auschwitz*, 224, 240.
59. Standortbefehl Nr. 33/43 Auschwitz, August 21, 1943, in *Standort- und Kommandanturbefehle*, 327.
60. Standortbefehl Nr. 38/43 Auschwitz, September 9, 1943, and Standortbefehl Nr. 13/44 Auschwitz, May 2, 1944, in *Standort- und Kommandanturbefehle*, 336, 441.
61. BArch 154-1084, Deutsche Arbeitsfront an Preussische Landesanstalt für Wasser-, Boden- und Lufthygiene, March 27, 1944; Preussische Landesanstalt für Wasser-, Boden- und Lufthygiene an die Deutsche Arbeitsfront, April 5, 1944.
62. Sebald, *On the Natural History of Destruction*, 34.
63. Kershaw, *The End*, 236
64. Stargardt, *The German War*, 473
65. Kershaw, *The End*, 56
66. Kershaw, *The End*, 147; Stargardt, *The German War*, 456–457.
67. BArch R8I-237, Reichsstelle für Textilwritschaft. "Lumpen. Rohstoffplan vom 1.10.1944 bis 30.6.1945," July 27, 1944; Bericht über die Textilplanungsbesprechungen, Belgien, August 19, 1944.
68. BArch R81-237, Ernst Huwe. Aktenvermerk, November 18, 1944.
69. BArch R8I-237, Aufstellung über im Gasthaus Generotzky, Schweicheln b. Herford lagernden Kisten mit Zellwollabfallgarn, October 31, 1944.
70. BArch R3001-24342, Der Reichsminister der Justiz an die Herren Generalstaatsanwälte, October 20, 1942.
71. Lohmann Werke AG, Werdegang einer Bedeutenden Industrie im Ravensberger Land (1942)
72. BArch R3001-25023, Dr. Ernst Scheld an Ministerialrat Dr. Nörr, Reichsjustizministerium, Berlin, March 20, 1944.
73. BArch R3001-25023, Dr. Ernst Scheld an Ministerialrat Dr. Nörr, Reichsjustizministerium, Berlin, March 20, 1944.
74. BArch R8I-237, Rohstoffhandelsgesellschaft an die Reichsstelle für Textilwirtschaft, April 21, 1944; R8I-239, Vermerk. Verlust durch Feindeinwirkung, March 26, 1945; Reichsstelle für Textilwirtschaft, "Grundsätze und Richtlinien der Reichsstelle für

Textilwirtschaft für die Behandlung von Verlusten durch Feindeinwirkung," February 28, 1945; BArch R8I-239, V. Vinciguerra Wien an Reichsstelle für Textilwirtschaft, February 2, 1945; Aktennotiz, November 10, 1944.
75. BArch R8I-239, V. Vinciguerra Wien an Reichsstelle für Textilwirtschaft, February 2, 1945.
76. BArch R8I-238, Rudolf Näser an Reichsstelle der Textilwirtschaft, November 22, 1944.
77. BArch R8I-240, Zusammenstellung der Räumungsgüter ohne Naturseide; R8I-239, An Ost-Faser-Gesellschaft, November 20, 1944.
78. Kershaw, *The End*, 169.
79. BArch R81-238, Eternit-Werke an Reichsstelle für Textilwirtschaft, January 31, 1945.
80. BArch R8I-238, Hitiac Hanf-Jute- und Textil-Industrie Aktiengesellschaft an Reichsstelle für Textilwirtschaft, February 6, 1945.
81. BArch R8I-238, A&R Mayer an Reichsstelle für Textilwirtschaft, February 1, 1945.
82. BArch R8I-407, Der Leiter der Bewirtschaftungsstelle für Spinnstoffe u.a. Spinnstoffwaren im Generalgouvernement, January 31, 1945.
83. See Führer Order, April 24, 1945, in *Führer-Erlasse*, 497.
84. See Führer Order, March 14, 1945, in *Führer-Erlasse*, 485.
85. BArch R1501-949, Der Reichsminister des Innern an Reichverteidigungskommissare, September 10, 1944.
86. BArch R5-ANH.I-48, Der Vorstand des Reichsbahn-Maschinen-Amts Aachen an den Präsidenten der Reichsbahndirektion Köln, "Räumungsbericht RMA Aachen," October 8, 1944.
87. BArch R1501-949, Der Reichsminister des Innern an Reichsverteidigungskommissare, September 15, 1944.
88. Stargardt, *The German War*, 509, 463.
89. Wette, Bremer, and Vogel, *Das letzte halbe Jahr*, 390.
90. Stargardt, *The German War*, 469–470.
91. Kershaw, *The End*, 236.
92. BArch R1501-3341, Bericht, June 10, 1944.
93. BArch R1501-3341, Bericht, June 10, 1944.
94. BArch R1501-3341, Der Reichsverkehrsminister und Generaldirektor der Deutschen Reichsbahn an Reichsminister des Innern, September 4, 1944.
95. BArch R1501-3341, Der Polizei-Präsident an Herrn Reichsminister des Innern, February 17, 1944.
96. BArch R1501-3341, Der Polizei-Präsident an Herrn Reichsminister des Innern, February 17, 1944.
97. BArch R1501-3341, Der Polizei-Präsident an Herrn Reichsminister des Innern, February 17, 1944.
98. BArch R1501-3341, Der Reichsminister des Innern. Entwurf zu einer Verordnung zur Vereinfachung auf dem Gebiete der Feuerbestattung, January 1945; Polizeipräsident an Herrn Oberbürgermeister der Reichshauptstatt Berlin, August 9, 1944.
99. BArch R1501-3341, Der Polizei-Präsident an Herrn Reichsminister des Innern, February 17, 1944.

NOTES TO PAGES 202–206   291

100. BArch R1501-3341, Der Polizei-Präsident an Herrn Reichsminister des Innern, February 17, 1944.
101. Kershaw, *The End*, 218–219.
102. Kershaw, *The End*, 379.
103. I am borrowing this turn of phrase from Samalin, *The Masses Are Revolting*.

Chapter 9

1. BArch NS19-3824, Der Chef des SS Wirtschafts-Verwaltungshauptamtes an den Reichsführer SS, January 10, 1945,
2. The term "*Menschenmaterial*" or human material appears ubiquitously in Nazi correspondence and was used in a variety of different contexts, sometimes referring to "excellent" *Menschenmaterial* available to the army or the Hitler Youth, for example, but also in references to the exploitation of humans as laborers or for scientific experiments. A particularly egregious example appears in a letter to Himmler from Dr. Sigmund Rascher requesting access to felons for dangerous altitude experiments. LOC_NT_Vol. XXVII Doc. 1602-PS, Letter from Dr. Sigmund Rascher to Reichsführer SS, May 15, 1941. For references to corpses as *Menschenmaterial* used for scientific purposes, also see R3001-2147. See, too, Hitler, *Monologe*, 161.
3. BArch NS19-3824, Der Chef des SS Wirtschafts-Verwaltungshauptamtes an den Reichsführer SS, January 10, 1945.
4. Blatman, *The Death Marches*.
5. Stargardt, *The German War*, 492.
6. For a comparison, see Achille Mbembe's discussion of the plantation economy and the slave as a "soilless body, a body of combustible energy, a sort of double of nature that could, through work, be transformed into an available reserve or stock," in *Necropolitics*, 10.
7. Mbembe defines the necropolitical regime as one that accrues power through "the instrumentalization of human existence and the material destruction of human bodies and populations." Mbembe, *Necropolitics*, 68.
8. For the concept of "violence work," see Micol, *Violence Work*.
9. Hanomag was a mechanical engineering company, building cars, race cars, and as of 1939 was increasingly involved in rearmaments manufacturing, from submarine parts to other heavy hauling equipment. Däbritz, *Hundert Jahre Hanomag*; Büllesbach and Görg, eds., *Fotografie bei Hanomag*.
10. BeA Yad Vashem 0.3/7563, Moshe Oster, undated.
11. BeA Yad Vashem 0.3/7563, Moshe Oster, undated.
12. BeA Yad Vashem 0.3/7563, Moshe Oster, undated.
13. BeA Yad Vashem 0.3/10510, Mendel Gur, undated.
14. BeA Yad Vashem 0.3/10510, Mendel Gur, undated.
15. Kolb, *Bergen-Belsen*, 36–37.
16. Wachsmann, *KL*, 335; Kolb, *Bergen-Belsen*; Bardgett and Cesarani, eds., *Belsen 1945*.
17. Kolb, *Bergen-Belsen*, 39.

18. Kolb, *Bergen-Belsen*, 44–61.
19. Kolb, *Bergen-Belsen*, 105.
20. Blatman, *The Death Marches*, 132; Kolb, *Bergen-Belsen*, 105–106.
21. BArch NS3 386, Chef des SS Wirtschafts- Verwaltungshauptamt Pohl an alle Lagerkommandanten. Geheim, October 26, 1943. Also Blatman, *The Death Marches*, 42.
22. Blatman, *The Death Marches*, 132–135; Kolb, *Bergen-Belsen*, 106; Cesarani, "A Brief History of Bergen-Belsen," in *Belsen 1945*, 13–21.
23. On December 1, 1944, there were 15,257 inmates in Bergen-Belsen. By March 1, 1945, the number had increased to 41,520. However, as Eberhard Kolb illustrates, since roughly 7,000–8,000 people died per month, mainly of hunger and disease, he estimates the total number of prisoners transported to Belsen between January 1945 and the camp's liberation by the British on April 15, 1945, was somewhere around 40,000–50,000. These estimates are conservative in light of the fact that the death toll increased during that period, and Kolb notes roughly 60,000 prisoners were in the camp at the time of liberation. Kolb, *Bergen-Belsen*, 127–128, 170.
24. Kolb, *Bergen-Belsen*, 140.
25. BeA BT 224, Katalin Frisch, July 26, 1945.
26. BeA Yad Vashem 0.3/4453, Zion Lavy, undated.
27. BeA BT 224, Katalin Frisch, July 26, 1945; BeA BT 620, Rosi Simon July 22, 1945; Lasker-Wallfisch, "A Surivor's Memories of Liberation," in *Belsen 1945*, 24.
28. BeA Yad Vashem 0.3/4453, Zion Lavy, undated; BeA BT 159, Helmut Mainz, September 1944; BeA BT 570, Cara Rijxman-van der Horst, undated; BeA BT 155, Manfred Rosenbaum, January 15, 1989.
29. BeA BT 155, Manfred Rosenbaum, January 15, 1989.
30. BeA BT 570, Cara Rijxman-van der Horst, undated.
31. BeA BT 240, Irvin Juda Van Gelder, undated.
32. BeA Archiv, BT 240, Irvin Juda Van Gelder, undated.
33. Stargardt, *The German War*, 361, for German practices of "compensating" themselves for their suffering from expropriated Jewish possessions; see p. 371.
34. BeA BT 581, Alexander Roseboom, January 15, 1989.
35. Kolb, *Bergen-Belsen*, 137.
36. Kolb, *Bergen-Belsen*, 139; BeA Yad Vashem 0.3/7563, Moshe Oster, undated.
37. Cited in Kolb, *Bergen-Belsen*, 139.
38. BeA BT 620, Rosi Simon, undated.
39. BeA BT 348, Hugh Jenkins, diary entries from April 21–May 25, 1945.
40. BeA BT 348, Hugh Jenkins, diary entries from April 21–May 25, 1945.
41. BeA BT 348, Hugh Jenkins, diary entries from April 21–May 25, 1945.
42. Blatman, *The Death Marches*, 259.
43. On court-martials and German terror against its own population, see Kershaw, *The End*, 220–225; Blatmann, *The Death Marches*, 260.
44. Blatman, *The Death Marches*, 268.
45. *Kommandant in Auschwitz*, 219.
46. *Kommandant in Auschwitz*, 220.

47. After the train station of Celle was bombed on April 8th, prisoners escaped from the train that had arrived from Neuengamme, roaming the city in search of food and shelter. The local population organized in putative defense and massacred the escaped prisoners who were hiding in the forest. Blatman, *The Death Marches*, 266–270.
48. BeA Yad Vashem 0.3/10510, Mendel Gur, undated.
49. BeA Yad Vashem 0.3/10510, Mendel Gur, undated.
50. BeA BT 224, Katalin Frisch, July 26, 1945.
51. BeA Yad Vashem 0.3/7563, Moshe Oster, undated.
52. BeA Yad Vashem 0.3/7563, Moshe Oster, undated.
53. Kolb, *Bergen-Belsen*, 147; Bardgett and Cesarani, eds., "The Medical Relief Effort: Eyewitness Accounts," in *Belsen 1945*, 53.
54. Kolb, *Bergen-Belsen*, 146–147.
55. BeA Yad Vashem 0.3/10510, Mendel Gur, undated.
56. BeA BT 1306, Valentina Bobina, July 9, 2000. On the corpses in the drainage ditches, see also Kolb, *Bergen-Belsen*, 167.
57. Kolb, *Bergen-Belsen*, 148.
58. Kolb, *Bergen-Belsen*, 148.
59. BeA Yad Vashem 0.3/10510, Mendel Gur, undated.
60. BeA Yad Vashem 0.3/7563, Moshe Oster, undated.
61. BeA 0.3/7563, Moshe Oster, undated. Dan Stone, *The Liberation of the Camps*, 83.
62. Stone, *The Liberation of the Camps*, 32.
63. Struk, *Photographing the Holocaust*, 142.
64. Stone, *The Liberation of the Camps*, 12.
65. Kolb, *Bergen-Belsen*, 170.
66. Flanagan and Bloxham, *Remembering Belsen*, 15.
67. Flanagan and Bloxham, *Remembering Belsen*, 13–14.
68. BeA BT 348. Hugh Jenkins, diary entries from April 21 to May 25, 1945. See Kolb, *Bergen-Belsen*, 168–171.
69. Kolb, *Bergen-Belsen*, 169.
70. Kolb, *Bergen-Belsen*, 169; Flanagan and Bloxham, *Remembering Belsen*, 14.
71. Flanagan and Bloxham, *Remembering Belsen*, 21.
72. Hargrave, *Bergen-Belsen 1945*, 36, 37, 41, 45.
73. Flanagan and Bloxham, *Remembering Belsen*, 24.
74. Hargrave, *Bergen-Belsen 1945*, 33, 57, 77.
75. BeA BT 348, Hugh Jenkins, diary entries from April 21 to May 25, 1945; Flanagan and Bloxham, *Remembering Belsen*, 27.
76. Flanagan and Bloxham, *Remembering Belsen*, 27.
77. Flanagan and Bloxham, *Remembering Belsen*, 21.
78. Cohen, "Between Relief and Politics"; Shepard, "'Becoming Planning Minded'"; Malkki, "Refugees and Exile."
79. Cohen, "Between Relief and Politics," 439–443; Cohen, *In War's Wake*, 66, 74, 77.
80. Cited in Cohen, "Between Relief and Politics," 443.
81. Cited in Cohen, "Between Relief and Politics," 447.

82. Grossmann, *Jews, Germans, and Allies*, 119.
83. BeA BA 2486, Der Bürgermeister an den Herrn Oberkreisdirektor in Celle, April 9, 1946.
84. Stone, *The Liberation of the Camps*, 67.
85. BeA BA 2486, Der Bürgermeister an den Herrn Oberkreisdirektor in Celle, May 8, 1946.
86. BeA BA 2486, Der Bürgermeister an den Herrn Oberkreisdirektor in Celle, April 9, 1946.
87. BeA BA 2466, "An den Oberkreisdirektor in Celle," May 10, 1946, accessed at Stiftung Niedersächsischer Gedenkstätten, Celle.
88. Crew, *Bodies and Ruins*, 31.
89. Quoted in Bessel, *Germany 1945*, 16.
90. Bessel, *Germany 1945*, 171.
91. Freudian, "Hannover Looted by Citizens Volkssturm and Police Join in" *New York Herald Tribune*, April 12, 1945.
92. Freudian, "Hannover Looted by Citizens."
93. Lippmann, "Today and Tomorrow," *New York Herald Tribune*, March 22, 1945.
94. Graham, "Junk Heap Marks Leuna Works Site," *New York Times*, April 21, 1945; Lyons, "8000 Germans a Day Come Home to Cologne, a City without Plumbing," *Daily Boston Globe*, May 30, 1945.
95. Lyons, "8000 Germans a Day."
96. Freudian, "Hannover Looted by Citizens."
97. Heineman, "The Hour of the Women," 362.
98. Holbrook, "Rubble of German Villages Is Used to Patch Highways," *The Sun*, February 19, 1945.
99. BArch R154-56, Landesgesundheitsamt an das Robert-Koch-Institute für Hygiene und Infektionskrankheiten, July 29, 1949.
100. Diefenbach, *In the Wake of War*, 13–14.
101. BArch R154-12366, Der Oberbürgermeister der Reichsmessestadt Leipzig an Preußische Landesanstalt für Wasser, Boden- und Lufthygiene, April 13, 1944.
102. BArch R3-3254, 41. Wochenbericht des Planungsamtes, October 20, 1944.
103. Bessel, *Germany 1945*, 185; Diefenbach, *In the Wake of War*, 22–23; Lyons, "German School Children Put to Work Two Hours a Day Cleaning Up Rubble," *Boston Globe*, May 26, 1945.
104. The Associated Press, "German Invents Process to Make Bricks of Rubble," *New York Times*, October 25, 1945.
105. Hill, "Berliners Give Peasants' Tools Metal Priority," *New York Herald Tribune*, September 23, 1945.
106. The Herald Tribune Bureau, "Berlin to Make Tiergarten into a Rubble Dump," *New York Herald Tribune*, November 1, 1945.
107. The Herald Tribune Bureau, "Berlin to Make Tiergarten into a Rubble Dump."
108. Adam-Tkalec, "So sah der Große Tiergarten in Berlin 1945 aus," *Berliner Zeitung*, September 5, 2017 at https://www.berliner-zeitung.de/mensch-metropole/

so-sah-der-grosse-tiergarten-in-berlin-1945-aus-li.24993. Also Diefendorf, *In the Wake of War*, 28.
109. Diefendorf, *In the Wake of War*, 26–28.
110. BArch R154-56, Landesgesundheitsamt an das Robert-Koch-Institute für Hygiene und Infektionskrankheiten, July 29, 1949.
111. Anderson, *Buried City*, 88.
112. Anderson, *Buried City*, 88. See also Smith and Shand, "Architectural Wounds: Teufelsberg," 185–192.
113. Anderson, *Buried City*, 92.
114. Grossmann, *Jews, Germans and Allies*; Hagemann, "History, Media and Collective Memory"; Tschiggerl, "Who Owns the 'Trümmerfrauen'?"

Conclusion

1. Rathje and Murphy, *Rubbish*, 45–46.
2. Chakrabarty, "Garbage, Modernity and the Citizen's Gaze"; Ward, *The Clean Body*; Zimring, *Clean and White*.
3. Shanks, Platt, and Rathje, "The Perfume of Garbage"; Berg, "Rubbished World."
4. BArch R3-3254 41, Wochenbericht des Planungsamtes, October 20, 1944.
5. Lieutenant Colonel Richard Taylor, who took over as the commander of Bergen-Belsen after the British decided to remove the SS officers from their post, addressed the camera in the film *Nazi Concentration Camps*, which was admitted as evidence Prosecution Exhibit #230 at the Nuremberg Trials. Available at https://collections.ushmm.org/search/catalog/irn616441.
6. Struk, *Photographing the Holocaust*, 191.
7. Cited in Struk, *Photographing the Holocaust*, 124.
8. Sontag, *Regarding the Pain of Others*, 24, 83.
9. Sontag, *Regarding the Pain of Others*, 26.
10. Zelizer, *Remembering to Forget*, 31.
11. Struk, *Photographing the Holocaust*, 138; Zelizer, *Remembering to Forget*; Shneer, *Grief*.
12. Struk, *Photographing the Holocaust*, 138.
13. Struk, *Photographing the Holocaust*, 133–134.
14. Most immediately, British relief efforts in Germany were informed by their experiences in Bengal in 1943–1944 where "[o]rders leading directly to famine came down from the War Cabinet in London," as Janam Mukherjee showed. The British medical regime fed surviving inmates a mush "made up of sugar, salt, flour and oatmeal, etc." that they termed the "Bengal mixture" and used to nurse starved prisoners back to life. See *Hungry Bengal*, 5; Hargrave, *Bergen-Belsen 1945*, 30. Also Davis, *Late Victorian Holocaust*; Zimmerer, *Von Windhuk mach Auschwitz?*
15. Moses, *The Problems of Genocide*, 277.
16. Césaire, *Discourse on Colonialism*, 36. Emphasis in the original.

17. Lehnstaedt and Traba, Die 'Aktion Reinhardt'; Arad, The Operation Reinhard Death Camps.
18. Struk, Photographing the Holocaust, 142.
19. See Aly and Roth, Die restlose Erfassung; A Film Unfinished, on Hersonski's 2010 film.
20. Stone, The Liberation of the Camps, 36, 38, 45.
21. See also Strzelecki, "The Plunder of Victims and Their Corpses," 128; Gedenkstätte Sachsenhausen Archiv, JSU 1 Bd 11 Teil 2, Gutachten der Sachverständigenkommission, June 4, 1946 and Protokoll, April 10, 1946.
22. Gedenkstätte Sachsenhausen Archiv JSU 1 Band 11 Teil 3, SS Wirtschafts-Verwaltungshauptamt an die Kommandanten der Konzentrationslager, August 6, 1942.
23. Moeller, War Stories, 12; see also Lüdtke, "Coming to Terms with the Past"; Neuman, Shifting Memories.
24. Berg, On Screen and Off, 94–95, 97–100; Moeller, War Stories; Weinreb, Modern Hungers.
25. Grossmann, Jews, Germans and Allies, 82–83; Hagemann, "History, Media and Collective Memory"; Tschiggerl, "Who Owns the 'Trümmerfrauen'?"
26. Washington, "Ball of Confusion"; Chad Montrie, The Myth of Silent Spring.
27. Mbembe, Necropolitics; Schrader, "A Carceral Empire"; Hinton, From the War on Poverty to the War on Crime; Seigel, Violence Work; Hönke and Müller, The Global Making of Policing; Weizman, Forensic Architecture; Davis, City of Quartz; Parenti, Tropic of Chaos; Kinney, Beautiful Wasteland; Sugrue, The Origins of the Urban Crisis; Alexander, The New Jim Crow; Frye, Walls: A History of Civilization in Blood and Brick; Osterweil, In Defense of Looting; Anderson, White Rage.

Bibliography

Archives

Archiwum Instytutu Pamieci Narodowej (AIPN)
Bundesarchiv Berlin (BArch)
Deutsches Tagebucharchiv Emmendingen (DTA)
Gedenkstätte Bergen-Belsen Archiv (BeA)
Gedenkstätte KZ-Mauthausen Archiv (MaA)
Gedenkstätte KZ-Sachsenhausen Archiv (SaA)
Film und Fernsehmuseum Hamburg (FFH)
Landesarchiv Berlin (LaB)
Landeshauptarchiv Potsdam (LhaP)
Library of Congress (LOC)
Memorial and Museum Auschwitz Archiv (AuA)
Staatsarchiv Hamburg (StAHH)
Stadtarchiv Bielefeld (BSta)
Stiftung Niedersächsicher Gedenkstätten (SNG)
United States Holocaust Memorial Museum (USHMM)

Published Primary Sources

Apelt, Kurt. "Gegenwartsfragen der deutschen Textilwirtschaft." *Jahrbücher für Nationalökonomie und Statistik* 143, no. 6 (June 1936): 678–703.
Associated Press. "German Invents Process to Make Bricks of Rubble." *New York Times*, October 25, 1945.
Backe, Herbert. *Um die Nahrungsfreiheit Europas: Weltwirtschaft oder Grossraum.* Leipzig: W. Goldmann, 1942.
Blum, O. *Städtebau.* 2nd ed. Berlin: Julius Springer, 1937.
Boberach, Heinz, ed. *Meldungen aus dem Reich. Die geheimen Lageberichte des Sicherheitsdienstes der SS, 1938–1945.* 17 vols. Berlin: Pawlag Verlag Herrsching, 1984.
Bockenmühl, Eric. *Volksgemeinschaft der Tat: Geschichten vom Hilfswerk 'Mutter und Kind', vom 'Winterhilfswerk' and von 'Kraft durch Freude'.* Halle: Carl Marhold Verlag, undated.
Böhme, C., Generaldirektor der Sächsischen Staatsgüter, Skass. "Wie Lässt sich im 4 Kriegsjahr ein Absinken der Erzeugung verhindern?" *Mittleilungen für die Landwirtschaft* 58, no. 3 (January 16, 1943): 37–38.
Buchert, Gerhart. *Der Marshallplan. Ein Weg in die Zukunft.* Frankfurt am Main: Wolfgang Metzner, 1949.

Cooke, Maude. *Three Meals a Day: The Great 20th Century Cook Book.* Chicago: L.W. Walter, 1902.
Daitz, Werner. *Lebensraum und gerechte Weltordnung: Grundlagen einer anti-Atlantikcharta.* Amsterdam: De Amsterdamsche Keurkamer, 1943.
Darré, Walther. *Neuland aus Blut und Boden.* Munich: J.F. Lehmann, 1935.
Der Reichskommissar für Altmaterialverwertung: Anordnungen und Richtlinien der Geschäftsgruppe Rohstoffverteilung und des Reichskommissars für Altmaterialverwertung in der Zeit vom November 1936 bis Februar 1940 (for internal use, not for publication).
Dresler, Adolf. *Deutsche Kunst und entartete "Kunst": Kunstwerk und Zerrbild im Spiegel der Weltanschauung.* Munich: Deutscher Volksverlag, 1938.
Eulenburg, Franz. *Grossraumwirtschaft und Autarkie.* Jena: G. Fischer, 1932.
Feder, Gottfried. *Die neue Stadt. Versuch der Begründung einer neuen Stadtplanungskunst aus der sozialen Struktur der Bevölkerung.* Berlin: Julius Springer, 1939.
Flanagan, Ben, and Donald Bloxham, eds. *Remembering Belsen: Eyewitnesses Record the Liberation.* London: Vallentine Mitchell, 2005.
Fleige, Kurt. "Städtebau-Gestern und Heute." *Monatshefte für Baukunst und Städtebau* 9 (September 1941): 229–230.
Frank, Hans. *Das Diensttagebuch Des Deutschen Generalgouverneurs in Polen 1939–1945.* Edited by Werner Präg and Wolfgang Jacobmeyer. Stuttgart: Deutsche Verlags-Anstalt, 1975.
Frank, Hermann, and Paul Frank. "Die Gartenstadt Klein-Borstel in Hamburg." *Monatshefte für Baukunst und Städtebau* 11 (November 1941): 317–324.
Frei, Norbert, et al. eds. Standort- und Kommandanturbefehle des Konzentrationslagers Auschwitz, 1940–1945. Munich: KG Saur, 2000.
Freudian, Seymour. "Hannover Looted by Citizens Volkssturm and Police Join In." *New York Herald Tribune* (April 12, 1945).
Goebbels, Joseph. "Ansprache des Reichsministers Dr. Goebbels vor den Filmschaffenden in der Krolloper am 10. Februar 1934." In *Der Aufbau des Deutschen Führerstaates. Das Jahr 1934. Dokumente der deutschen Politik.* Vol. II, edited by Paul Meier-Benneckenstein, 258–266. Berlin: Junker und Dünnhaupt, 1936.
Goebbels, Joseph. *Die Zeit ohne Beispiel. Reden und Aufsätze aus den Jahren 1939/40/41.* Munich: Zentralverlag der NSDAP, 1941.
Goebbels, Joseph. *Die Tagebücher von Joseph Goebbels,* edited by Elke Fröhlich. Munich: Saur, 1993.
Graham, Frederick. "Junk Heap Marks Leuna Works Site." *New York Times,* April 21, 1945.
Grimm, Hans. *Volk ohne Raum.* Munich: A. Langen 1926.
Heck, Hans. *Der Reichskommissar für Altmaterialverwertung: Anordnungen und Richtlinien.* 1940.
Hederich, Karl-Heinrich. *Die Reden des Führers nach der Machtübernahme, eine Bibliographie.* Berlin: Zentralverlag der NSDAP, 1939.
Heiber, Helmut, ed. *Goebbels-Reden.* Vol. 1: *1932–1939.* Düsseldorf: Droste, 1971.
Heiss, Fridrich. *Bei uns in Deutschland. Ein Bericht.* Berlin: Volk und Reich Verlag, 1938.
Henkel, (unknown). "Einsatz städtischer Abfallstoffe zur Bodenverbesserung und Düngung." *Mittleilungen für die Landwirtschaft* 58, no. 3 (January 1943): 50–51.
Herald Tribune Bureau. "Berlin to Make Tiergarten into a Rubble Dump." *New York Herald Tribune,* November 1, 1945.
Hill, Russel. "Berliners Give Peasants' Tools Metal Priority." *New York Herald Tribune,* September 23, 1945.

Hiller, Friedrich. *Deutscher Kampf um Lebensraum*. Leipzig: Armanen Verlag, 1933.
Hitler, Adolf. *Der Führer vor dem ersten Reichstag Großdeutschlands. Reichstagsrede vom 30. Januar 1939*. Munich: Zentralverlag der NSDAP, 1939.
Hitler, Adolf. *Monologe im Führer-Hauptquartier 1941–445*. Hamburg: Albert Knaus Verlag, 1980.
Holbrook, Bradley. "Rubble of German Villages Is Used to Patch Highways." *The Sun*, February 19, 1945.
Justizministerium. *Zuchthaus Straubingen: Ein Führer durch eine Neuzeitliche Strafanstalt*. 2nd ed. Straubing: 1935.
Kapp, Rolf. *Weltkrieg um Grossräume*. Munich: Deutscher Volksverlag, 1942.
Kempowski, Walter. *Das Echolot: Barbarossa '41: Ein kollektives Tagebuch*. Munich: Knaus, 2002.
Killus, Heinz. "Der Totalitätsgedanke im neuen Städtebau." *Monatshefte für Baukunst und Städtebau* 4 (April 1940): 85–88.
Köttgen, Arnold. *Deutsche Verwaltung*. 2nd ed. Berlin: Weidemannsche Verlagsbuchhandlung, 1937.
Krüger, Herbert "Der Raum als Gestalter der Innen- und Aussenpolitik." *Reich, Volksordnung, Lebensraum* 1 (1941).
Die Lageberichte der Geheimen Staatspolizei über die Provinz Brandenburg und die Reichshauptstadt Berlin 1933 bis 1936. Teilband I. Der Regierungsbezirk Potsdam. Cologne: Böhlau, 1998.
Landesamt, Statistisches, ed. *Statistisches Jahrbuch für die Freie und Hansestadt Hamburg, 1934/35*. Hamburg: Lütcke & Wulff, 1935.
Landesamt, Statistisches, ed. *Statistisches Jahrbuch für die Hansestadt Hamburg, 1937/1938*. Hamburg: Lütcke & Wulff, 1939.
Ley, Robert. *Ein Volk erobert die Freude*. Berlin: Verlag der Deutschen Arbeitsfront, 1937.
Lidbetter, Ernest James. *Heredity and the Social Problem Group*. London: Edward Arnold & Co, 1933.
Lippmann, Walter. "Today and Tomorrow." *New York Herald Tribune*, March 22, 1945.
Ludorf, Stadtrat A. D. "Luftschutz durch Städtebau." *Monatshefte für Baukunst und Städtebau* 5 (May 1935): 59–60.
Lyons, Louis. "8000 Germans a Day Come Home to Cologne, a City without Plumbing." *Boston Globe*, May 30, 1945.
Lyons, Louis. "German School Children Put to Work Two Hours a Day Cleaning Up Rubble." *The Boston Globe*, May 26, 1945.
Mächler, Martin. "Die Großstadt als Kultur- und Raumproblem und die Grenzen ihrer Größe." *Monatshefte für Baukunst und Städtebau* 6 (June 1939): 63.
Mackenroth, Gerhard. "Bericht über den Vierjahresplan." *Jahrbücher für Nationalökonomie und Statistik* 148, no. 6 (December 1938): 697–726.
Meier-Benneckenstein, Paul, and Axel Friedrichs, eds. *Dokumente der deutschen Politik. Der Aufbau des deutschen Führerstaates. Das Jahr 1934*. Vol. 2. Berlin: Junker und Dünnhaupt, 1936.
Meyer, Konrad, ed. *Volk und Lebensraum: Forschungen im Dienste von Raumordnung und Landesplanung*. Berlin: Kurt Vowinckel Verlag, 1938.
Migge, Berecht. *Deutsche Binnenkolonisation: Sachgrundlagen des Siedlungswesen*, edited by Deutsche Gartenstadt-Gesellschaft. Berlin: Deutscher Kommunal-Verlag, 1926.
Moll, Martin, ed. *Führer-Erlasse*. Hamburg: Nikol Verlag, 2011.

Noack, Viktor. "Die Umgestaltung des Gängeviertels in Hamburg." *Bauen, Siedeln, Wohnen* 23–24 (1934): 390ff.

Petersen, Käthe. "Entmündigung Geistesschwacher Prostituierter." *Zeitschrift für psychische Hygiene* 15, no. 4/6 (January 1943): 67–76.

Pinkley, Virgil. "Ruhr Area Aglow from Explosives." *New York Times*, April 12, 1945.

Schenck, Ernst Günther. *Das Notlazarett unter der Reichskanzlei: ein Arzt erlebt Hitlers Ende in Berlin*. Neuried: Ars Und, 1995.

Schenck, Ernst Günther. *Patient: Hitler: eine medizinische Biographie*. Düsseldorf: Droste, 1989.

Schirach, Baldur von. *Die Hitler-Jugend. Idee und Gestalt*. Berlin: Zeitgeschichte Verlag, 1934.

Schlange-Schöningen, Hans. *Im Schatten des Hungers: Dokumentarisches zur Ernährungspolitik und Ernährungswritschaft in den Jahren 1945–1949*. Hamburg: Paul Parey, 1955.

Schmitt, Carl. *Der deutsche Staat der Gegenwart*. Hamburg: Hanseatische Verlagsanstalt, 1935.

Schmitt, Carl. *Der Nomos der Erde: im Völkerrecht des Jus Publicum Europaeum*. 4th ed. Berlin: Duncker & Humblot, 1997.

Schmitt, Carl. *Land und Meer, eine weltgeschichtliche Betrachtung*. Leipzig: Philipp Reclam, 1942.

Schmitt, Carl. *Staat, Großraum, Nomos: Arbeiten aus den Jahren 1916–1969*, edited by Günther Maschke. Berlin: Duncker & Humblot, 1995.

Schubert, Werner, ed. *Akademie für Deutsches Recht 1933–1945. Protokolle der Ausschüsse*. Berlin: De Gruyter, 2001.

Sennett, A. R. *Garden Cities in Theory and Practice. Being an Amplification of a Paper on the Potentialities of Applied Science in a Garden City. Read before Section F of the British Association*. Vol. I. London: Bemrose and Sons Ltd., 1905.

Speer, Albert. *Inside the Third Reich: Memoirs by Albert Speer*. Translated by Richard and Clara Winston. New York: Macmillan, 1970.

Speer, Albert, Generalbauinspektor für die Reichshauptstadt, ed. *Neue deutsche Baukunst*. Berlin: Volk und Reich, 1943.

Spengler, Oswald. *Decline of the West*. New York: Knopf, 1979.

Starcke, Gerhard. *Die Deutsche Arbeitsfront*. Berlin: Verlag für Sozialpolitik, Wirtschaft und Statistik, 1940.

Storjohann, Uwe. *"Hauptsache: Überleben" Eine Jugend im Krieg 1936–1945*. 2nd ed. Hamburg: Dölling und Galitz Verlag, 1994.

Thiele, Walter. *Die Idee der Grossraumwirtschaft in Geschichte und Politik*. Dresden: Dittert, 1938.

Uexküll, Jakob von. *Staatsbiologie: Anatomie Physiologie und Pathologie des Staates*. Berlin: Verlag Gebrüder Patael, 1920.

Ungewitter, Claus. *Science and Salvage*. Translated by L.A. Ferney and G. Haim with an introduction by Dr. E. Franland Armstrong. London: Scientific Book Club, 1944.

Ungewitter, Claus. *Verwertung des Wertlosen*. Berlin: Wilhelm Lippert Verlag, 1938.

Unwin, Sir Raymond. *Nothing Gained by Overcrowding. How the Garden City Type of Development May Benefit Both Owner and Occupier*. London: P.S. King & Sons, 1912.

Walther, Andreas. *Neue Wege zur Großstadtsanierung*. Stuttgart: Verlag von W. Kohlhammer, 1936.

Wehner, Gerhard. *Die rechtliche Stellung der Hitler-Jugend.* Dresden: Verlag M. Dittert, 1939.
Wette, Wolfram, Ricarda Bremer, and Detlef Vogel, eds. *Das letzte halbe Jahr: Stimmungserichte der Wehrmachtspropaganda 1944/45.* Essen: Klartext, 2001.

Published Memoirs

Adelson, Alan. ed. *The Diary of Dawid Sierakowiak: Five Notebooks from the Lodz Ghetto.* New York: Oxford University Press, 1996.
Broszat, Martin, ed. *Kommandant in Auschwitz: Autobiographische Aufzeichnungen des Rudolf Höß.* Frankfurt am Main: DTV, 2000.
Hargrave, Michael John. *Bergen-Belsen 1945: A Medical Student's Journal.* London: Imperial College Press, 2014.
Kehrl, Hans. *Krisenmanager im Dritten Reich.* Düsseldorf: Droste, 1973.
Klemperer, Victor. *Lti. Notizbuch eines Philologen.* Berlin: Aufbau-Verlag Berlin, 1947.
Klüger, Ruth. *Still Alive: A Holocaust Girlhood Remembered.* New York: Feminist Press, 2001.
Klüger, Ruth, *Unterwegs verloren: Erinnerungen.* Munich: DTV, 2010.
Krogmann, Carl Vincent. *Es ging um Deutschlands Zukunft: 1932–1939. Erlebtes täglich diktiert von dem früheren regierenden Bürgermeister von Hamburg.* Leoni am Starnberger See: Druffel-Verlag, 1976.
Levi, Primo. *Survival in Auschwitz.* New York: Simon & Schuster, 1996.
Lévy-Hass, Hanna, *Tagebuch aus Bergen-Belsen, 1944–1945.* Munich: C.H. Beck, 2009.
Nossack, Hans Erich. *Der Untergang: Hamburg 1943.* Hamburg: Ernst Kabel Verlag, 1981.
Nossack, Hans Erich. *The End: Hamburg 1943.* Translated by Joel Agee. Chicago: University of Chicago Press, 2004.
Venezia, Shlomo. *Meine Arbeit im Sonderkommando Auschwitz.* 2nd ed. Munich: Karl Bessing Verlag, 2008.

Secondary Sources

Aalders, Gerard. *Nazi Looting: The Plunder of Dutch Jewry During the Second World War.* Oxford: Berg, 2004.
Adam-Tkalec, Maritta. "So sah der große Tiergarten in Berlin 1945 aus," *Berliner Zeitung,* September 5, 2017, at https://www.berliner-zeitung.de/mensch-metropole/so-sah-der-grosse-tiergarten-in-berlin-1945-aus-li.24993.
Adorno, Theodor W., Else Frenkel-Brunswik, Daniel J. Levinson, R. Nevitt Sanford. *The Authoritarian Personality.* New York: Norton, 1950.
Adorno, Theodor W. "Kulturkritik und Gesellschaft," in *Prismen. Kulturkritik und Gesellschaft,* 7–26. Munich: DTV, 1963.
Agamben, Giorgio. *Homo Sacer: Sovereign Power and Bare Life.* Stanford, CA: Stanford University Press, 1998.
Agamben, Giorgio. *State of Exception.* Chicago: University of Chicago Press, 2005.
Aguiar, Luis L. M., and Andrew Herod. *The Dirty Work of Neoliberalism: Cleaners in the Global Economy.* Malden, MA: Blackwell, 2006.

Alberti, Michael. *Die Verfolgung und Vernichtung der Juden im Reichsgau Wartheland, 1939–1945*. Wiesbaden: Harrassowitz Verlag, 2006.

Alexander, Catherine, and Joshua Reno. *Economies of Recycling: The Global Transformation of Materials, Values and Social Relations*. London: Zed Books, 2012.

Alexander, Michelle. *The New Jim Crow: Mass Incarceration in the Age of Colorblindness*. 10th ed. New York: The New Press, 2020.

Allen, Michael Thad. *The Business of Genocide: The SS, Slave Labor, and the Concentration Camps*. Chapel Hill: University of North Carolina Press, 2002.

Allen, Michael Thad. "Flexible Production in Ravensbrück Concentration Camp." *Past & Present* 165 (November 1999): 182–217.

Allen, Theodore W. *The Invention of the White Race*. Vol. II: *The Origin of Racial Oppression in Anglo-America*. 2nd ed. New York: Verso, 2012.

Allen, William Sheridan. *The Nazi Seizure of Power: The Experience of a Single German Town, 1922–1945*. 2nd and rev. ed. New York: F. Watts, 1984.

Aly, Götz. *Aussonderung und Tod: Die klinische Hinrichtung der Unbrauchbaren*. Berlin: Rothbuch, 1985.

Aly, Götz. *'Endlösung': Völkerverschiebung und der Mord an den europäischen Juden*. Frankfurt am Main: S. Fischer, 1995.

Aly, Götz. *Hitler's Beneficiaries: Plunder, Racial War, and the Nazi Welfare State*. New York: Metropolitan Books, 2007.

Aly, Götz. *Hitler's Volksstaat: Raub, Rassenkrieg und Nationaler Sozialismus*. Frankfurt am Main: S. Fischer, 2005.

Aly, Götz, and Susanne Heim. *Architects of Annihilation: Auschwitz and the Logic of Destruction*. Princeton, NJ: Princeton University Press, 2002.

Aly, Götz. Peter Chroust, and Christian Pross. *Cleansing the Fatherland. Nazi Medicine and Racial Hygiene*. Baltimore: Johns Hopkins University Press, 1994.

Aly, Götz, and Karl Heinz Roth. *Die restlose Erfassung. Volkszählen, Identifizieren, Aussondern im Nationalsozialismus*. Frankfurt am Main: Taschenbuchverlag, 2000.

Amato, Joseph A. *Dust: A History of the Small & the Invisible*. Berkeley: University of California Press, 2000.

Ames, Eric, Marcia Klotz, and Lora Wildenthal, eds. *Germany's Colonial Pasts*. Lincoln: University of Nebraska Press, 2005.

Anderson, Benedict. *Buried City, Unearthing Teufelsberg: Berlin and Its Geography of Forgetting*. New York: Routledge, 2017.

Anderson, Carol. *White Rage: The Unspoken Truth of Our Racial Divide*. New York: Bloomsbury, 2016.

Anderson, David M., and David Killingray. *Policing the Empire: Government, Authority and Control, 1830–1940*. Manchester, UK: Manchester University Press, 1991.

Anderson, Warwick. *Colonial Pathologies: American Tropical Medicine, Race, and Hygiene in the Philippines*. Durham, NC: Duke University Press, 2006.

Anderson, Warwick. *The Cultivation of Whiteness: Science, Health, and Racial Destiny in Australia*. Durham, NC: Duke University Press, 2006.

Anderson, Warwick. "Excremental Colonialism: Public Health and Poetics of Pollution." *Critical Inquiry* 21, no 3 (Spring 1995): 640–669.

Andrews, Thomas G. *Killing for Coal: America's Deadliest Labor War*. Cambridge, MA: Harvard University Press, 2022.

Angrick, Andrej. *Aktion 1005: Spurenbeseitigung von NS-Massenverbrechen*. Göttingen: Wallstein, 2018.

Ankele, Monika. "The Patient's View of Work Therapy: The Mental Hospital Hamburg-Langenhorn During the Weimar Republic." In *Work, Psychiatry and Society, c.1750– 2015*, edited by Waldtraut Ernst, 238–261. Manchester, UK: Manchester University Press, 2016.
Arad, Yitzhak. *The Operation Reinhard Death Camps: Belzec, Sobibor, Treblinka*. Bloomington: Indiana University Press, 1987.
Arboleda, Martin. *Planetary Mine: Territories of Extraction Under Late Capitalism*. New York: Verso, 2020.
Arendt, Hannah. *Eichmann in Jerusalem: A Report on the Banality of Evil*. New York: Viking Press, 1963.
Arendt, Hannah. *The Origins of Totalitarianism*. San Diego: Harcourt Brace Jovanovich, c1979.
Ault, Julia E. *Saving Nature Under Socialism: Transnational Environmentalism in East Germany, 1968–1990*. Cambridge, UK: Cambridge University Press, 2021.
Auzanneau, Matthieu. *Oil, Power, and War: A Dark History*. Translated by John F. Reynolds. White River Junction, VT: 2015.
Ayass, Wolfgang. *'Asoziale' im Nationalsozialismus*. Stuttgart: Klett-Cotta, 1995.
Bachrach, Susan D. *Deadly Medicine: Creating the Master Race*. Washington, DC: United States Holocaust Memorial Museum, 2004.
Bahr, Ehrhard. "The Anti-Semitism Studies of the Frankfurt School: The Failure of Critical Theory." *German Studies Review* 1, no. 2 (May 1978): 125–138.
Bajohr, Frank, ed. *Nordeutschland im Nationalsozialismus*. Hamburg: Ergebnisse Verlag, 1993.
Bajohr, Frank. "Gauleiter in Hamburg. Zur Person und Tätigkeit Karl Kaufmanns (1900– 1969)." *Vierteljahreshefte für Zeitgeschichte* 43 (1995): 267–295.
Bajohr, Frank. *"Arisierung" in Hamburg: Die Verdrängung der jüdischen Unternehmen 1933-1945*. Hamburg: Christians, 1997.
Bajohr, Frank. "Die Zustimmungsdiktatur: Grundzüge nationalsozialistischer Herrschaft in Hamburg." In *Hamburg im "Dritten Reich"*, edited by FZH, 69–120. Göttingen: Wallstein Verlag, 2005.
Bajohr, Frank, Werner Johe, and Uwe Lohalm, eds. *Zivilisation und Barbarei: Die widersprüchlichen Potentiale der Moderne*. Hamburg: Christians, 1991.
Baranowski, Shelley. *Nazi Empire: German Colonialism and Imperialism from Bismarck to Hitler*. Cambridge, UK: Cambridge University Press, 2011.
Baranowski, Shelley. *Strength Through Joy: Consumerism and Mass Tourism in the Third Reich*. Cambridge, UK: Cambridge University Press, 2004.
Bardgett, Suzanne, and David Cesarani, eds. *Belsen 1945: New Historical Perspectives*. London: Vallentine Mitchell, 2006.
Barkai, Avraham. *Das WirtschaftssystemdDes Nationalsozialismus: Der historische und ideologische Hintergrund, 1933–1936*. Cologne: Verlag Wissenschaft und Politik, 1977.
Barnouw, Dagmar. *Weimar Intellectuals and the Threat of Modernity*. Bloomington: Indiana University Press, 1988.
Barnes, Nicole Elizabeth. *Intimate Communities: Wartime Healthcare and the Birth of Modern China, 1937–1945*. Oakland: University of California Press, 2018.
Barth, Erwin. *Joseph Goebbels und die Formierung des Führer-Mythos 1917–1934*. Erlangen: Palm & Enke, 1999.
Barthes, Roland. *Camera Lucida: Reflections on Photography*. New York: Hill and Wang, 1980.

Bashford, Alison. *Imperial Hygiene: A Critical History of Colonialism, Nationalism and Public Health.* Basingstoke, Hampshire, UK: Palgrave Macmillan, 2004.

Bashir, Bashir, and Amos Goldberg, eds. *The Holocaust and the Nakba: A New Grammar of Trauma and History.* New York: Columbia University Press, 2019.

Bataille, Georges. *The Accursed Share: An Essay on General Economy.* New York: Zone Books, 1988.

Bauer, Raimund. *The Construction of A National Socialist Europe During the Second World War: How the New Order Took Shape.* New York: Routledge, 2020.

Bauer, Yehuda. *Rethinking the Holocaust.* New Haven, CT: Yale University Press, 2001.

Bauman, Zygmunt. *Modernity and the Holocaust.* Ithaca, NY: Cornell University Press, 1989.

Becerril, Michael Wilson. *Resisting Extractivism: Peruvian Gold, Everyday Violence, and the Politics of Attention.* Nashville, TN: Vanderbilt University Press, 2021.

Beckert, Sven. *Empire of Cotton: A Global History.* New York: Vintage Books, 201.

Benedict, Susan, and Linda Shields, eds. *Nurses and Midwives in Nazi Germany: The "Euthanasia Programs."* New York: Routledge, 2014.

Benninghaus, Christina, and Deborah Laurie Cohen. "Mother's Toil and Daughters' Leisure: Working Class Girls and Time in 1920s Germany." *History Workshop Journal* 50 (2000): 45–72.

Benson, Etienne S. *Surroundings: A History of Environments and Environmentalisms.* Chicago: University of Chicago Press, 2020.

Benz, Wolfgang. *Von der Besatzungsherrschaft zur Bundesrepublik: Stationen einer Staatsgündung 1946–1949.* Frankfurt am Main: Fischer, 1984.

Benz, Wolfgang. *Herrschaft und Gesellschaft im Nationalsozialistischen Staat: Studien zur Struktur- und Mentalitätsgeschichte.* Frankfurt am Main: Fischer, 1990.

Benz, Wolfgang. "Zwangsarbeit im Nationalsozialistischen Staat." *Dachauer Hefte* 16 (November 2000): 3–17.

Benzler, Susanne. "Auschwitz als Zivilisationsbruch." *Tribüne* 31, 1992: 109–116.

Berg, Anne. "A Rubbished World: White Supremacy's Complicated Love Affair with Garbage." *Journal of Genocide Research* 25, no. 1 (July 2021): 1–16.

Berg, Anne. "The Nazi Rag-Pickers and Their Wine: The Politics of Waste and Recycling in Nazi Germany." *Social History* 40, no. 4 (November 2015): 446–472.

Berg, Anne. *On Screen and Off: Cinema and the Making of Nazi Hamburg.* Philadelphia: University of Pennsylvania Press, 2022.

Berg, Anne. "Waste Streams and Garbage Publics in Los Angeles and Detroit." In *Global Garbage: Urban Imaginaries of Excess, Waste, and Abandonment,* edited by Christoph Lindner and Miriam Meissner, 80–98. London: Routledge, 2016.

Berg, Manfred, and Simon Wendt, eds. *Racism in the Modern World: Historical Perspectives on Cultural Transfer and Adaptation.* New York: Berghahn Books, 2011.

Bergerson, Andrew. *Ordinary Germans in Extraordinary Times: The Nazi Revolution in Hildesheim.* Bloomington: Indiana University Press, 2004.

Berghahn, Volker R. "Hamburg im Frühjahr 1945: Stimmungsberichte aus den letzten Wochen des Zweiten Weltkrieges." *Geschichts- und Heimatblätter* 8/9 (December 1969): 193–211.

Berlage, Matthias Iver Alexander. "Der Anatom. Prof. Dr. Rudolf Spanner in der Zeit von 1939 bis 1945." Dissertation, Medizinische Fakultät der Heinrich-Heine-Universität Düsseldorf, 2016.

Bernhard, Patrick. "Hitler's Africa in the East: Italian Colonialism as a Model for German Planning in Eastern Europe." *Journal of Contemporary History* 51, no. 1 (2016): 61–90.
Bernstein, R. J. *Radical Evil: A Philosophical Interrogation*. Cambridge, UK: Polity Press, 2002.
Bessel, Richard, ed. *Life in the Third Reich*. Oxford: Oxford University Press, 1987.
Bessel, Richard. *Nazism and War*. New York: Modern Library Edition, 2004.
Bessel, Richard. *Germany 1945: From War to Peace*. London: Simon & Schuster, 2009.
Biernacki, Stanislaw, Hans Henning Hahn, Michael Muller, Eligiusz Janus, Karin Borck, Blanka Meissner, and Czeslaw Madajczyk. *Vom Generalplan Ost Zum Generalsiedlungsplan: Dokumente*. Vol. 80. Berlin: De Gruyter, 1994.
Biggeleben, Christoph, Beate Schreiber, and Kilian J. L. Steiner, eds. *Arisierung in Berlin*. Berlin: Metropol, 2007.
Biller, Maxim. "Die neuen Relativierer." *Die Zeit*, September 1, 2021.
Binner, Jens. *"Ostarbeiter" und Deutsche im Zweiten Weltkrieg*. Munich: Martin Meidenbauer, 2008.
Blackler, Adam A. *An Imperial Homeland: Forging German Identity in Southwest Africa*. Philadelphia: University of Pennsylvania Press, 2022.
Blank, Ralf. *Hagen im Zweiten Weltkrieg: Bombenkrieg, Kriegsalltag und Rüstung einer westfälischen Großstadt*. Essen: Klartext, 2008.
Blatman, Daniel. *The Death Marches: The Final Phase of the Nazi Genocide*. Cambridge, MA: Belknap Press of Harvard University Press, 2010.
Bleuel, Hans Peter. *Das saubere Reich: Theorie und Praxis des sittlichen Lebens im Dritten Reich*. Bern: Scherz, 1972.
Bloxham, Donald. *The Final Solution: A Genocide*. New York: Oxford University Press, 2009.
Bloxham, Donald. "From the International Military Tribunal to the Subsequent Nuremberg Proceedings: The American Confrontation with Nazi Criminality Revisited." *History* 98 no. 332 (2013): 567–591.
Bönisch, Georg, and Klaus Wiegrefe, eds. *Die 50er Jahre: Vom Trümmerland Zum Wirtschaftswunder*. Munich: DTV, 2006.
Bose, Michael, et al. *"Ein neues Hamburg entsteht." Planen und Bauen von 1933–1945*. Hamburg: VSA, 1986.
Brady, Lisa M. *War Upon the Land: Military Strategy and the Transformation of Southern Landscapes During the American Civil War*. Athens: University of Georgia Press, 2012.
Bramwell, Anna. *Blood and Soil: Walther Darré and Hitler's Green Party*. Abbotsbrook, UK: Kensal Press, 1985.
Brandenburg, Hans-Christian. *Die Geschichte der HJ*. Köln: Verlag für Wissenschaft und Politik Berend von Nottbeck, 1982.
Brantz, Dorothee. "Environments of Death." In *War and the Environment: Military Destruction in the Modern Age*, edited by Charles E. Closmann, 68–91. College Station: Texas A&M University Press, 2009.
Braun, Hans, Uta Gerhardt, and Everhart Holtman, eds. *Die lange Stunde Null: Gelenkter sozialer Wandel in Westdeutschland nach 1945*. Baden Baden: Nomos, 2007.
Bridenthal, Renate, Atina Grossmann, and Marion Kaplan, eds. *When Biology Became Destiny: Women in Weimar and Nazi Germany*. New York: Monthly Review Press, 1984.
Briggs, David. *Footprints of War: Militarized Landscapes in Vietnam*. Seattle: University of Washington Press, 2018.
Brodeur, Jean-Paul. *The Policing Web*. Oxford: Oxford University Press, 2010.

Broszat, Martin. *Der Staat Hitlers.* Mumich: DTV, 1969.
Browning, Christopher. *Ordinary Men: Reserve Police Battalion 101 and the Final Solution in Poland.* New York: HarperPerennial, 1992.
Browning, Christopher. *The Origins of the Final Solution.* Lincoln: University of Nebraska Press, 2004.
Browning, Christopher R. "The Nazi Decision to Commit Mass Murder: Three Interpretations: The Euphoria of Victory and the Final Solution: Summer–Fall 1941." *German Studies Review* 17, no. 3 (October 1944): 473–481.
Browning, Christopher R. *Remembering Survival: Inside a Nazi Slave-Labor Camp.* New York: W.W. Norton, 2010.
Brüggemeier, Franz-Josef, Mark Cioc, and Thomas Zeller, eds. *How Green Were the Nazis? Nature, Environment, and Nation in the Third Reich.* Athens: Ohio University Press, 2005.
Bruns, Claudia. "Toward a Transnational History of Racism: Wilhelm Marr and the Interrelationships between Colonial Racism and German Anti-Semitism." In *Racism in the Modern World: Historical Perspectives on Cultural Transfer and Adaptation,* edited by Manfred Berg and Simon Wendt, 122–139 New York: Berghahn Books, 2011.
Brunswig, Hans. *Feuersturm über Hamburg: Die Luftangriffen auf Hamburg im Zweiten Weltkrieg und ihre Folgen.* 3rd ed. Stuttgart: Motorbuch Verlag, 1979.
Buder, Stanley. *Visionaries and Planners: The Garden City Movement and the Modern Community.* New York: Oxford University Press, 1990.
Buggeln, Marc. "Were Concentration Camp Prisoners Slaves?: The Possibilities and Limits of Comparative History and Global Historical Perspetives." *International Review of Social History* 53 no. 1 (2008): 101–129.
Büllesbach, Alfred, and Horst-Dieter Görg, eds. *Fotografie bei Hanomag: Menschen und Maschinen in Hannover-Linden.* München: Morisel, 2016.
Burbank, Jane, and Frederick Cooper, *Empires in World History: Power and Politics of Difference.* Princeton, NJ: Princeton University Press, 2010.
Burchardt, Hans-Jürgen, and Kristina Dietz. "(Neo-)extractivism--A New Challenge for Development Theory from Latin America." *Third World Quarterly* 35, no. 3 (2014): 468–486.
Burke, Timothy. *Lifebuoy Men, Lux Women: Commodification, Consumption, and Cleanliness in Modern.* Durham, NC: Duke University Press, 1996.
Burleigh, Michael. *Death and Deliverance: "Euthanasia" in Germany c. 1900–1945.* Cambridge, UK: Cambridge University Press, 1994.
Burleigh, Michael, and Wolfgang Wippermann. *The Racial State: Germany 1933–1945.* Cambridge, UK: Cambridge University Press, 1991.
Burnard, Trevor, and John Garrigus. *The Plantation Machine: Atlantic Capitalism in French Saint-Domingue and British Jamaica.* Philadelphia: University of Pennsylvania Press, 2016.
Butler, Judith. "Torture and the Ethics of Photography." *Environment and Planning* 25, no. 6 (2007): 951–996.
Büttner, Ursula. *Hamburg in der Staats- und Wirtschaftskrise.* Hamburg: Christians, 1982.
Büttner, Ursula. "Der Aufstieg der NSDAP." In *Hamburg im "Dritten Reich,"* edited by FZH, 27–65. Göttingen: Wallstein, 2005.
Büttner, Ursula. "'Gomorrha' und die Folgen. Der Bombenkrieg." In *Hamburg im "Dritten Reich,"* edited by FZH, 613–632. Göttingen: Wallstein, 2005.

Cecil, Robert. *The Myth of the Master Race: Alfred Rosenberg and Nazi Ideology.* New York: Dood Mead, 1972.
Césaire, Aimé. *Discourse on Colonialism.* Translated by Joan Pinkham. New York: Monthly Review Press, 2000.
Cesarani, David. *Final Solution: The Fate of the Jews, 1933–49.* New York: Macmillan, 2016.
Chakrabarty, Dipesh. "Garbage, Modernity and the Citizen's Gaze." *Economic and Political Weekly* 27, no. 10/11 (March 7–14, 1992): 541–547.
Chakrabarty, Dipesh. *Provincializing Europe: Postcolonial Thought and Historical Difference.* Princeton, NJ: Princeton University Press, 2000.
Chickering, Roger. *The Great War and Urban Life in Germany. Freiburg, 1914–1918.* Cambridge, UK: Cambridge University Press, 2007.
Chickering, Roger. *Imperial Germany and the Great War, 1914–1918.* Cambridge, UK: Cambridge University Press, 1998.
Childers, Thomas. "'Facilis Descensus Aveni Est': The Allied Bombing of Germany and the Issue of German Suffering." *Central European History* 38, no. 1 (2005): 75–105.
Chin, Rita, Heide Fehrenbach, Geoff Eley, and Atina Grossmann. *After the Nazi Racial State: Difference and Democracy in Germany and Europe.* Ann Arbor: University of Michigan Press, 2009.
Clinefelder, Joan L. *Artists for the Reich: Culture and Race from Weimar to Nazi Germany.* New York: Oxford University Press, 2005.
Chioveanu, Mihai. "Transnistria, the 'General Plan East', and the Shoah by Bullets." *Studia Politica (Bucuresti)* 10, no. 3 (2010): 427–446.
Cocks, Geoffrey. *The State of Health in Nazi Germany.* Oxford: Oxford University Press, 2012.
Cohen, Deborah. *The War Come Home: Disabled Veterans in Britain and Germany, 1914–1939.* Berkeley: University of California Press, 2001.
Cohen, G. Daniel. "Between Relief and Politics: Refugee Humanitarianism in Occupied Germany 1945–1946." *Journal of Contemporary History* 43, no. 3 (July 2008): 437–449.
Cohen, Gerard Daniel. *In War's Wake: Europe's Displaced Persons in the Postwar Order.* New York: Oxford University Press, 2011.
Collingham, Lizzie. *The Taste of War: World War II and the Battle for Food.* New York: Penguin, 2011.
Confino, Alon. *A World Without Jews: The Nazi Imagination from Persecution to Genocide.* New Haven, CT: Yale University Press, 2014.
Confino, Alon. *The Nation as a Local Metaphor: Württemberg, Imperial Germany, and National Memory, 1871–1918.* Chapel Hill: University of North Carolina Press, 1997.
Connelly, John. "The Uses of Volksgemeinschaft: Letters to the NSDAP Kreisleitung in Eisenach." *Journal of Modern History* 68, no. 4 (December 1996): 899–930.
Connelly, John. "Nazis and Slavs: From Racial Theory to Racist Practice." *Central European History* 32, no. 1 (1999): 1–33.
Conrad, Sebastian. "Entangled Memories: Versions of the Past in Germany and Japan, 1945–2001." *Journal of Contemporary History* 38, no. 1 (2003): 85–99.
Conrad, Sebastian, and Jürgen Osterhammel. *Das Kaiserreich transnational: Deutschland in der Welt 1871–1914.* Göttingen: Vandehoeck & Ruprecht, 2004.
Corni, Gustavo, and Horst Gies, *Brot. Butter. Kanonen: Die Ernährungswirtschaft in Deutschland unter der Diktatur Hitlers.* Berlin: Academy Verlag, 1997.
Cox, Mary Elisabeth, *Hunger in War and Peace: Women and Children in Germany, 1914–1924.* Oxford: Oxford University Press, 2019.

Crane, Susan. "Memory, Distortion and History in the Museum." *History and Theory* 36, no. 4 (1997): 44–63.
Crew, David, ed. *Nazism and German Society*. New York: Routledge, 1994.
Crew, David F. *Bodies and Ruins: Imagining the Bombings of Germany, 1945 to the Present*. Ann Arbor: University of Michigan Press, 2017.
Crew, David F. *Germans on Welfare: From Weimar to Hitler*. New York: Oxford University Press, 1998.
Crew, David F. "*Alltagsgeschichte*: A New Social History 'from Below'?" *Central European History* 22, no. 3 (September/December 1989): 394–407.
Cronon, William. "A Place for Stories: Nature, History, and Narrative." *Journal of American History* 78, no. 4 (1992): 1347–1376.
Cronon, William. *Uncommon Ground: Rethinking the Human Place in Nature*. New York: W.W. Norton, 1996.
Crouthamel, Jason. "War Neurosis versus Savings Psychosis: Working-Class Politics and Psychological Trauma in Weimar Germany." *Journal of Contemporary History* 37, no. 2 (April 2002): 163–182.
Däbritz, Walther. *Hundert Jahre Hanomag: Geschichte der hannoverschen Maschinenbau-Aktien-Gesellschaft vormals Georg Egestorff in Hannover 1835 bis 1935*. Düsseldorf: Stahleisen, 1935.
Dafinger, Johannes, and Dieter Pohl, eds. *A New Nationalist Europe Under Hitler: Concepts of Europe and Transnational Networks in the National Socialist Sphere of Influence, 1933–1945*. New York: Routledge, 2019.
Dahlman, Dittmar, and Gerhard Hirschfeld, eds. *Lager, Zwangsarbeit, Vertreibung und Deportation: Dimensionen der Massenverbrechen in der Sowjetunion und in Deutschland 1933–1945*. Essen: Klartext, 1999.
Daniel, Ute. *The War from Within: German Working-Class Women in the First World War*. Oxford: Berg, 1997.
Davie, H. G. W. "The Influence of Railways on Military Operations in the Russo-German War 1941–1945." *Journal of Slavic Military Studies* 30, no. 2 (2017): 3211–3246
Davis, Angela. *Are Prisons Obsolete?* New York: Seven Stories Press, 2003.
Davis, Belinda. *Home Fires Burning: Food, Politics, and Everyday Life in World War I Berlin*. Chapel Hill: University of North Carolina Press, 2000.
Davis, Mike. *City of Quartz: Excavating the Future in Los Angeles*. New York: Vintage, 1992.
Davis, Mike. *Ecology of Fear: Los Angeles and the Imagination of Disaster*. New York: Vintage, 1999.
Davis, Mike. *Late Victorian Holocaust: El Niño Famines and the Making of the Third World*. London: Verso, 2002.
Dean, Martin. *Robbing the Jews: The Confiscation of Jewish Property in the Holocaust, 1933–1945*. Cambridge, UK: Cambridge University Press, 2008.
DeCoste, F. C., and Bernard Schwartz, eds. *The Holocaust's Ghosts: Writings on Art, Politics, Law, and Education*. Edmonton, Canada: University of Alberta Press, 2000.
Degler, Stephanie. "Die Verlorene Erzeugungsschlacht: Die Nationalsozialistische Landwirtschaft Im Systemvergleich." *Jahrbuch für Wirtschaftsgeschichte* 49, no. 1 (2008): 161–181.
Deichmann, Ute. *Biologists Under Hitler*. Cambridge, MA: Harvard University Press, 1996.
Deighton, Anne. "Cold-War Diplomacy: British Policy Towards Germany's Role in Europe, 1945–9." In *Reconstruction in Post-War Germany: British Occupation Policy and the Western Zones, 1945–1955*, edited by Ian D. Turner, 15–34. Oxford: Berg, 1989.

Demuth, Bathsheba. *Floating Coast: An Environmental History of the Bering Strait*. New York: W.W. Norton, 2019.
Denton, Chad. "'Récupérez!' The German Origins of French Wartime Salvage Drives, 1939–1945." *Contemporary European History* 22, no. 3 (2013): 399–430
Denton, Chad. "Steel of Victory, Scrap of Defeat: Mobilizing the French Home Front, 1939–1940." *War & Society* 33, no. 2 (2014): 98–130.
Denton, Chad, and Heike Weber. "Bones of Contention: The Nazi Recycling Project in Germany and France During World War II." In *Coping with Hunger and Shortage Under German Occupation in World War II*, edited by Tatijana Tönsmeyer, Peter Haslinger, and Agnes Laba, 119–139. Switzerland: Palgrave Macmillan, 2018.
Dewey, Susan, ed. *Policing Pleasure: Sex Work, Policy, and the State in Global Perspective*. New York: New York University Press, 2011.
Dick, Charles. *Builders of the Third Reich: The Organisation Todt and Nazi Forced Labour*. London: Bloomsbury Academic, 2021.
Dickinson, Edward Ross. *German Child Welfare: From the Empire to the Federal Republic*. Cambridge, MA: Harvard University Press, 1996.
Diefendorf, Jeffry M. *In the Wake of War: The Reconstruction of German Cities After World War II*. New York: Oxford University Press, 1993.
Diehl-Thiele, Peter. *Partei Und Staat Im Dritten Reich*. Munich: Beck, 1969.
Dikotter, Frank, and Ian Brown, *Cultures of Confinement: A History of the Prison in Africa, Asia and Latin America*. Ithaca, NY: Cornell University Press, 2007.
Diner, Dan. *Beyond the Conceivable: Studies on Germany, Nazism, and the Holocaust*. Berkeley: University of California Press, 2000.
Diner, Dan, ed. *Zivilisationsbruch: Denken nach Auschwitz*. Frankfurt am Main: Fischer, 1988.
Dingell, Jeanne. *Zur Tätigkeit der Haupttreuhandstelle Ost, Treunhandstelle Posen 1939–1945*. Frankfurt am Main: Peter Lang, 2003.
"Discussion Forum: Holocaust Memory and Postcolonialism: Transatlantic Perspectives on the Debate." *Central European History* 53 (2023): 270–297.
Dobroszycki, Lucjan, ed. *The Chronicle of the Lodz Ghetto 1941–1944*. Translated by Richard Lourie, Joachim Neugroschel, and others. New Haven, CT: Yale University Press, 1984.
Douglas, Mary. *Purity and Danger: An Analysis of the Concepts of Pollution and Taboo*. New York: Routledge, 2000, 1966.
Drobisch, Klaus. "Hinter Der Torinschrift 'Arbeit macht frei.' Häftlingsarbeit, wirtschaftliche Nutzung und Finanzierung der Konzentrationslager, 1933-1939." In *Konzentrationslager und deutsche Wirtschaft 1939–1945*, edited by Hermann Kaienburg, 17–28. Opladen: Leske & Budrich, 1996.
Du Bois, W. E. B. "The Negro and the Warsaw Ghetto [1949]." *Raisons politiques: études de pensée politique* 1 (2006): 131–135.
Duffy, Aoife. "Bearing Witness to Atrocity Crimes: Photography and International Law." *Human Rights Quarterly* 40, no. 4 (November 2018): 776–814.
Durth, Werner, and Niels Gutschow. *Träume in Trümmern: Planungen zum Wiederaufbau Zerstörter Städte im Westen Deutschlands, 1940–1950*. Vols. I and II. Braunschweig: Friedr.Vieweg & Sohn, 1988.
Ebbinghaus, Angelika, ed. *Opfer und Täterinnen. Frauenbiographien des Nationalsozialismus*. Frankfurt: Fischer, 1997.
Ebbinghaus, Angelika, Heidrun Kaupen-Hass, and Karl-Heinz Roth, eds. *Heilen und Vernichten im Mustergau Hamburg: Bevölkerung und Gesundheitspolitik im Dritten Reich*. Hamburg: Konkret Literatur Verlag, 1984.

Ebbinghaus, Angelika, and Karsten Linne, eds. *Kein abgeschlossenes Kapitel: Hamburg im "Dritten Reich."* Hamburg: Europäische Verlagsanstalt, 1997.
Eichholtz, Dietrich. *Geschichte der deutschen Kriegswirtschaft 1939–1945.* Band 1. Berlin: Akademie-Verlag, 1969.
Eichholtz, Dietrich. *Geschichte der deutschen Kriegswirtschaft 1939–1945.* Band 2, *1941–1943.* Reprint ed. Boston: De Gruyter, 2022.
Eichholtz, Dietrich. *Geschichte der deutschen Kriegswirtschaft 1939–1945.* Band 3, *1943–1945.* Reprint ed. Berlin: Akademie Verlag, 1996.
Eichholtz, Dietrich. *War for Oil: The Nazi Quest for an Oil Empire.* Translated by John Broadwin. Washington, DC: Potomac Books, 2012.
Eley, Geoff. *Labour History-Social History-Alltagsgeschichte: Experience, Culture, and the Politics of the Everyday. A New Direction for German Social History?* Ann Arbor: University of Michigan Press, 1989.
Eley, Geoff. *Nazism as Fascism: Violence, Ideology, and the Ground of Consent in Germany 1930–1945.* London: Routledge, 2013.
Eley, Geoff. "Nazism, Politics and the Image of the Past: Thoughts on the West German Historikerstreit 1986–1987." *Past & Present* 121 (November 1988): 171–208.
Eley, Geoff. "Hitler's Silent Majority? Conformity and Resistance under the Third Reich." *Michigan Quarterly Review* 42, nos. 2 and 3 (Spring 2003): 389–425.
Eley, Geoff, ed. *The "Goldhagen Effect": History, Memory, Nazism—Facing the German Past.* Ann Arbor: Michigan University Press, 2000.
Eley, Geoff, and Jan Palmowski, eds. *Citizenship and National Identity in Twentieth-Century Germany.* Stanford, CA: Stanford University Press, 2008.
Epstein, Catherine. *Model Nazi: Arthur Greiser and the Occupation of Western Poland.* Oxford: Oxford University Press, 2010.
Erichsen, Casper W. "Namibia's Island of Death." *New African* 421 (August/September 2003): 46–49.
Evans, Andrew D. *Anthropology at War: World War I and the Science of Race in Germany.* Chicago: University of Chicago Press, 2010.
Evans, Richard J. *Death in Hamburg: Society and Politics in the Cholera Years.* New York: Penguin, 2005.
Evans, Richard J. *The Third Reich at War: How the Nazis Led Germany from Conquest to Disaster.* New York: Allen Lane, 2008.
Fanon, Frantz. *Black Skin, White Mask.* New York: Grove Press, c1967.
Fanon, Frantz. *A Dying Colonialism.* New York: Grove, 1965.
Fechner, Max. *Wie konnte es geschehen?* Berlin: Dietz Verlag, 1945.
Feiter, Wolfgang, and Alexandra Boy. *90 Jahre Persil: Die Geschichte einer Marke.* Düsseldorf: Henkel KGaA, 1997.
Ferdinand, Malcom. *A Decolonial Ecology: Thinking from the Caribbean World.* Cambridge, UK: Polity Press, 2021.
Ferk, Gabriele. "Judenverfolgung in Norddeutschland." In *Norddeutschland im Nationalsozialismus,* edited by Frank Bajohr, 280–309. Hamburg: Ergebnisse, 1993.
Fest, Joachim C. *Das Gesicht des Dritten Reiches: Profil einer totalitären Herrschaft.* Munich: R. Piper, 1963.
Fischer, Fritz. *Bündnis der Eliten: Zur Kontinuität der Machtstrukturen in Deutschland 1871–1945.* Düsseldorf: Droste, 1998.
Fischer, Jaimey. "Wandering in/to the Rubble-Film: Filmic Flanerie and the Exploded Panorama after 1945." *German Quarterly* 78, no. 4 (Fall 2005): 461–480.

Flachowsky, Sören. *Saubere Stadt. Saubere Weste?: Die Geschichte der Berliner Stadtreinigung von 1871 bis 1955 mit dem Schwerpunkt Nationalsozialismus.* Berlin: Berliner Wissenschaftsverlag, 2021.

Flachowsky, Sören, and Holger Stoecker, eds. *Vom Amazonas an die Ostfront: Der Expiditionsreisende und Geograph Otto Schulz-Kampfhenkel 1910-1988.* Cologne: Böhlau, 2011.

Foote, Stephanie, and Elizabeth Mazzolini. *Histories of the Dustheap: Waste, Material Cultures, Social Justice.* Cambridge, MA: MIT Press, 2012.

Forschungstelle für Zeitgeschichte in Hamburg, ed. *Hamburg im "Dritten Reich."* Göttingen: Wallstein Verlag, 2005.

Forth, Aiden, and Jonas Kreienbaum. "A Shared Malady: Concentration Camps in the British, Spanish, American and German Empires." *Journal of Modern European History* 14, no. 2 (January 2016): 245-267.

"Forum: The German Colonial Imagination." *German History* 26, no. 2 (2008): 251-271.

Foschepoth, Josef, and Rolf Steiniger. *Die britische Deutschland- und Besatzungspolitik.* Paderborn: F. Schöningh, 1985.

Foster, John Bellamy, Brett Clark, and Richard York. *The Ecological Rift: Capitalism's War on the Earth.* New York: Monthly Review Press, 2010.

Foucault, Michel. *Discipline and Punish: The Birth of the Prison.* New York: Vintage, 1977.

Frauenholz, Uwe. "'Verwertung des Wertlosen': Biotechnologische Surrogate aus unkonventionellen Eiweissquellen im Nationalsozialismus." *Dresdener Beiträge zur Geschichte der Technikwissenschaften* 32 (2008): 95-116.

Frei, Norbert. "German Zeitgeschichte und Generation, or how to Explain the Belated Career of the Nazi *Volksgemeinschaft*." *Social Research* 18, no. 3 German Perspectives on the Social Sciences (Fall 2014): 571-584.

Freund-Widder, Michaela. *Frauen unter Kontrolle: Prostitution und ihre staatliche Bekämpfung in Hamburg vom Ende des Kaiserreichs bis zu den Anfängen der Bundesrepublik.* Berlin: LIT Verlag, 2003.

Frewer, Andreas, and Günther Siedbürger, eds. *Medizin und Zwangsarbeit im Nationalsozialismus: Einsatz und Behandlung von 'Ausländern' im Gesundheitswesen.* Frankfurt am Main: Campus, 2004.

Frickel, Scott. "Missing New Orleans: Tracking Knowledge and Ignorance through an Urban Hazardscape." In *Histories of the Dustheap: Waste, Material Cultures, Social Justice*, edited by Stephanie Foote and Elizabeth Mazzolini, 119-146. Cambridge, MA: MIT Press, 2012.

Friedrich, Jörg. *The Fire: The Bombing of Germany, 1940-1945.* New York: Columbia University Press, 2006.

Friedländer, Saul. "A Fundamentally Singular Crime." *Journal of Holocaust Research* 36, no. 1 (2022): 39-43.

Friedländer, Saul. *Nazi Germany and the Jews, 1933-1939.* Vol. 1: *The Years of Persecution.* New York: HarperPerennial, 1998.

Friedländer, Saul, ed. *Probing the Limits of Representation: Nazism and the "Final Solution."* Cambridge, MA: Harvard University Press, 1992.

Friedländer, Saul, Norbert Frei, and Sybille Steinbacher, eds. *Ein Verbrechen ohne Namen: Anmerkungen zum neuen Streit über den Holocaust.* Munich: C.H. Beck, 2022.

Frieser, Karl-Heinz. *Blitzkrieg Legend: The 1940 Campaign in the West.* Annapolis, MD: Naval Institute Press, 2004.

Fritzsche, Peter. *An Iron Wind: Europe Under Hitler.* New York: Basic Books, 2016.

Fritzsche, Peter. *Germans Into Nazis*. Cambridge, MA: Harvard University Press, 1997.
Fritzsche, Peter. *Life and Death in the Third Reich*. Cambridge, MA: Belknap Press of Harvard University Press, 2008.
Frommelt, Reinhard. *Paneuropa oder Mitteleuropa: Einigungbestrebungen im Kalkül deutscher Wirtschaft und Politik 1925-1933*. Stuttgart: Oldenburg Wissenschaftsverlag, 2010.
Gabriel, Ralph. "Nationalsozialistische Biopolitik und die Architektur der Konzentrationslager." In *Auszug aus dem Lager: Zur Überwindung des modernen Raumparadigmas in der politischen Philosophie*, edited by Ludger Schwarte, 201-219. Bielefeld: Verlag, 2015.
Gandy, Matthew. *Recycling and the Politics of Urban Waste*. London: Earthscan, 1994.
Garland, David. *The Culture of Control: Crime and Social Order*. Chicago: University of Chicago Press, 2001.
Gellately, Robert. *Backing Hitler: Consent and Coercion in Nazi Germany*. Oxford: Oxford University Press, 1998.
Gellately, Robert, and Nathan Stoltzfus. *Social Outsiders in Nazi Germany*. Princeton, NJ: Princeton University Press, 2001.
Georg, Enno. *Die Wirtschaftlichen Unternehmungen der SS*. Stuttgart: Deutsche Verlagsanstalt, 1963.
Genschel, Helmut. *Die Verdrängung der Juden aus der Wirtschaft im Dritten Reich*. Göttingen: Musterschmidt, 1966.
Gerhard, Gesine. "Food as a Weapon: Agricultural Sciences and the Building of a Greater German Empire." *Food, Culture, & Society* 14, no. 3 (2011): 335-351.
"German Textile Industries during 1939-1945." *Nature* 64 (1949): 948-949, at https://www.nature.com/articles/164948e0.
Gerwarth, Robert, and Stephan Malinowski. "Der Holocaust als 'kolonialer Genozid'? Europäische Kolonialgewalt und nationalsozialistischer Vernichtungskrieg." *Geschichte und Gesellschaft* 33, no. 3 (2007): 439-466.
Geyer, Michael. "Insurrectionary Warfare: The German Debate about a Levée En Masse in October 1918." *Journal of Modern History* 73, no. 3 (2001): 459-527.
Giaccaria, Paolo, and Claudio Minca. *Hitler's Geographies: The Spatialities of the Third Reich*. Chicago: University of Chicago Press, 2016.
Gies, Horst. *Richard Walther Darré: der "Reichsbauernführer," die nationalsozialistische "Blut und Boden"--Ideologie und Hitlers Machteroberung*. Vienna: Böhlau Verlag, 2019.
Gillard, David. *Appeasement in Crisis: From Munich to Prague, October 1938-March 1939*. New York: Palgrave Macmillan, 2007.
Gille, Zsuzsa. *From the Cult of Waste to the Trash Heap of History: The Politics of Waste in Socialist and Postsocialist Hungary*. Bloomington: Indiana University Press, 2007.
Gilmore, Ruth Wilson. "Globalization and US-Prison Growth." *Race & Class* 40, no. 2/3 (1998/1999): 171-188.
Gilmore, Ruth Wilson. *Golden Gulag: Prisons, Surplus, Crisis and Opposition in Globalizing California*. Berkeley: University of California Press, 2007.
Glantz, David. *Barbarossa: Hitler's Invasion of Russia, 1941*. Stroud: Tempus, 2001.
Glantz, David M., and Jonathan M. House. *When Titans Clashed: How the Red Army Stopped Hitler*. Lawrence: University of Kansas Press, 1995.
Glensk, Evelyn. *Die Aufnahme und Eingliederung der Vertriebenen und Flüchtlinge in Hamburg 1945-1953*. Hamburg: Verlag für Hamburgische Geschichte, 1994.

Goldberg, David Theo. *Racist Culture: Philosophy and the Politics of Meaning.* Oxford: Blackwell, 1993.
Goldhagen, Daniel J. *Hitler's Willing Executioners: Ordinary Germans and the Holocaust.* New York: Knopf, 1996.
Gosh, Amitav. *The Great Derangement: Climate Change and the Unthinkable.* Chicago: University of Chicago Press, 2016.
Gotto, Bernhard. *Nationalsozialistische Kommunalpolitik: Administrative Normalität und Systemstabiliserung durch die Augsburger Stadtverwaltung, 1933–1945.* Munich: Oldenburg Verlag, 2006.
Gottwald, Alfred, and Diana Schulle. *Die 'Judendeportationen' aus dem Deutschen Reich, 1941–1945.* Wiesbaden: Marix Verlag, 2005.
Grabitz, Helge, and Wolfgang Scheffler. *Letzte Spuren.* Berlin: Edition Hentrich, 1988.
Graham, Stephen, and Simon Marvin. *Splintering Urbanism: Networked Infrastructures, Technological Mobilities and the Urban Condition.* London: Routledge, 2001.
Graml, Herman. *Die Alliierten und die Teilung Deutschlands: Konflikte und Entscheidungen, 1941–48.* Frankfurt am Main: Fischer, 1985.
Gräser, Marcus. *Der blockierte Wohlfahrtsstaat.* Göttingen: Vandehoeck & Rupprecht, 1995.
Gregor, Neil. "A Schicksalsgemeinschaft? Allied Bombing, Civilian Morale, and Social Dissolution in Nuremberg, 1942–1945." *The Historical Journal* 43, no. 4 (2000): 1051–1070.
Greve, Michael. *Die organisierte Vernichtung 'lebensunwerten Lebens' im Rahmen der Aktion T4: dargestellt am Beispiel des Wirkens und der strafrechtlichen Verfolgung der NS- Tötungsärzte.* Paffenweiler: Centaurus-Verlagsgesellschaft, 1998.
Gies, Horst. *Richard Walther Darré: Der 'Reichsbauernführer', die nationalsozialitische 'Blut und Boden'-Ideologie und Hitlers Machteroberung.* Vienna: Böhlau Verlag, 2019.
Grobecker, Kurt, Hans-Dieter Loose, and Erik Verg, eds. *Mehr als ein Haufen Steine. Hamburg 1945–1949.* Hamburg: Ernst Kabel, 1981.
Gross, Jan Tomasz, and Irena Grudzińska Gross. *Golden Harvest: Events at the Periphery of the Holocaust.* New York: Oxford University Press, 2012.
Grossbölting, Thomas. *Volksgemeinschaft in der Kleinstadt: Kornwestheim und der Nationalsozialismus* Stuttgart: Verlag W. Kohlhammer, 2017.
Grossmann, Atina. *Jews, Germans, and Allies: Close Encounters in Occupied Germany.* Princeton, NJ: Princeton University Press, 2007.
Guha, Ramachandra. "Radical American Environmentalism and Wilderness Preservation: A Third World Critique." *Environmental Ethics* 11 (1989): 71–83.
Gutman, Israel. "Introduction: The Distinctiveness of the Lodz Ghetto." In Isaiah Trunk, *Łódź Ghetto: A History,* xxix–lvii. Bloomington: Indiana University Press.
Gutman, Israel, and Michael Berenbaum. *Anatomy of the Auschwitz Death Camp.* Bloomington: Published in association with the United States Holocaust Memorial Museum, Washington, DC by Indiana University Press, 1994.
Hachtmann, Rüdiger. *Berlin im Nationalsozialismus: Politik und Gesellschaft 1933–1945.* Göttingen: Wallstein, 2012.
Hagemann, Karen. "Geschichtswissenschaft, Medien and kollectives Gedächtnis. Zum 'Mythos Trümmerfrauen.'" *Neue Politische Literatur* 2 (2015): 203–212.
Haggith, Toby, and Joanna Newman. *Holocaust and the Moving Image.* New York: Wallflower, 2005.

Haley, Sarah. *No Mercy Here: Gender Punishment and the Making of Jim Crow Modernity*. Chapel Hill: University of North Carolina Press, 2016.
Hanebrink, Paul. *A Specter Haunting Europe: The Myth of Judeo-Bolshevism*. Cambridge, MA: Harvard University Press, 2018.
Hansen, Jennifer. "The Art and Science of Reading Faces: Strategies of Racist Cinema in the Third Reich." *Shofar* 28 no.1 (2009) 80–103.
Harris, Victoria. *Selling Sex in the Reich: Prostitutes in German Society, 1914–1945*. Oxford: Oxford University Press, 2010.
Hartmann, Christian. *Wehrmacht im Ostkrieg: Front und militärisches Hinterland 1941/42*. Berlin: Oldenburg Wissenschaftsverlag, 2012.
Harvey, Elizabeth. *Youth and the Welfare State in Weimar Germany*. Oxford: Clarendon Press, 1993.
Haug, Albert. *Von der Kloake zur Kanalisation: Geschichte der Abwasser-Entsorgung in Ulm*. Stuttgart: Kommissionsverlag, 2012.
Hayes, Peter. *From Cooperation to Complicity: Degussa in the Third Reich*. Cambridge, UK: Cambridge University Press, 2004.
Hayes, Peter. *Industry and Ideology: IG Farben in the Nazi Era*. Cambridge, UK: Cambridge University Press, 1987.
Hayes, Peter, ed. *How Was It Possible? A Holocaust Reader*. Lincoln: University of Nebraska Press, 2015.
Headrick, Daniel R. *The Tools of Empire: Technology and European Imperialism in the Nineteenth Century*. New York: Oxford University Press, 1981.
Hearne, Siobhán. *Policing Prostitution: Regulating the Lower Classes in Late Imperial Russia*. Oxford: Oxford University Press, 2021.
Hecht, Gabrielle. "Human Crap: The Idea of Disposability Is a New and Noxious Fiction." *Aeon*, March 2020.
Heim, Susanne. *Plant Breeding and Agrarian Research in Kaiser-Wilhelm-Institutes 1933–1945: Calories: Caoutchouc, Careers*. Göttingen: Springer, 2003.
Heinz, Rainer. "Fritz Hippler." *Film-Dienst* 55, no. 17 (2002): 14.
Helm, Sarah. *Ravensbrück: Life and Death in Hitler's Concentration Camp for Women*. U.S. edition. New York: Nan A. Talese/Doubleday, 2015.
Helmer, Stephen D. *Hitler's Berlin: The Speer Plans for Reshaping the Central City*. Ann Arbor: University of Michigan Press, 1985.
Herbert, Ulrich. *Hitler's Foreign Workers: Enforced Foreign Labor in Germany under the Third Reich*. Cambridge, UK: Cambridge University Press, 1997.
Herbert, Ulrich. "'Die guten und die schlechten Zeiten.' Überlegungen zur diachronen Analyse lebensgeschichtlicher Interviews." In *"Die Jahre weiß man nicht, wo man die heute hinsetzen soll." Faschismus Erfahrungen im Ruhrgebiet*, edited by Lutz Niethammer, 2nd ed., 67–96. Berlin: J.H.W. Dietz, 1986.
Herbert, Ulrich. "Good Times, Bad Times." *History Today* 36, no. 2 (February 1986): 42–48.
Herbert, Ulrich, ed. *Europa und der 'Reichseinsatz': ausländische Zivilarbeiter, Kriegsgefangene und KZ-Häftlinge in Deutschland 1938–1945*. Essen: Klartext, 1991.
Herf, Jeffrey. *Divided Memory: The Nazi Past in the Two Germanys*. Cambridge, MA: Harvard University Press, 1997.
Herf, Jeffrey. *Reactionary Modernism: Technology, Culture, and Politics in Weimar and the Third Reich*. Cambridge, UK, and New York: Cambridge University Press, 1986.
Herf, Jefferey. *The Jewish Enemy*. Cambridge, MA: Harvard University Press, 2006.

Herzog, Dagmar, ed. *Sexuality and German Fascism*. New York: Berghahn Books, 2005.
Herzog, Dagmar. *Unlearning Eugenics: Sexuality, Reproduction and Disability in Post Nazi Europe*. Madison: University of Wisconsin Press, 2018.
Heynen, Robert, and Emily Van der Meulen. *Making Surveillance States: Transnational Histories*. Toronto: University of Toronto Press, 2019.
Hilberg, Raul. *The Destruction of the European Jews*. New Haven, CT: Yale University Press, 2003.
Himmler, Katrin, and Michael Wildt. *Himmler privat: Briefe eines Massenmörders*. Munich: Piper, 2014.
Hinton, Elizabeth. *From the War on Poverty to the War on Crime: The Making of Mass Incarceration in America*. Cambridge, MA: Harvard University Press, 2017.
Hirschfeld, Gerhard, and Lothar Kettenacker, eds. *Der "Führerstaat": Mythos und Realität. Studien zur Struktur und Politik des Dritten Reichs*, Stuttgart: Klett, 1981.
Höffkes, Karl. *Hitlers politische Generale: Die Gauleiter des Dritten Reiches: Ein biographisches Nachschlagewerk*. Tübingen: Grabert-Verlag, 1986.
Holmsten, Georg. *Die Berlin-Chronik. Daten. Personen. Dokumente*. Düsseldorf: Droste, 1984.
Hönke, Jana, and Markus M. Müller. *The Global Making of Policing: Postcolonial Perspectives*. Abingdon, Oxon: Routledge, 2016.
Horowitz, Gordon J. *Ghettostadt: Lodz and the Making of a Nazi City*. Cambridge, MA: Harvard University Press, 2008.
Housden, Martyn. *Hans Frank: Lebensraum and the Holocaust*. New York: Palgrave Macmillan, 2003.
Huchting, Friedrich. "Abfallwirtschaft im Dritten Reich." *Technikgeschichte: Beiträge zur Geschichte der Technikgeschichte* 48, no. 3 (1981): 252–273.
Hull, Isabell. *Absolute Destruction: Military Culture and the Practices of War in Imperial Germany*. Ithaca, NY: Cornell University Press, 2005.
Hüttenberger, Peter. "Nationalsozialistische Polykratie." *Geschichte und Gesellschaft: Zeitschrift für historische Sozialwissenschaft* 2 (1976): 417–442.
Hüttenberger, Peter. *Die Gauleiter: Studie zum Wandel des Machtgefüges in der NSDAP*. Stuttgart: Deutsche Verlagsanstalt, 1969.
Ingrao, Charles W., and Franz A. J. Szabo, eds. *The Germans and the East*. West Lafayette: Purdue University Press, 2008.
Jacobeit, Wolfgang. *Die Biologisch-Dynamische Wirtschaftsweise im KZ: Die Güter der "Deutschen Versuchsanstalt für Ernährung und Verpflegung" der SS von 1939–1945*. Berlin: Trafo, 1999.
Jacobson, Matthew Frye. *Whiteness of a Different Color: European Immigrants and the Alchemy of Race*. Cambridge, MA: Harvard University Press, 1998.
Jahn, Peter, ed. *Stalingrad Erinnern: Stalingrad im deutschen und russischen Gedächtnis*. Berlin: Ch. Links Verlag, 2003.
James, Harold. *Krupp: A History of the Legendary German Firm*. Princeton, NJ: Princeton University Press, 2012.
Jarausch, Konrad H., and Michael Geyer. *Shattered Past: Reconstructing German Histories*. Princeton, NJ: Princeton University Press, 2003.
Jaskot, Paul B. *The Architecture of Oppression: The SS, Forced Labor and the Nazi Monumental Building Economy*. New York: Routledge, 2000.
Jenks, Andrew. "Model City USA: The Environmental Cost of Victory in World War II and the Cold War." *Environmental History* 12, no. 3 (July 2007): 552–577.

Judt, Tony. *Postwar: A History of Europe since 1945.* New York Penguin, 2006.
Kaden, Eric. *'Kommandeur der deutschen Bauernschaft' Richard Walther Darré: Eine politische Biographie.* Naunhof: Edition Philalethes, 2018.
Kaienburg, Hermann. *Die Wirtschaft der SS.* Berlin: Metropol, 2003.
Kaienburg, Hermann, ed. *Konzentrationslager und deutsche Wirtschaft, 1939–1945.* Opladen: Lenke & Budrich, 1996.
Kamenetsky, Ihor. *Secret Nazi Plans for Eastern Europe: A Study of Lebensraum Policies.* New York: Bookman Associates, 1961.
Kaplan, Marion A. *Between Dignity and Despair: Jewish Life in Nazi Germany.* New York: Oxford University Press, 1998.
Kater. Michael. "Dr. Leonardo Conti and His Nemesis: The Failure of Centralized Medicine in the Third Reich." *Central European History* 18, no. 3/4 (September/December 1985): 299–325.
Kehr, Eckart, and Hans-Ulrich Wehler. *Der Primat Der Innenpolitik.* Berlin: de Gruyter, 1965.
Keller, Rolf. *Sowjetische Kriegsgefangene im Deutschen Reich 1941/1942.* Göttingen: Wallstein, 2011.
Keller, Rolf, and Silke Petry, eds. *Sowjetische Kriegsgefangene im Arbeitseinsatz 1941–1945: Dokumente zu den Lebens und Arbeitsbedingungen in Norddeutschland.* Göttingen: Wallenstein, 2013.
Keller, Sven. *Volksgemeinschaft am Ende: Gesellschaft und Gewalt 1944/45.* Munich: Oldenbourg Verlag, 2013.
Kelley, Victoria. *Soap and Water: Cleanliness, Dirt and the Working Classes in Victorian and Edwardian Britain.* London: I.B. Tauris, 2010.
Kershaw, Ian. *Hitler, 1889-1936: Hubris.* New York: W.W. Norton, 1999.
Kershaw, Ian. *Hitler, 1936–45: Nemesis.* New York: W.W. Norton, 2000.
Kershaw, Ian. *The End: The Defiance and Destruction of Hitler's Germany, 1944–1945.* New York: Penguin, 2011.
Kershaw, Ian. *The "Hitler Myth": Image and Reality in the Third Reich.* Oxford: Oxford University Press, 1989.
Kershaw, Ian. "Hitler and the Uniqueness of Nazism." *Journal of Contemporary History* 39, no. 2 (2004): 239–254.
Kershaw, Ian. "Hitler: 'Master in the Third Reich' or 'Weak Dictator'?" In *The Nazi Dictatorship: Problems and Perspectives of Interpretation*, edited by Ian Kershaw, 69–92. London: E. Arnold, 2000.
Kershaw, Ian. "'Working Towards the Führer.' Reflections on the Nature of the Hitler Dictatorship." *Contemporary European History* 2, no. 2 (1993): 103–118.
Kiernan, Ben. *Blood and Soil: A World History of Genocide and Extermination from Sparta to Darfur.* New Haven, CT: Yale University Press, 2007.
Killen, Andreas. "From Shock to Schreck: Psychiatrists, Telephone Operators and Traumatic Neurosis in Germany 1900-26." *Journal of Contemporary History* 38, no. 2 (April 2003): 201–220.
Kißener, Michael, and Joachim Scholtyseck, eds. *Die Führer der Provinz: NS-Biographien aus Baden und Württemberg.* Konstanz: UVK, 1999.
Kitchen, Martin. *Nazi Germany: A Critical Introduction.* Gloucestershire, UK: Tempus, 2004.
Klee, Ernst. *Auschwitz, die NS-Medizin und ihre Opfer.* Frankfurt am Main: Fischer, 2004.

Klee, Ernst. *Das Personenlexikon zum Dritten Reich: Wer war was vor und nach 1945*. Frankfurt: Fischer, 2005.

Kline, Nolan. *Pathogenic Policing: Immigration Enforcement and Health in the U.S. South*. New Brunswick, NJ: Rutgers University Press, 2019.

Knoch, Habbo. *Die Tat als Bild: Fotografien des Holocaust in der deutschen Erinnerungskultur*. Hamburg: Hamburger Edition, 2001.

Kocka, Jürgen. *Facing Total War: German Society, 1914-1918*. Cambridge, MA: Harvard University Press, 1984.

Kogon, Eugen. *The Theory and Practice of Hell: The German Concentration Camps and the System Behind Them*. Translated by Heinz Norden. New York: Farrar, Straus and Giroux, 1950.

Kolb, Eberhard. *Bergen-Belsen: Geschichte des "Aufenthaltslagers" 1943-1945*. Berlin: Lit Verlag, 2011.

Kollmeier, Katrin. *Ordnung und Ausgrenzung. Die Disziplinarpolitik der Hitler-Jugend*. Göttingen: Vandenhoeck & Ruprecht, 2007.

König, Wolfgang. *Volkswagen, Volksempfänger, Volksgemeinschaft. "Volksprodukte" im Dritten Reich: Vom Scheitern einer nationasozialistischen Konsumgesellschaft*. Paderborn: Ferdinand Schöningh, 2004.

Koonz, Claudia. *The Nazi Conscience*. Cambridge, MA: Belknap Press, 2003.

Koonz, Claudia. *Mothers in the Fatherland: Women, the Family and Nazi Politics*. London: Routledge, 2013.

Koop, Volker. *Das schmutzige Vermögen: Das Dritte Reich, I.G. Farben, und die Schweiz*. Munich: Siedler Verlag, 2005.

Koop, Volker. *"Dem Führer ein Kind schenken:" Die SS-Organisation* Lebensborn.e.V. Cologne: Böhlau, 2007.

Köster, Roman. *Müll: Eine schmutzige Geschichte der Menschheit*. Munich: C.H. Beck, 2023.

Köstering, Susanne. "Müllspülung im Golmer Luch. Ein Beitrag zum Verhältnis von Naturschutz und Nationalsozialismus." In *Müll von gestern? Eine umweltgeschichtliche Erkundung in Berlin und Umgebung, 1880-1945*, edited by Susanne Köstering und Renate Rüb, 76-89. Münster: Waxmann, 2003.

Köstering, Susanne. "'Pioniere der Rohstoffbeschaffung' Lumpensammler im Nationalsozialismus 1934-1939." *Werkstatt Geschichte* 17 (1997): 45-65.

Koven, Seth. *Slumming: Sexual and Social Politics in Victorian London*. Princeton, NJ: Princeton University Press, 2004.

Kröger, Markus. *Iron Will: Global Extractivism and Mining Resistance in Brazil and India*. Ann Arbor: University of Michigan Press, 2020.

Kundrus, Birthe. "From the Herero to the Holocaust? Some Remarks on the Current Debate." *Africa Spectrum* 40, no. 2 (2005): 299-308.

Landau, Paul S., and Deborah D. Kaspin. *Images & Empires: Visuality in Colonial and Postcolonial Africa*. Berkeley: University of California Press, 2002.

Lange, Ralf. *Hamburg: Wiederaufbau und Neuplanung, 1943-1963*. Königstein: Hans Köster, 1994.

Larsson, Lars Olof. *Die Neugestaltung der Reichshauptstadt: Albert Speers Generalbebauungsplan für Berlin*. Stockholm: Almqvist & Wiksell International, 1977.

Lebzelter, Gisela. "Die 'Schwarze Schmach.' Vorurteile Propaganda Mythos." *Geschichte und Gesellschaft* 11, no. 1 (1985): 37-58.

Lehnstaedt, Stephan, and Robert Traba, eds. *Die "Aktion Reinhardt:" Geschichte und Gedenken*. Berlin: Metropol, 2019.
Lekan, Thomas M. *Imagining the Nation in Nature: Landscape Preservation and German Identity, 1885–1945*. Cambridge, MA: Harvard University Press, 2004.
Lekan, Thomas M., ed. *Germany's Nature: Cultural Landscapes and Environmental History*. New Brunswick, NJ: Rutgers University Press, 2005.
Lemke, Thomas. *Biopolitics: An Advanced Introduction*, Translated by Eric Frederick Trump. New York: New York University Press, 2011.
Leroy, Justin, and Destin Jenkins, eds. *Histories of Racial Capitalism*. New York: Columbia University Press, 2021.
Liboiron, Max. "Waste Is Not 'Matter Out of Place.'" *Discard Studies*, September 9, 2019, at https://discardstudies.com/2019/09/09/waste-is-not-matter-out-of-place.
Lilla, Joachim. *Die Stellvertretenden Gauleiter und die Vertretung der Gauleiter der NSDAP im "Dritten Reich."* Koblenz: Bundesarchiv, 2003.
Lilla, Joachim, ed. *Der Preußische Stadtrat, 1921–1933: Ein biographisches Handbuch*. Düsseldorf: Droste, 2005.
Lindner, Stephan H. *Hoechst. Ein I.G. Farben Werk im Dritten Reich*. Munich: C.H. Beck, 2005.
Löffelsender, Michael. *Das KZ Buchenwald 1937-1945*. Erfurt: Landeszentrale für politische Bildung, 2020.
Lohalm, Uwe. "Für eine leistungsbereite und 'erbgesunde' Volksgemeinschaft: Selektive Erwerbslosen- und Familienpolitik." In *Hamburg im "Dritten Reich,"* edited by FZH, 379–431. Göttingen: Wallstein, 2005.
Longerich, Peter. *Heinrich Himmler*. New York: Oxford University Press, 2012.
Longerich, Peter. *Holocaust: The Nazi Persecution and Murder of the Jews*. Oxford: Oxford University Press, 2010.
Lower, Wendy. *Nazi Empire-Building and the Holocaust in Ukraine*. Chapel Hill: University of North Carolina Press, 2005.
Lubrich, Oliver, ed. *Travels in the Reich, 1933-1945: Foreign Authors Report from Germany*. Chicago: Chicago University Press, 2010.
Lüdtke, Alf. *Alltagsgeschichte: Zur Rekonstruktion historischer Erfahrungen und Lebensweisen*. Frankfurt: Campus, 1989.
Lüdtke, Alf. "'Coming to Terms with the Past': Illusions of Remembering, Ways of Forgetting." *Journal of Modern History* 65, no. 3 (1993): 542–572.
Lüdtke, Alf. *Eigen-Sinn: Fabrikalltag, Arbeitererfahrungen und Politik. Vom Kaiserreich bis in den Faschismus*. Hamburg: Ergebnisse Verlag, 1993.
Lumans, Valdis. *Himmler's Auxiliaries: the Volksdeutsche Mittelstelle and the German National Minorities of Europe, 1933–1945*. Chapel Hill: University of North Carolina Press, 1993.
Madley, Benjamin. "From Terror to Genocide: Britain's Tasmanian Penal Colony and Australia's History Wars." *Journal of British Studies* 47 (January 2008): 77–106.
Malkki, Liisa. "Refugees and Exile: From 'Refugee Studies' to the National Order of Things." *Annual Review of Anthropology* 25 (1995): 495–523.
Marcuse, Harold. *The Legacies of Dachau: The Uses and Abuses of a Concentration Camp, 1933-2001*. Cambridge, UK, and New York: Cambridge University Press, 2001.
Martin, Alexander. "Sewage and the City: Filth, Smell and Representations of Urban Life in Moscow, 1770-1880." *Russian Review* 67, no. 2 (2008): 234–274.

Mason, Timothy. *Social Policy in the Third Reich. The Working Class and the "National Community."* New York: Berg, 1993.
Mazower, Mark. *Dark Continent: Europe's Twentieth Century.* New York: Alfred A. Knopf, 1999.
Mazower, Mark. *Hitler's Empire: How the Nazis Ruled Europe.* New York: Penguin Press, 2008.
Mbembe, Achille. *On the Postcolony.* Berkeley: University of California Press, 2001.
Mbembe, Achille. *Necropolitics.* Durham, NC: Duke University Press, 2019.
Mbembe, Achille. "The Society of Enmity." *Radical Philosophy* 200 (2016): 23–36.
McLennan, Rebecca M. *The Crisis of Imprisonment: Protest, Politics, and the Making of the American Penal State, 1776–1941.* Cambridge, UK: Cambridge University Press, 2008.
McNeill, John Robert. *Something New Under the Sun: An Environmental History of the Twentieth-Century World.* New York: W.W. Norton, 2000.
Medina, Martin. *The World's Scavengers: Salvaging for Sustainable Consumption and Production.* Lanham, MD: Altamira, 2007.
Melamed, Jodi. *Represent and Destroy: Rationalizing Violence in the New Racial Capitalism.* Minneapolis: University of Minnesota Press, 2001.
Melosi, Martin V. *Effluent America: Cities, Industry, Energy, and the Environment.* Pittsburgh, PA: University of Pittsburgh Press, 2001.
Melosi, Martin V. *Garbage and the City: Refuse, Reform, and the Environment.* Rev. ed. Pittsburgh, PA: Pittsburgh University Press, 2005.
Merritt, Anna J., and Richard L. Merritt, eds. *Public Opinion in Occupied Germany. The Omgus Surveys, 1945–1949.* Urbana: University of Illinois Press, 1970.
Meyer, Winfried, and Klaus Neitmann, eds. *Zwangsarbeit während der NS-Zeit in Berlin und Brandenburg: Formen, Funkton und Rezeption.* Potsdam: Verlag für Berlin-Brandenburg, 2001.
Mildenberger, Florian, and Bernd Herrmann. "Nachwort." In *Umwelt und Innenwelt der Tiere*, edited by Jakob Johann von Uexküll, 261–330. Berlin: Springer, 2014.
Mills, Charles. *The Racial Contract.* Ithaca, NY: Cornell University Press, 1997.
Mills, Charles W. "Black Trash." In *Faces of Environmental Racism: Confronting Issues of Global Justice*, edited by Laura Westra and Bill E. Lawson, 73–91. New York: Rowman & Littlefield, 2001.
Mintz, Sidney. *Sweetness and Power.* New York: Viking, 1985.
Mitchell, Timothy. *Carbon Democracy: Political Power in the Age of Oil.* London: Verso, 2013.
Mitman, Gregg. *Empire of Rubber: Firestone's Scramble for Land and Power in Liberia.* New York: The New Press, 2021.
Moeller, Robert G. *War Stories: The Search for a Usable Past in the Federal Republic of Germany.* Berkeley: University of California Press, 2003.
Moiser, John. *The Blitzkrieg Myth: How Hitler and the Allies Misread the Strategic Realities of World War II.* New York: HarperCollins, 2003.
Mommsen, Hans. "Hitler's Stellung im nationalsozialistischen Herrschaftssystem." In *Der 'Führerstaat': Mythos und Realität*, edited by Gerhard Hirschfeld and Lothar Kettenacker, 43–72. Stuttgart: Klett-Cotta, 1981.
Montrie, Chad. *The Myth of Silent Spring: Rethinking the Origins of American Environmentalism.* Oakland: University of California Press, 2018.

Moore, Paul. "'And What Concentration Camps Those Were!': Foreign Concentration Camps in Nazi Propaganda 1933-9." *Journal of Contemporary History* 45, no. 3 (July 2010): 649–674.
Moses, A. Dirk. *The Problems of Genocide: Permanent Security and the Language of Transgression.* Cambridge, UK: Cambridge University Press, 2021.
Moses, A. Dirk. "The German Catechism." *Geschichte der Gegenwart,* May 23, 2021, at https://geschichtedergegenwart.ch/the-german-catechism.
Moyd, Michelle R. *Violent Intermediaries: African Soldiers, Conquest, and Everyday Colonialism in German East Africa.* Athens: Ohio University Press, 2014.
Moyd, Michelle, "Color Lines, Front Lines: The First World War from the South" *Radical History Review* 131 (May 2018): 13–35.
Mukherjee, Janam. *Hungry Bengal: War, Famine and the End of Empire.* New York: Oxford University Press, 2015.
Muhammad, Khalil Gibran. *The Condemnation of Blackness: Race, Crime, and the Making of Modern Urban America.* Cambridge, MA: Harvard University Press, 2010.
Müller, Rolf-Dieter. *Der Feind steht im Osten: Hitlers geheime Pläne für einen Krieg gegen die Sowjetunion im Jahr 1939.* Berlin: Ch. Links Verlag, 2011.
Müller, Rolf-Dieter. *Der Manager der Kriegswirtschaft: Hans Kehrl: Ein Unternehmer in der Politik des Dritten Reiches.* Essen: Klartext, 1999.
Müller, Rolf-Dieter. *Hitlers Krieg im Osten 1941-1945: Ein Forschungsbericht.* Darmstadt: Wissenschaftliche Buchgesellschaft, 2000.
Müller, Thomas. "Between Therapeutic Instrument and Exploitation of Labor Force: Patient Work in Rural Asylums in Württemberg c. 1810–1945." In *Work Psychiatry and Society, c. 1750–2015,* edited by W. Ernst, 220–237. Manchester, UK: Manchester University Press, 2016.
Muschalek, Marie. *Violence as Usual: Policing and the Colonial State in German Southwest Africa.* Ithaca, NY: Cornell University Press, 2019.
Muscolosi, Micah. *The Ecology of War in China: Henan Province, the Yellow River and Beyond, 1938–1950.* New York: Cambridge University Press, 2015.
Musial, Bogdan, ed. *"Aktion Reinhardt" Völkermord an den Juden im Generalgouvernement 1941–1944.* Osnabrück: Fibre, 2004.
Naranch, Bradley, and Geoff Eley, eds. *German Colonialism in a Global Age.* Durham, NC: Duke University Press, 2014.
Nash, Linda. "The Agency of Nature or the Nature of Agency." *Environmental History* 10, no. 1 (2005): 67–69.
Nasser, Walter. *SS-Wirtschaft und SS-Verwaltung: Das SS-Wirtschafts-Verwaltungshauptamt und die unter seiner Dienstaufsicht stehenden wirtschaftlichen Unternehmungen.* Düsseldorf: Droste, 1998.
Neander, Joachim. "The Danzig Soap Case: Facts and Legends around 'Professor Spanner' and the Danzig Anatomic Institute, 1944–1945." *German Studies Review* 29, no. 1 (February 2006): 63–86.
Necker, Sylvia. *Konstanty Gutschow, 1902–1978: Modernes Denken und volksgemeinschaftliche Utopie eines Architekten.* Hamburg: Dölling und Galitz Verlag, 2012.
Needham, Andrew, *Power Lines: Phoenix and the Making of the Modern Southwest.* Princeton, NJ: Princeton University Press, 2014.
Němec, Richard. "Hitler's 'Generalsiedlungsplanung Ost': A Case Only for Poland? A Forgotten Dimension of National-Socialist Spatial and Town Planning in the Former Czechoslovakia." *Planning Perspectives* 31, no. 1 (2016) 1–29.

Neumann, Klaus. *Shifting Memories: The Nazi Past in the New Germany*. Ann Arbor: University of Michigan Press, 2000.
Newell, Stephanie. *Histories of Dirt: Media and Urban Life in Colonial and Postcolonial Lagos*. Durham, NC: Duke University Press, 2020.
Nickelsen Kärin, and David P. D. Munns. *Far Beyond the Moon: A History of Life Support Systems in Space*. Pittsburgh, PA: University of Pittsburgh Press, 2021.
Noaks, Jeremy, ed. *Nazism*. Vol. IV. Exeter, UK: University of Exeter Press, 1998.
Nolzen, Armin. "Die Gaue als Verwaltungseinheiten der NSDAP." In *Die NS-Gaue: Regionale Mittelinstanzen im zentralistischen Führerstaat*, edited by Jürgen John and Horst Möller, 199–217. München: Oldenbourg Verlag, 2007.
Nyhardt, Lynn. *Modern Nature: The Rise of the Biological Perspective in Germany*. Chicago: University of Chicago Press, 2009.
O'Brien, Martin. *A Crisis of Waste: Understanding Rubbish Society*. New York: Routledge, 2008.
Ofer, Dalia, and Lenore J. Weitzman, eds. *Women in the Holocaust*. New Haven, CT: Yale University Press, 1998.
Olusoga, David, and Casper W. Erichsen. *The Kaiser's Holocaust: Germany's Frogotten Genocide*. London: Faber and Faber, 2010.
Orth, Karin. *Das System der nationalsozialistischen Konzentrationslager*. Hamburg: Hamburger Edition, 1999.
Osterweil, Vicky. *In Defense of Looting: A Riotous History of Uncivil Action*. New York: Bold Type Books, 2020.
Otto, Gerhard, and Johannes Houwink ten Cate, eds. *Das organisierte Chaos: "Ämterdarwinismus" und "Gesinnungsethik." Determinanten nationalsozialistischer Besatzungsherrschaft*. Berlin: Metropol, 1999.
Overy, Richard J. "Business in the Grossraumwirtschaft: Eastern Europe, 1938–1945." In *Enterprise in the Period of Fascism in Europe*, edited by Harold James and Jakob Tanner, 151–177. New York: Routledge, 2002.
Overy, Richard. J. *War and Economy in the Third Reich*. Oxford: Clarendon Press, 1994.
Parenti, Christian. *Tropic of Chaos: Climate Change and the New Geography of Violence*. New York: Bold Type Books, 2011.
Park, M. A. Jinhee. "Von der Müllkippe zur Abfallwirtschaft: Die Entwicklung der Hausmüllentsorgung in Berlin (West) von 1945–1990." Dissertation, Facultät der Geisteswissenschaften, Technische Universität Berlin, 2004.
Parsons, Kermit C., and David Schuyler, eds. *From Garden City to Green City: The Legacy of Ebenezer Howard*. Baltimore: Johns Hopkins University Press, 2002.
Paul, Gerhard, and Klaus-Michael Mallmann. *Die Gestapo—Mythos und Realität*. Darmstadt: Primus, 1996.
Pellow, David Naguib. *Garbage Wars: The Struggle for Environmental Justice in Chicago*. Cambridge, MA: MIT Press, 2002.
Pelzer-Reith, Birgit, and Reinhold Reith. "Fischkonsum und 'Eiweisslücke' im Nationalsozialismus." *Vierteljahresschrift für Sozial- und Wirtschaftsgeschichte* 96, no. 1 (2009): 4–26.
Pendas, Devin O, Mark Roseman, and Richard F. Wetzell, eds. *Beyond the Racial State: Rethinking Nazi Germany*. Cambridge, UK: Cambridge University Press, 2017.
Peters, Olaf., ed. *Degenerate Art: The Attack on Modern Art in Nazi Germany, 1937*. Munich: Prestel, 2014.

Petropolous, Jonathan. *Art as Politics in the Third Reich*. Chapel Hill: University of North Carolina Press, 1996.

Petsch, Joachim. *Baukunst und Stadtplanung im Dritten Reich*. München: Carl Hanser Verlag, 1976.

Petzina, Dietmar. *Autarkiepolitik im Dritten Reich: Der nationalsozialistische Vierteljahresplan*. Berlin: Oldenbourg Wissenschaftsverlag, 1968.

Peukert, Detlev. *Inside Nazi Germany*. New Haven, CT: Yale University Press, 1986.

Peukert, Detlev. *Grenzen der Sozialdisizplinierung: Aufstieg und Krise der deutschen Jugendfürsorge von 1878–1932*. Köln: Bund-Verlag, 1986.

Peukert, Detlev. "Zur Erforschung der Sozialpolitik im Dritten Reich." In *Soziale Arbeit und Faschismus: Volkspflege und Pädagogik im Nationalsozialismus*, edited by Hans-Uwe Otto and Heinz Sünker, 123–132. Bielefeld: K.-T. Verlag, 1986.

Peukert, Detlev. "The Genesis of the 'Final Solution' from the Spirit of Science." In *Nazism and German Society, 1933–1944*, edited by David Crew, 274–299. New York: Routledge, 1994.

Peukert, Detlev. *The Weimar Republic: The Crisis of Classical Modernity*. London: Allen Lane, 1991.

Pezzullo, Phaedra C. "What Gets Buried in a Small Town: Toxic E-Waste and Democratic Frictions in the Crossroads of the United States." In *Histories of the Dustheap: Waste, Material Cultures, Social Justice*, edited by Stephanie Foote and Elizabeth Mazzolini, 119–146. Cambridge, MA: MIT Press, 2012.

Pine, Lisa. *Nazi Family Policy, 1933–1945*. New York: Berg, 1997.

Pine, Lisa. *Hitler's 'National Community': Society and Culture in Nazi Germany*. London: Bloomsbury Academic, 2017.

Pini, Udo. *Leibeskult und Liebeskitsch: Erotik im Dritten Reich*. Munich: Klinkhardt & Biermann, 1992.

Piper, Ernst. *Alfred Rosenberg: Hitlers Chefideologe*. Munich: Karl Blessing Verlag, 2005.

Pitzer, Andrea. *One Long Night: A Global History of Concentration Camps*. New York: Little, Brown, 2017.

Pohl, Dieter. *Die Wirtschaft der Wehrmacht: Deutsche Militärbesatzung und einheimische Bevölkerung in der Sowjetunion 1941–1944*. 2nd ed. Munich: Oldenbourg, 2009.

Pohl, Dieter, and Tanja Sebta. *Zwangsarbeit in Hitlers Europa: Besatzung, Arbeit, Folgen*. Berlin: Metropol, 2013.

Porter, Dorothy. *Health Citizenship: Essays in Social Medicine and Biomedical Politics*. Berkeley: University of California, Medical Humanities Consortium, 2011.

Porter, Dorothy. *Health, Civilization and the State: A History of Public Health from Ancient to Modern Times*. London: Routledge, 1999.

Proctor, Robert. *Racial Hygiene: Medicine Under the Nazis*. Cambridge, MA: Harvard University Press, 1988.

Proctor, Robert. *The Nazi War on Cancer*. Princeton, NJ: Princeton University Press, 1999.

Rabinowitz, Paula. "Wreckage Upon Wreckage: History, Documentary and the Ruins of Memory." *History and Theory* 32, no. 2 (May 1993): 119–137.

Radkau, Joachim. *Nature und Macht: Eine Weltgeschichte der Umwelt*. 2nd ed. Munich: Beck, 2012.

Rathje, William. "The Garbage Decade." *American Behavioral Scientist* 28, no. 1 (1984): 9–30.

Rathje, William, and Cullen Murphy. *Rubbish: The Archaeology of Garbage*. Tucson: University of Arizona Press, 2001.

Rawlings, Philip. *Policing: A Short History.* Portland, OR: Willan, 2002.
Reagin, Nancy. *Sweeping the German Nation: Domesticity and National Identity in Germany, 1870–1945.* Cambridge, UK: Cambridge University Press, 2007.
Reagin, Nancy. "Marktordnung and Autarkic Housekeeping: Housewives and Private Consumption under the Four-Year-Plan, 1936–1939." *German History* 19, no. 2 (2001): 162–184.
Reagin, Nancy. "Comparing Apples and Oranges: Housewives and the Politics of Consumption in Interwar Germany." In *Getting and Spending: European and American Consumer Societies in the Twentieth Century,* edited by Susan Strasser, Charles McGovern, and Matthias Judt, 241–262. Cambridge, UK: Cambridge University Press, 1998.
Rebentisch, Dieter. *Führerstaat und Verwaltung im Zweiten Welkrieg.* Stuttgart: Franz Steiner, 1989.
Reid, Donald. *Paris Sewers and Sewermen: Realities and Representation.* Cambridge, MA: Harvard University Press, 1991.
Reiter, Richard Holzinger. *Der narrative Ausdruck des Grauens: Eine Filmanalytische Aufarbeitung des* Atrocity-Films *German Concentration Camps Factual Survey.* Stuttgart: ibidem-Verlag, 2020.
Renneberg, Monika. *Science, Technology, and National Socialism.* Cambridge, UK: Cambridge University Press, 1994.
Reno, Joshua O. "Toward a New Theory of Waste: From 'Matter out of Place to Signs of Life." *Theory, Culture, Society* 31, no. 3 (2014): 3–27.
Reuth, Ralf Georg. *Goebbels.* Translated by Krishna Winston. New York: Harcourt Brace, 1993.
Roberson, Cliff. *Police Misconduct: A Global Perspective.* Boca Raton, FL: CRC Press, 2016.
Robinson, Cedrik J. *Black Marxism: The Making of the Black Radical Tradition.* 3rd ed. Chapel Hill: University of North Carolina Press, 2020.
Roseman, Mark. "National Socialism and the End of Modernity." *American Historical Review* 116, no. 3 (2011): 688–701.
Roseman, Mark. *The Villa, the Lake, the Meeting: Wannsee and the Final Solution.* London: Allen Lane/Penguin, 2002.
Rosen, George. *A History of Public Health.* Rev. expanded ed. Baltimore: Johns Hopkins University Press, 2015.
Rosen, George. *From Medical Police to Social Medicine: Essays on the History of Health Care.* New York: Science History Publications, 1974.
Rossino, Alexander B. *Hitler Strikes Poland: Blitzkrieg, Ideology and Atrocity.* Lawrence: University of Kansas Press, 2003.
Rössler, Mechthild, and Sabine Schleiermacher, eds. *Der "Generalplan Ost": Hauptlinien der nationalsozialistischen Planungs- und Vernichtungspolitik.* Berlin: Akademie Verlag, 1993.
Rothberg, Michael. *Multidirectional Memory: Remembering the Holocaust in the Age of Decolonization.* Stanford, CA: Stanford University Press, 2009.
Rouette, Susanne, and Pamela Selwyn. "Mothers and Citizens: Gender and Social Policy in Germany after the First World War." *Central European History* 30, no. 1 (1997): 48–66.
Rüb, Renate. "Müll und Städtehygiene um 1900: Über Entstehung und Entsorgung eines Neuen Problems." In *Müll von Gestern: Eine umweltgeschichtliche Erkundung in Berlin und Brandenburg,* edited by Susanne Köstering and Renate Rüb, 19–29. Münster: Waxmann, 2003.

Rubins, Ashley. *The Deviant Prison: Philadelphia's Eastern State Penitentiary and the Origins of America's Modern Penal System.* Cambridge, UK: Cambridge University Press, 2021.

Russell, Edmund. *War and Nature: Fighting Humans and Insects with Chemicals from World War I to Silent Spring.* Cambridge, UK: Cambridge University Press, 2001.

Said, Edward W. *Orientalism.* New York: Pantheon Books, 1978.

Samalin, Zachary. *The Masses Are Revolting: Victorian Culture and the Political Aesthetics of Disgust.* Ithaca, NY: Cornell University Press 2021.

Sandler, Willeke. *Empire in the Heimat: Colonialism and Public Culture in the Third Reich.* New York: Oxford University Press, 2018.

Scarry, Elaine. *The Body in Pain: The Making and Unmaking of the World.* New York: Oxford University Press, 1985.

Schafft, Gretchen. *From Racism to Genocide: Anthropology in the Third Reich.* Urbana: University of Illinois Press, 2004.

Schalkowsky, Samuel, trans. *The Clandestine History of the Kovno Jewish Ghetto Police: By Anonymous Members of the Rovno Ghetto Police.* Bloomington: Indiana University Press, 2014.

Schanetzky, Tim. *"Kanonen statt Butter": Wirtschaft und Konsum im Dritten Reich.* Munich: C.H. Beck, 2015.

Schenk, Dieter. *Hans Frank: Hitlers Kronjurist und Generalgouverneur.* Frankfurt am Main: S. Fischer, 2006.

Schepermann, Kathrin, and Horst Dilling. *Schicksale psychiatrischer Patienten der Lübecker Heilanstalt Strecksitz im Dritten Reich.* Lübeck: Schmidt-Römhild, 2005.

Schmidt, Ingrid. "Der lange Weg zur Kommunalisierung der Berliner Müllabfuhr: Von Genossenschaft zum Eigenbetrieb der Stadt." In *Müll von Gestern: Eine umweltgeschichtliche Erkundung in Berlin und Brandenburg,* edited by Susanne Köstering and Renate Rüb, 29–38. Münster: Waxmann, 2003.

Schmiechen-Ackermann, Detlef, ed. *"Volksgemeinschaft": Mythos, wirkunsmächtige soziale Verheißung oder soziale Realität im "Dritten Reich?"* Paderborn: Ferdinand Schöiningh, 2012.

Schmitz, Helmut, ed. *A Nation of Victims? Representations of German Wartime Suffering from 1945 to the Present.* Amsterdam and New York: Rodopi, 2007.

Schmuhl, Hans-Walter. *The Kaiser Wilhelm Institute for Anthropology, Human Heredity, and Eugenics 1927–1945.* Dodrecht: Springer, 2008.

Schrader, Stuart. "A Carceral Empire: Placing the Political History of U.S. Prisons and Policing in the World." In *Shaped by the State,* edited by Brent Cebul, Lily Geismer, and Mason B. Williams, 289–316. Chicago: University of Chicago Press, 2019.

Schulte-Sasse, Linda. "The Jew as Other under National Socialism: Veit Harlan's Jud Süss." *German Quarterly* 61, no. 1 (Winter 1988): 22–49.

Schürmann, Katrin, and Horst Dilling, *Schicksale Psychiatrischer Patienten der Lübecker Heilanstalt Strecksitz im Dritten Reich.* Lübeck: Schmidt und Römhild, 2005.

Scott, James C. *Seeing Like a State: How Certain Schemes to Improve the Human Condition Have Failed.* New Haven, CT: Yale University Press, 1998.

Sebald, Winfried Georg. *On the Natural History of Destruction: With Essays on Alfred Andersch, Jean Améry and Peter Weiss.* London: Hamish Hamilton, 2003.

Segal, Raz. *Genocide in the Carpathians: War, Social Breakdown, and Mass Violence, 1914–1945.* Stanford, CA: Stanford University Press, 2016.

Seigel, Micol. *Violence Work: State Power and the Limits of Police*. Durham, NC: Duke University Press, 2018.
Shanks, Michael, David Platt, and William Rathje. "The Perfume of Garbage: Modernity and the Archeological." *Modernism/Modernity* 11, no. 1 (January 2004): 61–87.
Shepard, Ben. "'Becoming Planning Minded': The Theory and Practice of Relief 1940-1945." *Journal of Contemporary History* 43, no. 3 (July 2008): 405–419.
Shneer, David. *Grief: The Biography of a Holocaust Photograph*. New York: Oxford University Press, 2020.
Simmons, Dana. "Waste Not, Want Not: Excrement and Economy in Nineteenth-Century France." *Representations* 96, no. 1 (Fall 2006): 73–98.
Singh, Julietta. *Unthinking Mastery: Dehumanize and Decolonial Entanglements*. Durham, NC: Duke University Press, 2018.
Smelser, Ronald. *Robert Ley: Hitler's Labor Front Leader*. New York: Berg, 1988.
Smelser, Ronald M., and Rainer Zitelmann. *The Nazi Elite*. New York: New York University Press, 1993.
Smith, Chris L., and Benjamin Jay Shand. "Architectural Wounds: Teufelsberg." *Architecture and Culture* 4, no. 2 (2016): 185–192.
Smith, Helmut Walser. "The Vanishing Point of German History: An Essay on Perspective." *History and Memory* 12, nos. 1/2 (Spring/Winter 2005): 267–295.
Smith, Woodruff. "The Colonial Novel as Political Propaganda: Hans Grimm's 'Volk Ohne Raum.'" *German Studies Review* 6, no. 2 (May 1983): 215–235.
Snyder, Timothy. *Black Earth: The Holocaust as History and Warning*. New York: Tim Duggan Books, 2015.
Sontag, Susan. *On Photography*. New York: Picador, 1973.
Sontag, Susan. *Regarding the Pain of Others*. New York: Picador, 2004.
Stähler, Axel. *Zionism, the German Empire, and Africa: Jewish Metamorphoses and the Colors of Difference*. Berlin: de Gruyter, 2018.
Stamatopouou-Robbins, Sophia. *Waste Siege: The Life of Infrastructure in Palestine*. Stanford, CA: Stanford University Press, 2019.
Stargardt, Nicholas. *The German War. A Nation Under Arms, 1939-1945*. New York: Basic Books, 2015.
Steege, Paul, Andrew Stuart Bergerson, Maureen Healy, and Pamela E. Swett. "The History of Everyday Life: A Second Chapter." *Journal of Modern History* 80 (2008): 358–378.
Steinbach, Peter. *Widerstand gegen den Nationalsozialismus*. Berlin: Akademie Verlag, 1994.
Stern, Alex Minna. *Eugenic Nation: Faults & Frontiers of Better Breeding in Modern America* 2nd ed. Oakland: University of California Press, 2016.
Stibbe, Matthew. *Germany 1914-1933*. New York: Routledge, 2010.
Stibbe, Matthew. *Women in the Third Reich*. New York: Oxford University Press, 2003.
Stöckle, Thomas. *Die "Aktion T4": Die "Vernichtung Lebensunwerten Lebens" in den Jahren 1940/41 und die Heilanstalt Christophsbad in Göppingen*. Stuttgart: Frank+Ranger, 1998.
Stokes, Raymond G., Roman Köster, and Stephen C. Sambrook. *The Business of Waste: Great Britain and Germany, 1945 to the Present*. Cambridge, UK: Cambridge University Press, 2013.
Stone, Dan. *Concentration Camps: A Short Introduction*. Oxford: Oxford University Press, 2019.

Stone, Dan. *The Liberation of the Camps: The End of the Holocaust and Its Aftermath.* New Haven, CT: Yale University Press, 2015.
Stone, Dan, ed. *The Historiography of the Holocaust.* New York: Palgrave Macmillan, 2004.
Strasser, Susan. *Waste and Want: A Social History of Trash.* New York: Holt, 1999.
Strobel, Bernhard. *Das KZ Ravensbrück: Geschichte eines Lagerkomplex.* Paderborn: Schöningh, 2003.
Strzelecki, Andrzej. "The Plunder of Victims and Their Corpses." In *Anatomy of the Auschwitz Death Camp*, edited by Ysrael Gutman and Michael Berenbaum, 246–266. Bloomington: Indiana University Press, 1994.
Stüber, Gabriele. *Kampf gegen den Hunger 1945-1950: Die Ernährungslage in der britischen Zone Deutschlands, insbesondere in Schleswig-Holstein und Hamburg.* Neumünster: K. Wachholtz, 1984.
Stüber, Gabriele, ed. *Zonenbeirat. Zonal Advisory Council, 1946-1948. Protokolle und Anlagen 1.-11. Sitzung 1946/47.* Düsseldorf: Droste Verlag, 1993.
Sudrow, Anne. *Der Schuh im Nationalsozialismus: Eine Produktionsgeschichte im deutsch-britisch-amerikanischen Vergleich.* Göttingen: Wallenstein, 2010.
Süss, Werner, and Ralf Rytlewski, eds. *Berlin. Die Hauptstadt: Vergangenheit und Zukunft einer europäischen Metropole.* Berlin: Nicolai, 1999.
Sutter, Paul. "The World with Us: The State of American Environmental History." *Journal of American History* (June 2013): 94–119.
Svampa, Maristella. *Neo-Extractivism in Latin America: Socio-Environmental Conflicts, the Territorial Turn, and New Political Narratives.* Cambridge, UK: Cambridge University Press, 2019.
Swett, Pamela. *Selling Under the Swastika: Advertising and Commercial Culture in Nazi Germany.* Stanford, CA: Stanford University Press, 2014.
Szöllösi-Janze, Margit. *Science in the Third Reich.* Oxford: Berg, 2001.
Tauber, Joachim. *Arbeit als Hoffnung: Jüdische Ghettos in Litauen.* Oldenburg: De Gruyter, 2015.
Teichert, Eckart. *Autarkie und Grossraumwirtschaft in Deutschland 1930-1939: aussenwirtschaftliche Konzeption zwischen Wirtschaftskrise und Zweitem Weltkrieg.* Munich: Oldenburg, 1984.
Templin, David. *Wasser für die Volksgemeinschaft: Wasserwerke und Stadtentwässerung in Hamburg im 'Dritten Reich.'* München: Dölling und Galitz Verlag, 2016.
Thomas, Julia Adeney. "History and Biology in the Anthropocene: Problems of Scale, Problems of Value." *Journal of American History* 111, no. 5 (December 2014): 1587–1607.
Thorsheim, Peter. *Waste Into Weapons: Recycling in Britain During the Second World War.* New York: Cambridge University Press, 2015.
Tomes, Nancy. *The Gospel of Germs: Men, Women, and the Microbe in American Life.* Cambridge, MA: Harvard University Press, 1998.
Tönsmeyer, Tatjana, Peter Haslinger, and Agnes Laba. *Coping with Hunger and Shortage Under German Occupation in World War II.* Cham, Switzerland: Palgrave Macmillan, 2018.
Tooze, Adam. *The Wages of Destruction: The Making and Breaking of the Nazi Economy.* New York: Penguin, 2008.
Traverso, Enzo. *The Origins of Nazi Violence.* New York: The New Press, 2003.
Trunk, Isaiah. *Łódź Ghetto: A History.* Bloomington: Indiana University Press, 2006.

Tschiggerl, Martin. "Who Owns the 'Trümmerfrauen'?" *Public History Weekly Blog Journal for History and Civics Education* 17 (2019): 1-10.
Tsing, Anna Lowenhaupt. *Friction: An Ethnography of Global Connection.* Princeton, NJ: Princeton University Press, 2005.
Tucker, Richard P. *At War: The Military and American Culture in the Twentieth Century and Beyond.* New Brunswick, NJ: Rutgers University Press, 2018.
Tucker, Richard P., and Edmund Russell, eds. *Natural Enemy, Natural Ally: Toward an Environmental History of War.* Corvallis: Oregon State University Press, 2004.
Uetkötter, Frank. "City Meets Country: Recycling Ideas and Realities on German Sewage Farms." *Journal for the History of Environment and Society* 1 (2016): 89-107
Uekötter, Frank. *The Green and the Brown: A History of Conservation in Nazi Germany.* Cambridge, UK: Cambridge University Press, 2006.
Uekötter, Frank. *The Greenest Nation? A New History of German Environmentalism.* Cambridge, MA: MIT Press, 2014.
Uekötter, Frank. *The Turning Points of Environmental History.* Pittsburgh, PA: University of Pittsburgh Press, 2010.
Vaupel, Elizabeth, and Florian Preiß. "Kinder, sammelt Knochen! Lehr- und Propagandamittel zur Behandlung des Themas Knochenverwertung an deutschen Schulen im 'Dritten Reich.'" *NTM Zeitschrift für Geschichte der Wissenschaften, Technik und Medizin* 26 (2018): 151-183.
Vincent, C. Paul. *The Politics of Hunger: The Allied Blockade of Germany, 1915-1919.* Athens: Ohio University Press, 1985.
Vogt, Timothy R. *Denazification in Soviet-Occupied Germany. Brandenburg, 1945-1948.* Cambridge, MA: Harvard University Press, 2000.
Volkmann, Hans-Erich, and Bernhard Chiari. *Ökonomie und Expansion: Grundzüge der NS-Wirtschaftspolitik.* Berlin: de Gruyter, 2003.
Wachsmann, Nikolaus. *Hitler's Prisons: Legal Terror in Nazi Germany.* New Haven, CT: Yale University Press, 2004.
Wachsmann, Nikolaus. *KL: A History of Nazi Concentration Camps.* New York: Farrar, Straus and Giroux, 2015.
Wachsman, Nikolaus. "Between Reform and Repression: Imprisonment in Weimar Germany." *The Historical Journal* 45, no. 2 (2002): 411-432.
Wagner, Bernd C. *IG Auschwitz: Zwangsarbeit und Vernichtung von Häftlingen des Lagers Monowitz 1941-1945.* Berlin and New York: K.G. Saur, 2000.
Walker, Mark. *Nazi Science: Myth, Truth, and the German Atomic Bomb.* New York: Plenum Press, 1995.
Ward, W. Peter. *The Clean Body: A Modern History.* Montreal: McGill-Queen's University Press, 2019.
Washington, Sylvia Hood. "Ball of Confusion: Public Health, African Americans and Earth Day 1970." In *Natural Protest: Essays on the History of American Environmentalism,* edited by Michael Egan and Jeff Crane, 205-222. New York: Routledge, 2009.
Wasser, Bruno. *Himmlers Raumplanung im Osten: Der Generalplan Ost in Polen 1940-1945.* Basel: Birkhäuser, 1993.
Watts, Sheldon. *Epidemics and History: Disease, Power and Imperialism.* New Haven, CT: Yale University Press, 1997.
Weber, Heike. "Towards 'Total' Recycling: Women, Waste and Food Waste Recovery in Germany, 1914-1939." *Central European History* 22, no. 3 (2013): 371-397.

Weber, Heike. "Nazi German Waste Recovery and the Vision of a Circle Economy: The Case of Waste Paper and Rags." *Business History* 64, no. 5 (2021): 882–903.
Webster, Donovan. *Aftermath: The Remnants of War.* New York: Vintage, 1998.
Weckel, Ulrike. *Beschämende Bilder: Deutsche Reaktionen auf alliierte Dokumentarfilme über befreite Konzentrationslager.* Stuttgart: Franz Steiner, 2012.
Weckel, Ulrike. "Watching the Accused Watch the Nazi Crimes." *London Review of International Law* 6, no. 1 (2018): 45–73.
Weckel, Ulricke, and Edgar Wolfrum, eds. *"Bestien" und "Befehlsempfänger." Frauen und Männer in NS-Prozessen nach 1945.* Göttingen: Vandenhoeck & Ruprecht, 2003.
Weindling, Paul Julian. *Epidemics and Genocide in Eastern Europe, 1890–1945.* Oxford: Oxford University Press, 2000.
Weinreb, Alice. *Modern Hungers: Food and Power in Twentieth-Century Germany.* New York: Oxford University Press, 2017.
Weiss, Sheila Faith. *The Nazi Symbiosis: Human Genetics and Politics in the Third Reich.* Chicago: University of Chicago Press, 2010.
Weiss-Wendt, Anton, and Rory Yeomans, eds. *Racial Science in Hitler's New Europe 1938–1945.* Lincoln: University of Nebraska, 2013.
Weizman, Eyal. *Forensic Architecture: Violence at the Threshold of Detectability.* New York: Zone Books, 2017.
Welch, David. *The Third Reich: Politics and Propaganda.* 2nd ed. London: Routledge, 2002.
Wempe, Sean Andrew. *Revenants of a Fallen Empire: Colonial Germans, the League of Nations, and the Redefinition of Imperialism, 1919–1933.* New York: Oxford University Press, 2019.
Wetzell, Richard F. *Inventing the Criminal: A History of German Criminology, 1880–1945.* Chapel Hill: University of North Carolina Press, 2000.
Whitman, James Q. *Hitler's American Model: The United States and the Making of Nazi Race Law.* Princeton, NJ: Princeton University Press, 2017.
Wildt, Michael. *Generation des Unbedingten.* Hamburg: Hamburger Edition, 2003.
Wildt, Michael. *Volksgemeinschaft als Selbstermächtigung. Gewalt gegen Juden in der deutschen Provinz 1919-1939.* Hamburg: Hamburger Edition, 2007.
Wildt, Michael. *Hitler's Volksgemeinschaft and the Dynamics of Racial Exclusion: Violence against Jews in Provincial Germany, 1919–1939.* New York: Berghahn Books, 2012.
Wilke, Sabine. "'Verrottet, verkommen, von fremder Rasse durchsetzt:' The Colonial Trope in the 'Nazi Kulturfilm' 'Ewiger Wald' (1936)." *German Studies Review* 24, no. 2 (May 2001): 353–376.
Wilkerson, Isabel. *Caste: The Origins of Our Discontents.* New York: Random House, 2020.
Williams, Eric. *Capitalism and Slavery.* Chapel Hill: University of North Carolina Press, 2021.
The "Willing Executioners/"Ordinary Men" Debate: Selections from April 8, 1996, Symposium. Washington, DC: United States Holocaust Research Institute, 1996.
Winant, Howard. *The World Is a Ghetto: Race and Democracy Since World War II.* New York: Basic Books, 2001.
Winter, Jay. "Shell-Shock and the Cultural History of the Great War." *Journal of Contemporary History* 35, no. 1 (January 2000): 7–11.
Wojak, Irmtrud, and Peter Hayes, eds. *"Arisierung" Im Nationalsozialismus: Volksgemeinschaft, Raub und Gedächtnis.* Frankfurt: Campus Verlag, 2000.

Wolff, Horst-Peter, and Arno Kalinich. *Zur Geschichte der Krankenanstalten in Berlin-Buch*. Berlin: Edition Hentrich, 1996.

Worboys, Michael. *Spreading Germs: Disease Theories and Medical Practice in Britain, 1865-1900*. New York: Cambridge University Press, 2000.

Worster, Donald. "History as Natural History: An Essay on Theory and Method." *Pacific Historical Review* 53, no. 1 (1984): 1-19.

Yelton, David K. *Hitler's Volkssturm: The Nazi Militia and the Fall of Germany 1944-1945*. Lawrence: University of Kansas Press, 2002.

Young, James E. *The Texture of Memory: Holocaust Memorials and Meaning*. New Haven, CT: Yale University Press, 1993.

Zantop, Susanne. *Colonial Fantasies: Conquest, Family, and Nation in Precolonial Germany, 1770-1870*. Durham, NC: Duke University Press, 1997.

Zelizer, Barbie. *Remembering to Forget: Holocaust Memory through the Camera's Eye*. Chicago: University of Chicago Press, 1998.

Zeller, Thomas. *Consuming Landscapes: What We See When We Drive and Why It Matters*. Baltimore: Johns Hopkins University Press, 2022.

Zeller, Thomas. *Driving in Germany: The Landscape of the German Autobahn 1930-1970*. New York: Berghahn Books, 2007.

Zepp, Mariane. *Redefining Germany: Reeducation, Staatsbürgerschaft und Frauenpolitik im US-amerikanisch Nachkriegsdeutschland*. Göttingen: Vandehoeck & Rupprecht, 2007.

Zimmerer, Jürgen. "Colonialism and the Holocaust--Towards an Archeology of Genocide." *Development Dialogue* 50 (2008): 95-124.

Zimmerer, Jürgen. *German Rule, African Subjects: State Aspirations and the Reality of Power in Colonial Namibia*. New York: Berghahn Books, 2021.

Zimmerer, Jürgen. "The Birth of the Ostland Out of the Spirit of Colonialism: A Postcolonial Perspective on the Nazi Policy of Conquest and Extermination." *Patterns of Prejudice* 39, no. 2 (2005): 197-219.

Zimmerer, Jürgen. *Von Windhuk mach Auschwitz? Beiträge zum Verhältnis von Kolonialismus und Holocaust*. Berlin: Lit Verlag, 2011.

Zimmerer, Jürgen, and Joachim Zeller. *Völkermord in Deutsch-Südwestafrika: Der Kolonialkrieg (1904-1908) in Namibia und seine Folgen*. Berlin: Ch. Links Verlag, 2003.

Zimmerman, Andrew. *Anthropology and Antihumanism in Imperial Germany*. Chicago: University of Chicago Press, 2001.

Zimring, Carl. *Aluminum Upcycled: Sustainable Design in Historical Perspective*. Baltimore: Johns Hopkins University Press, 2017.

Zimring, Carl. *Cash for Your Trash*. New Brunswick, NJ: Rutgers University Press, 2005.

Zimring, Carl A. *Clean and White: A History of Environmental Racism in the United States*. New York: New York University Press, 2016

Zimring, Carl, and William Rathje, eds. *Encyclopedia of Consumption and Waste: The Social Science of Garbage*. Thousand Oaks, CA: SAGE, 2012.

Zolling, Peter. *Zwischen Integration und Segregation: Sozialpolitik im "dritten Reich" Am Beispiel der "nationalsozialistischen Volkswohlfahrt" (NSV) In Hamburg*. Frankfurt am Main: Lang, 1986.

Zysiak, Agata, Kamil Śmiechowski, Kamil Piskała, Wiktor Marzec, Kaja Kaźmierska, and Jacek Burski. *From Cotton and Smoke: Łódz--The Industrial City and Discourses of Asynchronous Modernity, 1897-1994*. Łódz: Wydawnictwo Uniwersytetu Łódzkiego, 2018.

Index

For the benefit of digital users, indexed terms that span two pages (e.g., 52–53) may, on occasion, appear on only one of those pages.

Figures are indicated by an italic *f* following the page number.

agriculture, 12, 25–26, 29, 102–3, 131, 138, 216, 219–20
   and Auschwitz, 178
   and DANO system, 186, 187–90
   and dumping, 45–46
   and farmers, 29
   and fertilizer, 23–24
   and food waste, 53
   and forced labor, 59, 166
   and Four-Year Plan, 50–51, 70–71, 98, 190
   and industrial wastes, 39
   and *Kampf dem Verderb* or "War against Rot," 64
   and Nazi Empire, 10, 98–99, 125–26
   and Ost-Faser, 128, 129
   and plunder, 100
   and POWs, 52, 166–67
   and vermin, 192–93
Ahrens, Arthur, 145
Allied Powers, 97, 181–82, 196, 204, 213, 216, 217–18, 225–27, 228
   and aerial bombardments by, 1, 2, 41, 199–200, 202, 210–11, 218
   and photography, 226–27, 228–29
   See also Britain; France; Soviet Union; United States
Altstoff/Altmaterial/secondary materials, 3, 32, 39–40, 116–17, 119, 123, 131, 197, 203, 204, 227–28
   and *Altstoffhändler* (rag-and-bone men), 37–38, 43, 44, 56, 57, 67–68, 69, 123
   and Claus Ungewitter, 28, 54–55, 62
   and collection of, 26–27, 37–39, 42–43, 57–58, 62–43, 63, 67–68, 71, 80, 142, 225
   and concentration camps, 139, 229–30
   and DANO system, 187–88, 189
   economy, 37–38, 68–69
   and extraction of, 7, 9, 10–11, 25, 31, 228–29
   and General Government, 92, 93
   and Hans Heck, 31
   and Hermann Göring, 67–68, 70–71, 91, 142, 191
   and hospitals, 56–57, 58
   and Jews, 38, 67–68, 69, 117, 266n.25
   and Office for, 76–77
   and Organization Schu, 87, 94–95
   and Ost-Faser, 128, 129, 132, 136
   and prison labor, 48, 54–55, 58–59
   and rags, 123, 129, 149, 266n.25
   and recovery of, 40–41, 69, 112–13, 115, 144, 187–88
   and recycling of, 10, 20, 58–59, 146
   and sorting of, 58, 189, 191, 204
   trade, 37–38, 57–58, 67–68, 69, 70–71, 81, 117, 120–21, 174
   and *Verwaltungs- und Verwertungsgesellschaft Ost m.b.H.* (VVG), 91
   See also Reichsbeauftragter für Altmaterial (Reich Commissioner for Secondary Materials)
anthropology, 21
antisemitism, 5–7, 21, 121–22
   and Adolf Hitler, 12–13, 19, 21
   and Jakob von Uexküll, 24
   and legal measures, 25, 38
   and Nazi waste regime, 12–13
   See also aryanization
Aretz Faserstoffplatten GmbH, 46, 50
armaments, 85, 91–92, 93, 115, 146–47, 157, 197, 200
   and concentration camps, 149

armaments (*cont.*)
  manufacturers, 1, 291n.9
  and metal scrap, 70–71
  and Ministry for Armaments and Ammunition, 144
  production, 15–16, 25, 93–94, 116
aryanization, 56, 67–68, 69, 91
  of secondary materials economy, 68–69
Auschwitz, 180–82, 205, 206, 209–10, 211, 227–28
  and crematoria, 178, 212
  and dust and ash, 13–14
  and hair, 134*f*
  and Heinrich Himmler, 154, 195
  and labor, 144–45, 178, 211, 212
  and liberation of, 213, 226
  and mass graves, 178
  and *Sonderkommando*, 152–53
  and recycling, 157
  and textiles, 157, 168–69
  See also concentration camp(s)
Auschwitz-Birkenau, 152–53, 178
austerity, 27–28, 61, 62–63
Australia, 140
Austria, 61–62, 174, 271–72n.4. *See also* Vienna
autarky/*Autarkie*, 3–4, 27, 31, 42–43, 92

Backe, Herbert, 185
  and Four-Year Plan, 29
  and labor, 39–40, 229
  and mass starvation, 100
  Nationalsozialistische Volkswohlfahrt, NSV (National Socialist People's Welfare), 51, 53
  and Nazi waste regime, 43–44
  and nutrition/food (waste), 29, 48, 51, 53
Baltics, 99, 126–27, 129, 130, 165
Bauer, Friedrich, 117–18
Bauwerker, Erich, 91–92
Bavaria, 79–80, 175
bedbugs, 195–96
Belgium, 196. *See also* Brussels
Belsen, 216–17
Bełżec, 177–78, 227–28
  dismantling of, 153, 284n.101
  and OSTI (*Ostindustrie GmbH*), 155
  as a "Reinhard camp," 153, 154, 283–84n.97
  and *Sonderkommandos*, 152–53
Bergen-Belsen, 16, 150, 151*f*, 176, 205–6, 212, 213–14, 226
  as displaced persons camp, 215
  establishment of, 206
  liberation of, 208*f*, 213, 216, 226
  and photographs of, 226, 227–28
  and piles, 204, 208*f*, 209
  as *Sterbelager*, 206–7
  and weaving mill, 207
Berlin, 55, 61, 75, 106–7, 144, 145, 162, 190–91, 195
  and aerial bombings of, 199–200
  and DANO system, 187–90
  and garbage, 45–46, 50, 51–52, 57–58, 59–60, 187–88, 191
  and "Green Week," 64
  Grunewald, 222–23
  and hospitals, 55–57, 58, 59
  and morgues and crematoria, 200–2
  municipal administration, 45
  and potato peels, 45
  and recycling, 58–59
  and rubble, 219–21, 221*f*, 222–23
  and schools, 80
  and scrap metal, 38, 56, 71–72, 74*f*, 93, 95
  and sewers/sewage, 44–45, 48–49
  See also Grunewald; Tiergarten
Berliner Müllabfuhr- Aktiengesellschaft (BEMAG), xiii, 45, 46–47
Białystok, 85–86, 111–12, 129, 185
Birnbaum, Johannes, 56
bones, 56–57, 67–68, 80, 169–70, 172–74, 197, 225, 230–31
  and concentration camps, 142, 176–77, 182, 183
  and DANO system, 187–88
  from animals, 30, 164–65, 172, 193, 194
  and postwar reconstruction, 223–24
  and soap, 169–70, 171–72, 181–82
  and visual record of Nazi crimes, 228
  and waste reclamation, 3, 6, 37–38
boots, 115, 133–35, 133*f*, 147, 213, 229–30
Brandenburg, 46, 59
Braunschweig, 167–68
Brest-Litowsk, 103–4, 106

INDEX   333

Britain, 26, 93–94, 97, 186–87, 212–13, 214f, 217, 218, 226, 243n.65, 295n.14
and concentration camps in Africa, 140
and Bergen-Belsen, 213–15, 226
and POWs, 209
Browning, Christopher, 75–76, 256n.54
Brunswick Institute for Economic Research (*Braunschweigisches Institut für Wirtschaftsforschung, BIWF*), 167–68
Brussels, 94–95, 196
Brzozowksi, Marian, 161, 163, 163f
Buchenwald, 40, 141, 176, 177
and armaments workshop, 149
establishment of, 176
and photographs of, 226
Bührmann, Robert, 89–90, 121–22, 123
as Commissioner for Raw Materials Requisitioning, 90–92, 93, 119
and Four-Year Plan, 90–91

Canaris, Wilhelm, 101
Celle, 205, 210–11, 215, 293n.47
Chelmno, 152–53, 178, 227–28
chemical(s), 119
fertilizers, 44–45, 186
industry, 28, 91, 173–74, 193
manufacturing, 28
methane, 179
waste, 123–24
See also I.G. Farben
children/youth, xvii, 3, 68, 75–76, 81, 114, 128, 150, 169–70, 214, 218
as ghetto laborers, 124, 125
and *Kampf dem Verderb* or "War against Rot," 64
and partisans, 132
and Wehrmacht, 166
See also Hitler Youth (*Hitler Jugend*, HJ); League of German Girls (*Bund Deutscher Mädel*, BDM); schools
cleanliness, 14–15, 42–43, 63, 149, 164–65, 168, 169–70, 175, 181, 185, 231
and Adolf Hitler, 19, 34–35
and concentration camps, 16, 175, 176, 177, 181–82
and *Haupt Treuhandstelle Ost* (HTO) or Main Trustee Section East, 121
and imperial expansion, 3–4
and Nazi waste regime, 16, 157, 229
and order, 20, 33–34, 35–36
and race, 21, 216–17
and recycling, 16
and survivors, 16
and wartime shortages, 163–64
collaborators, 14–15, 39–40, 100–1, 119–20
Cologne, 64, 199–200, 221
colonialism, 10–11, 140
and Aimé Césaire, 226–27
European, 8–9, 21
and General Government, 90–91
and German Empire, 8–9, 21, 140
and Nazism, 8–9, 10–11, 15–16, 87, 98–99, 112–13, 125–26, 140, 179
See also empire
Commissioner for Raw Materials Requisitioning, 90, 91–92, 119, 120–21. *See also* Bührmann, Robert
compost, 186, 187–88, 189–90
concentration camp(s), 16, 20, 40, 59–60, 153–54, 155–56, 170, 203, 204, 205, 214–15, 226
British, 140
and cleanliness, 16, 164–65, 169, 175, 176, 177, 181–82, 196
and clothing, 115, 124–25, 147, 148, 150, 162, 167, 168–69
and corpses, 13–14, 176, 178, 183, 195, 205, 212, 216–17
and death marches, 2
and *Deutsche Ausrüstungswerke* (DAW), 145, 146
and diet, 137, 167, 212
and disease, 175, 176, 181, 209, 212
as dumping grounds, 149, 177–78, 229–30
and evacuations of, 208–9
and German Earth and Stone Works (*Deutsche Erd- und Steinwerke, DESt*), 145
and hair, 133–34, 135
and Inspectorate of the Concentration Camps, 141, 151, 154
and labor, 3, 4, 15–16, 29–30, 39, 58, 124–25, 139–42, 144–45, 146, 157, 162, 165, 178

concentration camp(s) (*cont.*)
    and liberation of, 196, 213–14, 216, 227–28
    and photography, 226
    prisoners, 2, 9–10, 38, 39–40, 179, 203, 222–23
    and recycling, 15–16, 33–34, 38, 39, 152–53
    and sanitary conditions, 176, 177–78, 179–82, 208–9
    and textiles, 115, 147, 225
    and vermin, 177, 182, 195–96
    and waste, 39, 60, 137, 142, 152, 157–58, 225, 230
    See also Auschwitz; Bełżec; Bergen-Belsen; Buchenwald; Chelmno; Dachau; Groß-Rosen; Gusen; KGL Lublin; Mauthausen; Ravensbrück; Sachsenhausen; Sobibor; Treblinka
conservation(ism), 11–12, 22–24, 27–28, 237n.60
Conti, Leonardo, 47–48, 58, 59–60
Coordination Center for Ethnic Germans (*Volksdeutsche Mittelstelle*), 199
Copenhagen, 187–88
copper, 58–59, 95, 96, 142, 143*f*
corpses, 13–14, 41, 177, 182, 183, 192, 195, 204, 205, 206, 213, 214–15, 216–17, 225
    and Bergen-Belsen, 209, 211, 212–13
    and concentration camp infrastructure, 176
    and *Einsatzgruppen*, 157
    and Nazi waste regime, 16, 157–58, 185–86
    and photographs of, 227–28
    and soap, 181–82
    and *Sonderkommandos*, 152–53, 154–55, 178
    and transport of, 177, 185–86, 199–201
crematoria, 149, 154–55, 176, 177, 178, 179–80, 182, 200–2, 203, 207
    at Auschwitz, 212, 213
Czechoslovakia, 61–62, 161. *See also* Protectorate of Bohemia and Moravia

Dachau, 141, 144–45, 146–47, 226
    as an early "model" camp, 141, 175

DANO system, 186, 187–90
Danzig, 87–88, 285–86n.139
Darré, Richard Walther, 29
Department of Public Health, 193, 195, 200
detergents, 40–41, 164–65, 169–70, 171, 172, 173–75, 179–80, 181–82, 185, 203
Deutsche Ausrüstungswerke (DAW) [German Equipment Works], 145–46, 153, 155, 156, 157
Deutsche Wirtschaftsbetriebe (DWB) [German Economic Company], xiii, 144–45, 153
Deutschesfrauenwerk (German Women's Work), 64–65, 68, 174
disease, 12, 41, 181, 185, 206, 209, 216–17, 230
    and garbage, 44–45
    and "ghetto disease," 125
    and racial science, 22
    and Soviet POWs, 101, 166, 206
    See also dysentery; typhus
displaced persons (DPs), xiii, 16, 215–16
Dorn, Friedrich, 130–31, 135–36
Dresden, 184, 199–200
dumping, 20, 21–22, 45–46, 47–48, 149–53, 209, 222–23
Düsseldorf, 95, 187–88, 199–200
dysentery, 172, 175, 214. *See also* disease

East Prussia, 174, 185
ecocide, 6
Economic Staff East. *See Wirtschaftsführungsstab Ost*
Eichmann, Adolf, 88–89
Eicke, Theodor, 141
Einsatzgruppen, 36, 75–76, 89–90, 122–23, 133, 152, 157
empire, 8, 94–97
    British, 26
    European, 21
    German, 8–9
    Nazi, 3–4, 8, 9–11, 87, 125–26, 128, 130, 156–57
Erzeugungsschlacht (subsistence battle), 25–26, 48–49, 50–51, 63–64
ethnic cleansing, 88–89, 121, 164–65

eugenics, 21–22, 23–25
euthanasia program (T4), 47–48, 59–60, 152
Evans, Andrew, 21

famine/mass starvation, 8–9, 98–100, 101, 131–32, 138, 169, 177–78, 207, 213–14, 226–27
Federal Republic of Germany, 97
Feldeisenbahn (Army Railway Authority), 102–3, 104–5, 107, 108, 110–11. *See also* railways
felt, 115, 133–36, 133f, 197–98, 228, 229–30, 266n.31
fertilizer(s), 23–24, 44–45, 138, 181–82, 186
film, 64–67, 76, 226, 228
flies, 12, 190, 192–93, 194–95
Florsted, Herman, 180
food independence. *See Nahrungsfreiheit*
food rations, 52–53, 188–89
Food Relief Works (*Ernährungshilfswerk*, EHW), xiii, 51–52, 53, 138–39
food scraps, 57, 65, 149–50, 170
food security, 25–26, 61, 188, 189–90, 216–17, 254n.9
food supply, 50–51, 63–64, 131, 168, 195–96
food waste, 51, 53
forced labor, xv, 1–2, 3, 85, 152, 167–68, 169, 190–91, 197, 212, 225
 and agriculture, 127–28
 and autarky, 31
 and bones, 193
 and cleanliness, 163–64, 169
 and clothing, 148, 162
 and collaborators, 100–1
 and concentration camps, 179, 204, 209–11
 and cremation, 201–2
 and death marches, 2
 and detergent, 174
 and diet, 139
 as displaced persons, 216
 expansion of, 29–30
 and extraction, 36–37
 and genocide, 5
 and liberation of, 217–18
 and Ost-Faser, 127–29, 130–31, 136
 and Poland, 92–93
 and POWs, 96, 153–54, 165
 and proximity to Germans, 163–64, 167–68, 169
 and railways, 103, 106–7, 111–12
 and recycling, 10, 15–16, 38
 and *Schrottschu*, 95, 96–97, 108, 108f, 109–10, 112–13
 and shoes, 150, 156–57
 and soap, 164–65
 and strategic industry, 9–10
 and total number in *Reich*, 165
 and war funding, 144
 and zero-waste economy, 15–16, 30
 See also slave labor
France, 93–95, 196
 and colonialism, 21
Frank, Hans, 39–40, 87–91, 92–93, 94, 120–21, 172, 179. *See also* General Government
Funk, Walther, 126–27

garbage, xvii, 43, 49–53, 49f, 80–82
 alchemy, 49–50
 and Claus Ungewitter, 39, 51, 138
 collection, 3, 20, 39, 44–45, 53, 59, 139–40, 176, 182, 189, 191–92
 community (*Müllgemeinschaft*), 61–82
 and compost, 187
 and corpses, 211, 216–17
 dumping/dumps, 46, 117–18, 172–73, 188–89, 192–93, 216, 222–23
 economy, 7, 26–27, 59–60, 225, 229
 empire, xxivf, 8–11
 flushing, 46–48, 47f, 50, 58
 and Four-Year Plan, 57, 190
 and genocide, 14–15
 and hospitals, household, 41, 56
 kitchen, 4, 35f, 44, 51–52, 53, 177
 and (in)visibility of, 225
 and language, 20, 31–36
 melioration, 45–46, 222–23
 and NSV (*Nationalsozialistische Volkswohlfahrt*), 52, 62, 194
 pickers (*Ausklauber*), 57–58
 piles, 212

garbage (*cont.*)
  practices, 62, 191, 229, 231
  processing, 23–24, 148, 155, 186, 187–88
  regime, 57, 58–59
  and regulation of, 37–38, 45
  reserves, 57
  as a resource, 32
  sausage (*Müllwurst*), 137, 138–39, 152, 230–31
  soil (*Müllerde*), 186, 189
  sorting, 57–58, 191
  technology, 16, 186
  urban, 26–27, 44–46, 50, 53, 188–90, 191
  and value of, 68
  and *Volksgemeinschaft*, 63–64
General Government, 120–21, 124–25, 149, 166, 172, 177–78
  and colonialism, 89–90
  and *Deutsche Ausrüstungswerke* (DAW), 146, 153, 157
  and German war economy, 91
  and ghettoization of Polish Jews, 89–90
  and *Haupt Treuhandstelle Ost* (HTO) or Main Trustee Section East, 90–91
  and mass murder of Jews, 148, 153, 154
  and metal reclamation, 92
  and plans for, 89, 90–91, 92–93
  and resettlement of Germans, 88–89, 97–98
  as slave colony, 87–88
  and soap, 171–72, 173–74
  See also Frank, Hans
General Plan East (*Generalplan Ost*), 10, 36, 98–99, 101–2
German Earth and Stone Works (*Deutsche Erd- und Steinwerke, DESt*), xiii, 145, 218–19
German Equipment Works. *See Deutsche Ausrüstungswerke* (DAW)
German Foreign Office, 206
German Labor Front (*Deutsche Arbeitsfront*, DAF), xiii, 71, 185, 195–96
German Tenements Relief Works (*Deutsches Wohnungshilfswerk*, DWH), xiii, 185
German Women's Work (*Deutsches Frauenwerk*), xv, 64–65

Gestapo, xiii, 2, 140–41
ghettoization, 89–90
ghettos, 4, 33–34, 41, 124–25, 146–47, 150, 153, 154, 155, 169, 196, 205, 229–30
  administration, 124
  and conditions, 125, 131–32, 164–65, 175, 177–78, 181–82
  economy, 146–47
  Łódz, 119, 123–24, 125
  and "undesirables," 20
  Warsaw, 181–82
  workshops, 129, 149
Globocnik, Odilo, 150, 153, 155, 156, 157, 195
Glücks, Richard, 154
Goebbels, Joseph, 63, 77, 78–80, 81–82, 88–89, 243n.69
gold, 8, 9, 55–56, 61, 144, 156, 170–71, 227
  teeth, 55–56, 152–53
Golm, 46–48, 49f, 50
Göring, Hermann, 31–32, 50, 80, 86–87, 89–90, 94, 191, 193, 229
  as Reich minister of aviation and *Luftwaffe* commander, 96
  and autarky, 27
  and DANO, 187–88
  and Economic Staff East (*Wirtschaftsführungsstab Ost*), 98–99, 101–2
  and food independence, 48
  and food waste, 51, 53
  and Four-Year Plan, 29, 37–38, 61, 98, 142
  and *Haupt Treuhandstelle Ost* (HTO) or Main Trustee Section East, 90–91
  and Herbert Backe, 29, 43–44, 48, 51, 53, 100
  and hog farms, 52
  and mass starvation, 100, 101
  and metal/junk campaigns, 71–75, 94–95
  and Nazi waste regime, 43–44
  and Ost-Faser, 126–27
  and Poland, 92–94
  and recycling, 39–40
  and secondary materials economy, 37–38, 39–40, 67–68, 70–71
  and textiles, 126–27
Gottesmann, Max, 57

Graf von Helldorf, Wolf-Heinrich, 200–1
Great Depression, 25, 27–28, 54–55, 67–68
Greater-German Cremation Association, 200–1
Greiner, Carl, 193
Groß-Rosen, 206, 210
Grunewald, 222–23
Gur, Mendel, 206, 210–11
Gusen, 205

Hagedorn, Hans Peter, 104, 106
Hamburg, 74f, 186–87, 188–89, 199
　bombing of, 187f, 199–200
　and DANO, 188–90
　and garbage incineration, 45–46
　and garbage sorting, 191
　and Institute of Environmental Research, 24
　and Nazi ideas about contamination, 23–24
　and rubble, 221
　and vermin, 194, 195
Hannover, 205, 217–18, 220f
Haupt Treuhandstelle Ost (HTO), 90–91, 119, 120–22, 123
Heck, Hans, 30, 31, 38, 75–76, 80, 81–82
Heil- und Pflegeanstalt Buch, 55–56, 57, 58, 59–60
Henkel, (*Landwirtschaftsrat*), 188–89
Heydrich, Reinhard, 88–90
　and Reinhard camps, 153, 154, 178, 227–28
Hildesheim, 210–11
Hilfswillige, 100–1
Hilgenfeldt, Erich, 51–52
Himmler, Heinrich, 69, 101–2, 139–40, 149, 154–55, 203
　and Auschwitz, 154, 178, 180–82, 195
　and cleanliness, 181
　and concentration camps, 29–30, 39–40, 154
　and Hans Frank, 90–91, 179
　and Herbert Backe, 29, 39–40
　and Hermann Göring, 92–93
　and junk reclamation, 85–87, 102, 112–13
　and labor exploitation/extraction, 6, 29, 229
　and Operation Reinhard, 154, 155, 157, 206
　and Poland, 87–90, 91, 179
　and Soviet POWs, 177–78
　as *Reichskommissar für die Festigung deutschen Volkstums* (Reich Commissioner for the Consolidation of German Nationhood), 87–88
Hippler, Fritz, 183
Hitler, Adolf, 78–79, 93–94, 165, 169, 183, 189–90, 199, 227
　and ammunitions plan, 94
　and *Anschluss*, 61–62
　and antisemitism, 12–13, 21
　and autarky, 27
　and cleanliness, 19, 21, 34–35
　and collapse of Nazi Germany, 2
　and concentration camps, 141
　and empire, 21, 26
　and filth, 21
　and garbage, 20, 139–40
　and General Government, 89
　and German Tenements Relief Works (*Deutsches Wohnungshilfswerk*, DWH), 185
　and Heinrich Himmler, 87–88, 89–90
　and Holocaust, 5–6
　and ideas about nature, 12, 24–25
　and Jewish Question, 5
　and metal reclamation, 72–75, 94
　popularity of, 42, 87–88, 97–98, 230
　and race, 32–33
　and Reichsmark, 116
　and SA, 71
　and Soviet Union, 26, 104–5, 125–26, 128, 145–46, 166
　and *Volkssturm*, 196
　and youth, 19
Hitler Youth (*Hitler Jugend*, HJ), 38, 42–43, 68, 69, 70f, 77, 78, 169–70, 291n.2
Hörrmann, Georg, 85–86, 87, 101–2, 106–7
Höss, Rudolf, 181–82, 209–10
Holocaust/Final Solution, xviii, 3–4, 5–6, 150, 153–54, 283n.96
hospitals, 54, 55–57, 58, 72–75, 79–80, 93–94, 122, 170, 203, 215. See also *Heil- und Pflegeanstalt Buch*
human laundry, 215
hunger, 100, 109–10, 131–32, 138, 206, 209, 212. See also famine/mass starvation

hygiene, 16, 33–34, 42, 163–64, 171–72, 176, 178
  and Hygienic Institute of the Waffen-SS, 180
  social, 21–22, 41
  See also cleanliness

I.G. Farben, 116–17, 178, 195–96
insecticide(s), 195
Inspectorate of the Concentration Camps (IKL), 141, 206

Jewish businesses, 121, 122–23
Jewish councils. See Judenrat
Jewish labor, 5, 41, 130, 133*f*, 153, 155, 156
Jewish property, 91, 121–22
Jodl, Ernst, 77
John, Harry, 50
Josten, Heinrich, 195
Judenrat (Jewish Council), 123
junk, xix, 13–14, 86*f*, 87, 112–13, 185–86, 208, 225, 227–28
  airplane, 3, 4, 146, 200, 225
  campaign, 70–71
  collection of, 81, 94–95, 102
  empire, 94–95
  and "evacuation" of, 185–86
  and forced labor, 9–10
  and ghettos, 124
  and HTO (Main Section East), 119
  and hunt for, 3, 39–40
  and loot, 96–97, 196
  metal, 3, 6, 30, 38, 57, 93, 95, 102, 107–8, 110–11, 146, 203
  and Nazi waste regime, 10–11
  reclamation/recovery, 72, 85, 91, 94–95, 96, 97, 101–2, 107–8
  and Soviet Union, 86–87
  and transport of, 72, 97
  and war effort, 5, 30, 70–71, 92, 204
  and Wehrmacht, 87, 111–12, 124
  yard(s), xv, 39–40, 87, 108, 110–11, 111*f*
  See also Organization Schu; *Schrottaktion*

Kampf, Otto, 120
Kampf dem Verderb or "War against Rot," 58, 63–67, 69

Karrenberg & Co. Feuerungsbau, 187–88
Kassel, 142–44, 143*f*, 199–200
Katowice, 90–91, 195
Kaufmann, Karl, 188–89
Kehrl, Hans, 126–28
Keitel, Wilhelm, 100–1
KGL Lublin, 144, 154, 178–80
  and airport/airfield, 155, 156–57
  and Globocnik, Odilo, 153
  and OSTI, 155
  See also Majdanek
Kiel University, 190
Kloth, Albert, 102
Knochenvernichtungsverbot (prohibition on the destruction of bones), 183. See also bones
Köhler, Walther, 37–38, 70–71
Konstanz, 193
Kore, Paul, 172–73
Kraków, 90–91, 146, 198
Kramer, Josef, 214
Krewoczejew, Dimitri, 161, 162*f*, 163

labor, xv, 54–55
  allocation, 96, 100–1, 115, 191
  camps, 39–40, 59–60, 140–41, 145, 150, 165, 195, 206–7
  and "complete" use of, 29
  exploitation, 6–7, 9–10, 29–30, 138, 139, 142, 231
  and extraction, 3, 5, 9, 10–11, 15–16, 20, 30, 53, 141, 164–65, 175, 181–82, 229, 230
  force, 4, 9–10, 70–71, 132, 138–39, 157–58, 225
  Jewish, 5, 6, 155, 156
  and medical institutions, 54, 55, 59–60
  minister, 52
  organizers, 140–41
  output, 6, 139
  policing, 140
  power, 29, 60, 155, 171–72, 199, 228
  and prisons, 29–30, 48, 58–60, 139, 141, 144, 197
  and recycling, 7–8, 13, 142, 157
  regimes, 9–10, 12–13, 26
  and *Russenlager*, 167
  and secondary materials, 43

shortages, 15–16, 59, 139, 141, 166, 169–70, 186, 190, 203
and waste, 4, 9–10, 20, 33–34, 53, 59–60, 139–40, 142, 149, 152, 204, 225
See also forced labor; *Ostarbeiter*; slave labor
Landsberg (prison), 19
Latvia, 165, 172–73. *See also* Baltics
Law for the Restoration of the Professional Civil Service of 1933, 56
League of German Girls (*Bund Deutscher Mädel*, BDM), 62, 68
Lebensraum (living space), 11–12, 24–25, 31, 44–49, 87
Lebzelter, Gisela, 21
Leroux, Pierre, 31–32
Levi, Primo, 180–81
Ley, Robert, 185
lice, 14, 19, 22, 171–72, 180–81, 195–96, 209, 212–13
Lichterburg, 141
Lidbetter, E.J., 23–24
Lingner, Reinhold, 222–23
Lippert, Julius, 50, 58–59
Litzmannstadt. *See* Łódź
locomotives, 105*f*, 106*f*, 110*f*, *See also* railways
Łódź, 90–92, 118–20, 121–24, 124*f*, 125, 129, 135, 198
Löffelsammlung (collection of baking supplies), xvii, 81. *See also* National Socialist Women's Organization
Lörner, Georg, 144–45
Lohse, Hinrich, 133
loot/booty, 2, 15–16, 91, 96–97, 111–12, 119–20, 198, 217–18, 223–24
and collapse of Nazi Germany, 196, 225
and concentration camps, 38, 39–40, 203
and *Deutsche Ausrüstungswerke* (DAW), 146
and Hans Frank, 92
and Hermann Göring, 39–40
and labor, 38, 39–40, 156, 197, 229–30
and metal requisitioning, 39–40, 85, 95–97
and Organization Schu, 87, 95–96, 108–10

and rags, 119–20, 129
and railways, 102–4, 107, 108
and Ukraine, 102–3, 107
and *Verwaltungs- und Verwertungsgesellschaft Ost m.b.H.* (VVG), 91, 119
and Wehrmacht, 119
See also plunder
Lublin, 144–45, 146, 154, 155, 156–57, 178–80, 195, 196
district, 153, 157

Majdanek, 144–45, 154, 178, 196, 213, 226. *See also* concentration camp(s); KGL Lublin
Maretsky, Oskar, 57, 58
Marschner, Erich, 91–92
Mauthausen, 137–39, 141, 145, 176, 205. *See also* concentration camp(s)
Metal
allocations, 189
and armaments, 115, 144
collection, 72–75, 81, 93–94, 95
dealers, 95
industry, 219–20
junk, 3, 6, 30, 71, 86–87, 93, 110–12, 146, 185–86, 203
precious, 26–27, 39, 55–56, 91
reclamation, 86–87, 92, 95
requisitioning, 15–16, 91, 112–13, 119
reserves, 70–71, 86–87
scrap, 3, 34–35, 38, 56–57, 58–59, 62, 68, 70–71, 70*f*, 94–95, 96–97, 102, 107–8, 142, 149, 219–20
shortages, 57, 189
workers, 219–20
workshops, 123–24, 157
See also Organization Schu; *Schrottaktion* (junk campaign); *Schrottschu*
Ministry for Armaments and Ammunitions, 144
Ministry of the Interior, 190–91, 200
Minsk, 104
Mitteldeutsche Seifenfabrik Gmbh, 57
mosquitoes, 107, 193
Müllbeseitigungsanstalt, 45, 57–58
Müllgemeinschaft. *See* garbage: community

Näser, Rudolf, 187
Nahrungsfreiheit (food independence), xvi, 3–4, 48, 65
National Socialist Motor Corps, 70–71, 81–82
National Socialist Women's Organization, 37–38, 81
Nationalsozialistische Volkswohlfahrt, NSV (National Socialist People's Welfare), xiii, 27–28, 38, 52–53, 62, 68–69, 79–80, 81, 199
  and food scraps, 49–50, 51–52, 53, 66
  and Herbert Backe, 51
  and hog farms, 33–34, 35f, 50, 51–53, 65–66, 194
  and recycling, 33–34
Nazism, 5–6, 8–9, 15, 43, 183, 230–31
Nossack, Hans Erich, 194
Nuremberg, 95, 135, 199–200
  Trials, 155–56

Operation Reinhard, 150, 153, 155–56, 157, 206
Oranienburg, 145, 206
Organization Schu, 87, 95, 96, 107–8, 112. *See also Schrottschu*
Organization Todt, 107
Oster, Moshe, 205–6, 211, 212–13
Osterkamp, Herbert, 78
Ost-Faser-Gesellschaft mbH, 126–31, 132–34, 135–36
Ostarbeiter (Eastern workers), xviii, 9–10, 115, 161, 165, 166–68, 195, 199, 237n.53
Ostbahn, xviii, 94, 95
Ostgesellschaften, xviii, 15–16, 97, 115
OSTI (*Ostindustrie GmbH*), 153–56, 157, 278n.125
Otto, Emil, 114–15, 126, 127–28

partisans, 100, 132, 166
peddling, 29, 37–39, 44, 67–69, 117, 118, 123
Pichovicz, Dimitro, 163, 164f
plunder, 5, 7–8, 15–16, 50–51, 87–88, 92, 125–26
  and metal collection, 94
  and Ost-Faser, 128
  and recycling, 10

  and (*Rohstoff und Handelsgesellschaft*, ROGES), 97
  and textiles, 118
  and Wehrmacht, 100
Pohl, Dieter, 125, 135–36
Pohl, Oswald, 138, 139, 144–45, 155–56, 168–69, 203, 206–7, 228
Poland, 6, 29–30, 100, 122–23, 133–34, 146, 205, 226
  and *Einsatzgruppen*, 75–76, 89–90
  and extraction, 92–94, 97–98
  and Final Solution, 150, 153–54
  and General Government, 92–93, 97–98
  and ghettos, 33–34, 41, 129, 153
  and *Haupt Treuhandstelle Ost* (HTO) or Main Trustee Section East, 90
  and invasion of, 72, 87–88, 117–18
  and labor, 41, 88–89, 129, 145, 146, 149, 165
  as a "model colony," 88–89
  and pillage of, 90, 92, 99
  and rag trade, 121
  and Red Army, 196
  and soap/detergent, 171–72, 174–75
  and spatial engineering of, 88–89, 92
  as testing ground, 97–98, 103–4, 125–26, 171–72
  and textiles, 117–20, 146–47
  and *Verwaltungs- und Verwertungsgesellschaft Ost m.b.H.* (VVG), 91, 94
  See also Łódź; Warsaw
police/policing, 20, 119–20, 121, 140–41, 155–56, 190, 217–18, 231
  battalions, 36, 75–76, 133, 157
  building, 71–72
  and cleanliness and order, 14–15
  and contamination, 9–10
  and cremation, 200–2
  and *Einsatzgruppen*, 36, 75–76, 89–90, 133
  and garbage, 45
  and genocide, 183
  and ghettos, 124
  and Heinrich Himmler, 29, 89–90
  and *Hilfswillige* (collaborators), 100–1
  and labor, 140
  medical, 171–72
  and metal collections, 72

municipal, 21–22, 44–45, 69
and Nazi waste regime, 26–27
and partisans, 132
science of, 21–22
social, 7
and Soviet Union, 125–26, 128, 132, 166
and urban growth, 21–22
potato(es), 207, 220, 230–31
and concentration camp kitchens, 40, 149, 177
and ghettos, 125
harvest, 25–26, 50–51
juice, 4, 42–43
peels, 42–43, 50
processing, 42
protein, 42
and Reich Food Estate (*Reichsnährstand*), 25–26
shortages, 53
Potsdam, 46, 48–49
POWs, 39–40, 52, 96, 153–54, 165, 174, 199, 209, 210–11, 216
and anthropologists, 21
camps, 154, 165, 166, 169, 177–79, 206, 213
and dirtiness/filth, 33–34
and Organization Schu/*Schrottschu*, 96–97, 109–10
and *Ostarbeiter*, 237n.53
as racial others, 60
as slave laborers, 9–10, 29–30
Soviet, 5, 9–10, 101, 108, 154, 163–64, 165–67, 169, 177–78, 229
Poznań, 90–91
propaganda, 70–71, 72–75, 92–93, 209–10, 230
and antisemitism, 183
and austerity, 27–28
and frugality and thrift, 31–32
and genocide, 77
and household waste, 38–39
and *Kampf der Verderb* or "War against Rot," 63–64, 66–67
and kitchen garbage, 50, 53
and language of, 183
ministry, 77, 79–80, 81–82
and Nazi waste regime, 26–27
and *Nationalsozialistische Volkswohlfahrt* (NSV), 68

peacetime, 15
and *Reichsnährstand* (Reich Food Estate), 67–68
and secondary materials, 37–38, 68
Soviet, 226
and Walter Tiessler, 75
and Winter Relief Works, 79–80
and woolens campaign, 78, 79–80
and women, 50, 65–66
See also Reich Propaganda Office
Protectorate of Bohemia and Moravia, xviii, 99, 161, 165, 174
Pstross, Jan, 176

racial capitalism, 6, 239n.5
Radom, 146, 156
rag(s), 1, 5–8, 81, 121, 123, 161, 172–73, 198
and *Altstoffhändler* (rag-and-bone men), 37–38, 43, 44, 56, 67–68, 69, 121, 123
and cleaning, 1–2, 15, 58–59, 114–15, 116–17, 265n.16
and concentration camps, 124–25, 148, 149–50, 152, 181, 203, 207, 214f, 215, 225
and DANO system, 187–88
economy, 117–18
farming, 114–36
and Four-Year Plan, 117
and *Fusslappen* (foot rags), 148
and ghettos, 124
hunt for, 118
and Ost-Faser, 129, 132, 135–36
and OSTI (*Ostindustrie GmbH*), 156
and photographs of, 228–29
pickers, 29
and plunder, 15–16
and postwar reconstruction, 223–24
and production, 121–22, 129
and raw materials, 114–15, 121–22, 124, 132, 148
and recycling, 1–2, 3, 4, 129, 146, 229–30
and reprocessing, 1–2, 119–20, 129, 148
trade, 121, 123
and waste, 117–18, 119
See also Altstoff/Altmaterial/secondary materials; textile(s)

342 INDEX

railways, xvi, 2, 3, 34*f*, 40–41, 59, 78, 102–3, 104, 128, 143*f*, 144, 172–73, 185–86, 204
    workers, 87, 103–4, 106, 109*f*, 110–11, 199
    See also Feldeisenbahn; locomotives; Reichsbahn
Ranis, Ernst, 91–92
rationing, 1, 25–26, 42, 61–62, 117–18
Rautenberg, Richard, 46
Ravensbrück, 141, 147, 148, 203, 273n.38.
    See also concentration camp(s)
recycling, 3–4, 26, 87, 225
    and armaments, 149
    of cables, 139, 143*f*
    and bones, 173–74
    and Claus Ungewitter, 28, 29, 62, 146
    and cleanliness, 16
    comprehensive, 15, 28
    and concentration camps, 15–16, 41, 142, 150, 152–53, 156–57, 229–30
    and deadliness of, 41, 77, 150
    and *Deutsche Ausrüstungswerke* (DAW), 146
    dirtiness of, 33–34
    economy, 153
    and extraction, 10
    and forced labor, 6–7, 10, 13–14, 15–16
    and Four-Year Plan, 20, 58, 142
    and Heinrich Himmler, 149, 154–55
    and histories of, 13, 230–31
    infrastructure, 152–53, 203
    and Jewish labor, 13–14, 156, 229–30
    and loot, 203
    and Nazi genocide, 3–4, 6–8, 14–15, 77
    and ordinary Germans, 7–8, 15, 37–38
    and OSTI, 156
    plant, 1, 221*f*
    and prisons and hospitals, 58
    of rags, 1–2, 146
    and recovery of fats, 41
    and resource extension, 185–86, 223–24
    and resource scarcity, 41
    of rubble, 218–19, 220*f*, 221, 223–24
    of secondary materials, 10, 20, 58, 129, 197
    of shoes, 148
    and *Sonderkommandos*, 152–53
    of textiles, 119–20, 129, 146, 148, 156
    total (*restlose Wiederverwertung*), 33–34
    and volunteers, 38
    as waste practice, 20, 37–38, 157–58
    *See also Altstoff/Altmaterial/*secondary materials; garbage; waste; wastewater
Red Army, 2, 85–86, 111–12, 128, 135–36, 197, 213
    and advance of in Germany, 41, 157, 199
    and ethnic Germans, 185
    and felt boots (*Valenki*), 133
    and liberation of Lublin (Majdanek), 196, 213, 227–28
    and retreat of Wehrmacht, 197
    See also Soviet Union
Regional Office for Water, Soil and Air Hygiene (Landesanstalt für Wasser-, Boden- und Lufthygiene), 42–43, 193, 195–96
Reich Air Raid Protection League, 62
Reich Commissioner for the Consolidation of German Nationhood. *See Reichskommissar für die Festigung deutschen Volkstums*
Reich Commissioner for Kitchen Garbage (*Reichsbeauftrager für die Erfassung und Verwertung von Küchen- und Nahrungsmittelabfällen*), xviii, 51–52
Reich Commissioner for Secondary Materials Recovery (*Reichsbeauftragter für Altmaterialverwertung*), xviii, 29, 30, 37–38, 69, 70–71, 118
Reich Food Estate. *See Reichsnährstand*
Reich Labor Service or *Reichsarbeitsdienst* (RAD), xiii, 124
Reich Ministry of Economic Affairs. *See Reichswirtschaftsministerium* (RWM)
Reich Ministry of Finance, 51–52
Reich Ministry of Food and Agriculture, 29, 186, 188, 190
Reich Ministry of Justice, 142–44, 197
Reich Ministry of Labor, 218–19
Reich Ministry of Transport, 78
Reich Propaganda Office, 75
Reichsarbeitsdienst (RAD). *See* Reich Labor Service

Reichsbahn (railway authority), xiii, 94, 120–21, 142, 144, 197–98, 228
and corpses, 199–200
and garbage collection, 189
and junk collection, 72
and woolens collections, 77, 78–79
Reichsbank, 116
Reichsbeauftrager für die Erfassung und Verwertung von Küchen- und Nahrungsmittelabfällen. See Reich Commissioner for Kitchen Garbage
Reichsbeauftragter für Altmaterialverwertung. See Reich Commissioner for Secondary Materials Recovery
Reichsflaschentag, 75
Reichskommissar für die Festigung deutschen Volkstums (Reich Commissioner for the Consolidation of German Nationhood), 87–88
Reichsnährstand, RNS (Reich Food Estate), xix, 25–26, 29, 64, 65–66, 67–68, 188, 193
Reichsstelle Chemie (Reich Office for Chemistry), 138
Reichsstelle für industrielle Fettversorgung (RIF) [as of 1942 *Reichsstelle für industrielle Fette und Waschmittel*], xiv, 40–41, 171, 173–75, 181–82, 185
Reichsstelle für Textilwirtschaft, 117–18
Reichsstelle für Wolle und andere Tierhaare (Reich Office for Wool and Other Animal Hair), 134–35
Reichstag fire, 140–41
Reichswirtschaftsministerium (RWM), xiv, 38, 57–58, 81–82, 90, 116, 156, 166
refrigerators, 65, 214
refugees, 2, 185, 204, 209–10, 216, 218
and Adolf Hitler, 199
and the "Albert Kommission," 199
and cremation, 201–2
in Hamburg, 186–87
and United Nations Relief and Rehabilitation Administration (UNRAA), 216
Reich Raw Materials Office (*Rohstoffamt*), xix, 1–2, 96, 102, 127
Reich Security Service, 76
Reumschüssel, Karl, 46

Rhineland, 61–62, 81–82
Riefenstahl, Leni, 61
Rigele, Hermann, 171
Robert Koch Institute, 195
ROGES (*Rohstoff und Handelsgesellschaft*) [Raw Material Trading Company], xiv, 97, 197–98
Roma, 13–14, 21, 88–89, 172
Roseboom, Alexander, 176, 207–8
Rothe, M.A., 1–4, 15
rubble, xx, 13, 16, 41, 104, 192, 223*f*
and Berlin, 219–20, 222–23
and clearing, 62, 191, 192, 217, 223–24
and corpses, 195
and forced laborers, 9–10
and Hamburg, 187, 189, 221
and Hannover, 217–18
and Hans Schu, 112
people, 217–24
and piles, 13–14, 204, 218, 219*f*
recycling, 220*f*, 221, 221*f*, 223–24, 225
and scarcity, 185–86
and transformation of, 218–19
women (*Trümmerfrauen*), 223–24
as waste, 13
Rumkowski, Mordecai Chaim, 123–24

SA (Storm Troopers), xiv, 70–72, 123, 140–41
Saar (region), 61–62
Sachsenhausen, 141–42, 145, 152
Sahm, Heinrich, 46, 55–57
sanitation, 21–22, 33–34, 42–43, 157, 175, 176, 209, 223–24, 229–30
history of, 44–45
Sauckel, Fritz, 5, 39–40, 78–79, 90–91, 106–7, 139, 166, 199
scarcity, 25, 26–27, 41, 42–43, 62, 138, 185–86, 229
and consumer society, 7–8
and food, 186
and planning for, 66–67
and recycling, 20
and resources, 6, 15–16, 100–1, 152, 229
and Ost-Faser, 130–31
and textiles, 114
and war economy, 1, 7–8, 191
Schacht, Hjalmar, 116

Scheld, Ernst, 197
Schenck, Ernst Günther, 137, 138
Schmidt, Bernhard, 142
schools, 72, 78, 79–81, 118, 169–70, 194, 204, 213, 221
Schrottaktion (junk campaign), 71, 101–2. *See also* Organization Schu
Schrottschu, 107–8, 109–10. *See also* Organization Schu; *Schrottaktion*
Schu, Hans, 94–95, 96–97, 108, 112–13
Schulz, Fritz, 193
Schwarz, Gustav, 190–91
Schwarzerdegebiet. See "surplus zones"
Schwela, Siegfried, 181–82
scrap collection, 28, 29, 70f, 80, 117–18
Sebald, W. G., 192
secondary materials. *See Altstoff/Altmaterial/*secondary materials
sewage, 16, 26–27, 48–49, 170, 174, 185–86, 188–89, 190–92
  and Claus Ungewitter, 28, 39
  and extraction, 4
  as fertilizer, 23–24, 32, 44–45
  gasification, 179
shoes, 3, 4, 9, 133, 146–48, 149–51, 152, 153, 155, 156–57, 172–73, 181, 196–97, 207–8, 208f, 213, 215, 227–30
Sierakowiak, Dawid, 123, 124, 125
silver, 9, 10
Sinti, 21, 88–89
slave labor, 2, 9–11, 12, 33, 41, 131–32, 204, 226–27
  and colonialism, 140
  complex, 4, 29–30, 139, 145–46, 148
  and *Deutsche Ausrüstungswerke* (DAW), 145–46
  Jewish, 149
  and loot, 223–24, 229–30
  and Lublin, 179, 180
  and management of, 4
  and *Ostarbeiter*, 167
  and recycling, 7–8, 16, 157–58
  and (*Rohstoff und Handelsgesellschaft*, ROGES), 97
  and Soviet POWs, 5
  and textiles, 118, 129, 148
  and waste, 132, 136
  and Wehrmacht, 128

Smolensk, 104, 105f, 107–8, 110–12, 111f, 135–36
soap, 39, 57, 61, 163–65, 169–70, 171–72, 173–74, 178, 179–80, 181–82, 214
  production, 16, 30, 40, 41, 164–65, 169–70, 172, 173, 174, 183
Sobibor, 152–53, 154, 155, 177–78, 227–28
social Darwinism, 21–22, 23–24
socks, 78–79, 114–15, 122–23, 127, 145–46, 148, 167–68
Soldiers and Veterans Association (*Kyffhäuserbund*), 71–72
Sonderkommandos, 139, 152–53, 154–55, 178, 182, 183
South Africa, 140
Soviet Union, 29–30, 79, 85–86, 97–99, 125–26, 132, 197–98, 213, 226
  and Adolf Hitler, 26, 125–26
  and *Einsatzgruppen*, 75–76, 152
  and forced labor, 165, 166, 168
  and German invasion of, 75–76, 95, 103, 125–27, 145–46, 166
  and Hans Schu, 95
  and invasion of Poland, 87–88
  and Nazi "Hunger Plan," 98–99
  and photography, 227–28
  and POWs, 5, 9–10, 101, 108, 153–54, 163–64, 165–67, 169, 177–78, 229
  and soap, 173
  and starvation, 100, 101, 131–32
  See also Red Army
Speer, Albert, 127, 145, 149, 191, 222–23, 222f
Spencer, Herbert, 23–24
SS-Bekleidungswerk (SS-Clothing Works), xix, 145, 155, 156
SS Main Economic and Administrative Office (SS-WVHA), xiv, 40, 133–34, 135, 138, 144–45, 150, 155–56, 157, 168–69, 203, 206
Stalingrad, 85, 110, 188–89
Steeg, Ludwig, 201–2
Stuttgart, 199–200
Stutthof, 181–82
"subsidy zones" (*Waldzone* or forest zone), xxi, 98–100, 102–3, 106
Sudetenland, 61–62, 162

"surplus zones" (*Schwarzerdegebiet* or black earth territory), 98–100, 102–3
Svärd, Lotta, 79–80

Technical Emergency Relief Association, 71–72
TexLed (*Gesellschaft für Textil und Leder Verwertung*) [Textile and Leather Utilization], xiv, 146–47, 148, 149–50
textile(s), 25–26, 32–33, 61–62, 68, 91, 115, 123, 150, 197
   collection, xix, 75, 77–78, 81, 118, 168
   companies/firms, 120, 122–23, 157
   factories, 146–47, 148
   fibers, 58–59, 119, 124–25, 128
   industry, 116–17, 118–19, 126–27, 129
   and law, 116, 121–22
   mining, 92
   and Nazi Empire, 8
   and plunder/loot, 15–16, 38, 157
   processing, 119, 134–35, 153, 155, 156
   production, 118–19, 121–22, 146–47
   provisioning, 168–69
   rations, 114–15
   recycling, 119–20, 146–47, 156–57
   repositories, 78
   and *Reichsstelle für Textilwirtschaft*, 115, 117–18, 196
   secondary, 102, 129, 168
   sector, 68, 114, 116, 119–20
   and soap, 181–82
   sorting, 78, 157
   trade, 117–18
   waste, 1, 3, 57, 114–15, 117, 118, 119–20, 129, 142, 146, 148, 163, 196, 198, 203, 225
   workshops, 118–19, 123–24, 124f, 146–47, 179–80
   See also rag(s)
Thierack, Georg, 197
thrift, 3–4, 20, 26–27, 62, 63, 68
   and collective performance of, 7, 229
   and propaganda, 31–32
   and rubble recycling, 223–24
Thüringen, 78–79
Tiergarten, 220. *See also* Berlin
Tiessler, Walter, 75, 78
Todt, Fritz, 144

Toepfer (Reich Commissioner for Wool), 117, 130
Tooze, Adam, 25, 100
Treblinka, 152–53, 154, 155, 177–78, 227–28
typhus, 22, 23–24, 156, 172, 176, 190, 206, 212
   epidemic in Bergen-Belsen, 213–14, 215

Uexküll, Jakob von, 24
Ufa, xiv, 64–65. *See also* film
Ukraine, 97–100, 102–3, 104–5, 126–27, 128, 130, 135–36, 165, 173, 185, 212
Ungewitter, Claus, 29, 31–32, 33, 39, 54–55, 146
   and book *Verwertung des Wertlosen* (*Utilization of the Worthless*), 28, 31–32, 51, 54, 62, 138
United Nations Relief and Rehabilitation Administration (UNRRA), xiv, 216–17
United States, 11–12, 36
   and Adolf Hitler, 26
   and Claus Ungewitter, 28
   and the Great Depression, 27–28

vermin, 14, 22, 36, 46, 167–68, 169–70, 177, 182, 192, 193, 194, 195
Versailles Treaty, 61–62
Verwaltungs- und Verwertungsgesellschaft Ost m.b.H. (VVG) [Administration and Utilization Corporation], xiv, 91–92, 94, 119
Vienna, 19, 76, 80. *See also* Austria
Vilnius, 85–86
Völkischer Beobachter, 34–35
Volksdeutsche, 88–89
Volksgemeinschaft (people's community), 1, 31, 43–44, 54, 59–60, 63, 70–71, 72–75, 77
   and *Kampf dem Verderb* or "War against Rot," 66–67
   and recycling, 38
Volksdeutsche Mittelstelle (Coordination Center for Ethnic Germans), 199
Volkssturm, xxi, 196, 198, 217–18

Wagner, Eduard, 78
Waldzone. See "subsidy zones"

Walther, Andreas, 23–24
Wannsee, 190–91, 283n.96
Warsaw, 93, 157, 171, 203
  ghetto, 181–82
Warthegau, xxi, 87–88, 92–93
waste, xvii, 13–14, 19, 22, 33, 35f, 36–37, 43–44, 60, 225
  and Adolf Hitler, 19, 94
  and animals, 44–45, 170, 172, 174
  and antisemitism, 12–13
  avoidance, 3, 7, 20, 28, 29, 32, 54, 229, 230
  and chemical, 123–24
  collection, 53, 191
  and concentration camps, 4, 20, 60, 139, 148, 149, 176, 183, 207
  and disorder, 62–63
  disposal, 45, 56
  and extraction, 13, 25
  and food, 51, 52–53
  and genocide, 5–6, 9–10, 12–13, 149, 155
  and ghettos, 4, 20, 124–25, 149
  household, xvii, 32, 38–39, 51, 54, 57–58
  human, 184
  industrial, 39, 51, 123, 138, 139
  infrastructure, 15, 175
  labor, 4, 9–10, 29, 30, 33–34, 59–60, 126, 138–40, 142, 152, 204, 228–29
  and loot/booty, 2, 39–40, 129
  management, xviii, 7, 15–16, 20, 28, 39, 54, 139, 185, 230–31
  municipal, 28, 45, 48–49, 187–89, 193
  and Ost-Faser, 128, 129, 132, 135–36
  and OSTI, 155, 156, 157
  paper, 56–57, 59, 142, 172–73, 225
  peddlers, 69
  products, 20, 25–26, 28, 33, 39, 48–49, 54, 56, 58, 127–28, 138, 170, 186
  reclamation, 3, 5–6, 7, 9–10, 26, 28, 31, 36–37, 41, 57–58, 69, 229
  recovery, 67–68, 87
  and recycling, 3–4, 10, 13, 14–15, 20, 28, 33–34, 37–38, 87, 115, 119–20, 157–58
  and resource independence/autarky, 26–27, 31–32
  and secondary materials, 7, 10, 25, 58, 67–68, 136, 228–29
  and shortages, 3, 112–13, 186
  and soap, 41, 169–70, 173
  and SS, 148
  and textiles, 1–2, 57, 114–15, 116–17, 118, 119–20, 121–22, 129, 142, 146, 148, 185–86, 196, 203
  and Wehrmacht, 87, 119–20
  See also zero-waste economics
wastewater, 40, 48–49, 137, 138, 169–71, 179–80, 212, 230–31
  and detergents, 174
  and food-processing plants, 42
  management, 42–43
  and mining of, 172
  and soap, 164–65
  and transport of, 40–41
  and treatment plant, 48–49, 179
Weber, Friedrich, 200, 201–2
Wegener, H. F., 121–22, 123
Wehrmacht, 41, 76–77, 86–87, 117–18, 124, 135–36, 146–47, 156–57, 169, 200, 210–11
  and boots/footwear, 133, 134–35, 147
  and Bottles for Our Army campaign, 76
  and concentration camps, 147, 177–78, 210–11, 215
  and detergent, 174
  and extraction, 97
  and food waste, 53
  and garbage, 198
  and Hans Heck, 75
  and *Hilfswillige*, 100–1
  and loot/booty, 87, 96, 111–12, 119
  and metal collection/recovery, 95, 101–2
  and National Socialist Women's Organization, 81
  and Organization Schu, 87, 95, 96, 112
  and partisans, 132
  and Poland, 103
  and Soviet POWs, 166, 177–78
  and Soviet Union, 75–76, 100, 101, 103, 110–12, 125–27, 128, 129, 132, 145–46, 197
  and SS, 151, 157
  and textiles, 78, 119–20, 127, 131
  uniforms, 41
Wehrtechnische Fakultät (military academy), 222–23

Weimar Republic, xx, 20–21, 32–33, 43, 46, 54, 65
West Prussia, 87–88
White supremacy, 6
Wilhelm Schumann Gmbh, 56
Winkler, Max, 90–91
Winter Relief Works, 27–28, 79–80
Wirtschaftsforschungsgesellschaft (Wifo), 91
Wirtschaftsführungsstab Ost (Economic Staff East), xix, 86–87, 98–99, 100, 101
Wise, Stephen S., 181–82
women, 62, 65, 66, 75–76, 78, 79–80, 123, 128, 130, 132, 215, 217–18
  in concentration camps, 147, 148, 205, 207, 209, 214–15
  and *Deutschesfrauenwerk* (German Women's Work), 62, 68, 174
  and German evacuees, 218
  and hair, 133–34, 152–53
  as homemakers/housewives, 65, 66, 68
  and *Kampf der Verderb* or "War against Rot," 64, 66
  and labor, 59–60, 109–10, 115, 130, 165, 167–68
  and Nazi propaganda, 65
  and *Trümmerfrauen*, 217, 223f
World War I, 7–8, 24, 28, 45–46, 63–64, 65, 93–94, 141, 226

Zeitzler, Kurt, 101–2
zero-waste economics, 31–32, 133
Ziegler, Wilhelm, 29, 30, 37–38, 69, 80
Zörner, Ernst, 103